The Tyndale Old Testament Commentaries

General Editor:
PROFESSOR D. J. WISEMAN, O.B.E., M.A., D.Lit., F.B.A., F.S.A.

JOSHUA

JOSHUA

AN INTRODUCTION AND COMMENTARY

by

RICHARD S. HESS, B.A., M.DIV., TH.M., PH.D.
Reader in Old Testament, Roehampton Institute London

INTER-VARSITY PRESS
LEICESTER, ENGLAND
DOWNERS GROVE, ILLINOIS, U.S.A.

InterVarsity Press
P.O. Box 1400, Downers Grove, Illinois 60515, U.S.A.
38 De Montfort Street, Leicester LE1 7GP, England

© *Richard S. Hess 1996*

InterVarsity Press®, U.S.A., is the book-publishing division of InterVarsity Christian Fellowship®, a student movement active on campus at hundreds of universities, colleges and schools of nursing in the United States of America, and a member movement of the International Fellowship of Evangelical Students. For information about local and regional activities, write Public Relations Dept., InterVarsity Christian Fellowship, 6400 Schroeder Rd., P.O. Box 7895, Madison, WI 53707-7895.

Inter-Varsity Press, England, is the publishing division of the Universities and Colleges Christian Fellowship (formerly the Inter-Varsity Fellowship), a student movement linking Christian Unions in universities and colleges throughout the United Kingdom and the Republic of Ireland, and a member movement of the International Fellowship of Evangelical Students. For information about local and national activities in Great Britain write to UCCF, 38 De Montfort Street, Leicester LE1 7GP.

All Scripture quotations, unless otherwise indicated, are taken from the HOLY BIBLE, NEW INTERNATIONAL VERSION®. NIV®. Copyright ©1973, 1978, 1984 by International Bible Society. Used by permission of Zondervan Publishing House and Hodder & Stoughton Ltd. All rights reserved.

UK ISBN 0-85111-849-6 (paper)
USA ISBN 0-8308-1433-7 (cloth)
USA ISBN 0-87784-256-6 (paper)
USA ISBN 0-87784-880-7 (set of Tyndale Old Testament Commentaries, cloth)
USA ISBN 0-87784-280-9 (set of Tyndale Old Testament Commentaries, paper)

Printed in the United States of America ∞

Library of Congress Cataloging-in-Publication Data

Hess, Richard S.
    Joshua: an introduction and commentary/by Richard S. Hess.
        p.   cm.—(Tyndale Old Testament commentary series; 6)
    Includes bibliographical references.
    ISBN 0-8308-1433-7 (alk. paper).—ISBN 0-87784-256-6 (pbk.:
alk. paper)
    1. Bible.   O.T.   Joshua—Commentaries.   I. Title.   II. Series:
Tyndale Old Testament commentaries; 6.
BS1295.3.H47   1996
222′.207—dc20   96-26846
                                                          CIP

British Library Cataloguing in Publication Data

A catalogue record for this book is available from the British Library.

14	13	12	11	10	9	8	7	6	5	4	3	2	1
07	06	05	04	03	02	01	00	99	98	97	96		

GENERAL PREFACE

THE aim of this series of *Tyndale Old Testament Comment-aries*, as it was in the companion volumes on the New Testament, is to provide the student of the Bible with a handy, up-to date commentary on each book, with the primary emphasis on exegesis. Major critical questions are discussed in the introductions and additional notes, while undue technicalities have been avoided.

In this series individual authors are, of course, free to make their own distinct contributions and express their own point of view on all debated issues. Within the necessary limits of space they frequently draw attention to interpretations which they themselves do not hold but which represent the stated conclusions of sincere fellow Christians.

Dr Richard Hess has brought his special knowledge of the languages, archaeology and culture of the ancient Near East to the elucidation of the book of Joshua. In doing this he faces problems which have concerned many thoughtful readers. These include Israel's entry into the promised land, the concept of 'holy war', the total ban on its Canaanite opponents, the fall of Jericho and the role of Rahab. At the same time he unhesitatingly makes the application of the book relevant to today's Christian church and reader.

In the Old Testament in particular no single English translation is adequate to reflect the original text. The version on which this commentary is based is the New International Version, but other translations are frequently referred to as well, and on occasion the author supplies his own. Where necessary, words are transliterated in order to help the reader who is unfamiliar with Hebrew to identify the precise word under discussion. It is assumed throughout that the reader will have ready access to one, or more, reliable rendering of the Bible in English.

Interest in the meaning and message of the Old Testament

continues undiminished, and it is hoped that this series will thus further the systematic study of the revelation of God and his will and ways as seen in these records. It is the prayer of the editor and publisher, as of the authors, that these books will help many to understand, and to respond to, the Word of God today.

D. J. WISEMAN

CONTENTS

CONTENTS

AUTHOR'S PREFACE

The stories of Joshua are among the most exciting in the Bible. Who has not thrilled to the drama of the march around Jericho and the collapse of the wall? Or who has not pictured in the mind the drama of the battle of the 'longest day', when the sun stood in its place and Joshua fought the kings of the south? Mixed in with these colourful accounts are the accounts of the founding of a nation in its land, the covenant ceremonies with all Israel meeting before Joshua and renewing their commitment to God, and the detailed allocations of land, that great visible symbol of the blessing of God to the chosen people. This is the book of Joshua and today more than ever its message bears hearing.

The exciting results of archaeology have provided the Bible reader with a sharper and more detailed view of the world of early Israel than was available even a few years ago. There are the great sites of generations of archaeological exploration: Jericho, Lachish and Hazor, and their insights and challenges to the interpretation of the period. There are analyses that probe into the structure and form of key textual sources from outside the Bible: the Merneptah stele and its first mention of 'Israel', the Amarna texts and their picture of the political world of Canaan, and the newly discovered cuneiform texts from Hazor, Hebron and elsewhere that add insights to the reader's understanding of the biblical text. And then there is the important emergence of social archaeology and, with it, the site surveys of the past few decades. For the first time there is available a more complete understanding of how people lived, of where they lived and of how many of them actually settled in the hill country and elsewhere. With this new evidence to draw upon, the book of Joshua can be rooted in the early Israelite world in a more accurate and detailed manner than was ever possible before.

In addition, the impact of literary approaches to the Bible in

9

general and to Joshua in particular has meant new under-
standings of old problems. Questions such as 'How many times
does Israel actually cross the Jordan?' and with it the inevitable
'How many sources make up this account?' can be approached
in more satisfying ways than by assuming incompetent writers
in order to answer them.

More important than all these opportunities, however, is the
message that this book contains for the Christian. Here is
encouragement to faith in God in the midst of impossible odds,
warning of the terrible consequences of sin upon family and
community, and the encouragement to receive and accept
God's new covenant in Christ and to appropriate its blessings in
the same way that the Israelites of Joshua dedicated themselves
to the occupation and allocation of the Promised Land.

I am grateful to the principal and staff of Glasgow Bible
College for their support during the preparation of this study,
and especially to the students with whom I was able to discuss
many of the ideas found here. Others have also contributed
thoughts and ideas to this small commentary, and so it is a
privilege to thank especially the following people: Revd David
Kingdon for his suggestions and comments on the initial drafts
of the manuscript; Dr K. Lawson Younger, Jr., for his careful
reading of much of the work and his important insights; and
Professor Donald Wiseman who continued to provide helpful
suggestions throughout the various phases of this manuscript. I
would also like to thank Dr Graeme Auld for bibliographic
suggestions. Professor Alan Millard and Dr Nicolai Winther-
Nielsen kindly shared with me portions of their unpublished
manuscripts. The work is dedicated to Jean who has helped me
to see beyond pages and screens of text to a life lived in
faithfulness.

24 October, 1995   *Richard S. Hess*
                                              Roehampton Institute London

CHIEF ABBREVIATIONS

AB	Analecta Biblica.
ABD	D. N. Freedman *et al* (eds.), *The Anchor Bible Dictionary*, 6 vols. (Garden City, New York: Doubleday, 1992).
Aharoni, *Land*	Y. Aharoni, *The Land of the Bible: A Historical Geography*, reviser and tr. A. F. Rainey (Westminster: Philadelphia, 1979).
ANEP	J. B. Pritchard (ed.), *The Ancient Near East in Pictures* (Princeton University Press, ²1969).
ANET	J. B. Pritchard (ed.), *Ancient Near Eastern Texts relating to the Old Testament* (Princeton University Press, ³1969).
AOAT	Alter Orient und Altes Testament.
ASOR	American Schools of Oriental Research.
BA	*Biblical Archaeologist.*
BAR	*Biblical Archaeology Review.*
Barthélemy	D. Barthélemy, *Critique textuelle de l'ancien testament. 1. Josué, Juges, Ruth, Samuel, Rois, Chroniques, Esdras, Néhémié, Esthèr*, OBO 50/1 (Fribourg Suisse: Editions Universitaires; Göttingen: Vandenhoeck & Ruprecht, 1982).
BASOR	*Bulletin of the American Schools of Oriental Research.*
BAT	A. Biran and J. Aviram (eds.), *Biblical Archaeology Today, 1990. Proceedings of the Second International Congress on Biblical Archaeology. Jerusalem, June–July 1990* (Jerusalem: Israel Exploration Society, 1993).
BETL	Bibliotheca Ephemeridum Theologicarum Lovaniensium.
Bib	*Biblica.*

Blaikie	W. G. Blaikie, *The Book of Joshua* (London: Hodder & Stoughton, 1908).
Boling and Wright	R. G. Boling and G. E. Wright, *Joshua. A New Translation with Introduction and Commentary*, Anchor Bible 6 (Garden City, New York: Doubleday, 1982).
BR	*Bible Review.*
Butler	T. C. Butler, *Joshua*, WBC 7 (Waco: Word, 1988).
BZ	*Biblische Zeitschrift.*
BZAW	Beiheft sur ZAW.
CAD	E. Reiner *et al.* (eds.), *Chicago Assyrian Dictionary* (Chicago: The Oriental Institute; Glückstadt: J. J. Augustin, 1956–).
CBOTS	Coniectanea Biblica Old Testament Series.
CBQ	*Catholic Biblical Quarterly.*
ch.	chapter.
Das Land	G. Strecker (ed.), *Das Land Israel in biblischer Zeit. Jerusalem-Symposium 1981 der Hebräischen Universität und der Georg-August-Universität*, Göttinger Theologische Arbeiten 25 (Göttingen: Vandenhoeck & Ruprecht, 1983).
Fritz	V. Fritz, *Das Buch Josua*, Handbuch zum Alten Testament I/7 (Tübingen: J. C. B. Mohr, 1994).
FTH	A. R. Millard, J. K. Hoffmeier and D. W. Baker (eds.), *Faith, Tradition, History: Old Testament Historiography in Its Near Eastern Context* (Winona Lake, Indiana: Eisenbrauns, 1994).
Garstang	J. Garstang, *The Foundations of Biblical History: Joshua, Judges* (London: Constable, 1931).
Gottwald	N. K. Gottwald, *The Tribes of Yahweh: A Sociology of the Religion of Liberated Israel 1250–1050 BCE* (London: SCM, 1980).
Gray	J. Gray, *Joshua, Judges, Ruth*, New Century Bible Commentary (Grand Rapids, Michigan: Eerdmans, 1986).
Hamlin	E. J. Hamlin, *Joshua. Inheriting the Land*, International Theological Commentary

	(Grand Rapids, Michigan: Eerdmans, 1983).
HAR	*Hebrew Annual Review.*
Hawk	L. D. Hawk, *Every Promise Fulfilled. Contesting Plots in Joshua,* Literary Currents in Biblical Interpretation (Louisville: Westminster/ John Knox, 1991).
Heb.	Hebrew.
Hertzberg	H. W. Hertzberg, *Die Bücher Josua, Richter, Ruth,* Das Alte Testament Deutsch 9 (Göttingen: Vandenhoeck & Ruprecht, 1973).
HHI	H. Tadmor and M. Weinfeld (eds.), *History, Historiography and Interpretation. Studies in Biblical and Cuneiform Literatures* (Jerusalem: Magnes; Leiden: Brill, 1983).
HSM	Harvard Semitic Monographs.
HTR	*Harvard Theological Review.*
IDB	G. Buttrick *et al* (eds.), *The Interpreter's Dictionary of the Bible* (Nashville: Abingdon, 1962).
IES	Israel Exploration Society.
IEJ	*Israel Exploration Journal.*
IOS	*Israel Oriental Studies.*
JBL	*Journal of Biblical Literature.*
JPOS	*Journal of the Palestine Oriental Society.*
JSOT/*JSOT*	Journal for the Study of the Old Testament/ *Journal for the Study of the Old Testament.*
KAI	H. Donner and W. Röllig, *Kanaanäische und Aramäische Inschriften,* 3 vols. (Wiesbaden: Harrassowitz, 1973–1979).
Kallai	Z. Kallai, *Historical Geography of the Bible: The Tribal Territories of Israel* (Jerusalem: Magnes; Leiden: Brill, 1986).
Keil and Delitzsch	C. F. Keil and F. Delitzsch, *Commentary on the Old Testament in Ten Volumes* II. *Joshua, Judges, Ruth, I and II Samuel,* tr. J. Martin (Grand Rapids, Michigan: Eerdmans, n.d.).
Kh.	Khirbet (Ḥirbet).
Koopmans, *Joshua 24*	W. T. Koopmans, *Joshua 24 as Poetic Narrative, JSOT* Supplement 93 (Sheffield: JSOT Press, 1990).

Koorevaar	H. J. Koorevaar, *De Opbouw van het Boek Jozua* (Heverlee: Centrum voor Bijbelse Vorming België, 1990).
KS	A. Alt, *Kleine Schriften zur Geschichte des Volkes Israel* (Munich: C. H. Beck, 1953).
LXX	Septuagint (pre-Christian Greek version of the Old Testament).
LXX A	Septuagint Codex Alexandrinus.
LXX B	Septuagint Codex Vaticanus.
Madvid	D. H. Madvid, *Joshua,* The Expositor's Bible Commentary 3 (Grand Rapids, Michigan: Zondervan, 1992).
Mazar	B. Mazar, *The Early Biblical Period. Historical Essays,* eds. S. Ahituv and B. A. Levine (Jerusalem: IES, 1986).
Mitchell	G. Mitchell, *Together in the Land. A Reading of the Book of Joshua, JSOT* Supplement 134 (Sheffield: JSOT Press, 1993).
Moab	A. Dearman (ed.), *Studies in the Mesha Inscription and Moab,* Archaeology and Biblical Studies 2 (Atlanta: Scholars Press, 1989).
MT	Massoretic Text (the standard Hebrew text of the Old Testament).
Na'aman, *Borders*	N. Na'aman, *Borders and Districts in Biblical Historiography,* Jerusalem Biblical Studies 4 (Jerusalem: Simor, 1986).
NIV	New International Version, 1984.
NJPS	New Jewish Publication Society, 1978.
Noth	M. Noth, *Das Buch Josua,* Handbuch zur Alten Testament, I/7 (Tübingen: Universitätsverlag, ^{2}1953).
NRSV	New Revised Standard Version, 1989.
OBO	Orbis Biblicus et Orientalis.
Ottosson	M. Ottosson, *Josuaboken: En programskrift for davidisk restauration,* Acta Universitatis upsaliensis, Studia biblica pusaliensia 1 (Stockholm: Almqvist & Wiksell, 1991).
OTS	*Oudtestamentische Studien.*
PEQ	*Palestine Exploration Quarterly.*
Polzin	R. Polzin, *Moses and the Deuteronomist. A Literary Study of the Deuteronomistic History:*

	Part One. Deuteronomy, Joshua, Judges (New York: Seabury Press, 1980).
POTT	D. J. Wiseman (ed.), *Peoples of Old Testament Times* (Oxford: Clarendon, 1973).
Power	M. T. Larsen (ed.), *Power and Propaganda. A Symposium on Ancient Empires*, MESOPOTAMIA, Copenhagen Studies in Assyriology 7 (Copenhagen: Akademisk Forlag, 1979).
RB	*Revue Biblique.*
RSV	Revised Standard Version, 1952.
SBLSCSS	Society of Biblical Literature Septuagint and Cognate Studies Series.
Schäfer-Lichtenberger	C. Schäfer-Lichtenberger, *Josu und Salomo. Eine Studie zu Autorität und Legitimität des Nachfolgers im Alten Testament, VT* Supplement 58 (Leiden: Brill, 1995).
SJOT	*Scandinavian Journal of the Old Testament.*
Soggin	J. A. Soggin, *Joshua. A Commentary*, Old Testament Library (Philadelphia: Westminster, 1972).
Steuernagel	C. Steuernagel, *Deuteronomium und Josua,* Hand Kommentar zum Alten Testament (Göttingen: Vandenhoeck und Ruprecht, ²1923).
Svensson	J. Svensson, *Towns and Toponyms in the Old Testament with Special Emphasis on Joshua 14 – 21*, CBOTS 38 (Stockholm: Almqvist & Wiksell, 1994).
SWBA	Social World of Biblical Antiquity.
T	Tell (Tel).
TDOT	G. J. Botterweck and H. Ringgren (eds.), *Theological Dictionary of the Old Testament* (Grand Rapids, Michigan: Eerdmans, 1974–).
TOTC	Tyndale Old Testament Commentaries.
TynB	*Tyndale Bulletin.*
UF	*Ugarit Forschungen*
Ugarit and the Bible	G. Brooke, A. Curtis and J. Healey (eds.), *Ugarit and the Bible: Proceedings of the International Symposium on Ugarit and the Bible. Manchester, September 1992*, Ugaritisch-Biblische Literatur Band 11 (Münster:

	Ugarit-Verlag, 1994).
v./vv.	verse/verses.
VT	*Vetus Testamentum.*
WBC	Word Biblical Commentary.
Weinfeld, *Promise*	M. Weinfeld, *The Promise of the Land. The Inheritance of the Land of Canaan by the Israelites,* The Taubman Lectures in Jewish Studies (Berkeley: University of California Press, 1993).
Winther-Nielsen	N. Winther-Nielsen, *A Functional Discourse Grammar of Joshua. A Computer-Assisted Rhetorical Structure Analysis,* CBOTS 40 (Stockholm: Almqvist & Wiksell, 1995).
World of Ancient Israel	R. E. Clements (ed.), *The World of Ancient Israel. Sociological, Anthropological and Political Perspectives* (Cambridge University Press, 1989).
Woudstra	M. H. Woudstra, *The Book of Joshua,* New International Commentary on the Old Testament (Grand Rapids, Michigan: Eerdmans, 1981).
WTJ	*Westminster Theological Journal.*
Younger	K. L. Younger, Jr, *Ancient Conquest Accounts. A Study in Ancient Near Eastern and Biblical History Writing, JSOT* Supplement 98 (Sheffield: JSOT Press, 1990).
ZA	*Zeitschrift für Assyriologie.*
ZAW	*Zeitschrift für die Alttestamentliche Wissenschaft.*
ZDPV	*Zeitschrift des Deutschen Palästina-Vereins.*

INTRODUCTION

TITLE AND TEXT

The title of the book is the same as its major human character, Joshua. The name 'Joshua' is composed of two parts. The first part is a shortened form of the divine name 'LORD', (Heb. *yhwh*). The second part is the Hebrew word for 'salvation'. Thus the name means 'the Lord is salvation'.[1] Names made of the word for 'LORD' are common in Israel for all of its later history. However, at the beginning of Israel's history these names are fewer. As might be expected (see Ex. 6:3), the new awareness of Israel's God and his salvation led later generations to name their children in ways that confessed the power and love of their God. But in the period of Moses this practice was rare.[2] The name describes a special role that Moses wished Joshua to have when he renamed him in Numbers 13:16. Joshua's earlier name, Hoshea, simply means 'he has saved'. In the name Hoshea, the person or god who saves is not made clear. Moses specified the LORD as the source of salvation by renaming Joshua.

The book of Joshua in the Massoretic Text (MT) of the Hebrew Bible, as preserved in Codex Aleppo and Codex Leningrad, is the primary text used in this commentary. These codices date from 925 and 1008 AD.[3] They represent a form of the Hebrew text that agrees for the most part with other Hebrew manuscripts and with most ancient versions. There are two important groups of ancient texts that differ from this

---

[1] J. D. Fowler, *Theophoric Personal Names in Ancient Hebrew. A Comparative Study*, *JSOT* Supplement 49 (Sheffield: JSOT Press, 1988), pp. 114–115. The Greek transliteration of this name is identical to 'Jesus' in the New Testament.

[2] J. C. de Moor, *The Rise of Yahwism. The Roots of Israelite Monotheism*, BETL 91 (Leuven: University Press and Peeters, 1990), pp. 13–34. De Moor identifies only one personal name in the Bible from the time of Moses (p. 33).

[3] E. R. Brotzman, *Old Testament Textual Criticism. A Practical Introduction* (Grand Rapids: Baker, 1994), pp. 56–57.

tradition: the Greek translation of Joshua preserved in the Septuagint (LXX) and the Dead Sea Scroll fragments from Cave 4 at Qumran, 4QJos[a] and 4QJos[b].[1]

Textual criticism of the LXX of Joshua owes a great deal to Margolis.[2] Further study has confirmed many of his restorations of the Old Greek. However, it has called into question earlier conclusions that the translator worked with a Hebrew text identical to the MT.[3] The LXX preserves a shorter text of Joshua than does the MT and, since many textual critics view longer texts as later, several scholars have proposed that the LXX preserves a more original text.[4] The LXX and the MT preserve two separate editions of the text of Joshua.[5] The differences between the two editions are minor. Textual critics identify secondary elements in both texts.

One should not assume the priority of one text over the other in any particular instance. For example, in Joshua 7, 'Achan' in the MT is replaced by the name 'Achar' in the LXX. Achar appears as Achan's name in 1 Chronicles 2:7 in both versions. However, Achan is the original reading in Joshua. This is because Achan occurs as a personal name elsewhere in the Ancient Near East but the root carries no meaning in Hebrew; Achar, however, is a wordplay on the Valley of Achor (see comments on Joshua 7, p. 155) and becomes a 'nickname' for Achan in 1 Chronicles 2:7. Thus,

---

[1] E. Tov, 'The Growth of the Book of Joshua in the Light of the Evidence of the LXX Translation', *Scripta Hierosolymitana*, XXXI. *Studies in the Bible 1986* (Jerusalem: Magnes, 1986), p. 321.

[2] M. L. Margolis (ed.), *The Book of Joshua in Greek* (Paris: Librairie orientaliste Paul Geuthner, 1931); *idem, The Book of Joshua in Greek. Part V: Joshua 19:39 – 24:33* (Philadelphia: Annenberg Research Institute, 1992). The restoration of the Old Greek translation relies upon Codex Vaticanus and upon the readings from Theodotion's translation in Origen's Hexapla.

[3] See, among others, L. J. Greenspoon, *Textual Studies in the Book of Joshua*, HSM 28 (Chico, California: Scholars Press, 1983).

[4] A. G. Auld, *Studies in Joshua: Text and Literary Relations* (Unpublished PhD thesis, University of Edinburgh, 1976); *idem,* 'Cities of Refuge in Israelite Tradition', *JSOT*, 10, 1978, pp. 26–40; *idem,* 'Textual and Literary Studies in the Book of Joshua', *ZAW*, 90, 1978, pp. 412–417; *idem,* 'The Levitical Cities: Text and History', *ZAW*, 91, 1979, pp. 194–206; A. Rofé, 'The End of the Book of Joshua in the Septuagint', *Henoch*, 4, 1982, pp. 17–35; *idem,* 'Joshua 20: Historico-literary Criticism Illustrated' in J. H. Tigay (ed.), *Empirical Models for Biblical Criticism* (Philadelphia: University of Pennsylvania Press, 1985), pp. 131–147.

[5] E. Tov, 'The Growth of the Book of Joshua in the Light of the Evidence of the LXX Translation', pp. 321–339.

while the development from Achan to Achar is easily explained by the Bible's tendency to nickname, a shift from Achar to Achan is anomalous. Nor is it likely that Achar is a scribal error for Achan, since the name occurs more than once in Joshua 7. In this instance, at least, the MT preserves a more original reading.[1]

Nevertheless, the LXX preserves early readings and interpretations of the biblical text. For this reason some of the more important additions (*e.g.* the one at the end of ch. 24) are included at their appropriate places in the commentary.

Fragments from two scrolls at Qumran contain the text of Joshua.[2] They may be dated to *c.* 100 BC. Greenspoon's analysis of a selection of readings from both scrolls led him to several conclusions, two of which are relevant here.

(1) This material shows a wide acquaintance with distinctive readings preserved in the MT, usually in the direction of full texts judged to be secondary expansions. (2) The scribe(s) responsible for these scrolls were not reluctant to incorporate material of their own creation, material I judge to be 'in the spirit' of the MT.[3]

A similar conclusion is reached by Tov in his analysis of 4QJos[b].[4] With regard to the relation of the Qumran texts to the LXX, Greenspoon concludes: 'In the absence of any (many?) 4Q-LXX agreements in the more significant area of secondary readings, it is not necessary to posit any acquaintance on the part of these scribes with the distinctive features of the LXX tradition.'[5]

The most significant Dead Sea Scroll variant is found in

---

[1]R. S. Hess, 'Achan and Achor: Names and Wordplay in Joshua 7', *HAR*, 14, 1994, pp. 89–98.

[2]L. J. Greenspoon, 'The Qumran Fragments of Joshua: Which Puzzle Are They Part of and Where Do They Fit?' in G. J. Brooke and B. Lindars (eds.), *Septuagint, Scrolls and Cognate Writings. Papers Presented to the International Symposium on the Septuagint and Its Relations to the Dead Sea Scrolls and Other Writings (Manchester, 1990)*, SBLSCSS 33 (Atlanta: Scholars Press, 1992), pp. 159–204; E. Tov, '4QJosh[b]', in Z. J. Kapera (ed.), *Intertestamental Essays in Honour of Józef Tadeusz Milik* (Cracow: Enigma, 1992), pp. 205–212.

[3]L. J. Greenspoon, 'The Qumran Fragments of Joshua: Which Puzzle Are They Part of and Where Do They Fit?', pp. 174–175.

[4]E. Tov, '4QJosh[b]', p. 212.

[5]L. J. Greenspoon, 'The Qumran Fragments of Joshua: Which Puzzle Are They Part of and Where Do They Fit?', p. 175.

4QJos[a]. Ulrich's publication of this text indicates that fragments contain the following verses and additional non-biblical text (= X) in this order: 8:34–35; X; 5:2–7; 6:5–10; 7:12–17; 8:3–14, (18?); 10:2–5, 8–11.[1] Joshua 8:34–35, the account of the building of the altar on Mount Ebal, is out of its Massoretic sequence in this text. It occurs immediately after the crossing of the Jordan River. In the Septuagint, 8:30–35 follows 9:1, a text similar to 5:1. This variation leads Rofé to see the presence of several different recensions or editions of the text.[2] Auld argues that this demonstrates that 8:30–35 is a late text inserted by different editors into different places in the text.[3] However, the fragmentary nature of this text and the difficulty of assigning any of the X material that follows to a biblical text in Joshua or elsewhere suggest that caution is necessary regarding even the nature of the Qumran document. Could this be a midrashic style of text or a 'parabiblical' text, containing a collection of various biblical quotations along with additional notes and explanations?

THE PERSON OF JOSHUA

(a) The Pentateuch

Joshua is mentioned twenty-seven times in the Pentateuch.[4] He is introduced in the account of the war with the Amalekites (Ex. 17:8–13) as a warrior who fights on behalf of Moses and who leads Israel to victory. In fact, this is Israel's first war after the exodus from Egypt. Joshua appears in what will become a characteristic role as general of the armies with an authority approved by Moses and is mentioned without introduction or epithet.[5] He personifies the struggle as he alone is mentioned

---

[1] E. Ulrich, '4QJoshua[a] and Joshua's First Altar in the Promised Land' in G. J. Brooke and F. García Martínez (eds.), *New Qumran Texts and Studies: Proceedings of the First Meeting of the International Organization for Qumran Studies, Paris 1992.* Studies in Texts from the Desert of Judea 15 (Leiden: Brill, 1994), pp. 89–104.

[2] A. Rofé, 'The Editing of the Book of Joshua in the Light of 4QJosh[a]' in G. J. Brooke and F. García Martínez (eds.), *op. cit.*, pp. 73–80.

[3] A Graeme Auld, 'Reading Joshua after Kings' in J. Davies, G. Harvey and W. G. E. Watson (eds.), *Words Remembered, Texts Renewed: Essays in Honour of John F. A. Sawyer, JSOT* Supplement 195 (Sheffield: JSOT Press, 1995), pp. 167–181.

[4] These include: Ex. 17:9, 10, 13, 14; 24:13; 32:17; 33:11; Nu. 11:28; 13:16; 14:6, 30, 38; 26:65; 27:18, 22; 32:12, 28; 34:17; Dt. 1:38; 3:21, 28; 31:3, 7, 14 (twice), 23; 34:9.

[5] Schäfer-Lichtenberger, p. 112, suggests that this attests to the importance of Joshua and his similarity to Moses, who is also introduced without a father's name. Schäfer-Lichtenberger emphasizes the twin roles of Joshua as under

as selecting the army and as fighting and overcoming the enemy. Israel is mentioned as an army once (v. 11). In Exodus 24:13, Moses ascends the mountain of God with Joshua, who is designated 'his assistant' (Heb. $m^e\check{s}\bar{a}r^et\hat{o}$)[1] and who first speaks with him of the noise in the camp when Moses returns from the summit (32:17). He is kept separate from Israel's sin with the golden calf.[2] Joshua appears to have had a place at the tent of meeting. In 33:11, he is described as 'the son of Nun' and as a 'youth' (Heb. na^car; perhaps a better translation would be 'squire'), as he prepares to succeed Moses.

Joshua does not appear again until Numbers 11:28 where he protests against the prophesying of Israelites not selected by Moses. As if to reintroduce him, he is once again described as 'son of Nun' and 'Moses' aide since youth'. Moses rejects the protest. Despite his closeness to Moses and his earlier presence on the holy mountain, Joshua still has much to learn before he will assume the leadership.

When the spies are sent to explore the land of Canaan, we learn for the first time that Moses renamed Hoshea from the tribe of Ephraim as Joshua (Nu. 13:16; also in Dt. 32:44). Moses' act of renaming may be compared with God's actions in re-naming the patriarchs Abram and Jacob. In such cases, a quality of the person's character or future role is discerned. Is this a confession of a special act of God's salvation of Joshua or a desire by Moses to affirm the salvation that the LORD gives to Israel?[3]

When only Joshua and Caleb provide a positive evaluation of Israel's ability to conquer Canaan, these two alone are spared the plague that puts to death the other spies and they alone of that generation are promised entrance to the land of Canaan (Nu. 14:6, 30, 38). Joshua is commissioned to succeed Moses in Numbers 27:18–23.[4] There he is referred to as someone in

---

authority to his (eventual) predecessor, Moses, and as acting as an independent military leader. These twin roles will reappear in the first chapter of Joshua.

[1] This is a legally free person who nevertheless functions in a relationship of service to another. See Schäfer-Lichtenberger, p. 121.

[2] Schäfer-Lichtenberger, p. 124, who also observes the correspondence between Joshua's distance from Israel and his closeness to the holy things of God (p. 130).

[3] *Ibid.*, p. 140, observes that the name Hosea suggests that Joshua had a tribal leadership role separate from his special relationship with Moses.

[4] *Ibid.*, pp. 144, 154, suggests that as of Nu. 14 it is unclear whether Caleb or Joshua will be chosen as Moses' successor. Nu. 27 makes clear that God, not Moses, does the choosing.

whom is the spirit. The public commissioning involves Moses' laying of his hands upon Joshua and commissioning him (Heb. *wayᵉṣawwēhû*, v. 23). The public transfer of Moses' authority (Heb. *hôḏ*) is partial, as Moses will continue to lead the people for a time.[1] As part of his responsibilities, Joshua will stand before Eleazar the priest who will discern God's will through the Urim. Joshua is to command the people. In 34:17, it becomes clear that the work of Eleazar and Joshua is specifically concerned with the assignment of the Promised Land. The instructions regarding the allotment of the Trans-jordanian tribes in chapter 32 are passed along to Joshua and to Eleazar.

The first appearance of Joshua in Deuteronomy is also heralded with a special epithet. In addition to his designation as the son of Nun, he is also described as one who 'stands before' Moses, just as he would stand before Eleazar. In 1:38, God commands Moses to 'strengthen' (Heb. *ḥazzēq*) Joshua because he will cause Israel to inherit the land. When this is retold in 3:28, and linked with the verb 'to encourage' (Heb. *'mṣ*), it creates the familiar double form 'encourage and strengthen'. This formula is repeated three times when Moses passes the leadership to Joshua (31:6, 7, 23). God speaks to Joshua in 31:23 with the encouragement to 'be strong and courageous' and with the promise of his presence. However, God's address centres on the promise to Joshua that 'you will bring the Israelites into the land I promised'. Here for the first time Joshua is told to 'bring' the people into the land.[2] As the end of Moses' time on earth approaches, God assures Joshua that his role will include leadership of the people as they enter the Promised Land. Deuteronomy 32:44 describes how 'Moses came with Joshua son of Nun' to teach the people the song of that chapter. However, Joshua's name is spelled 'Hoshea', like his original name (Nu. 13:16). In contrast to the kings of other lands, Joshua does not take a new name as he prepares to assume leadership. Instead, he reverts to his first name, a sign of his own independence from Moses even at the point where

---

[1] *Ibid.*, pp. 166, 174–175, suggests that the full authority of Moses, received directly from God, is unique and cannot be completely transferred. See Dt. 34:10.

[2] See Dt. 31:7 where Joshua is told, 'You must go with this people into the land.' Schäfer-Lichtenberger, pp. 177–178.

he is about to succeed him.[1] In Deuteronomy 34:9 the spirit of wisdom fills Joshua when Moses lays hands on him. The intention of these events in Deuteronomy is to demonstrate that Joshua's leadership is based upon God's instructions, through Moses, to appoint him.

Barstad has identified the 'prophet like Moses' of Deuteronomy 18:15–19 as Joshua.[2] He separates 18:20–22 from verses 15–19. The later verses address the unrelated issue of false prophets and their detection. Deuteronomy 3:23–29 had already prepared the reader to accept Joshua as Moses' successor. Deuteronomy 34:10, which describes the absence of someone like Moses whom the Lord knew face to face, anticipates the book of Joshua and Joshua's stewardship of the Mosaic law. The similarities between Joshua and Moses further demonstrate the distinctive relationship of the two.[3] Barstad uses this argument to support his thesis that Deuteronomy places prophets in a secondary relationship to the law of Moses. However, there is nothing in the argument that Joshua is a fulfilment of Deuteronomy 18:15–19 that excludes the possibility that other prophets might also have been envisaged.[4]

For the Christian, this background exemplifies the preparation of a leader for Christian ministry. The leader is someone who, like Joshua, has already undertaken specific tasks successfully and who has demonstrated a loyalty to God's Word even when that means standing out from the crowd. Such a leader, who acts with independent judgment, can make mistakes. However, it is important to learn from those mistakes. A leader like Joshua is someone recognized by the people of God and, most important of all, someone whom God clearly chooses.

(b) The book of Joshua

Joshua 1 has a view of its chief character that is repeated throughout the book. It is found in God's charge, *Only be strong and courageous* (1:7, 18). This serves three purposes: (1) to confirm Joshua's leadership with a statement exhorting him to lead; (2) to recognize God's choice of Joshua as Moses'

[1] Schäfer-Lichtenberger, pp. 186–187.

[2] H. M. Barstad, 'The Understanding of the Prophets in Deuteronomy', *SJOT*, 8, 1994, pp. 236–251.

[3] Barstad cites Polzin, pp. 74ff., and Ottosson, pp. 21–23.

[4] A point made by K. Jeppesen, 'Is Deuteronomy Hostile Towards Prophets?', *SJOT*, 8, 1994, pp. 252–256.

successor by repeating this to both Moses and Joshua; and (3) to bring to a close the first two actions of Joshua in which he effectively exerts his leadership over all the people through (1) commanding the officers of Israel and thereby implicitly all of Israel, and (2) gaining full recognition of his leadership from the Transjordanian tribes. Joshua sends the spies to Jericho and receives their report (2:1, 23–24; see 7:2–3; 18:3–10). Joshua continues to receive and obey directions from God (3:7–13). The opening sentence of Joshua 4:10 specifies the place of Joshua in guiding the people. Repeated statements in this passage confirm these actions as a response to earlier instructions of Moses and to God's plan for his people. This culminates in verse 14 where God exalts Joshua before all Israel. Joshua's role as the chosen intermediary between the LORD and the people continues in the crossing of the Jordan with its miracle of the stopping of the waters, itself a response to Joshua's instructions (chs. 3 – 4). Once across the Jordan and encamped at Gilgal (ch. 5), Joshua is again leader and God's representative to Israel. His position is confirmed in Canaan, just as he had been confirmed as Moses' successor in Transjordan.

In Joshua 5:13 – 6:27, the confrontation with the commander of the LORD's army suggests a scene not unlike that of the commissioning of Moses and of later prophets. It thus gave Joshua new authority and responsibility before God, which continued in Israel's defeat of Jericho and in the salvation of Rahab. Israel obeyed God's word through Joshua.

Joshua 7 enhances the role of Israel's leader in several ways: (1) he is not named in the disastrous assault on Ai; (2) he leads the elders in penitence before God; (3) he receives divine instructions on how to identify the perpetrator and what to do when he is identified; and (4) he leads Israel in carrying out those instructions. Thus Joshua's religious and political leadership is not marred by the incident with Achan. On the contrary, it is enhanced. This is surprising when compared with Moses' time. With each new problem that Israel faced in the wilderness, they complained and grumbled. The difference is in the object of the complaint. Israel in the wilderness constantly complained about what God had provided, whether food, or the Promised Land, or the leadership of Moses. In the case of Achan's sin, the concern focused on following the divine direction. Israel could not do this unless they removed the sin from their midst. Thus Israel in the wilderness brought sin into their midst whereas the Israel of Joshua 7 sought to remove it. The purpose of Joshua in seeking direction to remove the sin coincided with Israel's desire to receive divine favour in order to possess the land.

In Joshua 8:1–29, Joshua receives God's word, instructs the Israelite army, deploys his forces, launches the attack with the signal from his weapon and directs the destruction of the enemy. In contrast to chapter 7, where he is not named in sending the forces who are defeated, chapter 8 positions Joshua as the initiator of each part of the battle. The repeated words 'see' and 'hand' describe Joshua's strategy. Because of divine revelation, he sees clearly what strategy to launch and he commands Israel to join him in 'seeing' this. Because of divine initiative, Joshua's 'hand' becomes the power by which the enemy is defeated. This occurs literally, as the weapon in his hand becomes the turning point in the narrative. It occurs symbolically, as the army of Israel, under his control, defeats the forces of Bethel and Ai.

The concern of chapter 9 to magnify Joshua's role as leader is evident. He appears at the beginning as the one in charge of negotiations. At the end of the account, he pronounces judgment on the Gibeonites, describing their servitude but thereby rescuing them from the wrath of Israel who wish to put them to death. Even though Israel's leadership is discredited in its dealings with outsiders, Joshua's position remains secure.

Chapters 10 – 12 argue that the southern and northern parts of Canaan were given to the nation by its God who fought for it. The key to this success was Joshua who heard God's word and obeyed it, just as God heard Joshua's prayer and answered it (11:12).

Joshua's key role continues as he presides over the allotments (chs. 13 – 21; especially 14:1, 6, 13–15; 18:1–10; 19:51; 20:1–3; 21:1–2), sends away the Transjordanian tribes (22:1–8), gathers Israel for a final exhortation (23:1–2), renews the covenant with Israel (24:1) and sends Israel to their inheritance (24:18). At the end of his life, like Moses, he receives the accolade *servant of the LORD* (24:29).

ANTIQUITY

The following items in the book of Joshua cannot otherwise be explained than, or can best be explained, by tracing their origin to the second millennium BC:[1]

1. The description of the borders of Canaan in the Pentateuch and in Joshua 1:4 matches the Egyptian understanding of Canaan in second-millennium BC sources, where the cities of Byblos, Tyre, Sidon, Acco and Hazor form part of the land.[2] The northern boundary never was clear because the Egyptians, who saw Canaan as part of their empire, were in conflict with the Hittites on the northern border of the land. The Mediterranean Sea formed the western border of Canaan and the Jordan River formed the eastern border (though north of the Sea of Galilee the region included areas farther east). The biblical concept of the Promised Land in Joshua agrees with the Egyptian usage of Canaan during their New Kingdom empire.

2. M. Weinfeld argues for the antiquity of Joshua 2, citing examples of parallels with Ancient Near Eastern cultures of the second millennium BC:[3]

Sending out men for reconnaissance was a widespread phenomenon in the east. Moreover, a prostitute's or inn-keeper's house was the accustomed place for meeting with spies, conspirators, and the like. Thus, for example, we read in Hammurabi's Code: 'If scoundrels plot together [in

[1] Some of this material is developed further in R. S. Hess, 'West Semitic Texts and the Book of Joshua', *Bulletin for Biblical Research*, forthcoming.

[2] See Mazar, pp. 192–193; Aharoni, *Land*, p. 69. The relevant sources are found in the satirical letter Papyrus Anastasi I and in the Amarna letters, especially EA 148 and 151 from the leader of Tyre, but including at least nine other letters from Byblos, Babylon, Alashia, and Amurru. See R. Hess, *Amarna Proper Names* (Ann Arbor, Michigan: University Microfilms, 1984), p. 460; E. Wente, *Letters from Ancient Egypt* (Atlanta: Scholars Press, 1990), pp. 106–109. The attempt of N. P. Lemche to dispute this depends on his alternative interpretation of a passage in EA 151, which he takes to mean that Cilician Danuna is part of Canaan. See N. P. Lemche, *The Canaanites and Their Land*, *JSOT* Supplement 110 (Sheffield: Sheffield Academic Press, 1991), pp. 25–52. Given the agreement of the other sources, however, A. F. Rainey's translation of this passage, which avoids such a conclusion, is to be preferred. See A. F. Rainey, 'Ugarit and the Canaanites again', *IEJ*, 14, 1964, p. 101.

[3] Weinfeld, *Promise*, pp. 141–143. On the laws of Hammurabi, see also P. Hieronymus Horn, 'Josua 2, 1–24 im Milieu einer "dimorphic society"', *BZ*, 31, 1987, pp. 264–270.

conspiratorial relationships] in an innkeeper's house, and she does not seize them and bring them to the palace, that innkeeper shall be put to death' (law § 109). In a Mari letter we read about two men who sow fear and panic and cause rebellion in an army. Also, the pattern of a three-day stay in an area when pursuing escapees has support in ancient eastern sources; for example the instructions to the Hittite tower commanders specify that if an enemy invades a place he must be pursued for three days. In the same collection of instructions we find that it is forbidden to build an inn (*arzana*) in which prostitutes live near the fortress wall, apparently because of the kind of danger described in Joshua 2.

3. Joshua 3:10 lists the groups of people whom God will drive out before Israel. Among these are three groups that have a distinctive association with the second millennium BC: the Hivites, the Perizzites and the Girgashites. The Hivites may be associated with Hurrian peoples who were among city leaders in Palestine in the fourteenth century and whose legacy remained to the time of David.[1] In Joshua 9:7 and 11:19, they are identified with the Gibeonites. A possible association has been observed with the place name Kue in Anatolia (1 Ki. 11:28).[2] A similar origin may exist for the Perizzites.[3] The association of Hivites and Perizzites with Hurrians is important

[1] This identification rests upon the interchange of 'Horite' and 'Hivite' in Gn. 36:2, 20 and the LXX rendering of 'Hivite' in Gn. 36:2 and Jos. 9:7. See E. A. Speiser, 'Hurrians', *IDB*, II, p. 665; H. A. Hofner, 'Hittites and Hurrians', *POTT*, p. 225. R. de Vaux, 'Les Hurrites de l'histoire et les Horites de la Bible', *RB*, 74, 1967, pp. 497–503, denied this relationship. However, the presence of Hurrian name bearers in nearby Jerusalem in the fourteenth century BC supports the equation. The attempt of O. Margalith, 'The Hivites', *ZAW*, 100, 1988, pp. 60–70, to identify them with the Ahhiyawa of Western Anatolia requires even greater linguistic shifts and finds little evidence in the hill country to support it.

[2] W. F. Albright, 'Cilicia and Babylonia under the Chaldean Kings', *BASOR*, 120, 1950, pp. 22–24.

[3] *Ibid.*, p. 25. M. Görg, 'Hiwwiter im 13. Jahrhundert v. Chr.', *UF*, 8, 1976, pp. 53–55, identifies it with the land of *pi-ri-in-du* in Cilicia. Others attempt a sociological definition, as people who dwell in unwalled villages and in the highland countryside. See R. F. Schnell, 'Perizzite', *IDB*, III, p. 735. While this association may have existed in Canaan, the name is attested in a personal name from fourteenth-century BC Mitanni, the Hurrian kingdom from northern Syria. Thus the name and presumably at least some of the people associated with it have a northern origin, however much the name becomes associated with 'foreigners' in general.

for dating. Hurrian peoples and names flourished in the Late Bronze Age (1550–1200 BC). Their presence diminished in the following two centuries and disappeared at the beginning of the first millennium BC. Girgashites may be attested in second-millennium BC Ugaritic and Egyptian sources.[1] These all may have migrated south from the Hittite empire and perhaps earlier, from the Hurrian kingdom of Mitanni.[2] Many peoples in addition to Israelites experienced migration during the latter half of the second millennium BC.

4. The act of God in bringing down the walls of Jericho (Jos. 6:20) has a parallel in a Hittite text:

> Shaushga of Shamuha, my lady, revealed also then her divine justice: in the very moment I reached him, the wooden fortifications fell down to the length of one *gipeššar*.[3]

5. The list of items that Achan stole fits best in the latter half of the second millennium BC. For the *beautiful robe from Babylonia*, see the commentary at Joshua 7:21 (p. 152). Two additional items from the list also support this conclusion. The term 'Shinar' designates Babylon in a variety of biblical passages. However, its cuneiform correspondent, Šanḫar, is used of Babylon in cuneiform texts only in the sixteenth to thirteenth centuries BC.[4] The description of *a wedge of gold weighing fifty shekels* finds a parallel in the fourteenth-century BC Amarna list of gifts from the king of Mitanni, 'an ingot of gold of 1,000 shekels in weight'.[5] Both use the same unusual word for 'ingot', literally 'tongue of'.[6] Both also follow the identical word order, ingot – gold – number – shekels – weight. These two

---

[1]M. Görg, *art. cit.*

[2]The preservation of the characteristic Hurrian -*zzi* suffix in 'Perizzite' may support this identification. For further discussion, see B. Mazar, 'The Early Israelite Settlement in the Hill Country', *BASOR*, 241, 1981, pp. 75–85, reprinted in Mazar, pp. 35–48; R. S. Hess, 'Cultural Aspects of Onomastic Distribution in the Amarna Texts', *UF*, 21, 1989, pp. 209–216.

[3]So M. Liverani, *Prestige and Interest. International Relations in the Near East ca. 1600–1100 BC*, History of the Ancient Near East/Studies 1 (Padova: Sargon, 1990), p. 155. The Hittite text is *Keilschrifturkunde aus Boghazkoy*, vol. VI, II 29–33.

[4]R. Zadok, 'The Origin of the Name Shinar', *ZA*, 74, 1984, p. 242.

[5]EA 29, lines 34 and 39. See H. P. Adler, *Das Akkadische des Königs Tušratta von Mitanni*, AOAT, 21 (Neukirchen-Vluyn: Neukirchener, 1976), pp. 234–235; A. R. Millard, 'Back to the Iron Bed: Og's or Procrustes'?', Congress Volume Paris 1992, Supplement to *VT*, 61 (Leiden: Brill, 1995), pp. 197–200.

[6]Hebrew *lešôn*, Akkadian *li-ša-an-nu ša.*

...he promises made to the Davidic line (2 Samuel 7). Joshua forms part of this history. A more positive perspective emphasizes God's promise and initiative in seeking new ways to bless the people when they reject him.[1] Literary approaches have sought to focus on some of the complex problems with which the people deal, the failure of simplistic theological solutions to deal with them and the record of this struggle in the Deuteronomistic history itself (Lasine).[2] Although Noth argued that the Deuteronomistic history was written by a single author in the exilic period, scholars since then have argued for authors working at two different periods,[3] or in stages of redactions or editions.[4]

The term 'Deuteronomistic' may be applied to Joshua in so far as it preserves a similar theological perspective and language as the other biblical texts mentioned above. Before Noth's hypothesis, emphasis was placed upon the relationship of Joshua to the Pentateuch. The similarities were felt to be so significant that the term 'Hexateuch' was used.[5] This affirmed Joshua as a continuation of the first five books. The similarities of language between Joshua and the Pentateuch have been noted in the person of Joshua as Moses' successor, and this and other relationships will be noted in the commentary.[6] This is nowhere more true than in the book's relationship with Deuteronomy and the law of Deuteronomy. It shares many concerns, especially in theological areas such as holy war, festivals, inheritance and covenant. However, it is also true that the work anticipates much of the history of Israel that follows. There are textual parallels between the last verses of the book

[1] T. F. Fretheim, *Deuteronomistic History*, Interpreting Biblical Texts (Nashville: Abingdon, 1983).
[2] S. Lasine, 'Jehoram and the Cannibal Mothers (2 Kings 6:24–33): Solomon's Judgment in an Inverted World', *JSOT*, 50, 1991, pp. 26–53.
[3] F. M. Cross, *Canaanite Myth and Hebrew Epic: Essays on the History of the Religion of Israel* (Cambridge, Massachusetts: Harvard University Press, 1973), pp. 217–289; R. D. Nelson, *The Double Redaction of the Deuteronomistic History*, JSOT Supplement 18 (Sheffield: Sheffield Academic Press, 1981); I. Provin, *Hezekiah and the Books of Kings: A Contribution to the Debate about the Composition of the Deuteronomistic History*, BZAW 172 (Berlin: Walter de Gruyter, 1988).
[4] M. A. O'Brien, *The Deuteronomistic History Hypothesis: A Reassessment*, OBO 92 (Freibourg: Universitätsverlag; Göttingen: Vandenhoeck & Ruprecht, 1989).
[5] J. Wellhausen, *Prolegomena to the History of Ancient Israel* (Gloucester, Massachusetts: Peter Smith, 1973), pp. 356–362.
[6] See also M. Weinfeld, *Deuteronomy and the Deuteronomic School* (Oxford: Clarendon, 1972), pp. 320–365.

items, in particular, make this parallel unique.[1] They suggest that this list betrays signs of an origin in the second millennium BC.

6. The Gibeonites of Joshua 9 occupied the Benjaminite plateau that extends from Jerusalem in the south to Bethel in the north. The acquisition of this area formed a key element in the strategy of the occupation of the land. Without it, Israel would be divided between the hill-country settlement of the north and the Judean hills to the south. Like other regions in the hill country, this area was not settled in the Late Bronze Age (1550–1200 BC). Eight Iron I (1200–1000 BC) villages have been identified, of which seven are in the eastern part of the region. These were settled early in Iron I. The only Gibeonite site that has been excavated is Gibeon itself. A partial excavation revealed a Late Bronze Age necropolis and Iron I habitation.[2]

7. The names of the defeated kings in Joshua 10 and 11 provide clues as to the origins of these narratives.[3]

a. That of the king of Jerusalem, *Adoni-Zedek*, means '(my) lord is Zedek', where Zedek (or Zadqu) is the name of a deity or a description of the deity as righteous (Heb. *ṣdq*). It may also be found in the biblical name of an earlier king, possibly of Jerusalem, in Genesis 14, Melchizedek, '(my) king is Zedek/ righteousness'. The structure of the name as well as the elements that compose it are found in personal names of the fourteenth-century Amarna letters in the names of town leaders from elsewhere in Palestine and Syria.[4]

b. Hoham and Piram, the leaders of Hebron and Jarmuth, possess names whose origins lie with the Hurrian culture to the north in northern Syria, a culture that influenced various

[1] *CAD*, vol. 9 L, p. 215, lists seven examples of the usage of *lišānu* as 'ingot'. Four of the seven examples are from the second millennium BC (Late Bronze Age).
[2] I. Finkelstein, *The Archaeology of the Israelite Settlement* (Israel Exploration Society: Jerusalem, 1988), pp. 56–65. The absence of evidence for habitation in the Late Bronze Age may call into question whether or not this site was inhabited. However, the partial excavation of the site and the problems with interpreting the stratigraphy suggest that the final verdict has not been rendered.
[3] R. S. Hess, 'Non-Israelite Personal Names in the Narratives of the Book of Joshua', *CBQ*, forthcoming.
[4] See the names of *a-du-na*, leader of Irqata, and *rabu-ṣí-id-qí*, a citizen of Byblos who is involved in its administration.

regions of Palestine, especially the inland valleys and the hill country, in the Late Bronze Age (1550–1200 BC).[1] Japhia and Debir, leaders of Lachish and of Eglon, have names that are similar to a fourteenth-century BC ruler of Gezer and to a name in contemporary Egyptian sources.[2]

c. Anak (Jos. 11:22; 14:6–15; 15:13–19) occurs as a place name in the Egyptian Execration texts from the first half of the second millennium BC.[3] From the region of Palestine three rulers are mentioned who are each called a ruler of Iy-'anaq.[4]

8. In Joshua 15:14, the names of the three Anakites appear, *Sheshai, Ahiman and Talmai.* Sheshai and Talmai are Hurrian names, originating in the Hurrian culture to the north of Palestine which was influential in 1550–1200 BC.[5] Ahiman is a West Semitic 'Canaanite' name. The land of the Anakites is the southern hill country around Hebron. This region included a population of mixed origin, as attested both in the biblical record and in contemporary extrabiblical evidence from this region, a testimony to the antiquity of this text.[6]

9. Joshua 24:2–27 contains a report of a covenant that, in its form and content, most closely resembles the Hittite vassal-

---

[1] For similarities of Hoham with *ḫuḫa* in some Nuzi names and for comparisons of Piram with Nuzi names such as *bi-ru* and *be-ru-wa*, see R. S. Hess, 'Non-Israelite Personal Names in the Narratives of the Book of Joshua'. For evidence of Hurrian influence at this time, see R. S. Hess, 'Cultural Aspects of Onomastic Distribution in the Amarna Texts', *UF*, 21, 1989, pp. 209–216.

[2] R. S. Hess, 'Non-Israelite Personal Names in the Narratives of the Book of Joshua' *CBQ*, forthcoming. The name of the ruler of Gezer in the Amarna texts is *ia-pa-ḫi.*

[3] See E. Lipiński, ''Anaq-Kiryat 'Arba' – Hébron et ses sanctuaires tribaux', *VT*, 24, 1974, pp. 41–48. See also M. Dothan, 'Ethnicity and Archaeology: Some Observations on the Sea Peoples at Ashdod', in *BAT*, pp. 53–55. Dothan identifies Anakites with the pre-Philistine stratum at Ashdod and suggests a Mycenean origin. This is not likely in view of their West Semitic and Hurrian personal names (see Jos. 15:14), nor is it correct if the Anakites are present in the early second millennium BC.

[4] *ANET*, p. 328; E. Lipiński, ''Anaq-Kiryat 'Arba' – Hébron et ses sanctuaires tribaux'. O. Margalit, 'The Origin of the Sons of Anak', *Beth Mikra*, 25, 1990, pp. 359–364, Hebrew, identified the Minoan word for 'king', *anak*, with the Anakites.

[5] See R. S. Hess, 'Non-Israelite Personal Names in the Narratives of the Book of Joshua'.

[6] *Ibid.* See also the Hurrian and West Semitic names on the second-millennium BC cuneiform tablet discovered there in M. Anbar and N. Na'aman, 'An Account Tablet of Sheep from Ancient Hebron', *Tel Aviv*, 13–14, 1986–1987, pp. 3–12.

---

treaty structure unique to the second millenniu
Theology: (c) The covenant between God and Isra
51) and the commentary on Joshua 24 (pp. 299–30(

This commentary will not attempt to 'prove' the h
any part of Joshua. However, it will accept th
preserving authentic and ancient sources that attes
in the late second millennium BC. In addition to
made here, notes throughout the commentary will ;
locate the text within this ancient context and so to u
its message.

COMPOSITION

(a) Traditional higher-critical methods

The book of Joshua makes no specific claim regarding
authorship or its composition. Scholars have sought to
the composition of Joshua from two perspectives o
criticism: Deuteronomistic sources and redactions, ;
history of traditions.[1]

1. Deuteronomistic sources and redactions. The Deute
istic History represents the books of Joshua, Judges, 1
Samuel, and 1 and 2 Kings. The narratives at the beginn
the end of Deuteronomy are also included. Martin
originally advanced the hypothesis that these all form a
literary work composed in the late seventh and the
centuries BC by an author who worked with various
historical sources.[2] The author added his personal views
sources of ancient Israelite history and created a work
essentially defended the theology of the books of Deutero
and Jeremiah. Central to this view was a rigid monotl
which King Josiah introduced to Judah. All rulers of (
people in the past were evaluated according to the degr
which they followed this monotheistic viewpoint. The fai
to follow this perspective were carefully catalogued by
Deuteronomists, who used it as the basis for explaining
God permitted the Northern Kingdom to fall. It also expla
why God later permitted the Southern Kingdom to fall, des

---

[1] See R. G. Boling, 'Joshua, Book of', *ABD*, III, pp. 1002–1015.

[2] M. Noth, *Überlieferungsgeschichte Studien* (Tübingen: Max Niemeyer Vei 1957), pp. 1–110. Translated and reprinted as *The Deuteronomistic History, J.* Supplement 15 (Sheffield: Sheffield Academic Press, 1981).

and the opening chapters of Judges. Joshua is a model leader who anticipates the best kings of Judah.[1] Many commentaries follow this analysis, dating the book's final composition to the post-exilic period.

Recent studies have revived an earlier hypothesis which identified priestly editorial work in Joshua, especially in the allotments of chapters 13 – 21.[2] However, the identification of a series of Deuteronomistic and priestly editorial layers in the book of Joshua cannot be accepted without qualification. There are difficulties with assumptions that Deuteronomistic theology must be confined to the period of Josiah and with the analysis of the Joshua narratives divorced from their Ancient Near Eastern context. Block has argued that many of the theological ideas traditionally associated with Deuteronomistic themes are not distinctive to Israel or confined to the seventh century, but are common in countries throughout the Ancient Near East.[3] This makes it difficult to draw conclusions about dating or about defining a particular period exclusive to the Deuteronomists in Israel. Younger has demonstrated that the relationship of the central historical section of Joshua 9 – 12 is too close to that of contemporary (1300–600 BC) conquest accounts (which themselves are normally used as historical sources – though biased – by historians of the Ancient Near East) to allow certainty of identification of later insertions. Thus statements about the work and words of God are not later insertions into a battle chronicle, but are an essential feature of all Ancient Near Eastern battle accounts. The theology and the narrative should not be separated.

2. History of traditions. Because many scholars recognized some historical value in the narratives of Joshua, they needed to find a means to associate the later written documents (Deuteronomistic, priestly, *etc.*) with the earlier origins of the

---

[1]R. D. Nelson, 'Josiah in the Book of Joshua', *JBL*, 100, 1981, pp. 531–540; R. S. Hess, 'Joshua 1 – 12 as a Centrist Document', in M. Augustin and K. D. Schunck (eds.), 'Dort ziehen Schiffe dahin . . .' Collected Communications to the XIVth Congress of the International Organization for the Study of the Old Testament, Paris 1992, Beiträge zur Erforschung der Alten Testaments und der Antiken Judentums 28 (Frankfort am Main: Peter Lang, 1996), pp. 53–67.
[2]See the discussion under 'The allotments of Joshua 13 – 21' (pp. 53–56).
[3]D. Block, *The Gods of the Nations: Studies in Ancient Near Eastern National Theology*, Evangelical Theological Society Monograph 2 (Jackson, Mississippi: Evangelical Theological Society, 1988).

material. It was noted that the first nine chapters of Joshua describe events in the region of Benjamin. Since they emphasize a central sanctuary at Gilgal, some have suggested that a priesthood at this site preserved the texts of Joshua. Chapters 8 and 24 describe covenant renewals at Shechem. This site became identified with an early assembly of tribes. Drawing on models from ancient Greece and Rome, Noth proposed an amphictyony or tribal league with its centre at Shechem. Social-science studies have since demonstrated the difficulties of transferring later models, such as the amphictyony, and applying them to ancient Israel.[1] However, this does not deny the possibility of a tribal confederation.[2] These hypotheses have merit in so far as they demonstrate a variety of historical possibilities in which such a text as Joshua could have been preserved until it came into the possession of the monarchy in Jerusalem.

Some recent studies of Joshua accept a date before the Monarchy for the composition of most or all of the book.[3] Others reflect attempts to date the Old Testament in the Hellenistic period. Strange advocates a second-century BC date for the book of Joshua.[4] He argues for this on the basis of the distribution of place names, the anti-Canaanite polemic, the presence of the priestly source, the fact that the book seems out of place in the narrative flow, and the emphasis on Shechem. These circumstantial arguments are not decisive. The absence of town lists from the central hill country may reflect the nature of the Manasseh and Ephraim allotments as related to family histories and to the first phase of the settlement.[5] The anti-Canaanite polemic is an argument for an earlier date. Canaanites do not appear after 1 Kings 9:20–21 in the historical literature.[6] The priestly source, if its existence is assumed, is not necessarily a Hasmonean document. There are good linguistic

[1]N. K. Gottwald, 'Israel's Emergence in Canaan – BR Interviews Norman Gottwald', *BR*, 5/3, October 1989, pp. 26–34.

[2]See the discussion and bibliography of Butler, pp. xxxiii–xxxv.

[3]Martin Holland, *Das Buch Josua*, Wuppertaler Studienbibel, AT. (Wuppertal/ Zurich: Brockhaus, 1993); Koorevaar.

[4]J. Strange, 'The Book of Joshua: A Hasmonean Manifesto' in A. Lemaire and B. Otzen (eds.), *History and Tradition of Early Israel: Studies Presented to Eduard Nielsen*, *VT* Supplement 50 (Leiden: Brill, 1993), pp. 136–141.

[5]See the introduction to these lists in the commentary (pp. 258–259).

[6]Mitchell, p. 127.

reasons for dating it before the exile.[1] The location of Joshua in its present context is not disruptive but fulfills the expected function of national histories which describe the conquest and occupation of their homeland.[2] The emphasis on the region of Shechem for the covenant is already found in Deuteronomy 27. Its strategic significance as the initial capital of the Northern Kingdom and its appearance in the Amarna letters attest to an early political and literary prominence for the site.[3]

It may be that future studies will establish a firmer base for the identification of sources and the history of traditions and redactions in the text of Joshua. That is not the purpose of this commentary. Although certainty is not possible regarding authorship and composition, specific evidence for antiquity already noted can be supplemented by the presence of literary forms of conquest accounts (chs. 9 – 12, see throughout this section), administrative town lists and boundaries that form part of a treaty text (see 'The allotments of Joshua 13 – 21', pp. 56–60) and the record of a treaty or covenant ceremony that resembles treaty forms (see 'Antiquity' 9, p. 30), and references there). This suggests that the presence of theological concerns commonly identified with the Deuteronomists did not compromise those literary forms and items of evidence whose identity has been observed. On the contrary, the picture that emerges from a study of this book in its canonical and Ancient Near Eastern context is one of authenticity and cohesion at many points. This may be exemplified by recent studies discussed in the next section.

(b) Literary strategies
An earlier generation of scholars examined the text of Joshua with a view to identifying different sources. For example, the apparent conquest of the whole land (Jos. 10:43; 11:23; 21:43–

[1] See Y. Kaufmann, *The Religion of Israel from Its Beginnings to the Babylonian Exile*, tr. M. Greenberg (New York: Schocken, 1972); A. Hurwitz, 'Dating the Priestly Source in Light of the Historical Study of Biblical Hebrew a Century after Wellhausen', *ZAW*, 100 (Supplement), 1988, pp. 88–100.

[2] See Weinfeld, *Promise*, pp. 22–51.

[3] See 1 Ki. 12:25; R. S. Hess, 'Smitten Ant Bites Back: Rhetorical Forms in the Amarna Correspondence from Shechem' in J. C. de Moor and W. G. E. Watson (eds.), *Verse in Ancient Near Eastern Prose*, AOAT 42 (Neukirchener-Vluyn: Neukirchener, 1993), pp. 95–111; 'Shechem' in *New International Dictionary of Old Testament Theology* (Grand Rapids: Zondervan, forthcoming).

45; 23:14), on the one hand, and clear statements that parts of the land were not conquered (Jos. 11:22; 13:1–7; 14:12; 15:14–17, 63; 16:10; 17:12–13, 16; 19:47; 23:5–13), on the other, suggested a contradiction. In order to resolve this, two or more sources were postulated: one that argued for a complete conquest of the land, and another, continued into Judges 1, that suggested only a partial conquest. This latter source was regarded as the more historically accurate of the two.[1]

Recent approaches have attempted new solutions to this and other questions. New literary studies seek to make sense out of the final form of the text without recourse to hypothetical sources. These methods provide important directions for understanding the book of Joshua.[2] Examination of them will consider some of the methods used as a prelude to their detailed application in the commentary. Scholars such as Polzin, Hawk and Mitchell have discerned literary strategies.[3] Koopmans has applied the same approach to the final chapter of the book, where Joshua renews God's covenant with Israel.[4] Ottosson and Svensson have attempted to look at the literary process at work in the allotments of Joshua 13 – 21. In linguistics, discourse grammar has emphasized the final form of other Old Testament texts. Winther-Nielsen applies this method to Joshua. Comparative literary approaches constitute a separate category of literary methods. Weinfeld extends the comparisons to Greek and Ancient Near Eastern literatures.[5]

Hawk's work follows the literary studies of Polzin and Gunn.[6]

---

[1]Thus passages related to Jdg. 1 might be assigned to the earlier J (Yahwist) source while those describing a complete conquest, such as most of Jos. 1 – 12, could be related to the slightly later E (Elohist) source. See R. Dillard and T. Longman III, *Introduction to the Old Testament* (Downers Grove and Leicester: Inter-Varsity Press, 1995), p. 109.

[2]Adapted from R. S. Hess, 'Studies in the Book of Joshua', *Themelios*, 20.3, May 1995, pp. 12–15.

[3]Hawk; Mitchell. On the views of Mitchell and Hawk regarding the 'ban', see 'Theology (a) Holy war and the ban'.

[4]Koopmans; *idem*, 'Josh. 23 and 24 Again: A Response to Klaas Spronk' in J. C. de Moor and W. G. E. Watson (eds.), *Verse in Ancient Near Eastern Prose*, AOAT 42 (Kevelaer: Butzon & Bercker; Neukirchen-Vluyn: Neukirchener, 1993), pp. 261–263.

[5]Weinfeld, *Promise*.

[6]Polzin; D. M. Gunn, 'Joshua and Judges' in R. Alter and F. Kermode (eds.), *The Literary Guide to the Bible* (Cambridge, Massachusetts: Belknap/Harvard, 1987), pp. 102–121.

Hawk emphasizes the discontinuities found in Joshua. This is especially true of what he recognizes as two conflicting threads that run through the book: emphatic assertions of complete obedience juxtaposed with statements of Israel's failure to obey and to achieve all that God had commanded them to do. Thus the first chapter of Joshua asserts Joshua's total dedication to God, but this must be contrasted with the reluctance on the part of the Transjordanian tribes to accept Joshua's authority except in so far as he obeys God (1:17–18). The story of Rahab is an example of disobedience on the part of Joshua in sending the spies, and on the part of the spies in making a covenant with Rahab. Joshua 11:16–23 begins and ends with statements about Joshua's conquest of the entire land, but places between them statements about the cities that were not conquered. Chapters 13 – 22 begin in an orderly manner with reference to Judah's allotment but gradually disintegrate as the other tribes are described. Chapter 22 (the altar of the Transjordanian tribes) is a model of ambiguity, and the concluding chapters strive to close the book with references to items found in the opening chapters, but also describe unresolved matters. Hawk explains these contrasting plots on the basis of different strategies ('desires') that he ascribes to Joshua, God, the author and the reader.

While there are tensions in the book of Joshua, it is not clear that Hawk has accurately identified them. There is no explicit evidence in the biblical text that the spies (or Joshua) were wrong in making and accepting their agreement with Rahab (see Winther-Nielsen, pp. 80–97). Younger has shown how phrases like 'all the land' were not intended to be taken with mathematical precision. Mention of areas not conquered appears alongside the claim of taking all the land. Younger's study is broader in scope than either Van Seters' attempt to compare Joshua 1 – 12 with Neo-Assyrian accounts or Hoffmeier's comparison with Egyptian New Kingdom narratives.[1] Younger compares conquest stories from a variety of Ancient Near Eastern peoples and periods. Both the Ancient Near Eastern treaty form and the covenant form of books such as Deuteronomy allow for the absence of elements of closure at

---

[1] J. Van Seters, 'Joshua's Campaign of Canaan and Near Eastern Historiography', *SJOT*, 4, 1990, pp. 1–12; J. K. Hoffmeier, 'The Structure of Joshua 1 – 11 and the Annals of Thutmose III' in *FTH*, pp. 165–179.

the end of the document. They include curses in the final chapters, something that Hawk finds problematic. Hawk's volume is important, however, for its serious treatment of the whole book of Joshua.

Mitchell attempts to incorporate form- and traditio-historical studies into a literary analysis of the text. He examines the question: why is the express divine will that all the enemy are to be slaughtered contradicted by the examples of Rahab, the Gibeonites and others who are not slaughtered? The first half of the book considers forms and phrases related to the command to destroy all the inhabitants of the land and Israel's failure to accomplish this. In the first part of his book, Mitchell moves through Joshua 8 – 21 without much consideration of the broader (other than Assyrian) Near Eastern context and with almost no mention of the historical-geographical context suggested by Kallai, Na'aman and Boling. While this may be understandable in a literary study, Mitchell's incorporation of historical comparative material elsewhere makes these omissions surprising. His literary conclusion, that the key theme of chapters 12 – 21 is the end of war, seems dubious in the light of chapter 22 and of Judges. While that emphasis does exist (Jos. 11:23; 14:15), comparisons of Joshua 1 with chapters 21 and 22 in terms of fulfilment say more about the literary closure of the book, as Hawk asserts (*cf.* his work's title, *Every Promise Fulfilled*), than they do about the expected cessation of warfare.

The second half of Mitchell's book considers expressions related to the enemy nations and their continued occupation of the land. His conclusions stress the change from a unified group of nations opposed to Israel at the beginning of Joshua to a collection of isolated pockets of resistance by the time of the allotments (chs. 13 – 21).[1] With Gottwald, Mitchell observes the emphasis upon the rulers of the nations that Israel conquered, as listed in Joshua 12. Survivors, such as Rahab and the Gibeonites, do not include the Canaanite rulers. Yet Mitchell cannot avoid an ambiguity in the text, in which Israel is to drive out the inhabitants of the land, but at the same time groups like Rahab and the Gibeonites are not killed but survive with orthodox Yahwistic confessions. Mitchell does not in the end resolve these ambiguities, although he does include a final

---

[1] See 'Additional Note: A partial or complete conquest?', at 21:43–45 (pp. 284–286).

paragraph that attempts to relate them to the historical realities of post-exilic Judaism. At times he moves from the literary device of juxtaposition of different perspectives to the charge of outright contradiction. For example, he maintains that Geshur and Maacah sometimes fall within the conquered territories of Transjordan (Jos. 13:11) and sometimes they lie outside those lands (Dt. 3:14; Jos. 12:5). However, a closer examination of the two latter passages reveals that these texts do not claim to describe all of Israel's conquered land in Transjordan. Mitchell seeks contradictions in the text in order to demonstrate an ideological bias. But this is not necessary, as theological 'bias' against 'Canaanites' or other groups can exist without the need for historical or literary contradictions.[1] These comments aside, Mitchell has provided a useful service by summarizing much of the best in continental scholarship and applying it to the study of key phrases in the text of Joshua.

Ottosson's work emphasizes the importance of ancient cultic material as original to the book of Joshua, rather than as something inserted by a later redactor. Ottosson's work on chapters 14 – 22 has been further developed by Svensson. Svensson also stresses the importance of the appearance of Eleazar, the priest, along with Joshua in the accounts of the distribution of the land. Ottosson's understanding of Joshua as a priestly figure is also developed by Svensson. Both find in these chapters an idealized land designed for a new David (prefigured by Joshua) who will restore the kingdom and expand it to include all the territory of the United Monarchy.

Ottosson and Svensson seek a motivation for the book of Joshua that stresses the positive value of rulership, especially David's reign. Kallai's dating of the boundaries of chapters 13 – 19, as well as his overall perspective on the unitary composition and purpose of these texts, agrees with this concern. Thus Svensson follows Kallai. Svensson describes his purpose as 'a literary-structural close reading of Joshua 14 – 21'. It is not clear that he achieves this, at least not in the terms of modern literary readings. No attempt is made to discern the role of the narrative segments in these chapters, nor is consideration given to the rationale for the order and organization of the text as it now appears. The only overall literary analysis occurs when

[1] R. S. Hess, 'Asking Historical Questions of Joshua 13 – 19: Recent Discussion Concerning the Date of the Boundary Lists' in *FTH*, pp. 191–205.

Svensson identifies two framing devices in chapters 13 and 22 – 23: the phrase 'Joshua was old and advanced in years' and the discussion of the two and a half Transjordanian tribes.

Ottosson, however, discerns a literary significance in the allotments. He suggests that the more towns named, the more positive the evaluation of the tribe. Thus Judah (ch. 15), with the most towns named, is most highly regarded by the author. Hawk also finds a positive evaluation for Judah. For him this is because Judah has a complete set of boundaries and a clearly distinguished town list. Other tribes, without boundaries or where boundaries and town lists are mixed (*e.g.* Ephraim and Manasseh), are targets of a negative evaluation by the author.

The form of the boundary descriptions and town lists reflects both the ideal of the early settlement and their usage as legal and administrative documents in later periods. The early origin that the text assigns to these documents is supported by their topographical similarity with Late Bronze Age city states of Palestine, by the need for some sort of boundaries – given the sociological dynamics present in the settlement of the land, and by the archaeological evidence of settlement in the hill country of Palestine from 1200 BC.[1] The similarity of the boundary descriptions to those found in treaties, and their context between the covenants of Joshua 8 and 24, suggest that the literary structure of these documents was as much determined by the legal and administrative realities of Israel and Judah as it was by some other overall literary structuring of the author. This is not to say that the documents served no literary purpose (as with the insertions of the narratives about Caleb, Acsah, the daughters of Zelophehad, and Joseph), but that purpose should be integrated within a covenantal context and theology.

Winther-Nielsen explores the first half of Joshua from a rhetorical-linguistic perspective. His work applies the discourse grammar approach of Robert Longacre to Joshua. The first hundred pages introduce this approach using the text of Joshua as a source for examples. A special study of the encounter with Rahab (Joshua 2) demonstrates how the dialogues elaborate central concerns of the narrative. The central role of the conquest theme is emphasized by the syntax

---

[1] R. S. Hess, 'Late Bronze Age and Biblical Boundary Descriptions of the West Semitic World' in *Ugarit and the Bible*, pp. 123–138.

of the chapter, as is Rahab's act of faith in throwing in her lot with Israel. The account of crossing the Jordan (chs. 3 – 4) is structured around the actions of the priests as they enter and emerge from the waters. The actions of these chapters have long been a source of debate due to their apparent repetition and contradiction. Winther-Nielsen proposes a unified and sequential structure to the whole. The conquest of Jericho focuses on the destruction of the site, an activity in which God serves as the major actor while Joshua and the Israelites obey. Winther-Nielsen applies his technique to the whole of Joshua, observing how God's speech of Joshua 1:2–5 sets forth the key themes of the book. As with past studies of other Hebrew texts, this application of functional discourse grammar demonstrates a textual and thematic unity to the book of Joshua.

Weinfeld moves the literary studies almost entirely into the realm of the comparative. He does not identify forms or discuss the usage of theologically significant words and phrases without recourse to comparative materials from the Ancient Near Eastern and classical worlds. Drawing together materials he has already published elsewhere and adding new insights, Weinfeld's work includes comparisons with a variety of materials in the Hebrew Bible. Of special interest for Joshua are his studies on Greek and Hebrew settlement traditions. Although other chapters detail Weinfeld's view on the history of the Joshua traditions and their origins, as well as the different accounts of this event as preserved in the Bible, it is in the area of comparative settlement traditions (pp. 22–51) that Weinfeld makes important contributions. Comparisons with the Greek traditions of settlement reveal a number of important similarities with the biblical accounts. For example, both include enquiries at the shrine, priestly guidance, divine obligations, the founder's tomb, naming and dividing the land, divine promises, setting up stones and building an altar. Both also follow a sequence: (1) oracular confirmation; (2) erection of monuments and altars, along with sacrifices; (3) the use of divine lot to allocate the land; (4) divinely given laws for the settlers; and (5) according a prominent position to a leader-founder who cooperates with a priest. The leader-founder (*e.g.* Joshua) is a leader of settlers, a builder of a city, and a legislator.

The use of literary techniques and close readings of the final or canonical form of the Hebrew text will form an important part of the commentary. The exaltation of Joshua, the holiness and graciousness of God and the covenantal context of the book all form features essential to understanding and appreciating the multifaceted aspects of this book.

Having considered the background and development of Joshua's leadership role, other theological themes to be noticed throughout the book include holy war and the ban; the inheritance of the land; God's covenant with Israel; and the holy and redeeming God.[1]

(a) Holy war and the ban

Few of the many issues raised by the book of Joshua create more difficulty than the question of how a loving God could command the wholesale extermination of nations that inhabited the Promised Land. There is no easy or simple solution to this problem. However, it is helpful to put Israel's actions in their biblical and Ancient Near Eastern context.

Joshua 2:10, with its reference to how Israel *completely destroyed* Sihon and Og, introduces the verb 'to devote to the ban' (Heb. *ḥrm*) to the vocabulary of Joshua. This verb is not used in the account of the defeat of Sihon and Og in Numbers 21:21–35, although the conduct in war is similar to 'the ban'.[2] However, it is used emphatically in the recounting of both wars in Deuteronomy 2:34 and 3:6. It appears elsewhere in the Pentateuch only to confirm that this is how the inhabitants of the land of Canaan are to be treated (Dt. 7:2 and 20:17). This verb will recur throughout the conquest accounts of Joshua as God claims those peoples and their possessions for himself despite their attempts to rebel against him. While this idea of returning to God that which is his from the beginning is significant in the warfare of Joshua and in other biblical wars, it is not unique to Israel.

At Mari, in the eighteenth century BC, a military commander

---

[1] See also R. Hess, 'Joshua' in W. Elwell (ed.), *Evangelical Dictionary of Biblical Theology* (Grand Rapids: Baker, forthcoming).

[2] It does appear in the account of Israel's defeat of armies from towns in the Negev, a few verses earlier (21:1–3). While it is used there to explain the name of a town in that region, Hormah, does the concept extend through the chapter to include the kings of the Amorites?

also proclaims a 'ban' on the spoils of war.[1] This twin idea of (1) total warfare against every living being and all property, and of (2) its understanding in the light of dedication to the national deity, is known in ninth-century Moab (where the same Hebrew root, *ḥrm*, is used), in contemporary Assyria, and in twelfth-century Egypt.[2] Mesha king of Moab records how he took the town of Nebo from Israel, killed everyone in it, and 'devoted' it to his god, Ashtar-Chemosh.[3] Thus the kind of warfare attributed to Israel in Joshua does not originate in a theology of 'holy war' peculiar to Old Testament theology.[4] Rather, it is a political ideology that Israel shared with other nations. All wars waged by a country were 'holy wars', dedicated to the glorification of its deity and the extension of the deity's reign.[5] If there is a distinctive feature of Israel's attitude towards war, it is that God did not approve of all wars. Those examples, such as the battle at Ai (Jos. 7), illustrate Israel's distinctive theology of warfare.

The devotion of the nations of Canaan to the 'ban' is described several times in Deuteronomy. It first appears in chapter 7. God warns Israel to destroy all the nations totally and without mercy (vv. 1–2, 23–24). However, it is clear from the text that the extermination of the Canaanites will be a gradual process and this is understood as part of the divine plan for

---

[1]A. Malamat, *Mari and the Early Israelite Experience*, The Schweich Lectures of the British Academy 1984 (Oxford: Oxford University Press, 1989), pp. 70–79. At Mari, the 'ban' was called *asakkum*. It could designate the property of a deity, a king or a military commander.

[2]For discussion and texts, see Younger, pp. 235–236; M. Liverani, *Prestige and Interest*, pp. 129–130.

[3]Line 17 of the Mesha inscription. See J. C. L. Gibson, *Textbook of Syrian Semitic Inscriptions*, I. *Hebrew and Moabite Inscriptions* (Oxford: Clarendon, 1971), pp. 75–76, 81.

[4]The usage of the term for 'ban' on the Moabite inscription and the texts which use it in the Old Testament and describe war are argued by some to possess a 'fixed structure'. However, this structure is in reality so general that any ancient description of a war would fit into it, *i.e.* one containing an oracle, departure of the army, battle, city capture, slaughter of the population, booty taken, and, of course, the use of the term for 'ban'! See G. L. Mattingly, 'Moabite Religion and the Mesha' Inscription' in *Moab*, p. 234. See also J. P. U. Lilley, 'Understanding the *Ḥerem*', *TynB*, 44, 1993, pp. 169–177; P. D. Stern, *The Biblical* Herem*: A Window on Israel's Religious Experience*, Brown Judaic Studies 211 (Atlanta: Scholars Press, 1991).

[5]See H. Tadmor, 'Autobiographical Apology in the Royal Assyrian Literature' in *HHI*, p. 42; M. Liverani, 'The Ideology of the Assyrian Empire' in *Power*, pp. 297–317 (301).

Israel (v. 22). Chapter 20 confirms that it is God who will fight for Israel and deliver the enemy into their hands.[1] For this reason Israel's army can exclude those who have built homes or vineyards recently, or become engaged to be married, or even those who are afraid (vv. 5–8). Since it is a divine war, the army's size is not important, only its dedication and commitment to God's cause. Verses 10–11 allow peace with enslavement for any fortified town that opens its gates to Israel and does not resist. Since the following section (vv. 12–15) describes the treatment of towns outside the Promised Land, this mercy may apply only to such towns and not the towns within the Promised Land where 'anything that breathes' is not to be left alive (vv. 16–18).[2] However, this is not certain within the context of Deuteronomy. It is clear that Deuteronomy's law anticipated wars by Israel in which prisoners of war would be taken (Dt. 21:10–14).

The question of Israel's obedience to the ban has arisen in its treatment of Rahab (Joshua 2) and in its exercise of the ban in its wars. Those who condemn the spies for making a treaty with Rahab and not following the theology of the ban (Dt. 20) do not mention Rahab's own use of the term (Jos. 2:10). In a speech that demonstrates a correct and precise knowledge of Israel's theology, it remains for Rahab's critics to explain why the author includes in her words the one term that would remind the spies of their supposed obligation to kill Rahab and her family. This fact calls into question the extraordinary lengths to which commentators go to impute to the spies of Joshua 2 'wickedness and lack of faith' and 'taking the place of God' because they accepted Rahab's conditions.[3] Nowhere in the text is this implied. Hawk notes that Joshua does not mention the spies' oath to the people of Israel.[4] However, this is astonishing if, as Hawk claims, the rescue of Rahab was an explicit contravention of God's covenant. The people would require more explanation than an act of mercy and gratitude to

---

[1]For this military role of God, see T. Longman III and D. G. Reid, *God Is a Warrior*, Studies in Old Testament Biblical Theology (Carlisle: Paternoster, 1995), pp. 31–47.

[2]This could explain the concern of the Gibeonites to pose as travellers from a distant land (Jos. 9:3–13). However, it is not clear that they appealed to this text. In any case, the concern of the passage is not the life of the Gibeonites but the failure of Israel to seek God before making a decision.

[3]See Polzin, pp. 88–90.

[4]Hawk, p. 73.

allow Rahab's family to live if they felt it would bring divine judgment against them. The fact that the oath goes unmentioned suggests that mercy for those who joined Israel was considered appropriate to God's covenant. Joshua's use of the word 'ban' in 6:16–19 supports this. In the same context in which he commands that Rahab should be spared, he commands that the remainder of Jericho should be devoted to the ban. If there were a contradiction here, one would expect that Joshua would address it. The reason for Rahab's salvation is not an error on the part of the spies. They and their oath are not mentioned. The reason is that *she hid the spies we sent.* Rahab switched her allegiance from Canaan and its deities to Israel and the God of Israel.

The fact that Rahab's salvation does not violate the ban does not mean that the force of the ban in Deuteronomy 20 is reduced. The defeat at Ai and the punishment of Achan and his family (Jos. 7) demonstrate this. The text states that Joshua *totally destroyed* the cities of Canaan *as Moses the servant of the LORD had commanded* (Jos. 11:12; see Dt. 20:16–17). This interpretation is opposed by Hawk, who understands the word with which 11:13 begins, *yet* (Heb. *raq*), to describe how the commands of the 'ban' were disobeyed.[1] He interprets this to mean that only at Hazor was everything destroyed. Thus the Israelites disobeyed God's commands. However, this would require a remarkable switch between verse 12 and verse 13, and again between verse 14 and verse 15. In verses 12 and 15 it is explicit that Joshua's obedience is complete. To assume that verses 13–14 describe disobedience requires a literalistic interpretation of the 'ban', one that is not justified by other usages such as that of Mesha of Moab, where some of the booty is taken by the victors. It seems that the 'ban' was applied differently in different situations, its one common element being the complete destruction of the inhabitants.[2] The phrase *anything that breathes* in Deuteronomy 20:16 refers only to human life, as it normally does elsewhere (and does in Jos. 11:14).[3] If so, then livestock need not necessarily be put to death, contra Hawk. Therefore *yet* (*raq*)

[1] Hawk, pp. 44–45.

[2] See Butler, p. 86; J. P. U. Lilley, 'Understanding the *Ḥerem*'; G. Mitchell, *Together in the Land*, pp. 52–82.

[3] J. P. U. Lilley, 'Understanding the *Ḥerem*', p. 174, refers to T. C. Mitchell, 'The Old Testament Usage of *nᵉšāmâ*', *VT*, 11, 1961, pp. 177–187.

functions as a clarification or specification of what precedes. It explains how Joshua took the royal cities and obeyed God (captured the royal cities *and specifically* burnt only Hazor), just as *raq* in 11:14 explains how they plundered the cities (*i.e.* plundered *and specifically* killed only the people).[1]

The New Testament development of the holy war theme moves in two directions. Firstly, there is the focus on God and his appointed Son as the Holy Warrior who fights for the people of God.[2] In his earthly ministry, Jesus battles against demonic forces (Mt. 12:24–29; Mk. 3:22–27; Lk. 11:15–22), endures death at the hands of his enemies (Mt. 26 – 27; Mk. 14 – 15; Lk. 22 – 23; Jn. 18 – 19), rises victorious from that death (Mt. 28; Mk. 16; Lk. 24; Jn. 20) and leads heavenly and earthly armies in a victorious war against all opponents (Rev. 1 – 2, 12, 14, 18 – 22). Although not resolving the philosophical issues associated with holy war and a good God's being involved in so many deaths, the death of Christ does add a new dimension to the problem.[3] Christ takes upon himself the sin of the world and becomes the victim of the holy war that God wages against sin (2 Cor. 5:21). The earthly army that Christ leads introduces the other focus of holy war: the engagement of Christians in a lifelong spiritual struggle against the powers of sin and evil (2 Cor. 10:3–5; Eph. 6:10–18). This war also requires the total extermination of the enemy. It allows for no involvement with sin, but demands a complete separation from it. Like the 'ban' of the Old Testament, the theme is that of surrendering all things to God. Total commitment to the army of Christ is the picture of discipleship that Jesus describes for his followers (Mt. 8:18–22; 10:37–39; Lk. 9:57–62; 14:25–35).

(b) The land as an inheritance

Throughout the stories of occupation in the first half of the book there is a continuous tension that has been noted in recent literary studies (see 'Composition' (b) 'Literary strategies', pp. 35–42). On the one hand, God has given the land to Israel in its entirety; on the other, they must occupy it. This

---

[1] See B. K. Waltke and M. O'Connor, *An Introduction to Biblical Hebrew Syntax* (Winona Lake, Indiana: Eisenbrauns, 1991), pp. 669–670 §39.3.5.

[2] T. Longman III and D. G. Reid, *God Is a Warrior*, pp. 91–192.

[3] C. H. Sherlock, 'Holy War' in D. J. Atkinson and D. H. Field (eds.), *New Dictionary of Christian Ethics and Pastoral Theology* (Inter-Varsity Press, 1995), pp. 448–449.

combination of challenge and opportunity is the way in which God works with believers. For Christians, the promise of victory over sin and death has been accomplished through Christ. However, this must be claimed through a life of faith in Christ's work and of faithfulness to him (Rom. 3 – 8). The theme of the inheritance of the land thus provides a model for the Christian life.

The allotments are supervised by Joshua, the divinely appointed leader. They represent God's gift to Israel.[1] Since land served as the primary capital resource for ancient peoples, the allocation of the land provided a material aspect to God's blessing. The people would experience peace and prosperity. However, this text is not primarily about the land itself. Instead, Joshua 13 – 21 presents the land as a divine gift. God has acquired the land, not Israel. Israel was permitted to participate in the process but the ownership of the land belongs to Israel's God. This land is now given to Israel through Joshua, as divinely chosen mediator, and through the casting of lots, as the means of expressing the divine will. Thus every family was given its land as a divine gift. God owned the land. Its use and enjoyment, and the life that it sustained, were gifts from God. All gratitude and worship were due to the LORD, Israel's God, alone.

This theological interpretation supports the formal identification of the boundary lists with those found in Ancient Near Eastern treaties, as noted above (p. 40). Like the Ancient Near Eastern treaties that established a relationship between two or more kings and their peoples, Joshua 13 – 21 defined the relationship between God and the divinely chosen covenant people. The covenants of Joshua 8 and 24 provide a context in which God gives the land. As boundary descriptions in other treaties occur where the stipulations appear, so the allotments of the land correspond to the legal stipulations of other biblical covenants (*e.g.* Ex. 20 – 23; Dt. 12 – 26). Joshua, in the same role as Moses, mediates the covenant to the people.[2]

---

[1] See E. W. Davies, 'Land: Its Rights and Privileges' in *World of Ancient Israel*, pp. 349–369; C. J. H. Wright, *God's People in God's Land. Family, Land, and Property in the Old Testament* (Grand Rapids, Michigan: Eerdmans; Exeter: Paternoster, 1990), pp. 3–70, 104–182.

[2] For this reason there is an artificiality to Ottosson's proposal to separate Jos. 13 from chs. 14 – 21. Whether Moses or Joshua was involved is incidental. Both fulfilled the same role as the opening chapters of the book of Joshua emphasize.

A second feature is that the land is a gift to families (and heads of families) rather than to individuals. The social basis of Israel was the family, and the land provided a binding tie for the family. As already noted, the demands of survival in the hill country required the participation of every living and capable member of the family. Thus all participated in using and benefiting from the divine gift. The many laws that relate to the land, its use and abuse, as well as the rights of inheritance, suggest that obedience to God's covenant with Israel and the maintenance of that fellowship with God that was every Israelite's privilege were integrally tied up with the proper use of the land. Proper and full use of the land was not simply the right and privilege of every Israelite family; it was a fundamental means by which they worshipped God in obedient response to the covenant. The land would also tie together previous generations of the family who had lived and farmed the land and worshipped the one God of Israel. These family members were now buried on the land. They and their descendants who were then alive provided an ongoing testimony of God's faithfulness to the covenant with Israel, 'showing love to a thousand generations of those who love me and keep my commandments' (Ex. 20:6). This would continue as long as there was faithfulness to God. When the people abandoned the worship of the one God and went after other deities, Israel broke its covenant. At that point the divine warnings came into effect. The land, whose ultimate owner had always been God, was now being used to subvert the purposes of its owner and to deny God's existence by affirming that it belonged to Baal and other deities. In contrast to the scholarship that argues that the Israelites were originally Canaanites, the Bible describes how the Israelites (who were distinct from the Canaanites by their allegiance to the LORD as alone the true God) actually became Canaanites, worshipping the false deities of the land.[1] Thus when God reclaimed the land, it was to remove Israel from it. Because they no longer recognized it as a divine gift, their generation could not receive it anew from

---

See Ottosson; Svensson, p. 11. The identification of an inclusio in the description of Reuben, Gad and the half tribe of Manasseh in chs. 13 and 22 does not separate these texts from the intervening ones, but integrates them, as the whole second half of the book anticipates ch. 24.

[1] R. S. Hess, 'Fallacies in the Study of Early Israel: An Onomastic Perspective', *TynB*, 45, 1994, pp. 345–353.

the hand of God's mediator, as the first generation had done.

Wright argues that the significance of the land for Israel applies to the Christian as a model of both socio-economic ethics and, more importantly, as a model of the basis of fellowship with Christ and with one another:[1]

> There are so many similarities which show that the experience of fellowship in its full rich New Testament sense fulfils analogous theological functions for the Christian as the possession of the land did for Old Testament Israelites. Both must be seen as part of the purpose and pattern of redemption – not just accidental or incidental to it. The explicit purpose of the Exodus was the enjoyment of the rich blessing of God in his 'good land'; the goal of redemption through Christ is 'for a sincere love of the brethren' (1 Pet. 1:22), with all its practical implications. Both are linked to the status of sonship and the related themes of inheritance and promise. Both thereby constitute a proof of an authentic relationship with God as part of his redeemed community. For fellowship, like the land, has limits, so that the person who departs permanently from it – or refuses to accept it – shows that he has no real part in God's people (see 1 Jn. 2:19; Mt. 18:15–17).

(c) The covenant between God and Israel

Israel's obedience provides the background for the covenant-making ceremonies of Joshua 8:30–35 and 24:1–27. Chapter 5 prepares the people for the covenant by their circumcision and their celebration of the Passover. This text demonstrates that the generation of Joshua 5 is no longer the generation which was judged and died in the desert. Instead, this Israel is heir to the promises that the LORD God made to the patriarchs and to Israel at Mount Sinai. The nation takes upon itself the covenant obligations and festivals, and so it prepares to lay claim to the divine promises.

Joshua 24 takes the form of a narrative report that describes the renewal of the covenant by the generation of Israelites which had come into the land with Joshua. This naturally relates to the covenant-making ceremony of Joshua 8:30–35, that is itself a fulfilment of earlier instructions. In chapter 24, however, a more

---

[1] C. J. H. Wright, *God's People in God's Land*, p. 113.

complete form of the covenant emerges. Following an earlier work, Mendenhall identified the vassal-treaty structure of the ancient Hittites (c. 1500–1200 BC) with that of the biblical covenants.[1] He did so by suggesting that both types of document established a formal relationship between an overlord and a vassal (in Israel's case, God and Israel) by setting forth a similar form. This form consisted of an introduction, a historical prologue, a set of stipulations, provision for depositing the document in the temple and its public reading, a list of divine witnesses, and curses (for disobedience) and blessings (for obedience). All this was done in the context of a formal oath ceremony. Subsequent discoveries identified treaty texts from the first millennium BC. However, these lacked both the historical prologue and the blessings promised for treaty obedience.

Attempts to apply this form to biblical covenants have met with some objection. In part, this may be because of a reluctance to follow the implications of such an identification. For example, if biblical covenants such as Deuteronomy and Joshua follow the Hittite treaty structure, questions must be raised about presuppositions that this material cannot predate the first millennium BC. There are no first-millennium treaties with historical prologues or blessings clauses. They occur only in the second-millennium BC texts. Some scholars have attempted to deny that the biblical covenants were ever intended to resemble treaties.[2] They suggest that the two have nothing in common. Others emphasize comparisons and contrasts with the first-millennium treaties, without due regard for the earlier forms.[3] However, structural similarities with these do exist, as Kitchen has continued to demonstrate.[4] Joshua 24,

---

[1] V. Korošec, *Hethitische Staatsverträge. Ein Beitrag zu ihrer juristischen Wertung,* Leipziger rechtswissenschaftliche Studien 60 (Leipzig, 1931); G. E. Mendenhall, 'Law and Covenant in Israel and the Ancient Near East', *BA,* 17, 1954, pp. 26–46, 50–76.

[2] Criticisms to various degrees may be found in L. Perlitt, *Bundestheologie im Alten Testament,* Wissenschaftliche Monographien zum Alten und Neuen Testament (Neukirchen: Neukirchener Verlag, 1969); M. Weinfeld, *Deuteronomy and the Deuteronomic School* (Oxford: Clarendon, 1972); E. W. Nicholson, *God and His People: Covenant and Theology in the Old Testament* (Oxford: Clarendon, 1986).

[3] D. J. McCarthy, *Treaty and Covenant. A Study in Form in the Ancient Oriental Documents and in the Old Testament,* AB 21A (Rome: Biblical Institute Press, ²1978).

[4] K. A. Kitchen, *Ancient Orient and Old Testament,* (London, Tyndale, 1966), pp. 90–102; *idem, The Bible in Its World* (Exeter: Paternoster, 1977), pp. 79–85; *idem,*

while not a covenant text itself, does report just such a covenant (v. 25). Evidence of terms and phrases that have a distinctive meaning in both treaties and biblical covenants are relevant for understanding these texts in Joshua.[1]

Joshua 24 brings to culmination all of God's dealings with his people in creating them and settling them in the land. It also introduces the history of Israel in the land by setting a standard of faith and unity that will seldom be attained in future generations.

(d) The holy and redeeming God

Each part of Joshua emphasizes the gracious and redemptive work of God on behalf of Israel and of Joshua. From chapter 1, God is in command of both. In chapter 2, Rahab's confession of God's salvation (vv. 9–11) provides the background for the whole story. This demonstrates the mercy of God in delivering Rahab. It also proves the justice of God in defeating and destroying all those who continued to resist God's plan for his people.

At the crossing of the Jordan (chs. 3 – 4), the power of God at work in bringing about *amazing things* (3:5) is enhanced by the sequence of the crossing. First, the priests enter the river. They are the special representatives of God and the ark is a unique symbol of God's presence. God precedes his people in the crossing of the Jordan and thereby enables them to cross. Then the representatives of the people cross. Finally, the people themselves cross. Thus the order of the presentation of groups begins with God's representatives, moves on to the representatives of the people and concludes with the people themselves. This order reflects the process of divine revelation throughout the Pentateuch and in Joshua. God reveals his will to an intermediary who passes it on to the representatives of the people and finally to the people themselves. The crossing of the Jordan also demonstrates divine power over nature.

In chapter 6, the fall of Jericho was a divinely ordained

'The Fall and Rise of Covenant, Law and Treaty', *TynB*, 40, 1989, pp. 124–135; *idem*, 'New Directions in Biblical Archaeology: Historical and Biblical Aspects' in *BAT*, pp. 43–44; *idem*, 'The Patriarchal Age, Myth or History?', *BAR* 21/2, March/April 1995, pp. 52–56.

[1] See the study and bibliography of P. Kalluveetil, *Declaration and Covenant*, AB 88 (Rome: Biblical Institute Press, 1982). For Joshua 24 in particular, see the summary of Koopmans, pp. 60–61.

judgment on its inhabitants for their failure to confess the true God, as Rahab did. The marching around Jericho recalled that the purpose of God, which began with Israel's march from Sinai, continued into the Promised Land and its occupation. It also affirmed that this purpose would not be thwarted as long as the people remained faithful.

In Joshua 7, Israel learned that God's holiness demands that his nation be holy. Thus the *devoted things* (v. 1) belonged to God alone and could not be kept by Israel, for that would be theft. Further, the restoration of the covenant sign of circumcision renewed the covenant relationship that the Israel of the exodus had enjoyed (see 5:9). The breaking of the ban by Achan demanded the restoration of the broken covenantal relationship with God. In the cutting off of Achan, the Israel that entered Canaan learned of the awful price of sin that God demanded, not only from the unrighteous Canaanites, but even from Israelite sinners. None was exempt. Although the divine wrath would not trouble Israel, Joshua had explained the implications of the sin of Achan in 7:9. Israel had already lost thirty-six men because of that sin. Its future battles would be that much more difficult. Now Canaan knew that Israel was not unbeatable.

In Joshua 8:1–29, Israel's God is both victorious in battle and just and gracious. When Israel removes the sin in its midst through the execution of Achan, it can then progress to new victories. The meeting of the requirements of divine holiness allows for blessing to follow. In this case, such blessing occurs in the form of success in battle. The LORD graciously guides the people. He provides a successful strategy, indicates to Joshua when to begin the crucial phase of the military action and allows for booty to be taken in order to provide for the people of God (v. 2). In the case of Jericho, disobedience led to the defeat and repentance of Ai. In the case of Ai, obedience leads to the covenantal celebration at Mount Ebal. Everything hinges on the word of God and the willingness of those who hear it to believe and obey.

In this most nationalistic of books, God's mercy finds room for non-Israelites in the covenant community, both for Rahab (Jos. 6:17–25) and for the Gibeonites (ch. 9). However difficult it was for them, they become associated with God's people. They can worship Israel's God. Furthermore, they preserve their lives and retain their holdings in the Promised Land.

Juxtaposed with the renewal of the Mosaic covenant in Joshua 8:30–35, these texts illustrate the international character of that covenant. Behind it lies the promise to Abram that through Israel all the nations of the world would find blessing (Gn. 12:1–3).

Chapter 10 develops four theological areas. Firstly, God fights for Israel and gives them the Promised Land, as part of the divine covenant. Without God they cannot succeed. With God's miracles they cannot fail. Secondly, only here are miracles performed, not in the north. The south, which will become the allotment of Judah and the Southern Kingdom, is specially blessed by God's presence. Thirdly, Israel remains faithful to the Gibeonite treaty, whatever the cost. This treaty was not God's will, yet God honours Israel's faithfulness and incorporates their response to the Gibeonite peril into the conquest of the south. Finally, the text suggests the important role that God played in all the political activities of Israel. They keep their vow before God to help Gibeon. Joshua receives divine aid in the midst of the battle, requests more help and receives that as well. Each battle and the capture of each town include the repeated refrain that God gave it into their hands. The account begins and ends in the sanctuary at Gilgal before the presence of the LORD. Joshua 11 shows God as ruler of the north as well as of the south and of the lowlands as well as of the hill country (contrast the Arameans' view in 1 Ki. 20:23). It demonstrates that not even the strongest of the fortified towns in Canaan can withstand the God of the Israelites.

God's holiness is in evidence at the conclusion of the book, in the erection of an altar east of the Jordan in order to remember the lordshp of Israel's God (22:26–27) and the establishment of a memorial stone at Shechem after the ceremony of covenant renewal (24:26–27). These acts and memorials point to God's special election of his people.

THE ALLOTMENTS OF JOSHUA 13 – 21

The reader approaching this material will perceive what appears as a complex maze of place names interspersed with occasional notes related to the acquisition and distribution of some of the places. Resisting the temptation to skip over this section of Joshua can result in an appreciation of important features of God's covenant with Israel. Beyond the obvious detail of the content of these chapters and the means by which God blessed those who remained faithful in the conquest of the land, this passage also addresses the question why the land formed so significant a part of God's promises to the patriarchs and remained a key feature of the covenant.

The study of these chapters raises questions that address four areas: the forms of the literature, the chronology of the texts, the identification of the sites, and the significance of these particular chapters in the book of Joshua. After a brief review of how scholars have answered these questions in the past, the first three items will be considered from the perspective of the overall allotment of the land.[1] For the theological significance of this allotment, see 'Theology' (b) 'The land as an inheritance' (pp. 46–49). Specific allotments will be examined at the appropriate section in the commentary.

Attempts have been made to locate this material within the traditional Pentateuchal sources. Noth, with his emphasis upon the unity of the Deuteronomistic history, long ago argued for these chapters as coming from the hand of a Deuteronomistic redactor.[2] Elliger concurred.[3] Mowinckel posited an oral tradition leading to a post-exilic Jerusalem document authored by the priestly redactor, P.[4] This view has been more recently advanced by Van Seters who stresses similar purposes (*e.g.* the occupation of the Promised Land) in the related P fragments of Numbers.[5] Cortese has argued for two priestly redactions, distinguishing emphasis upon the land, its distribution and the addition of narrative notes.[6] This results

[1]R. S. Hess, 'Tribes, Territories of' in G. W. Bromiley *et al.* (eds.), *The International Standard Bible Encyclopedia*, Revised edition, 4 vols. (Grand Rapids: Eerdmans, 1979–1988), IV, pp. 907–913; *idem*, 'Asking Historical Questions of Joshua 13 – 19: Recent Discussion Concerning the Date of the Boundary Lists'; *idem*, 'Late Bronze Age and Biblical Boundary Descriptions of the West Semitic World'.

[2]M. Noth, 'Studien zu den historisch-geographischen Dokumenten des Josuabuches', *ZDPV*, 58, 1935, pp. 185–255.

[3]K. Elliger, 'Tribes, Territories of' in *IDB*, IV, pp. 701–710.

[4]S. Mowinckel, *Zur Frage nach dokumentarischen Quellen in Josua 13 – 19* (Oslo, 1946).

[5]J. Van Seters, *In Search of History. Historiography in the Ancient World and the Origins of Biblical History* (Yale University Press, 1983), pp. 331–337.

[6]E. Cortese, *Josua 13 – 21: Ein priesterschriftlicher Abschnitt im deuteronomistischen Geschichtswerk*, OBO 94 (Fribourg: Universitätsverlag; Göttingen: Vandenhoeck & Ruprecht, 1990). See the review of this work by S. L. McKenzie, *JBL*, 110, 1991, pp. 713–715.

in a complex array of glosses, joins and links, far removed from the simplicity of Noth's single editor.[1] In fact, for several reasons source criticism is not helpful for answering the questions posed by this material. Firstly, the nature of most of this material as place names means that source-critical theories are useful only with respect to final redactions. They say nothing about the origins of the material. Secondly, recent questions about the nature and viability of source criticism for the Pentateuch apply just as much to the use of the method here.[2] It is not possible to evaluate the sequence of literary editions or the evolution of a written document by using only evidence gathered from within the final document. Some sort of external controls are necessary in order to ground the hypotheses. As with the Pentateuch and the remainder of Joshua, the absence of reference to external data by the source critics renders source-critical hypotheses highly subjective. Thirdly, as will be shown, the application of external controls through comparison with other Ancient Near Eastern boundary descriptions and through the site identifications themselves leads to conclusions about the integrity of the documents. Therefore this study will restrict itself to an examination of the literary forms of the documents and, within the context of comparative Ancient Near Eastern texts as well as consideration of the origins of the place names that appear in the chapter, it will also consider the broader implications for the dating and purpose of the documents in their present location.

The context of chapters 13 – 21 includes the first twelve chapters in so far as they describe a conquest of the land. There then follows the stage of the distribution of that land as a necessary precondition for its occupation.[3] This sequence has parallels in conquest descriptions of other ancient peoples in the Mediterranean, especially in accounts of founders of new colonies in Greek literature.[4] The actual sequence of tribal allotments follows the general order of the conquest, beginning

[1]See the review of K. L. Younger, Jr., *CBQ*, 55, 1993, pp. 105–106.

[2]See the discussion on the origins of the whole book of Joshua (pp. 26–42).

[3]Z. Kallai, 'The United Monarchy of Israel – A Focal Point in Israelite Historiography', *IEJ*, 27, 1977, pp. 103–109 (106).

[4]M. Weinfeld, 'The Extent of the Promised Land – The Status of Transjordan' in *Das Land*, pp. 63–65; *idem*, 'The Pattern of the Israelite Settlement in Canaan' in *Congress Volume. Jerusalem 1986. VT Supplement XL* (Leiden: Brill, 1988), pp.

in Transjordan and then moving to the southern region of Canaan before turning north. It is modified by the tendency to give priority to these allotments that Moses allocated (Transjordan) or whose claimants trace their rights to Moses (Caleb and the daughters of Zelophehad). This sequence cannot be explained by historical or political factors at any other time in Israel's history.[1]

(a) Form and dates of the literature

Alt advanced the study of Joshua 13 – 21 through the distinction of boundary descriptions from town lists. East of the Jordan there appear territorial lists.[2] Alt's identification of towns distinguished them from the territories that they controlled. When they lay along a boundary, he suggested that the territory and the town may belong to different tribes.[3] The boundary descriptions were preserved in a late premonarchic or early monarchic document. They served to adjudicate disputes between tribes concerning land ownership. Only the description of Judah's boundary dates later, to the period of Josiah. Noth observed the prepositions and verbs that connected these fixed points in the boundary descriptions;[4] he noted that in some of the southern boundary descriptions there are duplicate descriptions of the same boundary but the connecting terms differ; and he suggested that these were the work of a later editor. For Noth, the boundary descriptions dated to the United Monarchy when rule over the whole region required that the land be understood as a divine gift. Elliger and Albright followed this dating scheme, while Y. Kaufmann followed Alt in assigning the boundary descriptions to the

---

270–283; *idem*, 'Historical Facts behind the Israelite Settlement Pattern', *VT*, 38, 1988, pp. 324–332; *idem*, *Promise*, pp. 22–51.

[1] Z. Kallai, 'Organizational and Administrative Frameworks in the Kingdom of David and Solomon', in *Proceedings of the Sixth World Congress of Jewish Studies*, 1 (Jerusalem: World Congress of Jewish Studies, 1977), pp. 213–220 (219).

[2] A. Alt, 'Judas Gaue unter Josia', *Palästinajahrbuch*, 21, 1925, pp. 100–116; *ibid.*, *KS*, II, pp. 276–288 (276).

[3] *Idem*, 'Das System der Stammesgrenzen im Buche Josua', *Sellin Festschrift: Beiträge zur Religiongeschichte und Archaeologie Palästinas* (Leipzig: A. Deichert, 1927), pp. 13–24; *ibid.*, *KS*, I, pp. 193–202 (200–202).

[4] M. Noth, 'Studien zu den historisch-geographischen Dokumenten des Josuabuches', *ZDPV*, 58, 1935, pp. 185–255; *idem*, *Das Buch Josua*, Handbuch zum Alten Testament I/7 (Tübingen: J. C. B. Mohr, ²1953).

period before the Monarchy, specifically to the time before Dan's migration to the north.[1] Kaufmann defined the boundary descriptions as an idealized outline of the complete occupation of the land. They had their origins in historical records of different ethnic groups. Kaufmann, like many others, noted problems with towns on the border of Benjamin which also seemed to belong to other tribes. He concluded that no administrative document would preserve such confusion. Aharoni solved this problem for Judah by suggesting that the borders of Judah do not appear in Joshua 15.[2] Instead of the northern border of Judah, that of Benjamin, which is contiguous, is given. The other borders are those of the land of Canaan as found in Numbers 34. Aharoni argued that the boundary descriptions date back to a pre-Monarchic covenant among the northern tribes. The unified nature of the boundary descriptions, describing the whole land without gaps or overlaps, led Cross and Wright to argue for their origin in a single document.[3]

Both Z. Kallai and N. Na'aman have argued for a date for the boundary descriptions during the period of the Monarchy.[4] There are two reasons for their conclusions: (1) the boundary descriptions describe an actual historical situation and the United Monarchy is the only time that Israel controlled all the land outlined in Joshua 13 – 21; and (2) there is no longer any reason for boundaries to have been created before the Monarchy.[5] The tribes were scattered and would not have confronted one another in claims over land. Both of these points, but especially the second, arise out of the collapse of the theory that Israel originally constituted a tribal amphictyony in Canaan. This model of a tribal league, which focused around a central sanctuary, was based upon classical Greek analogies. Recent sociological research has questioned the validity of the

[1]K. Elliger, 'Tribes, Territories of'; W. F. Albright, 'The Administrative Divisions of Israel and Judah', *JPOS*, 5, 1925, pp. 17–54; Y. Kaufmann, *The Biblical Account of the Conquest of Canaan*, tr. M. Dagut (Jerusalem: Magnes, 1985).
[2]Aharoni, *Land*, pp. 248–262.
[3]F. M. Cross and G. E. Wright, 'The Boundary and Province Lists of the Kingdom of Judah', *JBL*, 75, 1956, pp. 202–226 (207); Boling and Wright, p. 338.
[4]Kallai, pp. 277–325; *idem*, 'Tribes, Territories of', *IDB Supplement*, pp. 920–923; Na'aman, *Borders*, pp. 75–117.
[5]N. P. Lemche, *Early Israel. Anthropological and Historical Studies on the Israelite Society before the Monarchy*, VT Supplement 37 (Leiden: Brill, 1985), pp. 285–290, used the same argument to date the boundary system to the time of Josiah.

model.[1] If the concept of a tribal league is rejected along with that of the amphictyonic model, then no reason exists for a boundary system before the period when the tribes joined together under a common leader, *i.e.* the United Monarchy. However, there is no evidence that a league of some sort must be excluded from consideration. On the other hand, if the testimony of other texts in Joshua is considered, there is reason to accept the existence of larger corporate units than the extended family or even the tribe.[2]

Alt dated the town lists that did not form part of the tribal boundaries to a variety of periods in Israel's history.[3] He argued that a southern source for the town lists of Judah should be dated to Josiah's time (later seventh century BC), just like the boundary descriptions. Aharoni found an administrative purpose in all of the town lists, which originated in two sources, a Judean list and one derived from the Solomonic districts.[4] Kallai also argued for more than one source for these lists, a Solomonic source for the northern lists and for those of Benjamin, and another for the Judean lists that he dated to the reign of Hezekiah (*c.* 700 BC).[5]

The Bible is clear that the occupation of the whole Promised Land was not realized until the period of David (1 Ki. 4:21). Full occupation was again realized in the eighth century under the leadership of Uzziah and Jeroboam II. The linking of tribal allotments for the whole of the Promised Land with the period of Joshua prompts a reconsideration of the date of the boundary lists as well as their original nature and purpose.

Within an Ancient Near Eastern context, boundary descriptions closest to the tribal boundaries in Joshua 13 – 21 are found in the treaty documents from Ugarit and from the Hittite capital (Hattusas) in the Late Bronze Age.[6] Three types

[6]For a review of recent research with bibliography, see J. W. Rogerson, 'Anthropology and the Old Testament', in *World of Ancient Israel*, pp. 27–31.

[2]See Jos. 2:12; 7:14; 8:30–35; and 24.

[3]A. Alt, 'Judas Gaue unter Josia', *Palästinajahrbuch*, 21, 1925, pp. 100–116; *ibid., KS*, II, pp. 276–288; *idem*, 'Die Landnahme der Israeliten in Palästina', *Reformationsprogramm der Universität Leipzig*, 1925; *ibid., KS*, I, pp. 89–125.

[4]Y. Aharoni, 'The Province List of Judah', *VT*, 9, 1959, pp. 225–246.

[5]Z. Kallai, 'Tribes, Territories of', *IDB Supplement*, p. 922.

[6]R. S. Hess, 'Late Bronze Age and Biblical Boundary Descriptions of the West Semitic World'.

of similarities occur. On a formal level, all these boundary descriptions possess: (1) an introduction and a conclusion indicating the land or lands on behalf of which the boundary is concerned; (2) brief historical notes that intersperse the boundary descriptions; and (3) in the case of duplicate descriptions of the same boundary, slight variations in the spellings, sequence and selection of the place names as well as in the appearance of prepositions and notes that occur between the place names.[1] A second area of similarity has to do with the parties involved with fixing the boundary. As in the case of the Israelite tribes, and in the case of the boundary descriptions from Ugarit and Hattusas, the parties involved and present at the point of decision represent the lands on both sides of the boundary. The third area of comparison addresses the purpose of the descriptions. In the Ancient Near Eastern texts, their context within a treaty suggests that they served to define a legal relationship between the political groups involved. In the case of the biblical text, God establishes a covenant with Israel and uses the boundary descriptions to define the fulfilment of promises made to the nation's ancestors in the context of formal covenant ceremonies that occur before (8:30–35) and after (24) the allotment. A similar cultural context and thus a similar date should be applied to the origin of the boundary descriptions in Joshua 13 – 21.

There is evidence of lists of towns in Late Bronze Age cuneiform cultures from sites such as Ugarit and Alalakh.[2] These cuneiform lists originated as part of census requirements in the city-states. They always occur as part of a list of people or objects, with the town names specifying their origin or destination. The town lists normally include an introduction, describing the significance of the items or persons listed, and a summary, again describing the list and sometimes providing a total number of persons or objects. These administrative lists can be long and complex. They are divided into subgroups with their own introductions and summaries. Many of the southern town lists, the northern town lists and the Levitical town lists

[1]For this latter point, see M. E. J. Richardson, 'Hebrew Toponyms', *TynB*, 20, 1969, pp. 97–98.
[2]R. S. Hess, 'A Typology of West Semitic Place Name Lists with Special Reference to Joshua 13 – 19', forthcoming.

resemble these administrative lists.[1] They often have their own introductions and summaries that indicate the total number of towns. Some of the longer lists are subdivided, just like the administrative lists. This may suggest their origin as administrative documents recording the town's, tribal allotments. However, unlike the town lists of Ugarit and Alalakh, the Joshua lists (1) are separated from any reference to persons or objects associated with the town; (2) contain glosses that tie them to narratives in Joshua; and (3) have been fully integrated into the land grant of Joshua 13 – 21 and the larger covenant context (Jos. 8:30–35; 24) that defines the whole land as God's gift to his people.

With the exceptions of the migration of the tribe of Dan, that is described in detail in Judges 18 (see Jos. 19:47), and of the later wars between the southern and northern kingdoms, there is little evidence to suggest that the planned boundaries saw much change. Some tribes, such as Issachar and Simeon, had no defined boundaries but only preserved a list of towns. The reasons for this may reflect their locations. Issachar, in the midst of the Canaanite centres of the Jezreel Valley, would find it difficult to settle and to draw boundaries around these mighty city-states. Simeon in the southern part of Judah would remain vulnerable to desert marauders and groups such as the Jerahmeelites and Cherethites whom David would encounter.[2]

Discussions of specific parts of the allotments are found accompanying the commentary for the relevant tribe.

(b) The identification of sites

The text of Joshua 13 – 21 is composed mostly of place names that form the boundaries and town lists just described. The commentary will introduce each tribal allotment with observations on the nature of place names. The narrative sections will

---

[1] The town lists for Benjamin (Jos. 18:21–28), Dan (19:41–46), Judah (15:21–62), Simeon (19:2–7), Issachar (19:18–21), Naphtali (19:35–38) and the Levitical list (21) share the characteristics of administrative lists. The central town lists of Manasseh (13:31; 17:2–3, 11) have a different form. See the commentary (pp. 258–259). The towns of asylum (20:7–8) and other small lists are so well integrated into their narrative context that they have no introductions and summaries, and so they do not resemble administrative lists.

[2] A. F. Rainey, 'Early Historical Geography of the Negeb' in Z. Herzog (ed.), *Beer-Sheba II: The Early Iron Age Settlements* (Ramot Publishing, Tel Aviv University Institute of Archaeology, 1984), pp. 88–104.

also receive brief comment. Otherwise the place names will be presented in a list in the order in which they occur in the text. Following each name, a chart will indicate whether the name occurs in the Hebrew text (MT), or in the Greek text (LXX, divided into A and B), or both.[1] This will be followed, where appropriate, by the Arab name, the Israeli name, and the grid number. The grid number refers to the Israeli and Jordanian systems for plotting locations in their countries. It pinpoints a site according to its west–east location in the first three numbers, and then according to its south–north location in the second group of three numbers. The larger numbers indicate sites farther east, for the first three digits, and farther north for the second three digits.

The procedure for site identification has become more and more sophisticated as knowledge of the land and its history has developed.[2] Normally, the historical geographer begins with a study of all the biblical and extrabiblical texts that mention the site, so as to ascertain the known periods of its occupation and its location relative to other sites or natural features. This is combined with a careful survey of the region to identify all known population centres of antiquity. The location of each is identified on a map, along with details such as proximity to known ancient roads and other topographical features (springs, rivers, mountains, *etc.*), as well as distances from other known sites. The locally preserved names of these centres, where they exist, are obtained. Sometimes such names can preserve the ancient name of the site; although it is possible that a name may 'shift' from one site to another over a period of centuries. The sites in the region should be carefully

---

[1]For a survey of attestations of the towns of Jos. 14 – 21 in all the ancient versions, see Svensson. The work also includes discussion of all the parallel passages in the Pentateuch and in Chronicles, as well as comparable listings of towns in particular regions as found in the historical books and the prophets.

[2]Aharoni, *Land*, pp. 105–130; H. J. Franken, 'The Problem of Identification in Biblical Archaeology', *PEQ*, 108, 1976, pp. 3–11; J. M. Miller, 'Site Identification: A Problem Area in Contemporary Biblical Scholarship', *ZDPV*, 99, 1983, pp. 119–129; A. F. Rainey, 'Sites, Identification of', *IDB Supplement*, pp. 825–827; *idem*, 'The Toponymics of Eretz-Israel', *BASOR*, 231, 1978, pp. 1–17; *idem*, 'Historical Geography – The Link between Historical and Archaeological Interpretation', *BA*, 45, 1982, pp. 217–223; *idem*, 'Historical Geography', in J. F. Drinkard, Jr, G. L. Mattingly and J. M. Miller (eds.), *Benchmarks in Time and Culture: Essays in Honor of Joseph A. Callaway*, Archaeology and Biblical Studies 1 (Atlanta: Scholars Press, 1988), pp. 353–368.

studied. In some cases this may involve simply identifying the pottery remains that may be located on the surface of an ancient site. These can provide an idea of the period of occupation. Occasionally excavation of sites has been or is being undertaken. This can reveal much information about a site's period of occupation, as well as its size and significance. Sometimes additional texts are discovered and, rarely, an inscription identifying the name of the site itself.

Using available textual, topographic, onomastic and archaeological data, historical geographers propose identifications of sites that best fit the data. Given the variety of data, it is not unusual to find that some sites are identified differently by various geographers. More surprising is the large number of sites whose identification has received general agreement. In the identifications provided in the lists that follow, Aharoni's masterful study of the names will receive first consideration. Where research has led to alternative proposals, this will also be noted.

ANALYSIS

I. THE CONQUEST (1:1 – 12:24)
    a. The book's goal and procedure (1:1–18)
        i. Past connections (1:1)
        ii. Promises: the book in outline (1:2–5)
        iii. Responsibilities: a call to courage and its source (1:6–9)
        iv. Obedience and the evidence of leadership: the organization of all Israel (1:10–11)
        v. The Transjordanian tribes (1:12–18)
    b. Rahab and the mission of the spies (2:1–24)
        i. Joshua sends two spies (2:1)
        ii. The house of Rahab (2:2–8)
        iii. The confession and request of Rahab (2:9–13)
        iv. The spies assure Rahab (2:14–21)
        v. The spies return (2:22–24)
    c. Rites of passage across the Jordan River (3:1 – 4:24)
        i. Joshua and all the Israelites set out (3:1)
        ii. Instructions for crossing, part 1 (3:2–5)
        iii. Instructions for crossing, part 2 (3:6–13)
        iv. The priests cross (3:14–17)
        v. The twelve stones (4:1–10)
        vi. The people cross (4:11–13)
        vii Joshua is exalted (4:14)
        viii Out of the Jordan (4:15–18)
        ix. The transition to Gilgal (4:19–24)
    d. Rites of preparation: circumcision (5:1–12)
        i. The fear of the Canaanites (5:1)
        ii. Joshua circumcises the people (5:2–3)
        iii. The reason for the circumcision (5:4–9)
        iv. Passover as the beginning of the inheritance of the land (5:10–12)
    e. The first assault: the capture of Jericho (5:13 – 6:27)
        i. The pre-capture instructions (5:13 – 6:5)

c. The covenant at Shechem (24:1–27)
    i. A new assembly at Shechem (24:1)
    ii. God's redemptive work for Israel (24:2–13)
    iii. The covenant agreement (24:14–24)
    iv. The ratification of the covenant (24:25–27)
d. The settlement in the land (24:28–33)

COMMENTARY

1. THE CONQUEST (1:1 – 12:24)

a. The book's goal and procedure (1:1–18)

i. Past connections (1:1). This statement joins the book of Joshua with the event narrated at the end of Deuteronomy. It is a time of transition in which Moses, who was the chief human character of the books of Exodus, Leviticus, Numbers and Deuteronomy, will no longer feature. The term *servant of the LORD* appeared in Deuteronomy 34:5, describing Moses at his death. This expression will occur another thirteen times in the book of Joshua as an epithet of Moses. The expression 'servant of X', where X is a deity, appears frequently outside the Bible.[1] However, until the death of Joshua (when it is also applied to him), only Moses is called *servant of the LORD*. Besides expressing the relationship of servanthood which Moses would have towards the LORD, it also stresses the personal relationship which the LORD had towards Moses, as described in the final verses of Deuteronomy.

Joshua, the book's main human character, is introduced as *son of Nun*. This identifies him with the Joshua of Deuteronomy who will succeed Moses. The designation of Joshua as *Moses' assistant* (Heb. *mᵉšārēt*) serves two purposes. Firstly, it links this Joshua with the figure in Exodus 24:13; 33:11 and in Numbers 11:28. This term does not appear again in Deuteronomy. This Joshua is the same person who ascended the mountain of God with Moses and who served as Moses' assistant in the wilderness wanderings. Secondly, this term is different from the more

---

[1] For example, in the fourteenth-century BC Amarna letters, at least ten West Semitic leaders from towns in Palestine and Syria bore personal names constructed as 'servant of X' where X is usually the name of a deity. See R. Hess, *Amarna Personal Names*, ASOR Dissertation Series 9 (Winona Lake, Indiana: Eisenbrauns, 1994), pp. 176, 209.

common word for *servant* (Heb. '*ebed*), which is used of Moses. Although the two terms overlap in their meaning and usage, the concern here is to preserve the distinctive relationship of Moses and the LORD and to affirm that the relationship between Joshua and Moses was different from this. However, it was a special relationship and one that further qualified Joshua for the task he received. In this verse, the LORD speaks directly to Joshua, just as he did with Moses. It further confirms the special role of Joshua as a successor of Moses.[1] Although the servant of the LORD was an honoured position in the Old Testament, Jesus introduces a whole new category of relationship. In John 15:15, he explicitly rejects the term *servants* for his disciples and replaces it with *friends*. For all those who follow Christ, this describes a new and fuller relationship with him. At the same time, the response of the apostle Paul is to continue to recognize that he is a 'slave' of Christ (Rom. 1:1; 1 Cor. 7:22; Eph. 6:6). Thus the Christian, elevated by Jesus to a new relationship, willingly submits to the discipleship to which God calls believers.

ii. Promises: the book in outline (1:2–5). This text summarizes the book. Verse 2 describes the crossing of the Jordan as found in 1:1 – 5:12. Verse 3 outlines the 'conquest' of 5:13 – 12:24. Verse 4 implies the distribution of the land in 13:1 – 22:34. The emphasis on *all the days of* Joshua's life in verse 5 is found at the end of Joshua's life in the final two chapters of the book. These verses also introduce the character of the LORD God of Israel. He is one of the main actors in the book. Here he reveals himself through his promises on behalf of Joshua and Israel.

2–3. A note of Moses' death is repeated to confirm that Joshua's leadership can now begin. The land is presented as a gift which the LORD is *about to give* to his people. However, the two occurrences of this verb alternate with verbs describing how Joshua and the Israelites are *to cross* (Heb. '*ābar*) the Jordan River and how they will possess wherever they *set* their

---

[1] As one concerned with the narrator, Polzin observes how the frequent quoting of divine instruction in this opening chapter establishes the authoritative role of the narrator. The narrator is a successor to Moses in so far as Moses previously cited God's word and now the narrator does the same. See Polzin, pp. 75–76. However, the role of Joshua as successor to Moses remains the key point of the opening chapter.

feet (*tidrōk*). There is a twofold aspect to this. God promises the land but the people must take it for themselves. They must fight in accordance with God's explicit direction and their allotment of the land must follow his guidance. The parallel passage of Deuteronomy 11:24–25 is also set within the context of commands of loyalty to God and his commandments. Joshua adds the command to 'cross over', something that the people are prepared to do.

A second twofold aspect of the book's message is implied in the two occurrences of the adjective *all* (Heb. *kol*) in *all these people* and in *every place.* The importance of the participation of all of the Israelites will become apparent in the responsibilities of the Transjordanian tribes and in the sin of Achan. The significance of God's gift of the whole land will explain the wars in both the south and the north and the allotment of the land with no gaps between tribal territories.

The reference to God's promise to Moses is surprising. Promises of land were first made to the patriarchs of Genesis (*e.g.* Gn. 15:18), but they are not often made to anyone else. God reaffirms this patriarchal promise to Moses in Deuteronomy 34:4 and it is alluded to in Jos. 1:6. The reason for the mention of Moses in 1:3 is to emphasize the closeness and certainty of Joshua's position as successor to Moses in leading the people according to God's plan. What God had promised Moses was now going to come true through the leadership of Joshua.

4. The detail of the land as comprising *the desert* and *Lebanon* and extending to the boundary of *the great river, the Euphrates,* may be compared with Gn. 10:19, Nu. 13:17, 21–22, and 34:3–12. In Genesis and Numbers, the southern territories of Canaan are specified since these are of concern in the contexts. In Gn. 10:19 and Nu. 34:3–5, the southern boundary of Canaan lies in an arc beginning in the region of Gaza and the Wadi of Egypt in the west[1] and proceeding eastward to the Dead Sea (Salt Sea) and the presumed region of Sodom and Gomorrah.

---

[1]The mention of Gaza in Gn. 10 may reflect the concern of that text to describe the boundaries only in terms of cities or city-states, without recourse to natural boundaries. The Wadi el-'Arish remains a likely identification for the Wadi of Egypt. See N. Na'aman, 'The Brook of Egypt and Assyrian Policy on the Border of Egypt', *TA*, 6, 1979, pp. 68–90; A. F. Rainey, 'Toponymic Problems (cont.): The Brook of Egypt', *TA*, 9, 1982, pp. 131–132; E. D. Oren, 'Ethnicity and Regional Archaeology: The Western Negev under Assyrian Rule', *BAT*, p. 103. Gaza is the closest city to the mouth of this river.

This is not contradicted by Numbers 13:17 and 21–22, where the southern border of Canaan must lie north of Kadesh Barnea but south of Hebron. This is true no matter how the Negev (which includes only the northern part of the modern Israeli Negev) and the Desert of Zin are understood to fit into the picture. The northern border of Canaan seems to vary, Lasha (= the town of Dan) in Genesis, Lebo Hamath (or Hamath) and Mount Hor in Numbers, and the Euphrates River in Joshua. The concern in all three cases is more with regions in southern Canaan than with the north. In no example is a northern boundary detailed.[1]

The desert (Heb. *hammidbār*) describes uncultivated land, but is not restricted to the Sinai desert and the other regions of the wilderness wanderings. In the book of Joshua, it includes the area around Bethel and Ai (8:15, 20; 16:1, 18:12) and the Judean desert (12:8; 15:61). It is a general description of the region west of the Jordan and to the south, just as the Lebanon describes the forested mountains that would form the region west of the Jordan and to the north. The Jordan defines the eastern border. The text designates the *Great Sea* or Mediterranean Sea as the western border, thereby including regions west of *the desert.* The reference to *all the Hittite country* is missing in the Septuagint. Located in what is now the country of Turkey, the Hittites were a 'superpower' during the age of Joshua. The area north of the Lebanon was under Hittite control at various times in the fourteenth and thirteenth centuries BC. Alternatively, perhaps the phrase intends the entire region west of the Jordan River occupied in the thirteenth and twelfth centuries by groups migrating south during the last days, or after the collapse, of the Hittite empire.[2]

---

[1] Weinfeld, pp. 52–75, distinguishes boundary descriptions according to whether land east of the Jordan was included. He uses the descriptions in Nu. 34 and in Jos. 13 – 19 as examples. He posits two different sources for these different boundary descriptions. However, none of the texts clearly indicates that the territories of Ammon and Moab were ever part of Canaan (or the Promised Land). Nor do any of the descriptions ever exclude Gilead and the Bashan. Jos. 13 – 19 is not intended as a description of the Promised Land or of Canaan. It includes areas outside Canaan but never designates them as Canaan or as the Promised Land. For the second-millennium BC context of this description of Canaan, see the Introduction: 'Antiquity' (p. 26).

[2] Some have interpreted it as a note from the first millennium BC, during which time Neo-Hittite states occupied the areas north of Lebanon and west of the Euphrates. See Noth, p. 20, who relates it to the Neo-Assyrian designation of

5. The promise of victory reaffirms the divine choice of Joshua's leadership and forms the basis by which others will discern that he enjoys a similar relationship with God and a similar role in Israel to those of Moses. The promise of God's presence recalls Deuteronomy 3:21–22, a previous occasion when God addressed Joshua. In both cases the emphasis lies with God's role as warrior fighting on behalf of Joshua and Israel. The promise occurs again in Deuteronomy 31:23, using similar language to that found in these verses. There it follows God's first assurance to Joshua that Joshua *will bring the Israelites into the land I promised them on oath.*

This text also looks forward. In addition to the reflection upon Joshua's entire life, which occurs in the final two chapters, the vivid verbs that affirm Joshua's invincibility and God's presence link this introduction with the variety of events depicted throughout the book. The promise that no-one will *be able to stand up against* (Heb. *yityaṣṣēḇ*) Joshua[1] contrasts with Joshua's assembling of all Israel who *presented themselves before God* at the covenant renewal in 24:1. The verb used in the promise that God will not *leave* Joshua appears again in 10:6, where the Gibeonites remind Joshua of their treaty and ask him not to *abandon* them when attacked. The second verb, the promise that God will not *forsake* (Heb. *'e'ezḇekā*) Joshua, occurs several times in the book. The warriors of Ai abandon their fortress (5:17), Joshua compliments the Transjordanian tribes for their loyalty to Israel (22:3), and most importantly all Israel confesses their loyalty to the LORD (24:16, 20).[2]

For the Christian, Christ's promise of his presence to his disciples resembles God's promise to Joshua. It forms the basis for sending his disciples on their worldwide mission (Mt. 28:18–20; Mk. 16:15; Acts 1:8).

---

this region. H. A. Hoffner, 'The Hittites and Hurrians' in *POTT*, pp. 213–214, distinguishes between *the Hittite country*, which he identifies with Syria in the Bible, and the Hittites of the Pentateuch and Joshua. He suggests that this group represents a people who bear Semitic names and whose designation as Hittite represents a 'chance conflation' with the Hittites of Anatolia. This analysis best suits the references in Joshua.

[1]The suffix 'you' is singular in the Hebrew, referring to Joshua. In the versions, it is plural, referring to all of Israel.

[2]The cognate form of this verb, *ezēbu*, occurs frequently in the Amarna letters, where it is also used with reference to loyalty. The fourteenth-century BC Canaanite city leaders use it to describe the disloyalty of other city leaders towards the Pharaoh.

iii. Responsibilities: a call to courage and its source (1:6–9). This continues the opening address from God to Joshua. Matters turn from the promises of the first half of the address to the responsibilities that Joshua must accept. The expression *be strong and courageous* (Heb. $h^a zaq$ $we^{,e} m\bar{a}s$) opens and closes this section. It describes the attitude that Joshua should possess. Its threefold repetition in these verses recalls the three times it appears in the Pentateuch, in Deuteronomy 31:6, 7, 23. Here it is applied to Israel (v. 6) and to Joshua, where it forms part of his commissioning. Deuteronomy 31:6 relates the expression to the promise of God never to *leave you or forsake you* as in Joshua 1:5. The occurrence in Deuteronomy 31:23 also recalls the language of Joshua 1:5–6, with its emphasis upon God's presence with Joshua. The same language appears in 1 Chronicles 28:20 (*cf.* 22:13) where David charges Solomon with building the Temple. The occurrence of *be strong and courageous* in Joshua 10:25 is set in the context of Joshua's encouragement to the people to fight against their opponents, similar to Hezekiah's usage of the expression in preparing the people to withstand the Assyrians (2 Ch. 32:7). Thus the term could be used in a variety of circumstances but always within a context of God's presence and support.[1] The promise that the people of Israel would inherit the land anticipates the division of the land in chapters 13 – 21 and the specifications regarding who receives what particular territory as their inheritance.

7–8. In Joshua 1, the appearance of *be strong and courageous* and its relationship to leading the people are overshadowed by the emphatic repetition of the command in the next sentence. There it is tied to the *law* (Heb. *tôrâ*) of Moses. Given the close parallels with Deuteronomy already noted, the reference is probably to Deuteronomic law. This is supported by the warning not to turn to the right or to the left, which also occurs

---

[1]Some have found here an 'installation genre' for the initiation of a new leader. It consists of encouragement, a description, and a promise of (divine) assistance. See N. Lohfink, 'Die deuteronomistischen Darstellung des Ubergangs der Führung Israels von Moses auf Josue', *Scholastik*, 37, 1962, pp. 32–44; J. R. Porter, 'The Succession of Joshua' in J. I. Durham and J. R. Porter (eds.), *Proclamation and Presence: Old Testament Essays in Honour of Gwynne Henton Davies* (London, SCM, 1970), pp. 102–132; Mitchell, p. 30. However, the outline is too general to be of use. Instead, specific linguistic parallels, such as those suggested here, elucidate the text and incorporate texts that might not otherwise be considered part of this hypothetical genre. See D. McCarthy, 'An Installation Genre?', *JBL*, 90, 1971, pp. 31–41.

throughout Deuteronomy (2:27, 5:29; 17:11, 20; 28:14). Verses 7–9 form a special instruction to Joshua in the light of the charge given to him in verse 6. He is to *be strong and very courageous* in order to lead the Israelites into their land. By itself, this could be interpreted as a charge to Joshua to prepare for military leadership. However, verses 7–9 reveal that he cannot do this without obedience to the law of Moses. Unless Joshua makes meditation upon, and obedience to, God's law his first priority, his leadership will fail (*cf.* Ps. 1:1–3). This is made clear by (1) the position of the two commands to *be strong and very courageous* in verses 6 and 7; (2) the clauses of result at the end of verses 7 and 8 which both promise success in his mission (*i.e. wherever you go* and *you will be prosperous and successful*); and (3) the threefold mention of the law of Moses in these verses: *the law* (Heb. *hattôrâ*), *the Book of the Law* (Heb. *sēper hattôrâ*), and *everything written in it* (Heb. *hakkātûb bô*).

9. *Have I not commanded you?* asserts that there can be no doubt in Joshua's mind. He has been chosen for this mission and he cannot avoid the responsibility. The final *be strong and courageous* signals that this divine address to Joshua of his responsibilities is now coming to a close. The last line, *the LORD your God will be with you wherever you go,* ends the second part of the divine address in a way similar to the conclusion of the first part, with the promise of God's presence. However, in the first part (v. 5), this was one more promise among several that had been made. In the second part of the address, it forms the only promise to Joshua. Cast with the last three words, *wherever you go,* it parallels the last line of verse 7 and the promise of success that is given as a result of Joshua's obedience. Structured in this manner, the text affirms that Joshua will not be alone in striving for obedience to the law. Rather, the obedience and the success will be enjoyed in the presence of the LORD God who gave both the law and the promises. Joshua will not succeed because he obeys God's instruction; he will succeed because God is with him to enable him to obey his instruction.

For Christian leaders, the importance of the study of God's Word was recognized in the apostle's charge to Timothy (1 Tim. 4:11–14). In Romans 5 – 6, Paul also addresses the role of God's grace in forgiveness and salvation and as a means to victory over sin. Like Joshua, Christians do not succeed spiritually because they obey God's law. Instead, God through Christ enables them to have victory over sin (1 Cor. 15:57).

The divine discourse ends and Joshua begins to speak and act for the people. He will complete five tasks before the LORD again addresses him (in Jos. 3:7–8): (1) commission officers to direct and to organize the Israelites; (2) confirm the participation of the Transjordanian tribes in the 'conquest' of the land; (3) send messengers to spy out the land and receive their report; (4) address the people concerning preparation for crossing the Jordan River; and (5) address the priests concerning the first act of crossing. None of these items is explicitly mentioned in the LORD's charge to Joshua. They all depend upon prior knowledge of the events of Numbers and Deuteronomy.

Joshua 1:1–9 introduces the entire book with promises and instructions for Joshua and for all Israel. The literary relationship with Deuteronomy suggests that what follows is the implementation of the Deuteronomic programme. These opening verses summarize the instruction of God to Moses by repeating it to Joshua. They also serve a political purpose which is found throughout the first few chapters, that Joshua is the leader of Israel recognized by God as the successor to Moses. Times of transition in leadership are occasions of potential instability and disaster for the security of any group. In these opening chapters of Joshua, the reader finds text after text that legitimates Joshua's authority and thus guarantees that Moses' passing would not be the beginning of a struggle for power, as had occurred repeatedly in the wilderness. Instead, the texts show Joshua as successor to Moses, receiving the divine promises and instructions for the leadership of the people which had also been given to Moses. Joshua's leadership roles in political, military and religious matters are in evidence before the crossing of the Jordan takes place.[1]

iv. Obedience and the evidence of leadership: the organization of all Israel (1:10–11). This is the first of five actions which Joshua performs after his initial instruction from the LORD. It is

---

[1]Both literary and political analyses of the text argue that vv. 7–9 are integral to the opening of the book and to the chapters which follow. The degree to which these verses share terms and ideas with Deuteronomy and the rest of the Pentateuch is not significantly more or less than with vv. 1–6. Thus the view that a separate deuteronomistic redactor inserted vv. 7–9 is speculative. See Fritz, pp. 26, 29–30. The same conclusion obtains for separate editorial editions of vv. 10–11 and vv. 12–18.

the only one in which Joshua *ordered* the people involved, although his instructions to the Transjordanian tribes use a verb with imperative force, *remember!* (v. 13). Who are *the officers of the people?* In Exodus 5:6–19 they appear as the *foremen* caught between Pharaoh's demands for extra work and the Israelites' inability to meet the new quota. In Numbers 11:16, some of their number are included in the seventy elders chosen by Moses who receive the Spirit of the LORD. They appear in Deuteronomy 1:15 (*cf.* 16:18) as those whom Moses chose to be judges over Israel. The *officers* are one of the groups specified to stand before God and to bear witness in the covenant ceremony of Moses (Dt. 29:10[9]; 31:28) and in the covenant renewal ceremonies of Joshua (8:33; 23:2; 24:1). However, the precedent most relevant for their function in Joshua 1:10 and 3:2 occurs in Deuteronomy 20:5–9, where the *officers* pronounce the exclusion clauses for those who do not need to fight in a war, and then appoint commanders over the army. Otherwise, this term occurs almost exclusively in the books of Chronicles where it describes royal officials involved in non-specified secular duties.[1] The roles of these 'officers' form a secular counterpart to those of the priests. Joshua will address both, beginning with the *officers*, whose tasks are greater since they involve all the people.

11. The first word with which Joshua instructs the officers is a command to *go through* the camp and to command the people to prepare to march. The verb used is the same as that in verse 2 where God instructs Joshua to *cross* the Jordan. It reappears later in verse 11 with the same implication for the Israelites. Its usage here with a different object, *i.e.* the camp instead of the Jordan, is not accidental. As a verb of action commanded and executed, it describes the key activity in the opening chapters.[2] Joshua and Israel cross over the Jordan. All other activities are understood in the light of this movement. The actions of the officers become part of the activity of crossing and are described in similar terms. The people are called upon to provision themselves in preparation for the journey. The term

---

[1]The Hebrew term, *šōṭēr*, seems related to the Akkadian *šaṭāru*, 'to write'. This may suggest a scribal function but it is not prominent in their descriptions of activities in the Pentateuch and Joshua. See M. Weinfeld, 'Judge and Officer in Ancient Israel and in the Ancient Near East', *IOS*, 7, 1977, pp. 65–88.

[2]The importance of this verb in Jos. 1:1 – 5:12 is discussed by Koorevaar, p. 117 *et passim*.

supplies (Heb. *ṣêḏâ*) appears when Joseph provides his brothers with provisions for their trip back to Canaan (Gn. 42:25, 45:21). The lack of time to prepare provisions is exemplified by the exodus, where the Israelites took with them dough without yeast, so that they baked unleavened bread (Ex. 12:39). The text thus signals that this second crossing of a body of water is similar to, but also different from, the first crossing. The word for *supplies* relates the two, as will further allusions, but it also serves to point out distinctions. This second crossing was not to be done in haste and in flight from an enemy. Instead, it would be done with sufficient preparation.

The second crossing takes the appearance of a ceremonial act of worship. The people are not fleeing an enemy but preparing to do battle. Therefore, they must join together in acts of preparation and in the crossing itself. Furthermore, the language of the text takes on a ritual aspect. This is already evident in this first act of Joshua with the record of his repetition of the same words which God spoke to him in verse 2: *cross the Jordan . . . the land I/the LORD your God am/is giving to them/you.* Joshua passes to the people, through their officers, the same message that he received from God. He adds the purpose of Israel's crossing, to take possession of the land. This was God's fulfilment of the promises given to the ancestors of Israel. It applied to all of them, not only to Joshua. The text does not describe the deeds of the officers although it may be assumed that they followed Joshua's instructions. They will reappear in chapter 3. Joshua's example of obedience to the teaching of God is a model for Christian discipleship (Mt. 28:18–20).

v. The Transjordanian tribes (1:12–18). Having spoken to representatives of all the people, Joshua turns to the next largest group. Moses had given the tribes of Reuben, Gad and a section of the tribe of Manasseh territorial allocation east of the Jordan (Nu. 32 and Dt. 3:12–20). By addressing the loyalty of these warriors, Joshua touches upon a theme that will emerge in various contexts throughout the book, that of the unity of all Israel.

12–15. The charge to *remember the command that Moses the servant of the LORD gave you* is more than a concern to recollect some history. Joshua must transform these words into reality. What follows is a near quotation of Deuteronomy 3:18–20. The most important differences are as follows:

(1) Joshua adds that *God is giving you rest.*

(2) He describes the Transjordanian fighters as *fully armed* (Heb. *ḥᵃmušîm*) while Deuteronomy describes them as *armed for battle* (Heb. *ḥᵃlûṣîm*). The former word suggests a division into squads of five fighters each (although the exact number may have changed with time), while the latter is a passive form of a verb describing those who are prepared for battle.

(3) In Deuteronomy, the list of people and livestock which may remain east of the Jordan is followed by a note recognizing that these tribes have much livestock or many possessions.

(4) Joshua adds the phrase, *You are to help your brothers.* This is at the centre of Joshua's instructions.[1] Joshua affirms that the two parts of the people of Israel are to remain a unity.

The first two differences may reflect Joshua's greater concern with the theological theme of 'rest' for all Israel and with the military theme of organization (*cf.* the other usages of this term in Jos. 21:44; 22:4; 23:1). The third may have been omitted in Joshua as unnecessary to the purpose of the narrative. Although verses 13–15 are not a literal repetition of Deuteronomy 3:18–20, they are close enough to indicate that this is an intentional repetition of the original command which Moses gave to these tribes. This is important for two reasons: (1) it establishes the literary link between the two books; and (2) it confirms once more Joshua's leadership role.

Joshua is in a potentially precarious position with respect to the Transjordanian tribes. They had already received their land by the authority of Moses; they had made their pledge and agreements with Moses; and their families and claim to land lay to the east of the Jordan River, not to the west. Before verse 12 it is not clear that Joshua has any authority over them. He exercises his authority as the figure who will lead Israel to claim its land west of the Jordan. No mention is made of his role east of the river. Therefore, it is essential that he define his relationship to the warriors of the Transjordanian tribes. This is also the reason for his appeal to Moses and his near quotation of Moses' words. Joshua must appeal to the agreement between these warriors and Moses, for he has no other basis on which to claim their loyalty and participation in the battles yet to come. Furthermore, Joshua's leadership must be accepted by all of

[1] Schäfer-Lichtenberger, pp. 206–207.

Israel if he is to function as the true successor of Moses. If the Transjordanian tribes do not recognize his leadership, his claim to it will be diminished and his exercise of it will divide the nation. Despite all this, however, his appeal to Moses' words is a 'trump card', for no-one in Israel would be so disloyal as to reject the authority of Moses, and it is right for Moses' successor to claim the leadership over those who had followed Moses.

The concern for 'rest' appears here in Joshua for the first time. It will recur with special reference to the land at rest from war.[1] 'Rest' is the goal of the created order in Genesis 1:1 – 2:3. It is celebrated by Israel in the Sabbath (Ex. 20:8–11) and associated with the nation's own redemption from Egypt (Dt. 5:12–15). The 'rest' from their enemies that Joshua's generation first enjoyed (Jos. 21:44; 22:4; 23:1) forms the model for the rest given to Israel in later generations (1 Ki. 5:4; 1 Ch. 22:9, 18; 23:25; 2 Ch. 4:6–7; 15:15; 20:30), for the prophetic expectation of a future time of peace (Is. 2:2–4; Mic. 4:1–4) and for the New Testament promise of a coming rest for those redeemed by Christ (Heb. 4). As in Joshua, it always follows upon victory in warfare.

16–18. The response of the Transjordanian warriors demonstrates that they are conscious of Joshua's ambiguous position and that they will affirm his leadership. This is done in three formulaic statements of promise followed by a curse. At the end of each of these two sections appears a clause begun by *only*, which serves as an exhortation to Joshua. Each of the three promises is made up of an initial *whatever/wherever/whoever*. Each of these is followed by a verb – *command, send* and *obey* – which is followed by a second clause made up of a corresponding verb, *i.e. whatever you have commanded us we will do*, and *wherever you send us we will go*.

17. The third statement also has this structure, but the subjects and objects have been reversed and there are additional phrases inserted: *just as we fully obeyed Moses, so we will obey you*. This last phrase is followed by the first *only* clause, so formulated that it reverses the order of the subjects Moses and Joshua. Thus verse 17 is arranged in an A–B–B–A fashion: Moses–Joshua–Joshua–Moses. This should not be understood as an implied threat, *i.e.* that only so long as God stays with Joshua as he was with Moses will the Transjordanian warriors

---

[1] See 11:23 and comment there as well as 14:15; 21:44; and 23:1.

obey Joshua.¹ Rather, it is a confession and prayer that the LORD may abide with Joshua just as he did with Moses.

18. The curse also begins with *whoever*. The verb *rebels* (Heb. *yamreh*) occurs only here in Joshua. In Deuteronomy, it describes Israel's rebellion at Kadesh Barnea (1:26; 9:23) and the nation's past history of rebelliousness (9:7, 24; 31:27). It also describes the rebellious son whose punishment is death (21:18–21). Thus its usage to describe behaviour towards Joshua is especially appropriate, for it is Moses' own description of how Israel acted in the past. It implicitly recognizes Joshua as Moses' successor because it recognizes the potential of his having the same problem. The death penalty is appropriate in the context of Israel's past experience. Throughout the wilderness wanderings, whenever Israel rebelled, the punishment of death was present. The same is true for the law of the rebellious son. The expression 'let him be put to death' is a legal one used in various laws that prescribe death. On the final expression, *Only be strong and courageous*, see Introduction: 'The Person of Joshua' (pp. 20–24).

Verses 12–18 may reflect a ceremony or public procedure for the transference of loyalty from Moses, who had now died, to Joshua. Loyalty oaths at the beginning of a new leader's reign were not unknown in the Ancient Near East. There is inscriptional evidence from Egypt and Palestine that during the latter part of the second millennium BC, new Egyptian Pharaohs could begin their reigns with campaigns into Canaan in order to administer loyalty oaths to the Canaanite city-state rulers who were vassals of the Pharaoh.² Perhaps this same loyalty oath took place between Joshua and all the tribes of Israel. The reason for recording the promise of loyalty from the Transjordanian tribes was their ambiguous position in relation to Joshua's leadership. This promise was put down in writing both in order to retain its witness with respect to those who made it and also to enhance the message of Joshua 1, that Joshua was Moses' divinely appointed successor as leader over all Israel.³

---

¹ *Contra* Hawk, p. 59. If Hawk were correct, one would expect the Hebrew particle *'im*, 'if', in addition to or in place of the *raq*, 'only'.

² W. Helck, *Die Beziehungen Ägyptens zu Vorderasien im 3. und 2. Jahrtausend v. Chr.* (Wiesbaden: Harrassowitz, ²1971), pp. 246–247.

³ Polzin, p. 79, asks whether vv. 16–18 records the response of the whole people. The context requires that it is only the Transjordanian tribes who respond here. Their response of loyalty exemplifies that of the other tribes,

For Christians, this opening chapter teaches that leadership of God's people must be recognized by the people as God's choice. The test for all such ministry is found in the knowledge of and obedience to God's Word, something that can meet the practical needs of God's people (1 Tim. 3:1–10; Tit. 1:6–9). Joshua's command to the Transjordanian tribes and their loyal promise provides an example of the importance of the unity of God's people and their support of his chosen leadership, as well as a sober note on the seriousness of any division (Jos. 22; Jn. 17; Acts 5:1–11; 1 Cor. 3).

b. Rahab and the mission of the spies (2:1–24)

The story about Rahab functions in several ways in its place in Joshua. From the perspective of the literary context, it provides a view of the Canaanites as chapter 1 did of the Israelites. As in chapter 1, one particular figure is highlighted. In this sense, Rahab corresponds to Joshua as the faithful one of her people who is chosen to lead them to salvation, or at least to offer it to those who are interested. Joshua 2 also anticipates the conquest of Jericho in chapter 6. In the broader context of the Pentateuch, ties are obvious with Numbers 13 – 14 and Deuteronomy 1 and the sending of the scouts from Kadesh Barnea with its disastrous results. In the contrasting account of Joshua 2, the role of Joshua is magnified as one who follows God and who leads the people. Joshua 2 thus justifies the character of Joshua as a leader concerned for his people, for he gathers intelligence before leading them into hostile territory. It also describes how Joshua gives Rahab and her family an opportunity to deliver themselves from the coming destruction. Finally, Joshua 2 affirms a theology of the mission of Israel. This is specified in the two longest monologues in the story: the confession and request of Rahab (vv. 9–13) and the conditional promise of the scouts (vv. 17–20). Together these provide the justification for

---

whose position is far more certain in terms of Joshua's authority and their need to respect it. Mitchell, pp. 27–28, 36, argues that the main point of ch. 1 is that the land is God's gift to Israel and thus the latter have a right to it. This had already been established and promised. In ch. 1, the divine commands and promises of vv. 1–11, the dialogue of vv. 12–18 and the verbal links with his selection in Numbers and Deuteronomy (especially ch. 31) establish the leadership of Joshua in his new role. This is the reason for the 'unmilitaristic' aspect of the opening of the book, rather than an emphasis on the land.

war, the provision of mercy for deliverance, and the expectations of Israel.

The structure of this story has evoked much discussion. It may be understood as a narrative interwoven with the two discourse passages referred to above. It begins and ends with Joshua and the spies on the east side of the Jordan. In between, there is a movement of the spies into and out of Jericho, into and out of the hills, and finally across the Jordan and back to Joshua. Although the spies spend *three days* in the hills, this is recorded briefly in two verses. The focus of the chapter lies on their time in Jericho. Besides the two monologues, there is a lengthy section detailing the search for the two spies and Rahab's success at hiding them. Several sentences are also devoted to Rahab's provision for their escape. The repetition of certain key elements in the narrative serves to focus upon them. As will be seen, these events are important for two reasons: (1) they explain what a great personal risk Rahab took in protecting the spies; and (2) along with her confession, her actions justify the offer of salvation to Rahab and her family and friends.

The story of Rahab confirms God's welcome to all people, whatever their condition. Christ died for all the world and the opportunity is available for all to come to him through faith, even the chief of sinners (1 Tim. 1:15). Like Paul, Rahab exhibits faith and understanding of the God who saves her. She becomes part of the family line that leads to the birth of Jesus (Mt. 1:5) and a model of faith for all Christians (Heb. 11:31).

i. Joshua sends two spies (2:1). Joshua initiates the action of this chapter. He *sent* and *addressed* the spies. The verbs of his address are both imperatives, *Go, look.* The reaction of the spies is in keeping with the first command. They *went.* Thus the opening statement enhances the status of Joshua as leader and co-ordinator of the advance plans for the military expedition. Shittim is a region where Israel made camp in Numbers 25:1. It may be located east of the Jordan River opposite Jericho, perhaps at Tell el-Ḥammām.[1] The word for *spies* (Heb. *mᵉraggᵉlîm*) appears on Joseph's lips when he accuses his brothers, 'You are spies! You have come to see where our land

---

[1]See N. Glueck, 'Some Ancient Towns in the Plains of Moab', *BASOR*, 91, 1943, pp. 7–26; J. M. Miller, 'Moab and the Moabites' in *Moab*, p. 27.

is unprotected' (Gn. 42:9). David sends out spies (NIV 'scouts') to ascertain Saul's whereabouts (1 Sa. 26:4). In 2 Samuel 15:10, the word appears with a different connotation. Absalom sends 'secret messengers' throughout Israel to inform his allies when they should proclaim him king. Thus in addition to gaining strategic information about an enemy, *spies* could also describe individuals who conveyed information secretly. In the case of the *spies* of Joshua 2, both functions seem applicable.

On the one hand, Joshua instructs them to *look over* the land and Jericho.[1] While this can be understood in terms of spying out the land, there is no indication from the narrative or from their final report to Joshua that they performed this function. The account of the conquest of Jericho makes no use of any information which might have been gained from this expedition. Further, the parallel account in Numbers 13 – 14 does not use the term *look over* for the twelve spies who spied out the land at that time. The verb *look over* appears in Moses' recollection of this event in Deuteronomy 1:24. It also occurs in the command to spy out places before they are attacked, in Joshua 7:2, and before they are robbed, in Judges 18:2, 14 and 17. On the other hand, the usage of the noun form in 2 Samuel 15:10, where it describes the private passing of information, favours the description of what actually happens in Joshua 2. The *spies* pass along information to Rahab as to how she and her family (and any others) might escape the imminent destruction of Jericho.[2]

The word translated *secretly* (Heb. *ḥereš*) does not appear elsewhere in biblical Hebrew. In Isaiah 3:3, a word spelled in exactly the same way in the MT occurs as a noun, translated as 'craftsman' (NIV, NJPS) or 'magician' (RSV), depending on which of several homonymic roots is preferred. While *secretly* is

---

[1] P. Wilton, 'More Cases of *Waw Explicativum*', *VT*, 44, 1994, p. 126, translates the phrase, 'Go, view the land, *that is*, Jericho'. This use of a waw explicativum explains the limitation of the spies' visit to Jericho.

[2] It is this positive function of the spies, along with the use of spies as an appropriate part of military preparations, that leads me to interpret Joshua's actions as a faithful response to God's commands. The view that Joshua is somehow lacking in faith because he sends out spies (see *e.g.* Polzin, pp. 85–86) has no explicit basis in this text nor is it condemned in the accounts of the spies sent from Kadesh Barnea. In that account, the problem is with the majority report and the people's response to it, not with the action of sending the spies. The same is true in Jos. 7:2. The spies are not condemned nor can it be said that their report leads to the defeat at Ai. That is explicitly ascribed to Achan's sin.

used in occurrences of this word in later Hebrew, the absence of a translation in the LXX and Syriac suggests that the original meaning of the occurrence in Joshua 2:1 may have been lost. Terms such as 'quietly' or 'skilfully' would describe the action and could translate the Hebrew.

The spies respond by going to Jericho (Tell es-Sultan), where they *entered the house of a prostitute.*[1] The text carefully avoids implying a sexual liaison between the spies and their hostess.[2] There is a common expression for going into buildings of all sorts (*cf.* Jdg. 9:5; 2 Sa. 12:20; 2 Ki. 19:1). It does not imply sexual relations with a prostitute. If the intention was to imply sexual relations, there would be no intermediate term, such as *the house of*, used when Samson visited a prostitute and 'went in to spend the night with her' (Jdg. 16:1).[3] Further, the last verb in the verse, *stayed there,* is not used for sexual relations without the occurrence of the preposition 'with' followed by the designation of a partner. Why then do the spies choose the house of a prostitute? This house was more likely a tavern, hostel or way station, which could be used by visitors, than a brothel.[4] There is

---

[1] H. Schulte, 'Beobachtungen zum Begriff der Zônâ im Alten Testament', *ZAW,* 104, 1992, pp. 255-262, argues that the pre-Monarchical usage of the term for 'prostitute', *zônâ,* should be understood as referring to a woman living in a matriarchal society with no male support. While the usage in texts such as Jos. 2 allows for a meaning of the term broader than 'prostitute', the need to argue selectively that texts such as Gn. 34 are secondary additions implies a weakness to this perspective. It is preferable to find a wider semantic range throughout the history of biblical Hebrew which may have been applied in contexts such as this one. D. J. Wiseman, 'Rahab of Jericho', *TynB,* 14, 1964, pp. 8-11, suggests that the meaning of the word here and in other Old Testament contexts may suggest one who conducts friendly dealings with alien persons. He also draws a comparison with the role of the Old Babylonian innkeeper, *sābîtu,* 'one who gives drink', and various laws regarding inns from the earlier law codes.

[2] This is crucial, since elsewhere the experience of Israel with prostitutes is condemned, especially at this time in Transjordan. See Nu. 25:1 and Je. 5:7; Hawk, p. 61. It would have been in the author's interest to state clearly if the spies had indulged in sexual immorality. It would have formed a further illustration of this practice by Israel.

[3] *Contra* P. A. Bird, 'The Harlot as Heroine: Narrative Art and Social Presupposition in Three Old Testament Texts', *Semeia,* 46, 1989, pp. 128-129; Hawk, p. 62. Bird argues that this is suggestive language which Rahab's actions contradict. The example of this verse is not suggestive, for the reasons given. The other example, v. 4, where Rahab confesses to the royal agents that the spies came to her, may suggest sexual language, but if it does it is part of her ruse to defeat the purpose of the agents. See comment on vv. 4-6.

[4] P. A. Bird, 'The Harlot as Heroine', pp. 128-129. See H. Schulte, 'Beobachtungen zum Begriff der Zônâ im Alten Testament', p. 256, who in n.

evidence for such overnight places of accommodation and their use by travelling caravans and royal messengers in Canaan of the fourteenth to twelfth centuries BC.[1] There is no reason to doubt that something like this existed in ancient Jericho. It may be attested later in New Testament times (Lk. 10:30–35). Such a place would naturally draw the vices of the region, as has been the case throughout history. The local 'hostel' would be an appropriate place for the spies to visit if they were going to learn about the area. It would also be the obvious spot for any attempt to discover a fifth column in the region and would provide an opportunity to communicate to interested parties a means of allying with the approaching Israelites. Finally, it would be a place to rest overnight, free from the dangers of the wilderness or those of the town (Gn. 19). In fact, the actions of the spies in verse 1 appear as a summary of what follows. Their lodging at Rahab's house may have been what they intended rather than what actually happened.[2] In that case, the translation of the NIV, *and stayed there,* may be accurate. The name of Rahab was known in Canaan during the centuries before Israel appeared in the land.[3]

ii. The house of Rahab (2:2–8). This was a public place that allowed agents of the local ruler to learn who the two men were and what their mission was. Their report to the ruler included the charge that the men had come *to spy out* (Heb. *lahpōr*) the land. This verb is normally used to describe the digging of wells. Its one other occurrence with the sense of spying is in Deuteronomy 1:22, which relates the earlier sending of scouts

---

9 cites other scholars who have held this view, beginning with Josephus (*Ant.* I, 2, 7) and the Targum.

[1] For texts and discussion, see C. Kühne, *Die Chronologie der internationalen Korrespondenz von El-Amarna*, AOAT 17 (Neukirchen-Vluyn: Neukirchener, 1973), pp. 108–110, n. 532; S. A. Meier, *The Messenger in the Ancient Semitic World*, HSM 45 (Atlanta: Scholars Press, 1988), pp. 93–96. On the historical background to Jos. 2, see the discussion in the Introduction (pp. 26–27).

[2] Commentators have noted the passive role of the spies throughout this narrative, in contrast to Rahab. Hawk, p. 64, sees that role beginning here with the spies 'lying down'.

[3] Taanach text no. 4, line 9. See A. Gustavs, 'Die Personennamen in den Tontafeln von Tell Ta'annek', *ZDPV*, 51, 1928, p. 189; D. Sivan, *Grammatical Analysis and Glossary of the Northwest Semitic Vocables in Akkadian Texts of the 15th–13th C.B.C. from Canaan and Syria*, AOAT 214 (Neukirchen-Vluyn: Neukirchener, 1984), p. 264.

to search out the land of Canaan. Repetition in this text emphasizes the key points of the narrative.

2–3. The first repetition is the message that the spies had come *to spy out the land.* This is relayed to the king, and his servants are told to repeat it to Rahab.[1] The text thus leads the reader to understand that the mission of the spies was known to the enemy at the highest levels. It was treason against Jericho and its king to aid these men. Rahab's helpful deeds indicate her renunciation of allegiance to the Canaanites of Jericho and her acceptance of the rulership of Joshua and his agents.

4–6. The second repetition is the reference to Rahab's hiding of the spies. This act demonstrates her loyalty to Israel as no other deed does. Its repetition in verses 4 and 6 is not an example of poor writing or editing.[2] It elucidates the story's plot. The tension rises as the agents of Jericho's king get closer and closer. At first, they are sent with a message to Rahab to give up the men. Then they are at the house listening to Rahab's attempt to divert them. After each of these junctures, the narrator pauses to inform the reader of what is happening with the spies. To begin with, Rahab hid them. But then the agents of the king come to speak with Rahab and the question occurs: will her hiding be effective? After Rahab's diversion, the text relates where and how she had hidden the spies. Will the royal agents believe her or will they search her house and find the spies? The critical point is the beginning of verse 7. The Hebrew narrative can be translated 'As for the men, they

[1] In v. 3, the purpose of the spies is *to spy out the whole land.* The addition of *kol,* 'whole', is not attested in the versions (LXX and Syriac), but is probably original, as there is no other explanation for its appearance only here. In fact, it serves to emphasize the danger of the spies to the security of the region. One can assume that the land the spies are assigned to *spy out* is that which they do examine. It need not be understood as the whole of Canaan, *contra* Mitchell, p. 38, who attempts to apply the broader sense here, in the activities of the spies in Jos. 7:2, and in Caleb's earlier adventures referred to in 14:7. Only the 14:7 reference should be understood as the whole of Canaan, and that is on the basis of the actual description of the land in Nu. 13:17–25.

[2] See Fritz, pp. 33–41, who regards these and other doublets in the chapter as unnecessary repetitions and additions. Proposed solutions for the two acts of lying down in vv. 1 and 8 are summarized by W. Moran, 'The Repose of Rahab's Israelite Guests', *Studi sull'Oriente e la Bibbia. Offerti al p. Giovanni Rinaldi nel 60j compleanno da allievi, colleghi, amici* (Genova Studio e vita, 1967), p. 275. With Moran, it is likely that v. 1 is anticipatory of v. 8. The former provides a summary of the elaboration of the latter.

pursued them'.[1] At this point it is not certain if this means a search of Rahab's house. Only with the fifth and sixth words of the Hebrew verse does the reader learn that the royal agents had departed and launched their search in the direction where it might be expected that the spies would go, *i.e.* back across the Jordan River.

A third repetition in this narrative is Rahab's assertion of ignorance, *I did not/don't know*. This is stated with regard to both the origin and the destination of the spies. It reinforces her commitment to Israel and its agents, a commitment for which she will risk her own life by attempting to deceive the representatives of the king of Jericho. The moral issue of whether or not Rahab was justified in lying has often been raised. Some may argue that it was no lie, but this is difficult to maintain in the light of statements in the text that are the opposite of what Rahab knew to be true. Perhaps it is felt that, if ever there was justification for lying, this was it. The entire mission of Joshua and Israel depended on the success of the initial expedition. The inhabitants of Jericho stood under God's judgment. Besides, the Bible never condemns Rahab, but admires her faith (Heb. 11:31). Nor does the Bible excuse lies because the person lied to is morally reprehensible. It cannot be said that the narrator condones the actions of Rahab at this point. Some may argue that Rahab, a Canaanite and a prostitute, would not be expected to have higher standards than she displays here, but there is no indication of this view in the text.

It is best not to excuse Rahab's actions, but neither to be troubled by them. In so far as they were wrong, the narrator and Israelite readers would understand that her acceptance among the people of Israel would also provide the means for forgiveness of such sin. The ethical issue is not the concern of the narrative. It stresses the deception, not in order to condemn Rahab but to magnify her personal risk in hiding the spies.[2] After all, she could have said nothing and allowed

---

[1] This is not clear in the NIV, which overlooks the narrative tension, dissolving it with an initial *So . . .* The reader is immediately reassured that the men have followed the false advice of Rahab.

[2] This emphasis is better than Prouser's view that 'deception is considered an acceptable and generally praiseworthy means for a weaker party to succeed against a stronger power.' See O. H. Prouser, 'The Truth about Women and Lying', *JSOT*, 61, 1994, pp. 15–28. All of Prouser's examples of deception stress

the agents to search her house. By pointing in another direction, she risked being caught, but in the end she delivered her new-found friends.

7. Another repetition occurs in the statement that *the gate was shut.* Rahab argues that the spies left before the gate was closed. The royal agents go out in search of the spies and the gates are shut behind them. This detail further emphasizes the vulnerability of the spies and their dependence upon Rahab for protection. There was no way out of the town for them. At any moment, Rahab could raise the alarm and have them arrested. Further, their escape from Jericho was now more urgent, for the agents could return at any time if they became satisfied that the spies had not left Jericho and concluded that they had been deceived. But the means of escape for the spies was no longer obvious to them: *the gate was shut.* This provides the background for Rahab's provision of another escape route, demonstrating how important her role was for the spies' deliverance.[1]

8. A final point, which is not repeated until verse 8, is the hiding place on the *roof* of Rahab's house. It is likely that this was the floor of the upper storey of her house. Verse 15 suggests that she lived in a house adjacent to the wall, perhaps built into one of the casemate walls that were common Israelite fortifications.[2] An upper storey such as this would have served as the sleeping quarters for occupants of the house. It was here that Rahab hid the spies. It was here that she related the fear of the citizens of Jericho and asked for her life and the lives of her family. This *roof* must have been the most private and secret part of the house, away from any unwanted listeners. Such a

---

personal risk and thus laud the courage of the person involved. They do not condone the deceit.

[1] W. Moran, 'The Repose of Rahab's Israelite Guests', p. 282, identifies a concentric structure in vv. 7–9 in which the closing of the gates lies at the centre and forms the conclusion of the preceding narrative section and the beginning of a new one.

[2] See L. E. Stager, 'The Archaeology of the Family in Ancient Israel', *BASOR*, 260, 1985, p. 16. Archaeologically, it is true that casemate walls are distinctive to the later Israelite period rather than the earlier Canaanite period of the second millennium BC. See Fritz, p. 37. However, this type of fortification has earlier examples in other Late Bronze Age Palestinian sites that were protected by 'a belt of houses' instead of a city wall. See Z. Herzog, 'Cities in the Levant', *ABD*, I, p. 1037, who mentions Megiddo, Lachish, Tel Batash, Tell Beit Mirsim, and most importantly Jericho.

detail emphasizes the way in which Rahab opened up everything that was hers to the spies. Just as she shared with them her heart's most secret belief and desire, so she led them into the most secret part of her house.

iii. The confession and request of Rahab (2:9–13). This represents one of the longest uninterrupted statements by a woman in a biblical narrative. The initial confession *I know* contrasts with the *I don't know* that introduced her statements to the agents of the king of Jericho.[1] It suggests that a true confession would replace the former deceit. This is followed by three subordinate clauses in verse 9, each beginning with the same Hebrew particle, *that* (Heb. *kî*). The first clause summarizes the basic theological message of the book: God has given the land to Israel. The verb 'to give' appeared in 1:2, 3, 6, 11, 13, 14 and 15 (twice) with reference to the land, whether east or west of the Jordan. The second and third clauses which begin with *that* describe the reaction of the Canaanites. The *great fear* was prophesied in the Song of the Sea (Ex. 15:16) as coming upon all the inhabitants of Canaan (the same verb and preposition are used, 'to fall on').[2] It appears as a divine promise at the end of the Covenant Code, where God is portrayed as sending forth 'fear of myself' (Ex. 23:27). In Rahab's confession, it is *a great fear of you, i.e.* of the Israelites, which has stirred the inhabitants of Canaan. *Melting in fear* occurs in the Pentateuch in the Song of the Sea (Ex. 15:15). The phrase is virtually identical, with 'Canaan' replacing *this country*. Thus Rahab confesses that what was foretold by the celebrants of the exodus has come to pass.

10–11. This identical phrasing is explained in verse 10. The 'we' in *we have heard* may include all the inhabitants of Canaan, but it certainly presupposes the citizens of Jericho. They have received accounts of the great deeds of the LORD on behalf of his people. These accounts represent the source of the knowledge of God by which Rahab was able to make her confession in verse 9. The two events that are described represent the

---

[1] See also W. Moran, 'The Repose of Rahab's Israelite Guests', p. 283.

[2] It may be that the expression for *all who live* should be understood as 'rulers' both here and in Ex. 15. The emphasis would then fall upon the rulers and their inability to respond. This corresponds to 5:1 and 10:1–2, where it is the rulers who are alarmed at the military successes of Israel. See M. Görg, '*yāšaḇ*', *TDOT*, 6, pp. 430–431; Gottwald, pp. 512–534; Boling and Wright, p. 146.

major acts that marked the beginning and the end of Israel's trek through the desert. The verb that describes how the LORD *dried up* the waters of the Red Sea appears here for the first time in the Bible. Its occurrence in 5:23 will link the crossing of the Jordan with the crossing of the Red Sea.

The verb 'to devote to the ban' (Heb. *ḥrm*) occurs in the reference to how Israel *completely destroyed* Sihon and Og.[1] This verb is not used in the account of the defeat of Sihon and Og in Numbers 21:21–35, although the conduct in war is similar to the ban.[2] However, it is used emphatically in the recounting of both wars in Deuteronomy 2:34 and 3:6. It appears elsewhere in the Pentateuch only to confirm that this is how the inhabitants of the land of Canaan are to be treated (Dt. 7:2; 20:17).

These historical reports of God's acts form the centre of the confession of Rahab. Although the two events recounted frame the whole sojourn in the wilderness, they do more. The account of the exodus has as its subjects the LORD who dries up the waters and Israel who comes forth from Egypt. Rahab believes that God has acted powerfully on behalf of his people to deliver them from the mighty nation of Egypt through miraculous deeds. The account of the destruction of Sihon and Og has as its subject Israel, who did something to these kings; specifically it 'destroyed/devoted' them. Here Rahab recounts the tragic fate of those who oppose Israel's plans under God's directions. Rahab has learned her history well and responds with a reaffirmation of the fear of those who oppose Israel and with the confession that only Israel's God controls the destiny of the world.

These sentiments were expressed in verse 9. They recur in reverse order in verse 11 and thus form a frame to the central historical confession of verse 10. The first word of verse 11 should be translated 'And so we heard', corresponding to the same verb which begins verse 10. It indicates that what was heard, in the sense of the news reports which came to Rahab and her fellow citizens, has now been reported to the spies. It does not introduce verse 11 but closes the report of verse 10.

[1] See the discussion on the ban in the Introduction: 'Theology (a) Holy war and the ban' (pp. 42–46).
[2] It does appear in the account of Israel's defeat of armies from towns in the Negev, a few verses earlier (21:1–3). While it is used there to explain the name of a town in that region, Hormah, does the concept extend through the chapter to include the kings of the Amorites?

The concentric or chiastic construction thus appears:

vv. 9b–10a

A. *the LORD has given this land to you*

  B. *a great fear of you has fallen on us*

    B. *all who live in this country are melting in fear because of you*

      C. *We have heard . . .*

v. 11

      C'. . . . *and so we have heard*

    B'. *our hearts melted* (NIV mg.)

  B'. *everyone's courage failed because of you*

A'. *the LORD your God is God in heaven above and on the earth below*

The contrast in the two halves is enhanced by the verb in B, 'fear of you has *fallen*' (Heb. *nāp̄ᵉlâ*), and that in B', 'courage has not *risen* again' (Heb. *qāmâ*). The confession of A, that the LORD God has control of the land of Canaan and has given it to his people, is extended to A' to describe God's dominion over the universe.[1] Yet the cosmological confession of verse 11 is also a personal one in which God is described as *your God*. This aspect prepares Rahab's discourse for the plea which follows. Since the God of the spies is the victor – past and future – then Rahab wants to make her faith a reality by extracting a promise of protection from 'the winning side'.

12–13. *Now then* prepares for a command as in 1:2. An occurrence of this interjection followed by a command to 'swear, take an oath' is found in 1 Samuel 24:21. There Saul has recounted to David his understanding of God's will for David to be king. He follows this with a request to David that he swear to Saul that he will spare the life of Saul's family. In a similar manner, Rahab has recounted to the spies her understanding of God's plan for Israel. She now requests that they give her their oath that they will spare her and her family. Of course, in Rahab's case she is able to add weight to the request by observing how she has treated the spies in sparing their lives. This is the opposite of Saul's situation, where David spares Saul's life despite Saul's attempt to kill him.

Rahab's statement that she has *shown kindness* is an expression composed of the verb 'to do, make' and the noun whose

---

[1]A similar phrase occurs in Dt. 4:39. See K. A. Deurloo, 'Spiel und Verweis auf *Torah*-Worte in Jos. 2–6; 9', *Dielheimer Blätter zum Alten Testament und seiner Rezeption in der Alten Kirche*, 26, 1989/1990, pp. 70–80.

rich meaning has been translated as 'covenantal loyalty' or 'commitment' (Heb. *ḥeseḏ*). This formulation appears when Abraham's servant asks for God's help in finding a wife for Isaac, that God may 'show kindness' to Abraham (Gn. 24:12). It also occurs in the self-identification formula of God as one who 'shows kindness' to thousands of generations of those who keep his covenant (Ex. 20:6; Dt. 5:10; Je. 32:18). Its closest parallel is found in Jdg. 1:22–26 where, like Rahab, the citizen of Bethel helps the Israelites and is allowed by them to escape the city's destruction. He and his family are shown kindness. Thus the showing of kindness means aid in keeping alive one's family for future generations. Rahab claims she has done this for the spies, no doubt by saving their lives. She asks the spies in return to 'show kindness' to her father's household. In accordance with the usage of this expression, this implies protection for her family and deliverance from death.[1] This is the very point that Rahab goes on to elaborate.

The term for *family* is literally 'house of the father'. This appears in the Bible as a description of an extended family governed by the eldest male. Members of a family often lived together in a cluster of dwellings, such as may be identified in the archaeological remains of small villages in the Palestinian hill country dating from the period of earliest Israel.[2] Rahab requests *a sure sign* (Heb. *'ôṯ 'ᵉmeṯ*) that this deliverance will be accomplished. The sign is the oath that she wants the spies to swear for the protection of her family. It is important to see the solidarity of the family, a concept that in this case ensures blessing and salvation for many in addition to the believer. As an oath of fealty,[3] this covenant would bring Rahab's family into Israelite society. As would happen with the Gibeonites, so

---

[1] G. R. Clark, *The Word* Hesed *in the Hebrew Bible*, JSOT Supplement 157 (Sheffield: JSOT Press, 1993), pp. 73–5, suggests that Rahab does not fully appreciate the depth of commitment and relationship this 'uniquely Hebrew' term implies and that she believes that it is simply a matter of 'one good turn deserves another'. However, her statements conform with the use of the term in the Pentateuch and Judges. The men do not rebuke her but only specify further the conditions that guarantee the act of salvation. Clark, p. 262, is correct to say that the men act as God's representatives and that it is ultimately God who delivers Rahab and her family.

[2] See L. E. Stager, 'The Archaeology of the Family in Ancient Israel', pp. 18–23.

[3] For this term applied here, see F. M. Cross, 'A Response to Zakovitch's "Successful Failure of Israelite Intelligence"' in S. Niditch (ed.), *Text and*

Rahab and her family here ceased to be Canaanite and became part of Israel's family. Rahab is acting as spokeswoman and agent for the family.[1] A female, rather than a male, leads this extended family and her faith delivers it.

For the Christian, Rahab represents the example of one who confesses God's historic acts of redemption and receives salvation. The confession of faith becomes the means to salvation (Rom. 10:9, 1 Jn. 4:15).

iv. The spies assure Rahab (2:14–21). In this passage, the spies speak for the first time in the text. Of course, the narrative assumes they have spoken before this but it does not record their words. In fact, a study of the first half of this chapter indicates that the spies have largely reacted rather than acted.[2] Their entrance into Jericho is a response to the initiative of Joshua. Once in Rahab's house, they are led around by her without taking any independent action.

14. It is only after her speech, which demands a response, that they speak. But even at this point, their words are a reaction. They affirm the request of Rahab and use language similar to her own. Their primary concern is to preserve secrecy, but what secrecy? The leader of Jericho already knows who they are and why they have come. It would be of no value to Rahab to reveal further details once the men had left the town. If she did, it would only threaten her own safety, as she would then be implicated in lying to the royal agents and in abetting the spies. Unless one assumes that the narrator inserted a contradiction or sought to make the spies look ridiculous, the answer must lie in the present circumstances of the spies. The secrecy they desire is for Rahab to enable them to escape before anyone learns that they are still in Jericho, and

Tradition. The Hebrew Bible and Folklore (Atlanta: Scholars Press, 1990), p. 103. For an attempt to see vv. 9–21 in the form of an Ancient Near Eastern treaty covenant, see K. M. Campbell, 'Rahab's Covenant', *VT*, 22, 1972, pp. 243–244. This is developed by M. Ottosson, for whom Rahab is a 'proselyte'. See M. Ottosson, 'Rahab and the Spies' in H. Behrens, D. Loding, and M. T. Roth (eds.), *DUMU-E₂-DUB-BA-A: Studies in Honor of Åke W. Sjöberg* (Occasional Publications of the Samuel Noah Kramer Fund 11 (Philadelphia: University Museum, 1989), pp. 419–427.

[1]D. J. Wiseman, 'Rahab of Jericho', *TynB*, 14, 1964, p. 8, observes: 'She was also a recognized member of her family group, a status not normally granted to a prostitute'.

[2]Hawk, p. 64.

for her to guarantee that escape by maintaining secrecy about it until they are across the Jordan and safe.

The reference to *tell what we are doing* appears twice in the account, in verses 14 and 20. As noted above, these duplicates are part of the narrative's way of emphasizing key aspects of the story. In this case, the expression demonstrates the vulnerability of the spies and their dependence upon the faithfulness of Rahab. Without her aid, the spies would not have been able to leave Jericho and eventually to return safely to Joshua.

15–16. The arrangement of the narrative in verses 15–21 has been a matter of much discussion, as have the questions surrounding the order of events in verses 3–8. Rahab first lets the spies escape out of her window and then converses with them regarding their oath. However, this seems unreasonable. Why would she not discuss the oath before letting them out of the window? Why would they wait until they were in a vulnerable position, on the wall of Jericho or at its base? Is one to imagine that the spies shouted up to Rahab from the ground, and thereby revealed their position to the inhabitants of Jericho? Or is it that they swore their oath while dangling by the rope that Rahab held? The narrator wished to stress certain features. In order to do so, it was not necessary to follow a linear sequence of events or to mention an event or a statement only once. There could be summaries of events before they were described in greater detail and there could be repetition of important matters. The NIV attempts to convey the sense by introducing Rahab's conversation in verse 16 with a pluperfect tense, *she had said to them.* Thus the conversation took place before they exited through the window.

In verse 14 the spies had found themselves called upon to answer Rahab. Without their affirmation at that point her continued aid would not have made sense. On the other hand, their full swearing of loyalty and help to Rahab can come only when they learn how to escape Jericho and how to avoid the royal agents who are looking for them near the Jordan. Thus Rahab, assured that they are ready to swear support for her family, overcomes the two barriers that are in the way of the spies' safety: the shut gate and the agents guarding the River. She overcomes the first obstacle by allowing the spies to escape through a window in her house which is attached to the wall of the city (see p. 87). She overcomes the second problem by advising the spies to hide in the hills for several days until the threat of discovery has passed.

17. It is at this point that the spies swear their oath of loyalty to Rahab, in verses 17–20. Since Rahab has already made the stipulations, it remains for the spies only to detail the qualifications. These had already been summarized in verse 14. In verses 15–16, the aid that Rahab provides was explained. It is then possible for the spies to list the qualifications, since they have now received all the help that Rahab is able to give. The nature of this statement as a qualification appears in the first two words that the spies utter in the Hebrew text, 'Innocent are we'.

18–20. Rahab must follow a threefold procedure to enable the spies to guarantee her protection.[1] The scarlet cord tied in the window may have been something that was already present, perhaps a means of advertising the purpose of her 'house'.[2] If so, then Rahab's tying of the cord in verse 21 was something that would not arouse attention among the returning agents and other citizens who might have had occasion to move about outside Jericho.[3] The second requirement is that she should gather everyone whom she wants to protect into her house, together with their property. The spies go to some lengths to declare their innocence if any of her family is discovered outside her house and killed. Finally, she must not report any information which could compromise the safety of the spies. This is a repetition of the statement in verse 14. However, in this case the detail of their hiding in the hill country for a few days is also part of what must remain secret.

21. Rahab agrees to these conditions. She has no further

---

[1] The verbs in vv. 17, 18 and 20, *you made us swear* and *you let us down*, have forms that are not expected in the light of their subject, Rahab. Rather than a textual error, it may be preferable to see here a stylistic device that occurs elsewhere in biblical Hebrew when the same verbs are repeated in a narrative and the speaker has changed. These verbs appeared in vv. 12 and 15, where the speakers were Rahab and the narrator. In vv. 17, 18 and 20, the speakers are the spies. Under such conditions the gender of a word may vary from its expected form in order to heighten the drama, a situation that pertains with the scouts as they are negotiating for their lives. For a collection of the evidence from biblical Hebrew, see R. J. Ratner, 'Morphological Variation in Biblical Hebrew Rhetoric', *Maarav*, 8, 1992, pp. 143–159.

[2] See P. Bird, 'The Harlot as Heroine', p. 130. Hawk, p. 70, suggests that the term 'scarlet cord' is a pun for the similar sounding Hebrew, 'hope for the two (spies)'.

[3] Since the spies had no trouble getting into Jericho, the town was not yet sealed as in 6:1.

need to detain the men and so sends them away. It is not the concern of the narrative where the spies were when the final agreement was reached, whether still in Rahab's house, or on the ground outside the walls, or in mid-air, rappelling down the side of the wall. In theory, any of these conditions is possible because the narrative does not specify the location of the spies. However, concerns of confidentiality and clear thought would be best preserved if the spies were still in Rahab's house. In such a case, the activities described in verses 15 and 21b are not separate or sequential. They are one and the same. Verse 15 introduces what is going to happen with the detail necessary to explain the reference to *the window through which you let us down* in verse 18. Verse 21 records that it happened. By tying the cord in the window, Rahab fulfilled the first of the conditions.

v. The spies return (2:22–24). The sequence of three verbs in the first four words of verse 22 reflects the hasty movement of the spies into the hill country, just as Rahab had advised. The *three days* during which they remain in the hill country resembles the 'three days' of 1:11 and 3:2. The same time period may be described in all three notices. The spies are west of the Jordan when the preparations are being made.[1] The description of the activities of the royal agents who were pursuing them is inserted to suggest the wisdom of Rahab's advice: had the spies attempted to cross the river, they would have been caught. Rahab continued to protect the spies. The agents returned, probably surmising that the fugitives had escaped across the Jordan before they reached it. Once the agents *returned* to Jericho, the spies 'returned' to Joshua. Their route down from the hill country and across the river was now a safe one. Upon reaching Joshua, the spies knew that Rahab had kept the second part of her agreement. The remaining part, that she and her family stay in her house, could not be fulfilled until the actual capture of the town. Their report to Joshua is almost a perfect quotation of Rahab's first and third statements in verse 9. The last half of their report is an exact quotation. It evokes three important points: (1) the fulfilment of the

---

[1] J. A. Wilcoxen, 'Narrative Structure and Cult Legend' in J. C. Rylaarsdam (ed.), *Transitions in Biblical Scholarship* (Chicago: University of Chicago Press, 1968), pp. 61–62. However, Woudstra, p. 79, suggests that the two periods of 'three days' are distinct.

prophecy made after the crossing of the Red Sea (Ex. 15:15), implying that the same powerful God at work there is about to take Israel to victory in their crossing of the Jordan River; (2) the contrast with the majority report of the twelve who explored Canaan from Kadesh Barnea (Nu. 12:26–33), a report that depended upon the personal impressions of the explorers rather than the confession of a native such as Rahab; and (3) the complete reliance of the spies upon Rahab, for their lives as well as their report.

With respect to this last point, it is not clear that the only purpose of the spies was to see whether or not the land could be conquered. They did not do this. Instead, they conveyed the hope of deliverance to any who would receive them. Strategically, such a move would serve to build up confidence among Israel's secret allies and therefore to erode the enemy's ability to present a united front. Politically, the account of Rahab would encourage Joshua and the rest of Israel to feel that news regarding the success of Israel's history since the exodus from Egypt had reduced the morale of the enemy. Like Rahab, others could presumably have escaped the threatened destruction. They needed only to believe and to confess the power of Israel's God. But to do so would mean ceasing to belong to their own people with their own gods. Such a transfer of allegiance might have created many difficulties. We learn only of Rahab as one who had the faith to do so, but there is no reason to doubt that others could and did join Israel under similar circumstances.[1]

In the story of Rahab (ch. 2), Joshua plays no role. It could easily have been omitted, along with its later reference in 6:22–25, and the main plot of the book would not have been affected. However, the story moves the focus from Joshua to Rahab. If Joshua represents the Israelite male who finds guidance and success through faith in the LORD God, does Rahab represent his counterpart, the Canaanite female who also finds guidance and success through faith in the LORD God?[2] In one of the most nationalistic books in the Hebrew Bible, does it not serve the

---

[1] See the interpretation found in early Rabbinic literature. According to *Leviticus Rabbah* 17:6, Joshua offered the Canaanites the possibility of flight or peace, as well as war.

[2] For the story of Rahab as part of a biblical genre in which a foreigner relates a *credo* acknowledging how Israel's God alone is the true God, see F. M. Cross, 'A Response to Zakovitch's "Successful Failure of Israelite Intelligence" ', p. 100.

purposes of the promise to Abraham that 'all peoples on earth will be blessed through you' (Gn. 12:3) to place side by side with the choice of a military leader and his initial preparations for battle, the story of a foreign woman who believed and was saved without arms or bloodshed?'[1]

For the Christian, Rahab's faith provides a model of one who believes in God's historic acts of redemption (whether the exodus of the Old Testament or the cross of the New Testament). Not only does she believe, but she confirms her faith and then acts upon it to preserve God's people and to advance God's kingdom (*cf.* Jas. 2:25–26).[2]

c. Rites of passage across the Jordan River (3:1 – 4:24)

These two chapters describe Israel's preparations for crossing the Jordan and the completion of the task. They describe the words and events that accompanied the crossing as well as the means by which the memory of it was preserved. Traditionally, scholars have found a collection of editorial layers in the apparent repetitions and complex structure of Joshua 3 – 4.[3] The presence of a distinctive grammar has also been noted, a fact that has led others to support a stylistic unity to the account.[4] Using the method of discourse linguistics, N.

[1] This is the theme and emphasis of Jos. 2. The question whether or not Israel sinned in accepting Rahab is subsidiary and cannot be answered without viewing it in the perspective of the text's positive evaluation of Rahab's faith. Unlike the events surrounding Achan and the Gibeonites, the story of Rahab does not lead to judgment, military loss or any lack of unity on the part of those who confess and follow Israel's God. Therefore, questions such as 'Why should Israel need Rahab when they have God?' miss the primary point of the passage. Jos. 2 is not an exegesis of Dt. 20, because the issue of the ban is not applicable here. That is why it is not mentioned. Rahab's confession moves her and her family from the status of Canaanite *enemy* to Israelite *friend.* The ban is not applied to the latter.

[2] A. F. Campbell, 'Old Testament Narrative as Theology', *Pacifica,* 4, 1991, pp. 165–180.

[3] The alternative view finds several hands at work in the writing of these chapters. This includes hypotheses of two deuteronomists and of as many as five redactors. For the former view, see Soggin, pp. 52–53 and Butler, pp. 41–44. For the latter view, in which the fifth redactor may be a composite of several additional hands, see Fritz, pp. 41–56. The most detailed analysis of this sort is that of F. Langlamet, *Gilgal et les récits de la traversée du Jourdain (Jos. III – IV),* Cahiers RB 11 (Paris: J. Gabalda, 1969).

[4] Boling and Wright, p. 171, suggest that Jos. 3 – 4 may reflect language different from exilic and post-exilic materials, implying pre-exilic archival

Winther-Nielsen has identified a coherency and structure according to boundary markers between the major episodes.[1]

Stylistic features include the development of instructions in ever greater detail as they are repeated, and the presentation of simultaneous actions in a sequential form. It is important to remember that this text is part of a ceremonial action on the part of Israel. Therefore, conventions for the description of ritual acts should be noted. For example, in Exodus 26 – 40 the construction and erection of the tabernacle occurs. In that passage, divine instructions are given first. This is followed by an often word-for-word repetition of those instructions in the form of a narrative, conveying the sense that God's directions were carried out exactly as planned. There is a similar form in these accounts. The actions of all three groups in Joshua 4 – 5 are repeated.

The repetitions and the miracle at the centre of the story emphasize the significance of the event of crossing the Jordan and entering into the new land. The events that follow the crossing also serve to focus on its importance. Israel enters into the land that God has promised and begins to lay claim to it. This entrance is a crossing of the boundary that separates the 'holy' land from the territory that lies outside the divine allocation. As such it represents a crucial transition.[2] It symbolizes the importance of all boundaries in the book, as found in the allocations of chapters 13 – 21 and as seen in the dispute of chapter 22. The ordering of the people in their land becomes part of their fulfilment of the divine covenant.

These events in Israel's history describe a time of preparation for this new generation who would be called upon to occupy the land. Although Christians are not called to carry out the same physical acts, preparation is necessary for any life of ministry and service. As with Israel's preparation, it involves

---

sources for the description of this event. However, to assign a date to this style seems speculative. More convincing is the assertion of B. Peckham, 'The Composition of Joshua 3 – 4', *CBQ*, 46, 1984, p. 423, that the disjunctive and resumptive style argues for 'the consistency and coherence of the account'.

[1] N. Winther-Nielsen, 'The Miraculous Grammar of Joshua 3 – 4', in R. D. Bergen (ed.), *Biblical Hebrew and Discourse Linguistics* (Dallas: Summer Institute of Linguistics; Winona Lake: Eisenbrauns, 1994), pp. 300–319; *idem, A Functional Discourse Grammar of Joshua. A Computer-Assisted Rhetorical Structure Analysis*, CBOTS 40 (Stockholm: Almqvist & Wiksell, 1995), pp. 169–190.

[2] See L. L. Thompson, 'The Jordan Crossing: *Șidqot* Yahweh and World Building', *JBL*, 100, 1981, pp. 355–358; Mitchell, pp. 41–42.

hearing and believing God's Word and the discipline of obedience to that word. As with the spies, confidence in God's calling and direction in life can provide the spiritual strength to face great obstacles (Mt. 17:20; Lk. 17:6).

i. Joshua and all the Israelites set out (3:1). Since their defeat of Sihon and Og, Israel had been encamped at Shittim (Nu. 22:1).[1] This had provided a strategic place of settlement. Once they had received the detailed prescriptions for crossing the Jordan, the Israelites needed to move as close as possible to the river so that no time would be wasted on the day of the crossing. Again, the key verb 'to cross' (Heb. '*br*) appears. It will recur throughout this account.

ii. Instructions for crossing, part 1 (3:2–5). With all but the final preparations out of the way, the narrative returns to the officers of the people, last mentioned in Joshua 1:10–11. In chapter 1, the first set of instructions that the people were to receive from the officers came from the lips of Joshua. In 3:2–4, the officers acted and spoke in accordance with what he had said. After the move from Shittim, the officers passed through the camp a second time, in order to prepare the people for the crossing.[2] As Joshua *ordered the officers* in 1:10, so the officers *went throughout the camp, giving orders to the people.*

3–4. The order of march was detailed before Israel departed from Sinai in Numbers 1 – 2 and 10. Numbers 10:33 explained the movement of the ark in front of the people to guide them to a place of rest.[3] This was probably known to the Israelites who prepared to cross the Jordan. Its repetition here may have been formulaic, perhaps part of the greater ceremony of crossing the river. The additional detail, that of allowing *about a thousand yards* between Israel and the ark, is not clear as to its origin. If the miracle of stopping the waters of the river was

---

[1] J. R. Porter, 'The Background of Joshua III – V', *Svensk Exegetisk Årsbok*, 36, 1971, 12, notes that the procession of Joshua 3 – 5 begins and ends at a pre-Israelite cult centre.

[2] On the *three days*, see also Jos. 1:11 and comment on 2:22 (p. 95.).

[3] This is the first mention of the ark of the covenant in Joshua. Its association with God's presence and with God's law is known from the period of the wilderness wanderings (Ex. 25:22; 30:6; Dt. 10:1–5; 31:26). The various titles given to the ark in Jos. 3 – 4 reflect the variety that are found throughout the Bible: ark of the covenant, ark of the testimony, ark of Yahweh. See Butler, p. 45.

understood as a special manifestation of the presence of Israel's God, it may be likened to the divine presence on Mount Sinai, from which people and animals were expected to keep their distance. But no specific distance is noted there (Ex. 19:10–25).[1]

5. Joshua addresses all the people for the first time. He commands them to *Consecrate yourselves*, to prepare for the next day. This instruction again evokes the image of Israel at Mount Sinai, where God commanded Moses to consecrate Israel. This involved washing their clothes and abstaining from sexual relations (Ex. 19:10–15). If these acts were repeated by the Israel of Joshua's generation, it would help to explain the reason for waiting until the people had come alongside the Jordan. They could wash their clothes in its waters, although its reputation as a muddy river, especially at flood stage, might have rendered this gesture little more than a symbolic act. The *amazing things* (Heb. *niplā'ôt*) that are promised appear in Exodus 3:20, with reference to the plagues against Egypt. They occur again in Exodus 34:10, where they seem to describe general acts done on behalf of the Israelites. However, in the following verse, they are related to driving out the inhabitants of Canaan. Thus *amazing things* are events designed to demonstrate the power of Israel's God over other peoples and on behalf of his own people. Compare Rahab's confession regarding God's acts (Jos. 2:9–11).

iii. Instructions for crossing, part 2 (3:6–13). Joshua addresses the priests for the first time. His instructions initiate the movement of the ark of the covenant which will become the means by which God enables Israel to cross the Jordan and to acquire the land which he has for them. The verb *pass on* (Heb. *'br*) again occurs, but it has to do with the passage of the priests before the people rather than with crossing the river. This positions the ark and the people so that all is ready for the actual crossing. Until this moment, the means by which that is to take place remains unclear.

Joshua has completed the preparations for entrance into the land. He has acted in accordance with his position as leader of

[1]The text specifies a distance of two thousand cubits. This distance appears in the Pentateuch in connection with the distance around each Levitical 'city' that is designated as pasture-land for the town (Nu. 35:5).

the people and successor to Moses. However, the people's continued acceptance of that leadership depends upon God's revelation to Joshua concerning his next steps.

7–8. God speaks to Joshua for the first time since his instructions in 1:1–9. In both cases the structure is similar: promises of God's presence and support followed by instructions. The basic promise of his presence with Joshua is repeated in verse 7.[1] Specific directions for Joshua's next move are given in the following sentence. The divine word that God *will begin to exalt* Joshua in the eyes of Israel introduces the crossing narrative itself. It explains that for Joshua the purpose of the miracle about to be performed is to confirm once more his position of leadership. The same form of *exalt* (Heb. *gdl*) is used in Genesis 12:2 where God promises to exalt the name of Abram. The specific instructions that follow concern only the role of the priests. Although all the people will participate in the miracle, the priests themselves will initiate it when they move the ark into the midst of the Jordan.

9–10. In verse 5, Joshua had alluded only to *amazing things* in general that would take place. As has been observed, God promises 'wonders' as a means of demonstrating his power over nations of the world and in order to preserve his own people. The structure of the instructions to Joshua also corresponds to that of Joshua's instructions to the people: specific directions follow promises of divine presence and support. The opening of Joshua's address has three parts: a call to listen to words of divine authority, a promise of God's presence, and a promise that God will dispossess the inhabitants of Canaan. The first part is a divine means of informing Israel that what is about to be said is important and therefore worthy of attention. The second part corresponds to God's promise of his presence with Joshua but the structure is slightly different from that of the first part, giving the sense of being more removed: God is *with* Joshua whereas he is *among* Israel. The *living God* (Heb. *'ēl ḥay*) is a phrase which occurs twice in the Psalms in parallel with God (42:2 [Heb. 3]; 84:2 [Heb. 3]) and once in Hosea 1:10 (Heb. 2:1) in a reference to the future renewal of Israel and their reunion with their covenant God.[2] This aspect of God,

---

[1] See Dt. 31:23; Jos. 1:5.

[2] *Contra* J. R. Porter, 'The Background of Joshua III – V,' pp. 21–22, there is no basis for associating this title with pre-Israelite fertility imagery.

one who is faithful and keeps his promises, seems to be involved when God promises to dispossess the inhabitants of Canaan. The verb *drive out* (Heb. *yrš*) occurs in an emphatic form, to confirm the divine guarantee. It often describes Israel's occupation of the land (*e.g.* Nu. 14:24; 32:21; 33:52–53, 55; Dt. 4:38; 7:17; 9:3–5; 11:23).

Lists of the peoples of Canaan, with some deleted or others added, appear in Genesis 15:19–21; Exodus 3:8, 17; 23:23; 33:2; 34:11; Deuteronomy 20:17; Joshua 9:1; 12:8; *etc.* Deuteronomy 7:1 contains the same peoples as are listed here, but in a different order. The differences suggest that there was no single list that was used to construct the narratives, but that the names of these peoples have their place in the origins of the narratives. The Canaanites and Hittites are those who occupy their respective lands as detailed in the notes above at 1:4 (pp. 69–70). The Amorites are associated with those who live in the hill country and include kings of major fortified centres in Joshua 10:5. The Hivites, Perizzites and Girgashites have associations with other peoples from the fourteenth and thirteenth centuries BC.[1] The Jebusites are not yet attested outside the Bible.

11–13. Verse 10 is more than a reiteration of promises. God assures Israel that *he will certainly drive out* the inhabitants of the land. A wonder will take place so that Israel can trust this assurance. The ark will go ahead of Israel into Canaan. Joshua refers to *the ark of the covenant of the Lord of all the earth*. The phrase *all the earth* appeared in the report of the spies' visit to Rahab (2:3). There it referred specifically to the land of Canaan, and that may be the understanding of the term in this verse.[2] God is *Lord* in the sense of 'master' or 'ruler'. The term describes his sovereignty over the land of Canaan. Although its inhabitants do not yet acknowledge it, they will do so as the symbol which represents God's presence and power enters their land.[3] Israel will witness a demonstration of this power at

[1] See Introduction: 'Antiquity' (pp. 27–28).

[2] See J. R. Porter, *art. cit.*, pp. 18–20. The title *šarri mātāti*, 'king of the lands', was used by princes of Canaan in the fourteenth century BC and applied to Pharaoh. As it was later applied to other Ancient Near Eastern monarchs, it implied real sovereignty over specific lands and potentially over all the earth.

[3] In v. 11, the verb '*br*, 'to cross over', again appears. This time it refers to the crossing over of the ark as the symbol of God's presence. M. J. Hauan, 'The Background and Meaning of Amos 5:17B', *HTR*, 79, 1986, pp. 341–346,

the miraculous crossing of the Jordan. Joshua then introduces the twelve men who are chosen, one from each tribe.

This is consistent with a narrative principle already begun in this chapter. In verse 6, the role of the priests is mentioned, but only with reference to their carrying of the ark. The reader learns more about the priests' role in verse 8 and still more in verse 13. Further details continue as the narrative develops. This technique of unfolding the instructions as the narrative itself unfolds is one that occurs with respect to the twelve men. In verse 12, the instructions are simply to choose twelve men from each tribe. Their task is not mentioned until chapter 4, where further details appear. Why is the narrative structured in this way? In the story of Rahab there was a repetition of themes. The same occurs here. But more than repetition is involved. There are three groups acting in this ceremony: the priests with the ark, the twelve men, and the people who will cross the river.

These groups are acting simultaneously. Like a film in which the camera switches back and forth between the various scenes of action, the narrative moves back and forth between these three groups. Joshua's address to the people in verses 11–13 describes these actions.

In verse 13, we learn for the first time what will happen when the priests carry the ark into the water. The miraculous parting of the waters may have evoked a reference to the *ark of the LORD*, using God's covenant name, rather than the *ark of the covenant* which Joshua used at the beginning of his discourse. The reference to the *heap* (Heb. *nēd*) in which the waters stood appears again in verse 16 and ties this event once more with the Red Sea crossing as described in Exodus 15:8 and in Psalm 78:13.[1] An *amazing thing*, akin to God's deliverance from the pursuing Egyptians, will take place.

iv. The priests cross (3:14–17). The narrative of the crossing begins. Verse 6, where the (earlier) movement of the priests had begun, signalled this. It took place *when the people broke*

---

compares this usage with Gn. 15:18–21 and Ex. 34:11, and concludes that it 'is a theophanic term used to describe Yahweh's role in a covenant ritual'. Although there are connections in this passage with covenant and Passover, the context of this verb in this section of Joshua must determine its primary meaning.

[1] On *nēd*, see L. L. Grabbe, 'Comparative Philology and Exodus 15, 8: Did the Egyptians Die in a Storm?', *SJOT*, 7, 1993, pp. 263–269 (265–266). He argues for retaining the meaning of a 'wall of water'.

camp. However, the emphasis in this passage is not on the people but on the priests: they *reached the Jordan and their feet touched the water's edge*. They remain standing while the people pass over to the other side (see 4:10, p. 112). At the centre of this picture are the waters of the Jordan. They are also in the centre of the narrative. The people of Israel are mentioned at the beginning (14a) and the end (17b). The priests also appear before (14b–15a) and after (17a) the description of the Jordan. This account focuses upon the drama of the waters of the Jordan that stop flowing. Winther-Nielsen refers to the 'miraculous grammar' of this passage, observing the unusual way that the Hebrew text portrays the events:[1]

> Several temporal clauses (14a–15a) culminate in a slow-motion portrayal of the waters stopping (16a), just as the feet of the priests touch the water (15b), but after a comment on the flooded Jordan . . . The 'miraculous' syntax of 3:14–17 and 4:18 grammatically twists the action into descriptive events. It lends depictive force to the situation, creating a dramatic pause of the sort that often occurs at peak climaxes and resolutions. All dialogue is faded out . . . This is quite similar to the Flood Story . . .

15. The text explains that this event took place *a great distance away* south of the town of Adam (v. 16). The time was in the spring of the year, when the river is in its flood stage and therefore wider than its normal width of 90–100 feet and deeper than its average 3–10 feet. The southern flow of the Jordan is turbulent. The ez-Zōr surrounds it. This is a thicket that makes the river itself difficult to reach, and that in ancient times contained wild animals.[2] From a geological perspective, the Jordan River Valley lies at the juncture of tectonic plates

---

[1] Winther-Nielsen, pp. 176, 179; *idem*, 'The Miraculous Grammar of Joshua 3 – 4', pp. 308, 310. For his comparison with the flood story, another miraculous event, he refers to a similar analysis of Gn. 6 – 9 by R. Longacre, 'The Discourse Structure of the Flood Narrative', *Journal of the American Academy of Religion Supplement Series*, 47.1, March 1979, pp. 89–133.

[2] See R. de Vaux, *The Early History of Israel* (Philadelphia: Westminster, 1978), pp. 12–13; E. K. Vogel, 'Jordan', *International Standard Bible Encyclopedia*, 2 (Grand Rapids, Michigan: Eerdmans, 1982), pp. 1119–1125; D. L. Christensen, 'Jordan River/Valley of the Jordan' in *Mercer Dictionary of the Bible*, W. E. Mills *et al.* (eds.), (Macon, Georgia: Mercer University Press, 1990), pp. 466–467. Christensen provides examples of recent earthquakes creating landslides that cut off the waters of the Jordan River.

that create an unstable region. Earthquakes can occur and have been known to block the flow of the river. No mention of an earthquake appears in the account in Joshua. Whatever secondary causes there were, the primary purpose was the exaltation of Israel's God and his people.

16. Much geographical detail appears. Adam is a site in the Jordan Valley, identified with Tell ed-Dāmiye, 18 miles north of Jericho.[1] Zarethan also lies east of the Jordan. Archaeologists have identified it with Tell es-Sa'idîyeh, 12 miles north of Adam, or with Tell Umm Ḥamîd, 3 miles north of Adam. The site of Adam, immediately south of the Jabbok River, is important as a convenient point for crossing the Jordan. South of Adam the river becomes more difficult to cross. The *Sea of the Arabah (the Salt Sea)* is the Dead Sea which lies 18 miles from Adam, although the meandering Jordan is several times longer. The flood affected 29% of the Jordan Valley. The text defines this length so as to emphasize the magnitude of the *amazing thing*. The mention of the crossing of the people at this point confirms that the spectacle was not designed only to impress. God's 'wonders' served a practical purpose.

17. The narrative focuses again on the priests. A series of wordplays relate their actions to the waters and the people. The priests *stood* (Heb. *wayya' am°dû*) in the midst of the river just as the waters *stopped flowing* (*wayya' am°dû*) at Adam. The priests stood *on dry ground* just as the people crossed *on dry ground*, and just as Moses turned the sea into dry land (Ex. 14:21). The water was *completely cut off* (Heb. *tammû*) *until the whole nation had completed* (*tammû*) *the crossing.* These wordplays demonstrate that all the actions were related to one another. The priests who bear the ark of the covenant initiate the action. Thus they receive the most attention among the three groups (*i.e.* priests, twelve men, and all the people)[2] in this first perspective on the crossing of the River Jordan.

Like the first generation of Israelites who entered the land

---

[1] See R. S. Hess, ''*ādām* as "Skin" and "Earth" ', *TynB*, 39, 1988, p. 148.

[2] Polzin, p. 98, rightly notices the distinctive usage of the participle to describe the people's movement at this point. However, the reason has less to do with a 'centrality of movement' in ch. 3 and more to do with the fact that the movement of the people will not be completed until they become the focus of attention in ch. 4. The verbal form is a participle, not an imperfect, so that Polzin's reference (p. 97) to Uspensky's discussion of the imperfect is puzzling.

and laid claim to the promises of God, the Christians of the early church also worked together in obedience to God's appointed leaders (Acts 5:1–11). Their experience of God's power and the respect and witness that they enjoyed (Acts 5:12–16) mirror the fear of the nations before Israel (Jos. 2:24; 5:1) who miraculously crossed the Jordan. It also challenges the church today to learn the lessons of faith in Christ and of faithfulness to his Word.

v. The twelve stones (4:1–10). This text focuses upon the memorial that the Israelites set up. There are three major emphases: (1) the divine initiative comes through the leadership of Joshua; (2) the tribes cross the Jordan; and (3) a permanent memorial enables future generations to remember the 'amazing things' (3:5) of the crossing.

1–5. (1) The first point continues the theme of Joshua's role as successor of Moses. The initiation of the task comes from the LORD, who speaks only to Joshua. Joshua closely follows (v. 4) God's directions for choosing the twelve representatives (v. 2). Joshua repeats the command to lift up the stones. It and the observation that the stones (and the priests) are in the midst of the Jordan demonstrate that he followed God's instructions. The actions of the twelve men (vv. 8–9) demonstrate that Joshua has also obeyed God's word in verse 3.[1] Divine instruction and its repetition in the narrative are features of cultic descriptions, as seen in the instruction and erection of the tabernacle in Exodus 26 – 40.[2] A note about the careful obedience to Joshua's commands appears at the beginning of verse 8, *So the Israelites did as Joshua commanded them.* Joshua

---

[1] There is a wordplay between the *place right* (Heb. *hākîn*) *where the priests* of v. 3 *stood* and how Joshua *set up* (Heb. *hēqîm*) the stones in v. 9. Butler, p. 40, is perplexed by its appearance in 3:17 and 4:3 and suggests that it is meaningless. However, the wordplay noted here associates the action of the priests that initiates the 'amazing things' and that of the memorial that remembers the 'amazing things'. Boling and Wright, p. 173, note the wordplay with 'had appointed' (Heb. *hēkîn*) in 4:4. They find a connection with the men who were to carry the stones into the river from the east bank and who are now to remove stones and to 'make a platform for the porters of the Ark'.

[2] See Polzin, p. 95, who describes 3:11–12 as 'a prefiguring connective which anticipates' 4:2–3. See also the discussion of B. F. Batto, *Slaying the Dragon: Mythmaking in the Biblical Tradition* (Louisville: Westminster/John Knox, 1992). A summary of research is found in J. R. Porter, 'The Background of Joshua III – V', pp. 5–7.

provides an explanation in verses 6–7. As the human initiator and authoritative interpreter of the memorial, Joshua follows Moses, whose song at the crossing of the Sea (Ex. 15) also provided both a memorial and an interpretation of the event. For the Christian, obedience to God's Word is an essential part of effective service and leadership among God's people (Acts 2:42; Rom. 16:19; 1 Cor. 4:1–2; 1 Thes. 4:1–2; 2 Tim. 3:15–16).

(2) Israel's crossing of the Jordan is, of course, the central plot of chapters 3 and 4. In this section, three new aspects of it are clarified. Firstly, these events take place *when the whole nation had finished crossing the Jordan.* The phrase that appears in verse 1 resembles the phrase that immediately precedes it (3:17), where it concludes the section concerning the priests' transport of the ark. The difference is that the former phrase is introduced by *until* and describes how long the priests remained in the Jordan. The phrase at the beginning of the account of the memorial begins with *when* and informs the reader that the following events took place as the people crossed the river. The verb *finished* (Heb. *tmm*) does not suggest that everyone had crossed before the next event took place. It is better understood as something still taking place and translated 'were finishing the task'.[1] Theologically, this verb describes the complete and precise fulfilment of God's will, as is illustrated in the next section.

Secondly, in this section the fourfold occurrence of the root 'to cross' (Heb. *'br*) describes the crossing of the Jordan. It appears in the causative sense in verses 3 and 8, as the twelve representatives are to *carry over* the stones from the river to their resting place. Used in this way, the stones become symbolic of Israel's crossing. It also appears in the first instruction which Joshua gives to the representatives, *Go over.* Finally, it appears in the explanation of the memorial. It was when the ark *crossed the Jordan* that the waters of the river were stopped.

Thirdly, a new aspect of Israel's crossing is emphasized throughout this section: the fact that the whole nation crossed. It begins with the phrase *the whole nation* (Heb. *kol-haggôy*) in verse 1. The twelve representatives from every tribe of Israel symbolize it. For the same reason the memorial requires twelve stones and it is a component of the explanation of the

---

[1] This is due to the Hebrew *ka'^ašer* that precedes it and can be translated 'as' in the sense of 'during the time when'.

memorial by Joshua. This crossing of the Jordan by all the Israelites is not just an experience of the present generation. Future generations of Israelites will also acknowledge it. They will 'participate' in it through observing the sign and through hearing the explanation. For Israel, crossing the Jordan symbolized the means to enter the 'new world' of God's promises. For the Christian, the picture of the new birth symbolizes entering into a new life of God's blessing and salvation (Jn. 3:1–21).

6–7. (3) The purpose of this text is to establish a memorial by which future generations will learn of the identity of the people of Israel as the one nation whose God could do such great wonders. The explanation occurs in the centre of this passage and is given by Joshua. The discourse itself has a chiastic structure, as the NIV translation suggests:

A. *to serve as a sign among you. In the future, when your children ask you,*
　　B. *'What do these stones mean?' tell them that*
　　　　C. *the flow of the Jordan was cut off*
　　　　　　D. *before the ark of the covenant of the* LORD.
　　　　　　D'. *When it crossed the Jordan,*
　　　　C'. *the waters of the Jordan were cut off.*
　　B'. *These stones are to be*
A'. *a memorial to the people of Israel for ever.*

The chiastic structure provides an explanation concerning the significance of the memorial. It is a sign that educates future generations about their heritage and, more importantly, about their God. They will see that sign in the stones that came from the Jordan when its waters were cut off. They were cut off because the ark of the covenant passed through the Jordan. The term *memorial* (Heb. *zikkārôn*), appearing only here in Joshua, is found twenty times in the Hebrew Bible, of which thirteen occurrences are in Exodus, Leviticus and Numbers. In those books, it describes the Passover and exodus (Ex. 12:14; 13:9), the record of the defeat of the Amalekites (Ex. 17:14), the stones and names on the priest's ephod (Ex. 28:12, 29; 39:7), atonement money (Ex. 30:16), feasts of trumpets (Lv. 23:24; Nu. 10:10), a grain offering (Nu. 5:15, 18), bronze censers (Nu. 16:38 [Heb. 17:5]) and other offerings dedicated to the LORD (Nu. 31:54). The connection of these memorials with Israelite cultic festivals and rituals forms a consistent motif. Its application to these stones reinforces the ceremonial significance of the crossing and points to the role of Gilgal, where the stones are erected, as significant in the religious life of early Israel. The choice of the stones from the place where the priests stood while the people crossed associates them with an Israelite priestly and ritual context. For the Christian, 'memorials' such as baptism and the Lord's Supper serve as milestones in the believer's life of faith, reviewing, teaching and encouraging to obedience (1 Cor. 11:23–32; 1 Pet. 3:18–22).

8–9. Joshua sets up twelve stones in the middle of the Jordan River. The text seems to suggest that this is a second memorial, in addition to the twelve stones mentioned already. The absence of purpose for this action, as well as its omission in any previous instructions and in all later accounts, raises questions. Why is it in the text? Perhaps it should be omitted as unnecessary.[1] Alternatively, it may refer to a platform for the priests to stand on, or a literary device to emphasize Joshua's excess of zealous obedience.[2] However, the best solution is to recognize the following features: (1) the style of repetition and review already begun in verse 8 and continued in verse 10; (2) the similarity in language to the erection of the first set of stones referred to in verses 8 and 20; (3) the use of grammatical repetition to focus on a key feature; and (4) the unique and unlikely feature (in Hebrew grammar) of introducing a completely new topic in midstream with only a single reference to it.[3] Thus a translation relating these stones to the first set is preferred: *Joshua set up the twelve stones that had been in the middle of the Jordan . . .*

10. Although largely repetitive, verse 9 provides new information that Joshua was ultimately responsible for the stone memorial. Verse 10, which continues the summary of verses 8–9, notes that the priests were standing in the river, ascribes the whole action to a divine command given through Joshua, and adds that this was all done *just as Moses had directed Joshua.* As with verse 9, the concern is to ascribe the ultimate responsibility for the actions to the divinely

[1]P. P. Saydon, 'The Crossing of the Jordan: Josue 3; 4', *CBQ,* 46, 1984, p. 203.
[2]Boling and Wright, p. 175; Polzin, p. 109.
[3]Winther-Nielsen, pp. 179–182; *idem,* 'The Miraculous Grammar of Joshua 3 – 4', pp. 313–314.

appointed leadership. However, here the parallel is drawn between Moses and Joshua: as Moses obeyed God so Joshua obeyed Moses. This is a further demonstration that Joshua is Moses' successor. More importantly, it anticipates the exaltation of Joshua in verse 14, where the people's honouring of Moses is applied to Joshua.[1]

Additional Note: Aetiologies

One additional feature deserves comment: the significance of the expression 'until this day' (Heb. '*ad hayyôm hazzeh*). Of the 83 occurrences of this expression, fifteen appear in the book of Joshua, more than in any other book. Although the expression can be used in a casual manner, as a reference to a continuing state of affairs until the time of the writer, scholars have argued that it has a distinctive role in historical books such as Joshua. They have suggested that this phrase signals an attempt by the author to use a legend to explain the name of a place or some notable feature of a region. For example, in Joshua 4 this phrase explains the true reason behind the story about the erection of the stone memorial. At Gilgal (v. 20) there was a pile of stones to which the narrator wished to draw attention and whose existence he wanted to explain. This story about Joshua was the result. It is called an aetiology. Other possible aetiologies in Joshua include the presence of Rahab and her family in Israel (7:26), Ai (8:28–29), the presence of the Gibeonites (9:27), the presence of Geshur and Maacah (13:13), Calebites in Hebron (14:14), the presence of Jebusites (15:63) and the presence of Canaanites in Gezer (16:10). However, the expression 'until this day' also appears in contexts that are not aetiologies. Joshua uses it to describe the faithfulness of the Transjordanian tribes (22:3), the continuing effects of the sin of Peor (22:17), the faithfulness of the people (23:8) and God's victories on their behalf (23:9).

From this evidence, a few conclusions seem clear. (1) The expression has a wide range of uses in Joshua, corresponding to the English expression 'until now', and therefore the burden of proof for any 'technical' formula rests with those

---

[1]The LXX removes the reference to Moses, perhaps out of zeal to avoid any appearance of contradiction, as Moses nowhere explicitly commands Joshua regarding the events of v. 10. See Barthélemy, pp. 3–4.

who argue for it.[1] (2) While the expression 'until this day' may be used to explain why certain things that appear in the present are the way they are, the texts themselves do not reveal any consistent literary form as would be expected for the identification of something like an aetiology.[2] (3) As in the case of its usage in chapters 23 – 24, where Joshua applies certain past history to his audience, the expression may signal that the writer wants to apply the story to the contemporary generation (for 4:9 see preceding paragraph).[3] (4) The term allows no conclusions regarding historicity or lack of historicity.[4] Thus the usage of this term throughout the historical and prophetic books of the Old Testament, coupled with its discrete application to specific passages (*e.g.* 4:9 is applicable only to the account in ch. 4), allows no generalization as to when it was 'inserted' in the book nor does it allow conclusions regarding when the book was written.

vi. The people cross (4:11–13). The narrative technique of noting features of the plot in brief before they appear in more detail has been observed with the story of the spies in chapter 2 and with the twelve representatives in chapters 3 and 4. The people have been mentioned several times earlier in anticipation of a greater emphasis upon them in this passage. The manner of presenting simultaneous actions has also been observed. The crossing by the people took place in the narrative after the priests who carried the ark had assumed

[1]Younger, pp. 224–225, finds a similar expression from the Annals of Thutmose III, a fifteenth-century BC Pharaoh: 'They are recorded on a scroll of leather in the temple of Amun to this day' (*m hrw pn*). As in Joshua, the phrase comes from the records of a miltary campaign.

[2]B. O. Long, *The Problem of Etiological Narrative in the Old Testament*, BZAW 108 (Berlin: Alfred Töpelmann, 1968), pp. 25–26; and Butler, p. 81, notes how Noth's classic example of an aetiology, the Achan narrative, deviates from other 'aetiologies' in many ways.

[3]B. S. Childs, 'A Study of the Formula "Until This Day"', *JBL*, 82, 1963, pp. 279–292. Weinfeld, *Promise*, pp. 148–149, suggests that it was used as a didactic tool to make the experience of the nation's heritage real for later generations.

[4]B. S. Childs, *art. cit.* The concept of the aetiology has been criticized as an unhelpful label that says nothing about the narrative itself and is used to describe narratives whose purpose is best understood as rhetorical (to heighten interest in the object or event) rather than as cultic. See H. C. Brichto, *Toward a Grammar of Biblical Poetics. Tales of the Prophets* (Oxford: Oxford University Press, 1992), pp. 28–30; P. J. van Dyk, 'The Function of So-Called Etiological Elements in Narratives', *ZAW*, 102, 1990, pp. 19–33.

their position. It may have taken place before, during and after the events of 4:1–10.

For the order of the crossing, see Introduction: 'Theology' (d) 'The holy and redeeming God' (p. 51). The response of God's people follows God's revelation and it remains an essential part of the covenantal relationship. This was true at Sinai and at the Jordan. For Christians, it is no less true of their response to the message of Jesus Christ (Rom. 10:9; 1 Jn. 1:1–3).

11. Two reasons are given for the crossing in this passage: obedience to God's directives and preparation for battle. The first, obedience to God's instruction, occurs in the repeated statements of Israel doing just what they were told to do. The verb *finished* (*tmm*), which was used of the whole nation crossing the Jordan (3:17 and 4:1), described the complete fulfilment of the LORD's commands (v. 10). This parallels the usage of the same verb to describe the completion of the crossing of the people (v. 11). It emphasizes that Israel's crossing was a complete response to God's command, *i.e.* Israel 'finished' obeying the divine instructions when it 'finished' crossing the Jordan. This also explains the detail that the Israelites *hurried over* (v. 10). They eagerly obeyed God's command.

As they witnessed the initial movement of the priests and ark into the Jordan, so the people witness their final movement across the river. In both cases (3:6; 4:11), the ark and the priests *came* (Heb. '*br*) *to the other side while the people watched.* The text emphasizes Israel's role in observing the actions of the priests.[1] Like the memorial, the witness of the people was the means of preserving this 'amazing thing' and the ceremony that surrounded it. Like the crossing of the Red Sea, all the people of Israel witness and participate in this act of God.

12–13. The preparation for war occurs in three separate notices. Firstly, the Transjordanian warriors cross. This begins the fulfilment of their oath to Joshua in 1:16–18, but it also confirms the promise they had made to Moses when he gave them allotments east of the Jordan (*cf.* comment on 1:12–15, pp. 76–78). They cross *armed* for war. This signals their participation in all the battles in Palestine in the following narratives. It also confirms the unity of all the tribes of Israel in the crossing.[2] All

---

[1] Winther-Nielsen, p. 182.

[2] A comparison with 1:16–18 demonstrates that the unity of Israel is at stake here. Thus the mention of the Transjordanian tribes is not 'superfluous', nor

Israel sees them cross. Secondly, the notice of forty 'armed groups'[1] clarifies the purpose of this crossing for all Israel. It is the beginning of their military venture in Canaan. In crossing the Jordan, Israel at last enters the land promised to their ancestors. At the same time, they enter enemy territory, with all the dangers and challenges that this might imply. Therefore, they appear armed and prepared for battle. Thirdly, the final statement of this passage, that they crossed over *before the LORD to the plains of Jericho for war*, summarizes the purpose of the crossing for the people. They crossed *before the LORD, i.e.* they were obedient to the LORD's commands and he witnessed their obedience. Therefore, they could expect his faithfulness to his promises that they would possess the land and that he would fight for them. They crossed *to the plains of Jericho*. Therefore, they established a strategic foothold in the lands west of the Jordan. Once on the plain, they could organize and defend themselves as they prepared for their movements to occupy Canaan. They crossed *armed for battle*. This demonstrates that here was not merely a religious ritual empty of significance. The crossing was the first part of the movement to occupy Canaan, and this was done with the necessary appearance of military preparedness.

Why did the inhabitants of Canaan not meet Israel at the river and do battle with them there? Three reasons may be suggested:

(1) They may have been uncertain if or when the Israelites would cross. They may have appeared established in Moabite territory at Shittim. When they did move to cross, it was sudden and their stay at the riverbank was brief. Thus the Canaanites may not have been prepared to meet them.

(2) They crossed at an unexpected place, south of Adam, a place where the river could not be forded easily. In this region, potential enemies would not have expected the Israelites to cross. If they were waiting for them, the Canaanites would have chosen the area to the north.

---

are they 'a military escort' distinct from the other tribes (so Boling and Wright, p. 175). Instead, they confirm the participation of 'all Israel'.

[1] For the word *thousand* (Heb. *'elep*) as a reference to a military group, see G. J. Wenham, *Numbers. An Introduction and Commentary* (Leicester and Downers Grove: IVP, 1981), pp. 60–66; Boling and Wright, p. 176. Both refer to G. E. Mendenhall, 'The Census Lists of Numbers 1 and 26', *JBL*, 77, 1958, pp. 52–66. Mendenhall states that originally the group may have numbered five to fourteen individuals.

(3) Canaan in the Late Bronze Age (1550–1200 BC) had only a few major centres of population, none of which would have been threatened by the movement of some peoples on to the plain of Jericho. Jericho, as will be seen, was not a major centre, so perhaps there was little that the inhabitants of that 'town' could have done to prevent the crossing.

For the Christian, these military preparations bring to mind the spiritual warfare that the New Testament describes as equally challenging (1 Pet. 5:8). It requires spiritual preparation and armour (Eph. 6:10–18).

vii. Joshua is exalted (4:14). This fulfils the divine promise of 3:7, using similar language. It also closes the account of the crossing of the Jordan. The LORD's exaltation of Joshua caused Israel to respect him just as they had respected Moses. The crossing was the first of Joshua's many responsibilities. Israel recognized him as successor to Moses and as their leader. The succeeding events confirmed the role of Joshua in leading the people to obtain their covenant promises.

viii. Out of the Jordan (4:15–18). These verses resemble Joshua 3:8, 13, 15–16. There, the LORD speaks to Joshua and promises his exaltation. He instructs him to command the priests who carry the ark to stand in the river and, when they do, the waters of the Jordan cease. In Joshua 4:15–18, the LORD speaks again to Joshua and instructs him to command the priests. This time, however, they are to bring the ark up from the Jordan on to the dry ground of Canaan. Again, Joshua instructs the priests in what the LORD has said. Again, they do exactly as instructed and move the ark. The waters of the Jordan respond to their actions and return to run in *flood as before.* Religiously, this action places the entire crossing in the context of a divinely ordained ceremony. The priests initiate and complete it. The laity participate and bear witness. The note about the soles of the priests' feet guarantees that this 'amazing thing' functions under priestly control. From a literary perspective, this text closes the scenes of crossing the river and the role of the priests in that crossing. As noted above, it interweaves with the exaltation of Joshua and signals the accomplishment of this goal. Theologically, the text inspires a confession of the power of God to control natural forces. God chooses to use these forces through his chosen instruments

(Joshua and the priests) to enable his people to attain his promises. For the Christian, this recalls the power of Jesus of whom the disciples testified: *Even the winds and the waves obey him!* (Mt. 8:26–27; Mk. 4:39–41; Lk. 8:23–24).

ix. The transition to Gilgal (4:19–24). Until now, the reader knows only that the crossing took place during the flood stage of the Jordan, that is in the spring. Now the text specifies *the tenth day of the first month.* The same date appears in Exodus 12:2–3, where it introduces the preparations for the Passover, which occurs on the fourteenth day. Thus the text again reviews the events of the exodus. However, this time the review prepares the reader for the coming celebration of the Passover in chapter 5. It also implies that, as events designed to prepare for the Passover begin on this day, so the crossing of the Jordan River prepares for the celebration of the Passover at Gilgal. No certain identification exists for the site of 'the Gilgal'. It is not necessary or even likely that all the occurrences of Gilgal in the Bible refer to the same location. The name means 'circle', and is a good description for a fortified camp such as must have been present in Joshua's time. Any of several small tells near Jericho serve as candidates, but the actual position of the camp has left no detectable remains for the archaeologist.

20–21. Joshua erects the memorial. His instructions enabled the crossing, and this memorial will commemorate the event. As in verses 6–7, the memorial will evoke questions from future generations.

22–23. Unlike the earlier explanation (vv. 6–7) that emphasized the ark of the covenant, this one focuses upon the *dry ground* that Israel *crossed.* The cutting off of the waters was the key factor in the obtaining of the stones. The people experienced the dry riverbed on which they walked. Verse 23 is the explicit link between the crossing of the Jordan and that of the Red Sea. Although the verb *dried up* does not appear in the Exodus account, Rahab uses it (2:10) in her reference to the Red Sea crossing. A change of person occurs. In the description of the crossing of the Jordan, the object is in the second person plural, *you.* Presumably, this refers to all the Israelites who have just crossed the Jordan. In the reference to the crossing of the Red Sea, the object is a first common plural pronoun, *us.* This refers to Joshua and other members of his generation who experienced this event. This change of person is consistent with the desert wandering for forty years, as mentioned in Joshua 5:6. Theologically, the experience of this 'new exodus' is also for each succeeding generation of Israel. They too can come to Gilgal, see the memorial, learn of the events of the crossing of the Jordan and of its relationship to the original exodus, and renew their commitment to the service of their God. It would be in this region that John the Baptist would come many years later to prepare the people anew for the coming of the kingdom of God.[1]

24. Joshua identifies two purposes, the first one being that these acts make known to all the inhabitants of the land (of Canaan) that God alone is the true God. The strength of *the hand of the LORD* is great. It frequently occurs when God acts against those who rebel (*e.g.* Ex. 9:3; 16:3; Nu. 11:23; Dt. 2:15; Jos. 23:31). The second purpose follows from this reference to *the hand of the LORD*. The second person plural *you* is used once again, referring to all Israel who heard Joshua. This sign has been accomplished in order that Israel might *fear* God throughout its life. To fear God is to give him wholehearted loyalty. Both the miracle and its remembrance, as well as the exaltation of Joshua, pointed to this purpose. The miracle directed the people's attention to loyalty towards God, his covenant, and his appointed leader of the people.[2] The gospels record the signs and wonders of Jesus of Nazareth for the same twofold purpose: that those who hear might believe and that this belief might lead to fullness of life in commitment to Christ (Jn. 20:30–31).

This final passage acts as a transition. It concludes the events of the crossing, to which it alludes and for which Joshua erects a memorial and explains its significance. It introduces the events that will follow. Israel is now in the land of Canaan with its base at Gilgal. God has performed 'wonders' on its behalf which will

[1]This and the following chapters have been thought to have been preserved at the Gilgal sanctuary near Jericho. Indeed, some have seen their origins in the celebration of the Red Sea crossing through re-enacting the procession across the waters. See F. M. Cross, *Canaanite Myth and Hebrew Epic. Essays in the History of the Religion of Israel* (Cambridge, Massachusetts: Harvard University Press, 1973), pp. 103–105. This is the conscious purpose of Israel at the point of crossing into Canaan. They, like Israel at the exodus, are preparing to begin a new life and a new commitment as the people of God. This should be distinguished from the Ugaritic myths where Baal defeats the water deities, Sea and River. Jos. 3 – 5 roots the event in early Israelite history.

[2]K. Aryaprateeb, 'A Note on YR' in Jos. IV 24', *VT*, 22, 1972, pp. 240–242; Boling and Wright, p. 187.

challenge the citizens of Canaan to choose either for or against Israel and its God. In either case, they will eventually be brought to confess that Israel's God is strong and able to overcome their resistance just as he has overcome the resistance of the Red Sea and of the Jordan River. Israel will know this success as they learn to *fear God, i.e.* to worship and obey him alone.

d. Rites of preparation: circumcision (5:1–12)

With the establishment of Joshua's authority and with the Israelites encamped west of the Jordan in the Promised Land, the narrative pauses to reaffirm the covenantal relationship between Israel and God. The chapter considers (1) the fear of Israel's enemies due to God's mighty acts; (2) Joshua as covenant initiator; (3) circumcision as an identification with the covenants of Abraham and Sinai; and (4) the ceremony as a separation from Egypt and the desert and an identification with the covenanted land of Canaan. The enemies of Israel are struck with fear at the news of Israel's God and his deeds; Joshua acts as leader of the people; Israel as a nation joins in a covenant ceremony that prepares them for the coming mission. Finally, the land of Canaan 'welcomes' Israel by providing the nation with its produce.

  i. The fear of the Canaanites (5:1). This description of the Canaanite reaction follows the miracle of chapter 4. It explains why the Canaanites did not attack at once, and thus allows time for the circumcision of the Israelites, a period of weakness when they would be susceptible to defeat (see Gn. 34). Its usage of language previously associated with the first exodus foreshadows the significance of circumcision (v. 4) and explains why the Israelite offensive actions against both Jericho and Ai went unopposed by Canaanites forces. 'Amorites' and 'Canaanites' are terms used to describe the same peoples. Their locations refer to peoples living between the Jordan and the Mediterranean. The descriptions, two parallel lines, identify all the areas of the land and emphasize the total number of the rulers in Canaan.[1] That is why both lines have an identical structure beginning with *all.* The second half of the verse describes the fearful effects of the LORD's *amazing things* upon

---

[1] In literary terms, this is a merism.

117

the kings. It uses language which is the same as that found in Rahab's confession of 2:10–11 (same wording in bold):

> . . . **heard how the LORD had dried up the** *water of the Red Sea/ Jordan for you/before the Israelites* . . . **our/their hearts melted and** *everyone's courage failed because of you/they no longer had the courage to face the Israelites.*

Rahab referred to the Red Sea. The note here refers to the crossing of the Jordan. Thus the similarities in the descriptions of the two crossings noted in the previous chapter are reinforced by this verse.

ii. Joshua circumcises the people (5:2–3).[1] The expression *at that time* appears in three additional places in Joshua (6:26; 11:10, 21), always to introduce a statement or specific act by Joshua. Only here does it introduce a statement that God makes, although the verse goes on to report Joshua's obedient action. The text uses the same words to describe Joshua's response (v. 3) as to describe the divine command (v. 2), indicating the complete obedience of Joshua. Four points are relevant for understanding the text: the nature of circumcision in the Bible, the command to do it *again*, the use of *flint knives*, and the location of Gibeath Haaraloth. Physical circumcision occurs in the Pentateuch in Genesis 17 and 34, and Exodus 4:24–26. For Abraham, it becomes a sign of his covenant with God. For the Shechemites, it is a demonstration of identity with the sons of Israel. Exodus 4:24–26 is a difficult passage in which Moses' son is prepared for the events that follow Moses' return to Egypt. These texts agree in associating Israelite circumcision with the community of Israel and with its divine covenant. This association applies in Joshua where the circumcision forms the necessary preparatory ritual to celebration of the Passover, which remembers the creation of the nation and God's covenant with it. Some suggest that the command to circumcise *again* may reflect the concern that, until the present time, Israelites had only been circumcised according to the Egyptian method, which did not involve a complete removal of the foreskin.[2] The LXX and later Jewish

---

[1] See Introduction: 'Title and text' (pp. 19–20) for a discussion of a Dead Sea Scroll fragment that contains 8:30–34 and positions it before 5:2.

[2] J. M. Sasson, 'Circumcision in the Ancient Near East', *JBL*, 85, 1966, p. 474; R. G. Hall, 'Circumcision', *ABD*, I, p. 1027.

interpretation suggest that this implies that Joshua had performed an earlier circumcision.[1] Fox suggests that Israelite circumcision was originally a puberty rite, as implied in the earliest form of this story, and that a priestly redactor reinterpreted this as a rite at childbirth. This reinterpretation explains the *again* as 'a clumsy effort at harmonization'.[2] However, none of these explanations is explicit in the text (see vv. 4–9).

The *flint knives* are best understood as obsidian. This is probably not a retrojection to the past, *i.e.* an attempt to identify a ritual as ancient by the usage of ancient implements.[3] Millard has demonstrated the widespread use of obsidian knives throughout the Ancient Near East for a variety of purposes.[4] The smooth and sharp surface of this sort of knife enjoyed popularity for ritual and non-ritual purposes long after the development of metal knives. This does not mean that Joshua's act was not a ceremony, only that obsidian knives do not prove that such was the case. Gibeath Haaraloth means 'hill of the foreskins'. Its location has not been identified. As with Gilgal, it may have been a temporary camp-site.

iii. The reason for the circumcision (5:4–9). Verses 4–9 are interwoven with repeated verbs and phrases. They form an argument for the circumcision of Israel. All the circumcised had died in the desert. Verse 6 describes the reason for the death of the circumcised and the following verse describes the reason for the lack of circumcision of those who were born. Verses 8–9 summarize the circumcision process and prepare for the celebration of the Passover.[5]

---

[1] D. W. Gooding, 'Traditions of Interpretation of the Circumcision at Gilgal', *Proceedings of the Sixth World Congress of Jewish Studies*, I (Jerusalem: World Union of Jewish Studies, 1977), pp. 149–164.

[2] M. V. Fox, 'The Sign of the Covenant', *RB*, 81, 1974, p. 593.

[3] Soggin, p. 71; Butler, p. 58.

[4] A. R. Millard, 'Back to the Iron Bed: Og's or Procrustes'?', *Congress Volume Paris 1992, VT* Supplement 61 (Leiden: Brill, 1995), pp. 195–197. See *ANET*, p. 326, for references to a scene from the Sixth Dynasty of Egypt which shows the use of a flint knife in circumcision (*ANEP*, p. 206), and to an Egyptian text of the twenty-third century which describes the simultaneous circumcision of 120 males.

[5] Z. Talshir, 'The Detailing Formula *wezeh(had)dābār*', *Tarbiz*, 51, 1981, pp. 27–29, Hebrew, identifies a structure based on the beginning of v. 4, 'Now this is why he did so'. Elsewhere in Hebrew, this formula identifies a detailed

4. The key verb is 'to die'. Every Israelite *who came out of Egypt
. . . died in the desert.* For this reason, a second circumcision of all
Israel had to take place. No-one among those who originally
participated in the exodus survived. The specific concern is the
men of war, *i.e.* those males of sufficient age to engage in battle.
Joshua circumcised these at Gilgal. Their counterparts of the
earlier generation had died in the wilderness.

5. These men had been circumcised. Again, the emphasis is
on *all the people that came out.* All the people of that generation
died, but, just as important, all of them had been circumcised.
Israel at its formation contained no uncircumcised warriors. No
uncircumcised members of the community passed through the
Red Sea and none stood at Mount Sinai and entered into
covenant with God. So it should be true with the new
generation. All should be circumcised. However, verse 5
contains a *but.* The reader learns that those born after leaving
Egypt were not circumcised. Again, the totality *all* suggests that
none was circumcised. In the earlier generation, all *had been
circumcised*; in the generation born in the desert, they *had not.*

6. That generation had all died; none was present at the
crossing of the Jordan, and therefore all this generation
needed to be circumcised at Gilgal.[1] The first group *had moved
about in the desert forty years.* This recalls God's judgment on that
generation for their unbelief (Nu. 14:33–34). This is confirmed
by the additional phrase *since they had not obeyed the LORD.*
Although Numbers recalls many examples of disobedience,
only the rebellion of chapter 14 includes both the disobedience
and the forty years of wandering. The second half of verse 6
goes on to make this point explicit. It concludes with a
digression from that generation to the patriarchal generation.
To them and to their descendants, God had promised the land.
Because the generation of the exodus had failed to enter
Canaan, the text notes that now the new generation led by
Joshua had the opportunity to do so.

7–8. Joshua acts because the present generation is not
circumcised. The pattern of these verses is A–B–A¹–B¹, where A

---

elaboration and repetition of the subject. This is the case here with circumcision.

[1]Butler, p. 59, suggests a wordplay for the *people* (Heb. *'am*) of God who
emerged from Egypt (vv. 4, 5) and the 'nation' (Heb. *gôy*) of God's enemies who
died in the desert (v. 6). The younger generation was but a *nation* in the desert
until it was circumcised (v. 8).

is the generation of the exodus and B is the present generation. This structure contrasts the two generations, a distinction reinforced by a wordplay with the verb 'to finish' (Heb. *tmm*) which functioned in this way in 4:1, 10 and 11. In verse 6, forty years are spent in the wilderness *until all the men . . . died* (*i.e.* 'finished'). On the other hand, in verse 8, as *the whole nation had been circumcised*, *i.e.* 'had finished' the process of circumcision, they rested in camp. Thus the earlier generation 'finished' in the death of disobedience, while the generation of Gilgal 'finished' the act of obedience.

The text nowhere indicates why Israel should be circumcised. However, there are clues, especially when verses 5–6 and 8 are compared. As just noted, verse 8 refers to the obedience of circumcision. In verses 5–6, a similar phrase refers to the opposite, their disobedience and the resulting death. The text describes this in three ways: (1) *they had not obeyed the LORD*; (2) they had not received the promise that the LORD *had solemnly promised their fathers*; and (3) they had not seen the *land flowing with milk and honey*. The first point is the opposite of what the LORD first commanded his people in their covenant with him at Sinai, that they should *hear* the LORD (Dt. 6:4 *et passim.*). The second point recalls the covenant that God made in Genesis 17. There, he commanded Abraham and all his descendants to be circumcised (vv. 9–14), after promising them, *The whole land of Canaan, where you are now an alien, I will give as an everlasting possession to you and your descendants after you* (v. 8). The third point describes the land. Although appearing only here in the book of Joshua, this expression occurs fifteen times in the Pentateuch and four times elsewhere in the Hebrew Bible (Je. 11:5; 33:22; Ezk. 20:6, 15). It describes the agricultural and pastoral abundance of Canaan. It is particularly appropriate to the highlands (where Israel would first settle), with orchards for date honey and grazing lands for cattle and goat herds.[1] It is also associated with the covenants between God and Israel, especially as a reward for Israel's obedience (*e.g.* Dt. 6:3; 11:9). The contrast with the generation of the exodus explains the reason for the circumcision of the generation of Joshua 5.[2] At

---

[1]See the description in the early-second-millenium Egyptian text of Sinuhe's visit to Canaan and the land of Yaa: 'Plentiful was its honey . . . There was no limit to any (kind of) cattle' (*ANET*, p. 19b).

[2]Mitchell, p. 45.

the beginning of its entry into the land, this generation identified itself with Abraham and his descendants and so with both the obligations and the promises given in God's covenant with Abraham. It also identified with the covenant given through Moses to all Israel by listening to God and by 'seeing' the promised land of Canaan. The generation of Joshua 5 took upon itself all the responsibilities of the covenant through the covenantal sign of circumcision. Through circumcision, it could lay claim to the promises of the land that God had given to Abraham and to his descendants.

9. God accepted this act as a means of ending *the reproach of Egypt*. Although other nations understood this as involving Israel's victory over Egypt (Jos. 2:10), the reference here is to verses 4–6. This describes the generation *who came out of Egypt* and *died in the desert*. *The reproach of Egypt* was the disobedience of the previous generation (the generation of Egypt) which brought about the period of wandering and death in the desert.[1] That generation could not inherit the land. Presumably, the same judgment lay upon the present generation. It was through their obedience to the covenant, their circumcision, that this judgment could be removed from the nation. Thus Israel was now permitted to inherit the land of Canaan. God would fight for Israel, not against her (contrast Nu. 14:40–45). The wordplay with the name of the site *Gilgal* takes advantage of the verbal root 'to roll' (*gll*) that sounds like the name Gilgal.

The New Testament encourages identification with the people of God through participation in the church. Ephesians 2:11–22 discusses circumcision as a means of entry into the Old Testament covenant community. It compares this to Christ's death on the cross, which provides the way to become part of the new-covenant community of Christians. This new way abolishes the old division between Jew and Gentile and allows both to come to God.

iv. Passover as the beginning of the inheritance of the land (5:10–12). With the last obstacle removed, Israel affirms its

---

[1] Polzin, pp. 110–111, interprets this as an application of Moses' account of Israel's disobedience in Dt. 1 – 2 and 9 – 10. To identify the *reproach* with an ignoble social position as slaves in Egypt (Hertzberg, p. 33; Butler, p. 59) introduces a category of thought that is not addressed elsewhere in the passage.

identity with God and with his covenantal promises. This is accomplished through a feast. Verse 10 notes the place and the time of the celebration. It contains four phrases that form an A–B–B¹–A¹ chiasm, as they appear in the following order in the Hebrew text.[1]

A. *while camped at Gilgal*
  B. *the Israelites celebrated the Passover*
  B¹. *On the evening of the fourteenth day of the month*
A¹. *on the plains of Jericho*

The first and last phrases describe the locations. Gilgal is the place where Israel has been circumcised. *The plains of Jericho* look forward to the possession of the land. The second and third phrases connect Israel's first Passover festival with the events of the previous four days. This is not merely through the implied reminiscence of crossing the Red Sea after the first Passover and crossing the Jordan before this Passover. It is also explicit, as the earlier note (about the crossing of the Jordan on the tenth day, 4:19) makes clear. Such a detail transforms the ceremony of crossing the Jordan and circumcising the people into a single act of preparation for the Passover. Although Numbers 9:1–15 remembers how Israel kept this feast in the desert, two aspects relate the celebration of Joshua 5 to that of the first Passover. Firstly, in both there is a preparation on the tenth day of the month: in Exodus 12:3, it is the selection of a lamb to be slaughtered; in Joshua 4:19, it is the crossing of the Jordan.[2] Secondly, the Passover regulations in Exodus 13:5 call for Israel to celebrate the feast when it enters Canaan, *a land flowing with milk and honey* (*cf.* Jos. 5:6). Thus the celebration identifies Israel at the Jordan with Israel at the exodus and Israel at Sinai. Israel at the Jordan inherits the covenantal promises of the previous generation.

11–12. Although roasted lamb figures prominently in all

[1] Those who understand information such as the date of the Passover to be later additions need to reckon with a literary structure as witnessed by the chiasm of vv. 11–12. It is not adequate to explain it as an addition to an earlier text. It requires substantial rewriting of the text. For a summary of critical views, see C. Brekelmans, 'Joshua V 10–12: Another Approach', *OTS*, 25, 1989, pp. 89–91.

[2] No mention of any significance attached to the tenth day of the month is found in the accounts of the Passover in the desert (or in the legal collections). See Ex. 23:15; 34:18; Lv. 23:4–8; Nu. 28:16–25; 33:3; and Dt. 16:1–8.

descriptions in the Pentateuch, it is not mentioned in Joshua. Why not? Scholars have sought to find in the Passover two original festivals, a nomadic one where a lamb was sacrificed and a settled agricultural one that involved eating *unleavened bread.*[1] On this explanation, the account of Joshua 5 should originate with the settled peoples. However, the theories that oppose nomadic and settled groups rest upon assumptions that are not valid. The peoples of the hill country at the time of Israel's appearance in Canaan could have been both (enclosed) nomads and settled village dwellers, changing their lifestyle according to the challenges of political and environmental forces.[2]

A better explanation lies in the literary structure and in the purpose of the foods that are mentioned. The staple diet throughout the desert wandering was manna; the basic food in the diet of Canaan was cereals, especially barley and wheat.[3] Verses 11–12 form four clauses, each beginning with a conjunction and followed by a verb: *they ate, the manna stopped, there was no longer,* and *they ate.* As in verse 10, a concentric A–B–B'–A' pattern results:

A. *The day after the Passover, that very day, they ate some of the produce*[4] *of the land: unleavened bread and roasted grain.*
   B. *The manna stopped the day after they ate this food from the land;*
   B'. *there was no longer any manna for the Israelites,*
A'. *but that year they ate of the produce of Canaan.*

The text is not concerned with a review of Passover foods. Rather, it describes the diet of Canaan, the cereals.[5] These are now what the Israelites eat, in part because the manna has stopped. This fact is repeated because it signals the end of any

---

[1] B. M. Bokser, 'Unleavened Bread and Passover, Feasts of' in *ABD*, VI, p. 756; Fritz, pp. 61–62; Soggin, p. 75.

[2] I. Finkelstein, *The Archaeology of the Israelite Settlement* (Jerusalem: IES, 1988).

[3] D. C. Hopkins, *The Highlands of Canaan*, SWBA Series 3 (Sheffield: JSOT Press, 1985), pp. 241–242.

[4] A. R. Millard (private communication) observes that this word occurs only here in the Bible. It also appears in inscriptions from the southern Judean fort of Arad, *c.* 600 BC. There it describes quantities of wheat issued or received. See text 31, line 10 in Y. Aharoni, *Arad Inscriptions*, Judean Desert Studies (Jerusalem: IES, 1981), pp. 56–58. See also text 111, line 6, on p. 124.

[5] See Steuernagel, p. 169; C. Brekelmans, 'Joshua V 10–12: Another Approach', pp. 91–92. Both also stress the context of Israel's new appearance in the land to explain these foods.

connection with the desert journey and with the *reproach of Egypt*.[1] A new page in Israel's experience begins: the wilderness has passed and the Promised Land has come. Therefore, the diet changes.[2] A second reason for the emphasis lies in the new connection of the Passover with the Promised Land. In Exodus 12 – 13, the Passover served as a reminder of the events of the exodus. Now it will also serve as a reminder of the entrance into the Promised Land. The crossing of the Jordan and the end of the manna took place at the Passover. The food of the Passover itself, the unleavened bread, became part of the harvest feast in Canaan. A third reason for the emphasis upon the cereals follows from the implications of the harvest season. The Passover, with its consumption of the produce of Canaan, suggests the initial possession of the land. Already, Israel enjoys the fruits of the land. These were initial 'down-payments' of the great abundance of blessing it could expect if it remained faithful to God.

From a literary standpoint, this text closes Israel's preparation for the possession of the land. The repetitive, ceremonial language of chapters 1, 3 and 4 appears again. The act of circumcision takes place, however, west of the Jordan as preparation for the coming events in Canaan. The language of the opening and closing verses emphasizes Canaanite peoples and agriculture.

For the Christian, the Easter celebration of the resurrection of Christ marks the new Passover event. Belief in this work of Christ inaugurates a life just as new as that of the Israelites celebrating their first Passover in the Promised Land. But this celebration is not confined to once a year, as was the Passover. Instead, week by week Christians have the opportunity to remember the saving work of Jesus Christ in their worship (Acts 2:42–46; 20:17–36; 1 Cor. 11:17–34).

e. The first assault: the capture of Jericho (5:13 – 6:27)

The description of Jericho's capture divides into three parts: the pre-capture instructions, the narrative of the capture itself,

---

[1] See C. Brekelmans, 'Joshua V 10–12: Another Approach', pp. 92–93, who connects this passage with Ex. 16:35.

[2] Butler, p. 60, identifies the *roasted grain* as 'grain ready to hand, growing wild in fields they had not planted.'

and the resulting effect of the capture upon Joshua. God's presence, the divine word, Joshua's response and the chronological notes connect the text with the preceding Passover celebration. The events occur within the seven-day period of the Feast of Unleavened Bread. The salvation of Rahab reminds the reader of the earlier events of the book. The final section interprets Jericho's defeat as a symbol of God's continuing preservation of Israel and blessing of Joshua.

i. The pre-capture instructions (5:13 – 6:5). The strange confrontation of 5:13–15 resembles that between Jacob and the man of God at Peniel (Gn. 32:22–32) and that between Moses and the burning bush (Ex. 3:1 – 4:17).[1] In each case, the human protagonist encounters a divine messenger before facing a life-and-death conflict, but there is a significant difference with Joshua. Unlike the other two figures, Joshua does not wrestle or argue with the messenger. He questions him and responds as he is told. There are three reasons for this difference. Firstly, Joshua is never doubting or accused of wrong by God, as contrasted with Jacob and Moses, who appear fallible. Further, neither Jacob nor Moses wishes the coming conflict. Joshua accepts it, perhaps looks forward to it. A second reason for Joshua's passive acceptance of the messenger occurs in the description *with a drawn sword*. This expression appears in two other places in the Bible, with reference to the angel who stops Balaam and his donkey (Nu. 22:23) and to the angel who stands ready to execute punishment for David's census (1 Ch. 21:16). A figure *with a drawn sword* is one not to be toyed with. He is one who threatens divine judgment.

14. The third reason recalls the figure's self-identification as *commander of the army of the LORD*. Elsewhere, the commander of an army is the general in charge (Gn. 21:22, 32; 26:26; Jdg. 4:2, 7; 1 Sa. 12:9; 14:50; *etc.*). The figure assumes a role of authority. Joshua, as leader of the Israelites, is in a comparable position, but he recognizes the superior rank of the stranger. However, the concern is not which leader is more important but Joshua's willingness to accept the figure's authority and to respect this as a divine sign.[2]

---

[1] Schäfer-Lichtenberger, p. 210.
[2] Joshua's initial question is a customary interrogation of any armed stranger before war. The warrior's answer introduces a third component into the coming

15. In language that duplicates God's command to Moses in Exodus 3:5, Joshua is instructed to remove his sandals because the place is *holy*.[1] As with Moses, the place is holy because it is where God meets with his chosen leader in a special way. Three points suggest that this is a manifestation of the divine presence, and therefore more than an angelic visitation. Firstly, Joshua worships the figure who accepts his worship. In the light of the covenantal requirements that only the LORD God should be worshipped (*cf.* Ex. 20 and Dt. 5 – 8), there can be no doubt who this is. Secondly, the holiness is a manifestation of the divine presence throughout the Bible.[2] Finally, the continuation of the narrative in chapter 6 blends the figure of the commander of *the army of the LORD* with God himself. As with the incident in Exodus 3:2–5, and with the accounts in the patriarchal narratives (*e.g.* Gn. 18 and 22), distinctions between the messenger (angel) of the LORD and the LORD himself evaporate. Therefore, the events of 5:13–15 should not be seen as a separate narrative embedded between two others. Rather, they form the logical introduction to the instructions that follow. Just as God informed Moses of his mission after confronting him with the holiness of the place, so God charges Joshua with his special task after informing him of the sacred place where he is. Compare this with the commissioning scenes of the prophets Isaiah (ch. 6) and Ezekiel (ch. 1). In both cases, the demonstration of God's holiness precedes the charge given.

In the New Testament, the same sequence occurs in the announcement to Mary (Lk. 1:26–38) and in the Transfiguration (Mt. 17:1–13; Mk. 9:2–13; Lk. 9:28–36). For the Christian, Christ's salvation, his saving presence, precedes his call to a life of discipleship (Rom. 5 – 6; Eph. 2:8–10; 4:1–16).

6:1. The reference to Jericho's defences as *tightly shut* makes sense in the context of the one earlier text in Joshua which uses

---

battle, in addition to the two human opponents. Joshua's response and the movement of the text on to other matters, without further comment, suggest that this is the case. Thus the warrior does not evade the question, nor is the text non-committal regarding Joshua (Hawk, pp. 21–24).

[1] For this act as one of servanthood towards God, in which the shoes symbolize power, dignity and ownership, see Mitchell, p. 49, who cites H. C. Brichto, 'Taking-off of the Shoe(s) in the Bible', *Proceedings of the Fifth World Congress of Jewish Studies*, I (Jerusalem: World Union of Jewish Studies, 1969), pp. 225–226.

[2] Woudstra, pp. 101–106.

the verbal root 'shut' (Heb. *sgr*). It occurs in Joshua 2:5 and 7, where it is also used of Jericho, shut up so that the *spies* cannot escape. If the mission of these spies had been, at least in part, to seek out those who believed in Israel's God, then the act of shutting the gates in Joshua 2 signified the official rejection of this opportunity. The shut gates in 6:1 serve the same purpose. Jericho has refused to hear the message of Israel, proclaimed in the great deeds of the exodus, in the crossing of the Red Sea and of the Jordan, and in the military victories that had already occurred. The act of shutting forms a physical barrier to Israel's divinely ordained movement to *take possession* of the land. As with the natural barrier of the Jordan, it must be overcome. If Israel is to realize the promises of God, Jericho's gates must be opened.[1] In this sense, the exception of Rahab is symbolically paralleled by her window, the one opening to Jericho which is not 'shut' against the Israelites. The reasons for the note at this point are as follows:

(1) As with the call of Moses, the divine word introduces the mission with an explanation of the problem that the mission will resolve (*cf.* Ex. 3:7).

(2) The focus on how to breach the walls reflects the concern of 6:1 where Jericho is *tightly shut up*. This may symbolize the attitude of the citizens of Jericho, also 'shut up' in their refusal to hear the message of Israel.

(3) Grammatically and stylistically, this note appears as an intrusion in the otherwise smooth flow of the dialogue of 5:13 – 6:5. All the other statements concern Joshua and the divine representative. The stylistic intrusion of 6:1 forms a narrative 'obstacle' that corresponds to the obstacle that Jericho presents to Israel's possession of the land.[2]

2. In Joshua 6:2–5, Joshua receives the divine instructions for the breaching of Jericho's defences. Verse 2 introduces and

---

[1] In this sense, 'go out and come in' may suggest the act of warfare as in 14:11. No one was able to wage war against the inhabitants, nor did they wage war as long as the gates were shut. See A. van der Lingen, '*bw'-ys*' ('to go out and to come in') as a Military Term', *VT*, 42, 1992, pp. 59–66. However, this is not the emphasis of the text, which concerns the defensive aspects of Jericho rather than the offensive ones.

[2] This understanding of 6:1 and seeing the promises that follow as a continuation of the scene of 5:13–15 (parallel to the call of Moses) mean that there is no 'abrupt ending' to 'lend an uncanny and ominous tone to the encounter'. See Hawk, p. 23.

summarizes the instructions. The victory over Jericho is a gift of God. It once again confirms the role of Joshua as divinely chosen leader of Israel. The references to the king and the warriors of Jericho suggest the human defences just as those to the walls describe the material defences. Joshua and the warriors of Israel who will march around Jericho correspond to the king and his defenders. Other than Rahab and her family, these are the only inhabitants of Jericho who are mentioned here and in chapters 1 – 5. However, the king and the warriors of Jericho are not addressed in the discussion of the conquest. The reader already knows that these individuals are no obstacle to Israel. The summary statement of verse 2 contains the perfect form of the verb, *I have delivered.* As was suggested by 2:8–11 and by 5:1, the victory has already been won. The inhabitants of Jericho and of the whole land live in fear of what God will do. Israel's God has already given Jericho over to Joshua's power. It is only necessary for him to claim that victory. Thus the king and the warriors are already at Joshua's mercy. Only the walls remain an obstacle.

3–5. A ceremony will overcome Jericho's walls. Elsewhere in the Ancient Near East among pre-battle rituals there is no comparison to it. The ceremony focuses upon a daily move-ment around Jericho until the climax of the seventh day. Warriors, priests and the ark of the covenant make up the procession. Trumpets are blown and the people raise a shout. Several of these elements point to God's leadership of a military expedition. Firstly, the presence of the warriors of Israel requires that the procession involve military action. The fact that they lead and follow the ark and the priests suggests that they may protect the ark. The note that all are to enter Jericho when the walls collapse describes an additional purpose. The armed guard is also an offensive force waiting to claim Jericho for Israel.

Secondly, *rams' horns* are used to prepare the people to go to war and to form sacred processions.[1] The sacred processions normally involve the ark, which symbolizes the presence of God journeying with his people to protect them.[2] The *loud shout* (Heb. *tᵉrûʿâ*) joins the sound of the trumpets with that of the warriors of Israel. They proclaim victory in war throughout the

[1]Nu. 10:9; 1 Sa. 4:5–6; 2 Sa. 6:15.
[2]In addition to the above references, see Nu. 10:35; Ps. 132.

Old Testament.[1] The *shout* described the noise of the trumpets when Israel began its journey in the wilderness (Nu. 10:2–6) and when the ark entered Jerusalem in procession (2 Sa. 6:15–16).

Thirdly, the *march around the city* uses the same verb (Heb. *nqp*) in Psalm 48:12 and 2 Kings 6:14. In Psalm 48, it describes the pilgrim who journeys around Zion/Jerusalem in order to admire its defences. In 2 Kings 6:14, it describes how the king of Aram surrounded Dothan with his army in order to capture Elisha. The action in Joshua may thus imply (1) a ceremonial inspection of the defences as a recognition of Jericho's refusal to allow admittance, and (2) a dramatic statement of the hostile intentions of the Israelites as their army daily surrounds the fortress.

Fourthly, the seven-day period corresponds to the Feast of Unleavened Bread. No leaven is to be eaten for seven days as a sign of Israel's consecration to the LORD (Ex. 12:14–20). It was during this season that Israel set forth from Egypt and witnessed the defeat of the Egyptian army (Ex. 12 – 14). The second detailed description of a Passover, in Numbers 9, is also followed by a procession from Mount Sinai into the desert (Nu. 10). The combination of the march around Jericho and the Passover of Joshua 5 recalls the first Passover. God will destroy Israel's enemies and consecrate the nation to himself. The battle becomes part of the Passover celebration, a memorial of the first exodus and a victory over enemies in the Promised Land. The capture of Jericho in seven days takes on greater significance than the traditional usage of the number 'seven' in Egyptian campaigns, *i.e.* the attack of a town on the seventh day, or the siege of one that falls on the seventh month.[2]

Thus the ceremony of the ark described in Joshua 6 creates a sacred procession into the Promised Land. Even though the people participate, it is God's divine work that will bring down the defences of the enemy and allow no obstacle to withstand the onward movement of God's people into their divine inheritance. The similarity with the role of the ark in the crossing of the Jordan is apparent. However, unlike the events of chapters 3 – 4, the ceremonial marching around Jericho adds the use of trumpets and the shout of the warriors. In so far

---

[1] See references and discussion in C. L. Seow, *Myth, Drama, and the Politics of David's Dance*, HSM 44 (Atlanta: Scholars Press, 1989), pp. 118–120.

[2] M. Liverani, *Prestige and Interest*, p. 174.

as it is seen as a procession of Israel, it invites comparison with the order of march in the desert as described in Numbers 10:11–28. Although finished with the desert, Israel continues to march in battle formation, but the context is different. The march has an immediate goal, entrance into Jericho. From this perspective, Joshua 6 may be compared with 2 Samuel 6 and the ceremony of bringing the ark into Jerusalem. Joshua 6 forms the intermediate stage in the ongoing history of Israel and of the ark of the covenant. The ark's movement, which began after the giving of the covenant at Mount Sinai, would continue in one continuous procession until it reached its climax in the entrance of the ark into Jerusalem. This goal would not change with the entrance into Canaan, but the fulfilment of the divine promise of Jericho and all the land of Canaan would form part of the great drama in which the divine will would continually guide the people.

Having thus studied the account, it is apparent that ritual processions such as that recorded in the Babylonian New Year's festival, the *akitu*, do not serve as adequate parallels (*ANET*, pp. 331–334). Such items as incantations, ritual confessions of the king, and leading the statue of the deity from temple to temple are not present in Joshua. Indeed, the opposite emphasis, in which God speaks and leads the people, provides a stark contrast. It should also be noted that processions in the Ancient Near East were not confined to religious ritual. A fascinating Hittite text, which describes the daily life of the royal bodyguard, outlines the procession of the king from the palace to where he would hold court and back again.[1] In the procession, details about attendants and guards and their positions are given. Such texts provide a political and military context for the procession in Joshua 6, as well as that in chapters 3 – 4. This context disassociates the biblical accounts from the world of

---

[1] See H. G. Güterbock and T. P. J. van den Hout, *The Hittite Instruction for the Royal Bodyguard* (Chicago: The Oriental Institute of the University of Chicago, 1991). The Hittite kingdom came to an end *c.* 1200 BC. This text would date some time before that. Its possibilities for comparison with the processions of the whole camp of Israel in Nu. 2 and 10 have not yet been addressed. God as Israel's true king and the ark of the covenant as the symbol of his presence would provide parallels to the Hittite king's journey in his cart surrounded by rows of guards and attendants. The use of trumpets in Jos. 6 compares with special 'chanters' who call out 'Welcome!' when the Hittite sovereign enters his palace.

cultic aetiologies and suggests a wider context.

The Christian may find in this journey and ceremony a picture of God's guidance of his people. Abram's journey (Gn. 12:1–3; Heb. 11:8–10), Jesus' travel to Jerusalem (Mt. 16:21), and Paul's movement to Jerusalem and then to Rome (Acts 19:21; 21:7–15; 23:11; 25:11–12; 27:23–24) all describe the pattern by which God leads his people by faith to himself (Heb. 13:7–16).

ii. The capture of Jericho (6:6–25).

6–15, 20. These verses repeat all the phrases in the divine instruction of verses 3–5. On these phrases, see the discussion above. Everything that God told Joshua, he communicated to the priests and warriors. This activity is punctuated by the frequently repeated phrase, *blew the trumpets*. All the activity begins and ends with the sounding of the trumpets. It and the daily marching around Jericho describe a spectacle of sight and sound. The expression 'cross over' (Heb. *ʿiḇrû*) appears three times in verses 7 and 8. Like the crossing of the Jordan, this was also a movement involving a transition of Israel from their position on the edge of the land of Canaan to possession of a part of that land. The army divides between those in front of and those behind the ark (vv. 9 and 13). Such a detail may imply an ordering similar to the procession in the desert (see Nu. 10), with some of the tribes going in front of the ark and some of them travelling behind it (Nu. 10:11–28). The insertion of verse 10 marks a contrast to the constant notices about sounding the horns. On the seventh day, Joshua forbids the people to speak or cry until his signal. Whatever other significance such silence might have had, it illustrates a disciplined force.

16–19, 21. The account breaks with the repetitive patterns of the preceding section. The seventh day has arrived and Joshua orders a different set of procedures for this last day. He introduces the concept of the 'ban' (Heb. *ḥērem*). The 'ban' involves the devotion of something to the LORD God of Israel for his exclusive use.[1] It appears in Deuteronomy 20:16–18 in the instructions to destroy completely all the population centres that are found in the land that God has given to Israel.

---

[1] See the discussion on the ban in the Introduction: 'Theology (a) Holy war and the ban' (pp. 42–46).

The reason given there is so that the inhabitants of the land will not teach Israel their 'detestable practices', those associated with the worship of their gods. Joshua placed all of Jericho under the ban: for the living creatures, this meant their death; for the valuable possessions, it meant their dedication to the house of God; for the rest, it meant destruction through fire. Nothing escaped that had been so dedicated.

Although the 'ban' meant total destruction for Jericho, this does not mean that there could not have been mercy. The 'ban' is only one aspect of God's plans for nations. Elsewhere it is clear that nations do have a choice. Even a people whose wickedness is reaching the point of no return (Gn. 15:16) can repent and find forgiveness and mercy from God (2 Ch. 7:14; Je. 18:5–10; Jon. 4:11).

22–23. The single exception was Rahab and all her family.[1] The reason given is her kind treatment of the spies, hiding them and thereby saving their lives. This is the agreement that Rahab made with the spies. It represents the recognition of their obligation on the part of Joshua and of Israel. Does this mean that the ban was not absolute? No, it means that those who ceased to be Canaanites and 'devoted' themselves to the God of Israel were already 'devoted'. Therefore they escaped the terrible destruction of the ban.

24. The command to devote everything to the ban is repeated several times. Those items that are to be placed in the treasury of the sanctuary are duplicated in lists found in verses 19 and 24. The list is formulaic, a kind of checklist for what belongs to the sanctuary, rather than an inventory of what was purported to have been actually taken at Jericho. Therefore, the text does not indicate what was taken in the defeat but indicates what would have been devoted to the sanctuary if it had been taken. Is the same also true of the list of those who were to be slaughtered in verse 21? Does the text tell the reader anything at all about the inhabitants of Jericho, other than the king, the army, and the family of Rahab?

Verses 16–25 begin with Joshua's command to destroy

---

[1]Although the fortifications of Jericho may have collapsed, it is not unthinkable that a house built at the wall could have survived, *contra* Soggin, p. 83. This is especially true if it formed part of a casemate wall or a belt of outer houses. See comment on Jos. 2:8 (pp. 87–88). In either case, the 'wall' would have collapsed section by section.

Jericho and conclude with the report of the destruction and of the rescue of Rahab. They form an alternating A–B–A–B–A–B structure. 'A' represents the descriptions of the destruction of Jericho, while 'B' represents the descriptions of the salvation of Rahab's family. Eighty-six words in the Hebrew text are devoted to Rahab's rescue, while the destruction of Jericho occupies 102. The account concludes with Rahab. The salvation of Rahab was as important as the destruction of Jericho. Once the walls collapsed, the divinely appointed ceremony had completed its goal; Israel and the ark might enter Jericho; the victory had been won. The absence of any mention of resistance agrees with 5:1, that the mighty deeds of God had already defeated Jericho. Israel need only follow the divine guidance to occupy it.[1]

25. The importance of Rahab's role and that of her family is explained in the last half of verse 25. The Hebrew text indicates firstly that she lives among Israel until the present, *i.e.* until the time of writing this text. She is not distinguished from, but is part of, Israel. She has ceased to be a Canaanite or non-Israelite and has now become an Israelite.[2] The reason for this is then stated for the second time, *because she hid the men Joshua had sent as spies to Jericho*. In the story of Rahab, this verb 'hide' (Heb. *ḥbʾ*) occurs only once, when Rahab explains how the spies should hide themselves in the mountains after they leave Jericho (2:16). Here, however, it describes her earlier actions in keeping the men away from the royal agents. The text stresses that Rahab rejected her past associations with the Canaanites and transferred her loyalty to Israel. By so doing, it demonstrates how Israel could receive others with kindness.[3]

For the Christian, the story of Rahab is the story of the

---

[1]For a similar conquest by the Hittite king, see Introduction: Antiquity (pp. 26–27).

[2]Hawk, p. 74, suggests that Rahab's initial place 'outside the camp' (v. 23) is an example of the awkward situation of allowing a Canaanite to live, while her presence in the midst of Israel (v. 25) is a statement as to how she seduces Israel. It seems that wherever the text puts Rahab she will be judged by those who condemn her rescue. Nor is it clear that her place outside the camp is only to be understood as a statement of her cultic impurity in response to Dt. 23:3, 10–15, as Butler, p. 71; Fritz, p. 73; Woudstra, p. 115. Verse 23 notes her initial position as unattached to any tribe of Israel whereas v. 25 affirms her place in Israel. Neither text prejudices her association with God's people, for which see Boling and Wright, p. 209.

[3]Butler, p. 71.

shepherd's search for the one lost sheep (Mt. 18:12–14; Lk. 15:4–7). It is the concern of Jesus for the despised of the world (Mt. 15:21–28; Jn. 8:1–11). It is the transformation of values to which Christianity calls disciples. Those rejected by the world are precious to God (1 Cor. 1:18–31; Jas. 2:5).

iii. **The consequences of Jericho for Joshua (6:26–27).** The curse that Joshua places upon anyone who would attempt to rebuild its foundations and gates represents the wish for the remains of the site to be left undisturbed. Thus it resembles Joshua's curse of the Gibeonites in 9:23. They also were to remain in their present state, always to be servants of Israel.

Comparison with curses in Phoenician inscriptions reveals interesting parallels. Ahiram and Eshmunezer were Phoenician kings. On their sarcophagi, they left inscriptions that cursed anyone who would disturb them. The curse warned of the loss of the offender's offspring.[1] In this sense, the rest of Jericho should not be disturbed. But this is not because of any dead who lie buried there. Rather, it emphasizes the totality of divine judgment against Jericho. Devoted to God by complete destruction, the city was to remain that way for ever, a symbol of the power of Israel's God to all who would see it. In 1 Kings 16:34, the words of the curse come true for Hiel of Bethel who loses his sons when he rebuilds Jericho in the ninth century. Although Deuteronomy 20:16–18 attests a theological rationale for the *ḥērem* in its concern to avoid Israelite involvement with the practices of worshipping the deities of the Canaanites, this is not explicit in Joshua. Joshua's intention that Jericho should remain uninhabited parallels Deuteronomy 13:16 (Heb. 17). In that text, any population centre where the citizenry counsels worship of other gods is to be destroyed and never inhabited again. In the light of Deuteronomy 13 and 20, the destruction of Jericho must be understood as punishment upon the people for their refusal to worship the God of Israel.

27. As with the previous notes regarding the reaction of the Canaanites, the reader learns how knowledge of Joshua and his deeds was made known throughout Canaan. No note is made of the reaction of the Canaanites, but this is not as important as the knowledge of Joshua's accomplishments. God's presence with Joshua is the reason for his fame, for without that presence

---

[1] *KAI*, nos. 1 and 14.

none of the miracles of chapters 3 – 6 could have taken place. In this note, it is Joshua who is emphasized rather than the LORD, in contrast to 2:8–11 and 5:1. Why is this? Perhaps it has to do with the role of military leader that Joshua began to play at Jericho. With the capture of Jericho, Joshua's name would be on everyone's lips. He marched with the army; he decided who lived and who died; and he pronounced the curse on Jericho, presumably in a public context. From a political standpoint, Joshua's fame would also be enhanced by this, his first military victory in Canaan. Of course, he had fought before, as early as the battle with the Amalekites in Exodus 17:10–14. In the case of Jericho, however, Joshua was the leader, not Moses. The outcome of a leader's first 'campaign' was considered important in the Ancient Near East. Thus a Hittite king writes to newly enthroned Assyrian rulers with advice such as:

> On whatever campaign he goes for the first time, where he is three or four times superior, or which is some overpowered place, let him go for the first time against such a place.[1]

The success of the first battle was considered essential in establishing leadership. Such a victory on the part of Joshua would secure him respect, not only among the Israelites (who already had ample evidence) but also among the Canaanites. If, as seems likely, this text was designed to present the case for Joshua's leadership, it would make an effective argument in the context of the rulers of Canaan.

From a literary perspective, the account of the capture of Jericho concludes the ceremonies which Israel undergoes in preparation for possessing the land. It also ties up the loose ends of chapter 2 and the incident regarding Rahab. The narrative prepares the reader for the following chapters of 'the conquest narrative', although its special concern is to prepare for chapter 7 and the failure of the whole nation to carry out the divine instructions. From a political perspective, Israel comes to see Joshua as a successful military leader who is led by God to great victories. The march around Jericho served as a 'propaganda device' to the citizens, warning them of the coming destruction for their failure to recognize Israel's God. In the same way, the fall and capture of Jericho served warning

---

[1] See M. Liverani, *Prestige and Interest*, p. 133 and notes there. The text quoted is from *Keilschrifturkunden aus Boghazkoy*, XXIII, no. 103, Rs 12–18.

on the remaining inhabitants of Canaan that this people and its God were serious about their occupation of the land.

The context of the ceremonial marching around Jericho and of its fall during the Feast of Unleavened Bread provided a present meaning for a feast that remembered God's deliverance from another foreign power. For the Christian, the fall of Jericho represents an example of the power of faith in God. Without this faith, nothing can happen. With this faith, however, and the faithful obedience that it brings about, the Christian can overcome any obstacle in life, no matter how great (*cf.* Heb. 11:30).

Additional Note: The archaeology of Jericho

The Jericho of Joshua is identified with Tell es-Sultân, 10 miles north of the Dead Sea in the Jordan Valley, west of the Jordan River. Occupation started in the ninth millennium BC. Excavation of this site began with the work of Sellin and Watzinger (1907–1913), John Garstang in the 1930s, and then Kathleen Kenyon.[1] The walls identified by Garstang as belonging to the fourteenth century BC, and therefore possibly to the events of Joshua 6, were redated by Kenyon to a period several centuries earlier. The results of Kenyon's excavations left little in the way of remains that could be identified with the period of Joshua's entrance into the land, whether to the fourteenth century or to the thirteenth century BC. Based on the pottery evidence, the site was destroyed *c.* 1550 BC. It was not reoccupied in a substantial manner before the Iron Age, possibly not before the first millennium BC. The only remains from the Late Bronze Age (1550–1200 BC) were three tombs with pottery dating from the fifteenth until the thirteenth centuries BC and traces of three structures on the tell itself. The latter group includes the ruins of a house floor with an oven, dated to the end of the fourteenth century on the basis of a juglet. Evidence of significant erosion on the tell makes it difficult to determine how much Late Bronze occupation there was at the site. The absence of fortifications is not surprising in the archaeological context, since most Canaanite settlements do not reveal evidence of Late Bronze Age walls, and, where they do, the

[1] For bibliography and summary, see T. A. Holland and E. Netzer, 'Jericho' in *ABD*, III, pp. 723–740.

walls usually do not circle the tell. Massive wall and defence construction in the eighteenth century (Middle Bronze Age) at Jericho and other sites in Canaan leaves open the question whether these continued to be used by the Late Bronze occupants.[1] Another possibility is that these towns were protected by outer walls adjoining belts of houses.[2] This could be possible in the light of Rahab's house which is described as built against the wall. Nevertheless, the evidence for a small settlement remains a difficulty for those who envisage the conquest of a large, well-fortified city at Jericho. The following should be noted:

(1) The biblical text does not describe Jericho as a major city, unlike a site such as Gibeon (Jos. 10:2) or Hazor (11:10).

(2) The 'king' (Heb. *melek*) of Jericho may have been the local leader. The term is used to describe leaders of towns and villages throughout the book of Joshua. It appears in fourteenth-century Amarna letters from Canaan (*ma-lik*) where it is paralleled with the term for a commissioner appointed by the Pharaoh to oversee a region or town.[3] In itself it says nothing about the size of the 'city'.

(3) The concern of the text to emphasize the victory of Joshua and Israel under God's direction may have led readers to confuse the stress upon the miraculous victory that God brought about with an emphasis upon the size of the obstacle to that victory.[4]

---

[1] See A. Mazar, *Archaeology of the Land of the Bible 10,000–586 BCE* (Garden City, NY: Doubleday, 1990), p. 331.

[2] I. Finkelstein and D. Ussishkin, 'Back to Megiddo', *BAR*, 20/1, January/February 1994, p. 32, suggest these two explanations for the city of Megiddo. Like Hazor, Shechem and Lachish, no fortification walls have been found from this period. Yet the Egyptian army claims to have laid siege to the city for seven months.

[3] The text is El Amarna letter 131, line 21. *CAD*, 10, 'M' part I, pp. 162–163, translates the term as 'counselor, advisor'.

[4] Boling and Wright, pp. 214–215, refer to the reference to Jericho's poor water in 2 Ki. 2:19 and relate the absence of settlement and the curse of Jericho to the disease schistosomiasis, found in contaminated water and causing depression and reduced fertility. They suggest that the march around Jericho was a protective ritual and that the collapse of the walls was part of a period of seismic activity also associated with the blockage of the Jordan River. However, evidence of the disease itself has not been found (despite the presence of a possible host species of snail), so this remains speculative. Whether seismic activity was involved or not, the text notes that the walls collapsed at a specific time and place at the end of Israel's ceremonies.

Additional Note: The date of the entrance into Canaan

The issues surrounding this question, and the corresponding question of the date of the exodus, are many. It is not possible to summarize all the data in this limited space. Some scholars question the existence of either an exodus from Egypt or an entrance into the land of Canaan. Among those who do ascribe some historical worth to the biblical text, two major interpretations prevail, the early date and the late date. Those who favour the early date accept a literal interpretation of 1 Kings 6:1 and count back 480 years from the building of Solomon's temple to arrive at 1447 BC as a date for the exodus. The Bible would then place the entrance into Canaan a generation later, *c.* 1400 BC. Exponents of the late date understand 1 Kings 6:1 in a symbolic sense, where the number reflects twelve generations of forty years each, but they accept that each generation might have been less than forty years in reality. This symbolic sense may occur in Genesis 15:13 and 16. In the former, 430 years are given for a period of time. In verse 16, this is described as four generations. (See also Ex. 6:16–27.)

The symbolic interpretation allows for a later date for the time of the entrance into Canaan. The one clear reference to Israel in the second millennium BC is that of the Merneptah stele, an account of an Egyptian Pharaoh's campaign into Canaan.[1] The campaign can be dated *c.* 1207 BC. Since Israel is mentioned among the enemies whom Pharaoh Merneptah defeated, Israel had to be in the land by the end of the thirteenth century BC.

Alternatively, the hypothesis of two or more entrances into the land at different times has been proposed.[2] The book of Joshua, however, focuses on a single entrance from the east. Although data from Egypt, the Sinai and the Negev may be taken into consideration in assessing the best option for the date of the exodus, the date of the entrance into Canaan concerns the narrative of Joshua. The data from both Transjordan and from Canaan itself favour a thirteenth-century entrance.

In the Transjordan, the earlier survey of Nelson Glueck found no evidence of Late Bronze Age settlement in the regions of Ammon and Moab. However, recent surveys allow for an earlier occupation. Tell Hesban is not the Hesban of the wilderness

---

[1] *ANET*, p. 378.
[2] For example, Aharoni, *Land*, pp. 209–215.

wanderings, nor is Tell Dhibân to be identified with biblical Dibon if the Israelites encountered these sites as fortified cities at any time before the tenth century BC. Sites did exist in the region of Amman and farther north in the Late Bronze Age. There is evidence for destruction levels of sites in Gilead in the thirteenth century, but very little evidence for occupation is to be found at present in Moab and Edom.[1] With respect to the land west of the Jordan River, the following points are relevant:

(1) Jericho and Ai remain problems for any of these periods, due to the lack of significant settlement evidence. (See, however, notes on the archaeology of these sites, pp. 137–138, 157–159.)

(2) Fourteenth-century BC Amarna letters, written from towns and villages in Canaan to the Pharaoh, mention certain Habiru/Apiru as groups of discontents without land who harrass the 'loyal' city-state leaders. These are not identical to the Hebrews. Instead, the term 'Habiru', which is used throughout the Ancient Near East in the second millennium, seems to describe a social group of outcasts in the Amarna letters, although even this is difficult, since the city-state leaders call one another Habiru. In other words, anyone they dislike is a Habiru.[2] In any case, their activities as described in the Amarna letters do not agree with the accounts of Joshua, nor do the Amarna letters mention any of the events or peoples recorded in the books of Joshua or Judges.

(3) There is no archaeological evidence of Israel's presence other than the possible identification of these peoples with some of the many new village settlements which appear in the hill country of Palestine in the twelfth century. Earlier attempts to identify distinctive Isreaelite pottery (collared-rim jar), technology (plastered lime cisterns and terraces), or architecture (four-roomed houses) have now been discredited, as all of these appear in and outside of Palestinian hill country sites before the period of Israel's appearance in the land.[3]

---

[1]W. G. Dever, 'Israel, History of (Archaeology and the 'Conquest')' in *ABD*, III, pp. 547–548.

[2]For a review of the evidence, see O. Loretz, *Habiru-Hebräer*, BZAW 160 (Berlin: Walter de Gruyter, 1984). For a discussion of the sociological and ideological aspects of the Amarna usage, see N. P. Lemche, 'Habiru, Hapiru' in *ABD*, III, p. 8; M. Liverani, 'Farsi Habiru', *Vicino Oriente*, 2, 1979, pp. 65–77.

[3]A summary of the older interpretation and a critique, as well as the most important collection of data on the settlement evidence, is found in I. Finkelstein, *The Archaeology of the Israelite Settlement* (Jerusalem: IES, 1988).

(4) The absence of destruction layers at most of the sites identified as conquered by Joshua has created problems for both dates. Only Jericho and Hazor, however, are described as set on fire and burnt (*cf.* Jos. 11:13 and comment there, p. 215). Therefore, it is not clear that the 'destruction' of a town was understood as physical destruction in a manner that would leave archaeological evidence.

(5) Hazor was destroyed in the thirteenth century and this fits the late date for the conquest. (See the note on Hazor, pp. 212–214.)

(6) Egypt had power over Canaan in the fourteenth and thirteenth centuries BC. This may have peaked around 1200 BC, when it extended to include southern Canaan, the coastal plain, the Jezreel Valley, and across the Jordan Valley to Tell es-Sa'idiyeh and Tell Deir'Alla.[1] According to the Amarna texts, however, Egypt's contact with the hill country was strongest in the earlier period. Therefore, absence of any mention of Egypt in Joshua or of the events of the book in the Egyptian records is difficult to explain if these events took place *c.* 1400 BC, whereas the Merneptah stele and possibly a contemporary relief in Egypt attest to the presence of Israel *c.* 1200 BC.[2] The absence of any mention of this event in the book of Joshua may be due to temporal or thematic selectivity; *i.e.* the battle with Egypt occurred at a time which was earlier or later than the events which are remembered in Joshua, or the battle was a defeat for Israel and therefore not of interest in a book that emphasizes the successful occupation of the land. Egypt's hold on every part of Canaan weakened considerably by the mid-twelfth century.

(7) The transition from the Late Bronze Age to the Iron Age

[1] For Egypt in Canaan, see J. M. Weinstein, 'The Egyptian Empire in Palestine: a Reassessment', *BASOR*, 241, 1981, pp. 1–28. For additional archaeological evidence of the southern and Transjordan Egyptian presence, see C. J. Bergoffen, 'Overland Trade in Northern Sinai: The Evidence of the Late Cypriot Pottery', *BASOR*, 284, 1991, pp. 59–76; O. Negbi, 'Were There Sea Peoples in the Central Jordan Valley at the Transition from the Bronze Age to the Iron Age?', *Tel Aviv*, 18, 1991, pp. 205–243.

[2] F. Yurco, 'Merneptah's Canaanite Campaign', *Journal of the American Research Center in Egypt*, 14, 1980, pp. 187–213; *idem*, '3,200-Year-Old Picture of Israelites Found in Egypt', *BAR*, 16/5, 1990, pp. 21–38; *idem*, 'Yurco's Response', *BAR*, 17/6, 1991, p. 61; L. E. Stager, 'Merenptah, Israel and Sea Peoples: New Light on an Old Relief', *EI*, 18, 1985, pp. 56*–64*; *idem*, 'When Canaanites and Philistines Ruled Ashkelon', *BAR*, 17/2, 1991, pp. 24–37, 40–43.

I (1200 BC) was a period of much migration and movement among peoples throughout the Levant. For example, at this period the migrations of the 'Sea Peoples', and among them the Philistines, are recorded in Egyptian records. This is also the time when the Arameans seem to have settled and become prominent around Damascus. The entrance into Canaan by Israel would fit well in the context of this unsettled world.

Two scholars have argued against the late date for the entrance into Canaan. John J. Bimson challenges the dating of the pottery and seeks to show evidence that the period of the end of the Middle Bronze Age and the destruction layers found in Palestine from that period should be redated from 1550 BC to *c.* 1450 BC.[1] In other words, he would lower the end of the Middle Bronze Age by 100 years. Reviewers who are pottery experts have not agreed.[2] Bimson argues that the Merneptah stele describes Israel a generation or more before the beginning of the settlement process in the hill country.[3] Thus Israel existed as a non-settled people in Palestine before they settled down, *i.e.* their settlement did not create the people of Israel, and so the date for their appearance in the land should be pushed back well before the beginning of the new settlement pattern in the hill country, before the twelfth century BC. However, Zertal's survey of Manasseh leads him to contend that the settlement 'explosion' in the hill country begins in the mid-thirteenth century in eastern Manasseh.[4] Thus settlement was already going on before Merneptah's stele. Bryant G. Wood argues for the presence of diagnostically reliable Late Bronze Age pottery at Jericho in levels other than those identified by Kenyon.[5] He has been challenged by Piotr Bienkowski.[6]

---

[1] J. J. Bimson, *Redating the Exodus and Conquest, JSOT* Supplement 5 (Sheffield: Sheffield Academic Press, 1978).

[2] For example, the review by A. F. Rainey, *IEJ*, 30, 1980, pp. 250–251.

[3] J. J. Bimson, 'Merneptah's Israel and Recent Theories of Israelite Origins', *JSOT*, 49, 1991, pp. 3–29.

[4] A. Zertal, 'Israel Enters Canaan: Following the Pottery Trail', *BAR*, 17/5, 1991, pp. 28–47.

[5] B. G. Wood, *The Sociology of Pottery in Ancient Palestine* (Sheffield: Sheffield Academic Press, 1989); *idem*, 'Did the Israelites Conquer Jericho?', *BAR*, 16/2, 1990, pp. 44–58; *idem*, 'Dating Jericho's Destruction: Bienkowski Wrong on All Counts', *BAR*, 16/5, 1990, pp. 45, 47–49, 68–69.

[6] P. Bienkowski, *Jericho in the Late Bronze Age* (Warminster, Aris and Phillips, 1986); 'Jericho Was Destroyed in the Middle Bronze Age, Not the Late Bronze Age', *BAR*, 16/5, 1990, pp. 45–46, 69.

Bienkowski's own work with the pottery excavated at Jericho led him to conclude that Kathleen Kenyon was right and that Jericho was destroyed *c.* 1550 BC and not rebuilt to any large extent until the first millennium. He charges Wood with incorrectly reading the pottery, *e.g.* as designating Late Bronze Age II local ware as Late Bronze Age I Cypriot bichrome ware. If the views of either Bimson or Wood are accepted, the entire question of the date of the entrance into Canaan will need to be re-evaluated.

f. The second assault, part 1: the defeat at Ai and its consequences (7:1–26)

There are three parts to the defeat: the sin of Achan, the anger of God, and the judgment against Israel. This is followed by the identification of the cause and the resolution in the death of the perpetrator. The chapter demonstrates the problem of sin in Israel's mission. It follows the account of Jericho because the sin occurred in the context of the capture of that town. It occupies so much space because the first breach of Israel's purity as a holy nation before God brings the harshest judgment and punishment. This also serves as a warning against yielding to future temptations.

i. The defeat at Ai (7:1–5). This part also divides into three sections: the mission and report of the spies, the attack and defeat of Israel, and the reaction of the people.

1. The first phrase summarizes what follows, *But the Israelites acted unfaithfully in regard to the devoted things.* The verbal root for *acted unfaithfully* (Heb. *m'l*) is used here.[1] As a noun it always describes unfaithfulness towards God. The same three Hebrew letters occur in the preceding verse in the phrase *his fame spread throughout the land.* There as well, Hebrew *m,* ', and *l* appear in the same sequence. There is an intentional contrast. Although Joshua's fame spread because of Jericho, Israel's unfaithfulness provoked God's anger. Although only one person acted in this unfaithful manner, all Israel is held liable. Thus all Israel suffers

---

[1] It appears with its accusative object, spelled with the same letters. This is called a cognate accusative. Boling and Wright, p. 220, comment on 'the construction of verb + cognate accusative, a device that is especially characteristic of popular narrative'.

punishment for the sin of one person.

This corporate punishment is suggested by the perpetrator's genealogy. No other figure has been introduced in the book of Joshua with such detail about his family background. Four 'generations' are listed. Achan's sin is part of the actions of the 'sons of Israel' who have acted unfaithfully. The specifics prepare the reader for the identification of Achan which proceeds in the opposite direction (from the general ancestor, Judah, to Achan) in verses 16–18.[1] The father of Achan is Carmi, a name whose root means 'vineyard'.[2] The name of the next figure in the line is Zabdi in the MT of Joshua 7. The root *zbd*, 'to give a gift', appears in other Hebrew names.[3] Zabdi is called Zimri in 1 Chronicles 2:6. Zabdi's father is Zerah, a name meaning 'brightness, sunrise'. A Zerah also appears as the son of Judah in Genesis 38:30. The identification of Achan concludes with a note of his sin. The translation of the NIV, *took some of them*, obscures the fact that Achan took from the *ban* (*ḥērem*), *i.e.* from those items of Jericho that were devoted to God.

2. Joshua prepares for the next move, against a place named Ai. The text mentions three new place names, Ai, Beth Aven, and Bethel. Ai should be identified with et-Tell, Beth Aven with Tell Maryam, and Bethel with the remains at the Palestinian town of Beitin.[4] These identifications agree with the geographical and topographical descriptions of the sites in the Bible and, in the case of Tell Maryam and Beitin, with the archaeological

---

[1] The name 'Achan' appears with an 'r' rather than an 'n' at the end of his name (as 'Achar') in the LXX of Jos. 7 and in the MT and LXX of 1 Ch. 2:7. The reason for this difference is the attraction of the name to the Valley of Achor, which similarity the Bible notes in Jos. 7:26 and in 1 Ch. 2:7. There is a Hebrew root for the name with the final 'r', meaning 'disaster, misfortune'. For more on this name, and attestations elsewhere, see R. S. Hess, 'Achan and Achor: Names and Wordplay in Joshua 7', *HAR*, 14, 1994, pp. 89–98.

[2] This same root appears in the name of a thirteenth-century BC inhabitant of Ugarit, *kar-mu-nu*. See D. Sivan, *Grammatical Analysis and Glossary of the Northwest Semitic Vocables in Akkadian Texts of the 15th–13th CBC* from Canaan and Syria (Neukirchen-Vluyn: Neukirchener, 1984), p. 236.

[3] Zabdi is the name of the son of Shimei the Benjaminite (1 Ch. 8:19), an official in David's day (1 Ch. 27:27) and a Levite (Ne. 11:17). For the role of wordplay here, see R. S. Hess, 'Achan and Achor: Names and Wordplay in Joshua 7'.

[4] For Ai, see J. A. Callaway, 'Ai' in *ABD*, I, pp. 125–130. For Beth Aven, see Z. Kallai, 'Notes on the Topography of Benjamin', *IEJ*, 6, 1956, pp. 180–183. For Bethel, see A. F. Rainey, 'Bethel is Still Beitin', *WTJ*, 33, 1971, pp. 175–178.

remains that date from this period. For the difficulty of the archaeology at Ai, see the Additional Note (pp. 157–159). Ai is one mile east-south-east of Bethel. Beth Aven is 3.3 miles south of Ai.

Why did Joshua choose Ai? Assuming that Joshua sought a strategic position, it would not be to his advantage to remain in the Jordan Valley. The hill country would provide a secure base that could not be reached by Egyptian and Canaanite chariotry. The region between Shiloh and Jerusalem presented the most direct route into the highlands that was not dominated by a Canaanite stronghold. D. Dorsey has identified three main roads that led from Jericho to the hill country in the Iron Age.[1] The southern road led to Jerusalem, a site that Joshua would naturally avoid until he had an adequate base from which to launch an attack. The northern road led to biblical Ophrah and the middle road to Bethel via Ai. The selection of the particular road that ran past Ai may have been made due to the main north-south route that ran through Bethel. The road to Bethel provided easier access to the area that would become Benjamin, lying between Jerusalem and Bethel. This region was a strategic centre for control of the hill country to the north and to the south. It is the region that the Philistines would seek to control, where Saul would build his capital, and which the southern kingdom would retain despite the secession of the north. This route is actually two routes that, beginning from Jericho, run parallel to one another as they move westward into the hill country. The northern branch passes through et-Tell.

The instructions given to the men, *Go up and spy out* (Heb. *'ªlû wᵉraggᵉlû*), are different from those given to the two who went to Jericho in 2:1, *Go, look* (Heb. *lᵉkû rᵉ'û*). The response of the spies and their report suggests that they perceived their mission differently. If the mission of the first group had been to report on the condition of the inhabitants and to discover supporters, that of the second seems to centre around the strength of the opposition and whether it can be overcome. The purpose of the mission to Ai resembles the instructions that Moses gave to the original group of spies (Nu. 13:17–20).

[1]D. A. Dorsey, *The Roads and Highways of Ancient Israel* (Baltimore: Johns Hopkins University Press, 1991), pp. 201–206. See also A. Mazar, D. Amit, and Z. Ilan, 'The "Border Road" between Michmash and Jericho and Excavations at Horvat Shilhah', *Eretz Israel*, 17, 1984, pp. 236–250, Hebrew.

Perhaps this similarity also prefigures the defeat.[1]

3. The response of the spies expresses a military strategy based upon human judgment. Unlike the report of the spies sent to Jericho (Jos. 2:24), but resembling the majority report of Moses' spies (Nu. 13:27–33), there is no mention of the divine promises but only an evaluation of the likelihood of military success on the basis of the perceived strength of the enemy. The *two or three thousand* (Heb. *'ªlāpîm*), whom the spies recommend should be understood as two or three companies (Heb. *'ªlāpîm*) of troops, as in Jos. 22:24; Jdg. 6:15; 1 Sa. 10:19–21; *etc.*[2] The explanation of the spies, that they do not wish to *weary* the other Israelites, seems odd in the light of the possession of Jericho. That victory did not weary the army. They had only to enter the town as it literally fell into their hands. This shows the folly of their plans made apart from God, and of their lack of faith.[3] If those in Numbers lacked faith because they did not believe they were strong enough, these lack faith because they believe that Israel is too strong to worry about such a small fortress. The form of the verbal root 'to weary' (Heb. *yg'*) ocurs only in Ecclesiastes 10:15, where its description of the fool who does not know the way to town could serve as a commentary on this passage in Joshua.

4–5. The description of the battle is unique among the military campaigns found in the first twelve chapters of Joshua. It alone makes no mention of Joshua's leadership. Rather than attempting to exonerate Joshua, it narrates an irregular campaign on the part of Israel. A decision reached apart from explicit divine directions and carried out without the explicit leadership of Joshua has all the ingredients of a defeat. When the defeat does come, the description provides details of the number of deaths as well as the extent to which the attack became a humiliating rout. The significance of the number *thirty-six* is not clear. Three companies went to the battle. The

---

[1]Boling and Wright, p. 221, note that Joshua's commissioning (Nu. 27:21) required that he consult the Urim before going to battle. The absence of consultation with God leads to the defeat that follows.

[2]See the discussion of the large numbers in the census of Numbers; G. E. Mendenhall, 'The Census of Numbers 1 and 26', *JBL*, 77, 1958, pp. 52–66; G. J. Wenham, *Numbers. An Introduction and Commentary* (Leicester and Downers Grove: IVP, 1981), pp. 62–64. However, the argument for Joshua 7 does not require this interpretation of the census figures in the book of Numbers.

[3]Butler, p. 79.

number could signify a significant loss from each of the three companies, *i.e.* twelve from each. If so, it may also foreshadow the twelve thousand citizens of Ai, all of whom would fall (8:25). The *Shebarim* or *stone quarries* to which the attackers were chased suggests a retreat along the road by which the attackers came, about three and a half miles east-south-east to the steep slopes of the Wadi el-Makkuk.[1] The repetition of the *men of Ai* and of the verb *killed* emphasizes the complete victory of the enemy. This repetition appears in the Hebrew text but not in the NIV. The result, that *the heart of the people melted* recalls the same expression in 2:11 and 5:1. There it applies to the Canaanites; here it applies to the Israelites. The addition *and became like water* enhances the image beyond that experienced by the Canaanites. In five short verses the narrator has overturned the story of unbroken success that occupied the previous six chapters.

For the Christian, the defeat at Ai describes the dangerous and destructive effects of sin. It challenges false assumptions about easy victories in struggles against sin and temptation. Like the struggle against addiction, victories over sin require discipline and reliance upon God's grace (Rom. 7:14–25). The sin of Achan affected the whole community as they lost the first battle with Ai and also their reputation as invincible. Like the sin of Ananias and Sapphira in the young church (Acts 5:1–11), Achan's rebellion had to be identified and dealt with decisively before the people of God suffered further defeat and death.

ii. Israel's humiliation (7:6–9). Joshua and the elders of Israel respond to the defeat with repentance. The chief concern is the honour of God.

6. The tearing of clothes, lying upon the ground, and the sprinkling of dust upon the head express grief that is often associated with mourning.[2] The ark of the covenant appears for the first time in the chapter. As a symbol of God's presence and of Israel's past victories, its absence in the first five verses demonstrated the lack of divine support and suggested the ensuing disaster.[3]

---

[1] B. P. Irwin, 'Ai' in *ABD*, V, pp. 1171–1172.

[2] R. de Vaux, *Ancient Israel: Its Life and Institutions* (Darton, Longman and Todd, 1961), p. 59. See Jb. 1:20, 2:12–13.

[3] For comparisons with the Benjaminite civil war of Jdg. 20, see Boling and Wright, pp. 223–224.

The *elders of Israel* are mentioned here for the first time in Joshua.[1] As in other tribal societies, Israelite elders were involved in political and military policy-making and leadership and in representing the whole tribe in dealings with other states. They also attended treaty or covenant ceremonies.[2]

7. The expression *Ah!* (Heb. *'ᵃhâ*) occurs fourteen times elsewhere in the Old Testament, always as part of a cry or complaint, and usually by a prophet. Of special interest are the instances in Jeremiah 4:10 and Ezekiel 11:13. As with Joshua, the prophets cry to the LORD fearful that the people of God will perish. The complaint that follows has three elements: (1) its repeated usage of the root 'to cross over' (Heb. *'br*) as part of a wish to reverse the process; (2) its similarity to complaints by the Israelites in the wilderness wanderings; and (3) its concluding statement that resembles Moses' arguments with God on behalf of the Israelites. The first point emphasizes the context of the complaint. Stylistically, it relates the complaint to all the preceding events in the book of Joshua, as they all contain the verbal root 'to cross over'. Politically, it implies a challenge by Joshua to the wisdom of his own leadership. Theologically, it questions the wisdom of God's guidance.

Joshua's complaint resembles Numbers 14:2–4 and 20:3–5. In both cases there is a problem that the Israelites find vexing. They complain in a similar fashion, using the particle 'if only' (Heb. *lû*) and following it with a wish for death. The Numbers 14 passage occurs immediately after the report of the spies. In Joshua 7, the complaint also follows the report of the spies. However, the wish is not for death, but to remain east of the Jordan. In all three examples, God's guidance is also questioned. The major difference with Joshua 7 is that the question of divine direction precedes the complaint, *If only . . .*

8. Nevertheless, Joshua challenges God's wisdom. The reader might expect a similar reaction of divine anger and punishment as in the complaint passages in Numbers. What prevents this is the appeal that follows. This transforms the complaint from a self-serving whine, such as occurred in Numbers, to a concern for the honour of God. In his covenant, God had

---

[1] They also occur in 8:10, 33; 23:2; 24:1, 31.
[2] H. Reviv, *The Elders in Ancient Israel. A Study of a Biblical Institution* (Jerusalem: Magnes, 1989), pp. 36–39, 183–186. Reviv compares the biblical accounts with the role of the tribal elders mentioned in the eighteenth-century BC Mari texts.

promised that Israel's enemies would turn the back of their
necks (Heb. *'ōrep*) and flee (Ex. 23:27). Now the enemy had
made Israel turn the back of its neck (*'ōrep*) and flee.

9. Joshua expressed bewilderment at what appeared to be
God's breach of the covenant. Such an ignominious defeat
would lead to the annihilation of Israel as other Canaanites
took advantage of the humiliation. To emphasize the significance of this, Joshua uses a wordplay based on the word for *name*
(Heb. *šēm*), here meaning 'reputation'. The elimination of
Israel's *name* (*šēm*) would challenge the *name* (*šēm*) of Israel's
God. This recalls Moses' appeal to the LORD's reputation after
he threatens to destroy Israel for its refusal to enter the land
(Nu. 14:13–19). Here is a further difference between Numbers
13 – 14 and Joshua 7. In the former, Israel angered God when
the nation refused to obey and enter the land. In Joshua 7, both
Joshua and Israel thought they were obeying God. The
problem was not wilful disobedience but ignorance of a hidden
transgression. For these reasons, God did not seek to destroy
the nation, but to warn it of the problem that rendered it
impotent.

iii. The identification of the transgression (7:10–21). Three
persons act in this section: God explains and directs; Joshua
obeys and searches; and Achan confesses. This re-establishes
the normal order of events in the book of Joshua, one that was
missing in the failed assault on Ai. The divine explanation and
direction are introduced by the command to Joshua to *Stand
up!* The first *Stand up!* (Heb. *qum*) introduces the explanation
of the dire situation in which Israel finds itself.[1] The second
'Stand up!' (v. 13; NIV translates *Go!*) explains what Israel must
do to resolve this situation.

10. God commands Joshua to get on his feet.[2] Prayer and
mourning remain unacceptable until the impediment is
removed. The command to Joshua to *Stand up!* contrasts with
Israel's inability to *stand* against its enemies (v. 12).

11–12. Two phrases frame the catalogue of Israel's sins. The
first, the transgression of the covenant, denies any guilt on the

[1] Boling and Wright, p. 224, compare the use of this same command in Jos.
1:2. 'The first introduces Joshua as the famous military leader, and the second
introduces Joshua as "judge".'
[2] Butler, p. 80, finds the beginning of a lawsuit between God and Joshua.

part of God. The verb *violated* has the same root as that for *cross* (*'br*) in Joshua 6:7 and thus magnifies the significance of the sin. Israel could not cross against any more enemies (Jos. 6:7) because they had crossed against God's covenant. The next statement, *they have taken some of the devoted things*, specifies the covenant violation. God owned the *devoted things* (*ḥērem*) in the capture of Jericho (Jos. 6:18–19, 24). To take God's property is theft. The denial of the theft is deceit. Having detailed Israel's sins as the reason for their defeat, the text now explains a chilling fact: as long as Israel possesses the devoted things, God will consider them as devoted things. He will not win victories for them. Instead, he will guarantee their defeat and destruction. Either Israel must destroy the devoted things that it possesses or it will be destroyed as devoted things.

13. The second 'Stand up' (NIV *Go*) moves from a statement about the gravity of the situation to explain how Israel can destroy its devoted things. Firstly, all the people must consecrate themselves. Secondly, they must identify who possesses the devoted things. Thirdly, the one who possesses them must be destroyed. The command for Israel to consecrate itself repeats the warning that Israel will face defeat until the devoted things are removed. No detail is given as to what it means for Israel to consecrate itself, but Leviticus 17 – 26 describes what it means to be a holy people. In the context of the book of Joshua and the 'warfare' terminology of the following verses, consecration for battle might be implied. In that case, the observation by David that his men consecrated themselves by abstaining from sexual intercourse might apply (1 Sa. 21:4–5). However, comparisons with the other battles and events in the book of Joshua suggest that all ceremonies and ritual actions (such as circumcision) are explicitly stated in the text. The absence of further detail here implies that the consecration was an examination within each Israelite family to determine who might possess the devoted things. If so, it could explain the punishment of Achan's family along with Achan in verses 24–25. This explanation, however, like all others, remains conjectural.

14–15. The instructions describe the examination of each group in Israel. It is not clear how the LORD signifies which group is guilty. The verb *take* (Heb. *lkd*), normally describes the capture of an enemy (see 6:20). The selection ceremony symbolizes God's act of warfare against the nation. In this way,

God captures or takes the person who stole the divine property.[1] The divisions of tribe (Heb. *šēḇeṭ*), clan (*Heb. mišpāḥâ*), and family (Heb. *bayiṭ*) form the basic building blocks of Israelite society. These terms occur in the Bible with a certain amount of fluidity, especially in the case of overlap between clan and family.[2] The extended family (*bayiṭ* or *bêṭ-'āḇ*), is attested archaeologically. In excavated Israelite villages, such as Ai and Raddana, the dwellings are clustered in compounds.[3] Each dwelling within a cluster could accommodate four or five people. Here was the nuclear family, in which lived a *man* (Heb. *geḇer*), a male of age for military service, such as would be called to stand before the LORD. Clusters of these structures bear witness to extended families.

The punishment of the guilty, *destroyed by fire*, anticipates Achan's fate as described in verse 25. It is a devotion of the guilty one to God (Dt. 13:15–16) just as Jericho had been devoted to the 'ban' (Jos. 6:24).

16–18. Having received the divine instructions, Joshua obeys. In narrating the events (vv. 16–18), the text uses language similar to that of the instructions to demonstrate the care with which they were carried out. The MT may be correct in recording that the clans came forth by *man* rather than by *family*. Each of the men represented either an extended family or his own nuclear family. The expression *Give glory to the LORD* occurs nowhere else, but something similar appears in Malachi 2:2, where priests are admonished to 'set your heart to honour my name', in the context of faithfulness to God's covenant with them. The covenantal context of Achan's sin has already been noted (v. 11). At this point, the only proper action remaining for him is to tell the whole story of his sin.

19–21. Achan's response begins with a general confession of sin. The specifics of the deed follow. Achan's sin took place when he *saw* (Heb. *r'h*) something that was *beautiful* (Heb. *ṭôḇ*).

---

[1]Fritz, p. 82, notes the use of this term in the choice of Saul for king (1 Sa. 10:20–21) and in the guilt of Jonathan (1 Sa. 14:41–42).

[2]This point is especially clear in N. P. Lemche, *Early Israel. Anthropological and Historical Studies on the Israelite Society before the Monarchy* (Leiden: Brill, 1985), pp. 245–285. This survey is also useful for its critique of earlier studies on the subject, even if the literary-critical assumptions necessary to establish the *mišpāḥāh* as a late term artificially retrojected into the past can be questioned.

[3]See L. E. Stager, 'The Archaeology of the Family in Ancient Israel', *BASOR*, 260, 1985, pp. 11–24. The distinction is also visible in the family tombs.

The same words describe the sin of the woman in the Garden (Gn. 3:6), who also *saw* something that appeared to be *good* (*ṭôb*). The *plunder* that Achan saw would be the spoils of war. The same word was used to describe the material won from the battle against Midian (Nu. 31:11–12), which, although taken by the warriors of Israel, was presented as an offering to the LORD.

Three items are described. Texts listing textiles, silver and gold are not uncommon in the Ancient Near East. Items such as these can be found in inventory lists from many places, including the West Semitic cities of fourteenth- and thirteenth-century BC Emar, Ugarit and Alalakh.[1] Such items are found in Amarna inventory lists of the fourteenth century which record gifts exchanged between Egypt's Pharaoh and the Mitannian and Babylonian sovereigns. Whether by trade or theft, it is easy to imagine such materials appearing in a Palestinian town.

The first item, *a beautiful robe from Babylonia*, is described in the fashion common on such inventory lists: firstly the item (*robe*, Heb. *'adderet*) and then the origin of the item (*Babylonia* = Shinar, Heb. *šin'ār*) followed by the quality (*beautiful*, Heb. *ṭôbâ*).[2] Millard has observed several ancient descriptions of garments followed by their place of origin. These come from the thirteenth-century BC coastal city of Ugarit that lay near the borders of Canaan.[3] His example of a cloth from Tyre is instructive since it is followed by a description of the type of wool in the garment. Such descriptions, with the quality of the cloth following them, are common at Ugarit.[4] The term 'Shinar' for Babylon and the peculiar description of the gold in the form of *a wedge* also suggest a second-millennium BC date

---

[1]West Semitic is a general term for languages and people who lived in and around Palestine and who spoke Hebrew and other similar languages (*e.g.* Phoenician, Aramaic, Moabite, Ammonite). The author thanks Lawson Younger for the observation that these items are also found on booty lists such as are attested from campaigns by Egyptian and Assyrian kings in the thirteenth and twelfth centuries BC.

[2]The position of the numeral 'one' (Heb. *'aḥaṭ*) after the construction of the garment is due to its usage as an attributive adjective, *i.e.* 'a certain garment'. See B. K. Waltke and M. O'Connor, *An Introduction to Biblical Hebrew Syntax* (Winona Lake, Indiana: Eisenbrauns, 1991), pp. 273–274.

[3]A. R. Millard, 'Back to the Iron Bed: Og's or Procrustes'?', pp. 197–200. The specific text is KTU 4.132 (RS 15.04), line 4.

[4]See *ktn.n'mm*, 'a linen cloth of good quality', (Ras Ibn Hani text, *Syria* 56, p. 306). This and Millard's examples may be found in W. H. van Soldt, 'Fabrics and Dyes at Ugarit', *UF*, 22, 1990, pp. 321–357 (331, 337).

for this list.[1] *Two hundred shekels of silver* comes to about 2.7 kg (6 lbs) of weight, while fifty shekels comes to about 560 g (1¼ lbs). Thus the whole inventory could have been transported and hidden with ease.

The verb 'to covet' (Heb. *ḥmd*) is identical to that found in the tenth commandment of the Decalogue (Ex. 20:17; Dt. 5:21). It describes the desire for that which one has no right to possess. The details, as well as the location of the hiding place, demonstrate the dishonesty of Achan and portray Joshua's obedience in identifying the specific sin that cost Israel its battle against the enemy. As with Joshua's earlier prayer, Achan's confession reveals a distinct attitude towards the identification of unknown or hidden sin in Israel, in comparison with other Ancient Near Eastern nations. Although other nations were reluctant to admit military defeat, the plague prayers of the Hittite king Mursili and the 'sin' catalogues from Mesopotamia provide examples of attempts to identify sins that brought divine wrath in the form of calamities.[2] However, the emphasis is upon a comprehensive list of possible sins, often of a cultic nature. The penitent hoped that the list would include the particular sin. If not, it might be revealed through omens or through dreams.

The absence of the use of lists, omens, and dreams for the purpose of revealing such sins in the biblical texts suggests a different attitude towards sin. The account of Joshua 7 places less emphasis upon the words of Joshua or upon the ritual for determining the identity of the sinner. God specifically criticizes the former, and the latter serves only as a means of identifying the guilty party, rather than as a means of identifying the sin itself. Instead, the emphasis in the text is twofold. Firstly, there is the importance of the word of God and obedience to it. In this case, Joshua is told of the procedure and follows it. The details of the procedure are unimportant, only the fact that it is God's word and that it is obeyed. Secondly, great importance is placed upon the words of Achan. By contrast with the practice in other cultures, these are not ascribed to a divine source, such as an omen. In Israel, the guilty party confesses the sin and bears the consequences.

---

[1] See Introduction: 'Antiquity' (p. 28).

[2] For the plague players, see *ANET*, pp. 394–396; for the Mesopotamian confession lists, see K. van der Toorn, *Sin and Sanction in Israel and Mesopotamia* (Assen/Maastrich: Van Gorcum, 1989), pp. 94–99.

Rather than penitence and ritual, the emphasis is upon obedience and confession. For the Christian, confession of sin brings the promise of forgiveness (1 Jn. 1:9). It is commended along with a life of prayer (Jas. 5:13–18).

iv. The resolution of the sin (7:22–26). The sending of the messengers to collect the booty is a natural consequence of verse 21. Joshua's earlier act of sending men to scout out Ai led to this dilemma (v. 2). This second act of sending messengers leads to its resolution.

23. The return of the goods and their display *before the LORD* suggest more than that the selection and interrogation had been done before the LORD (*cf.* Ex. 21:6, 22:7–8). It also symbolizes the return by Israel of these items to God's possession. The act called upon God to bear witness that Israel held back nothing that belonged to him.

24. Both the patronym (*son of Zerah*) and the record of all of Achan's property and offspring indicate that the correct individual was punished along with all that belonged to him. As long as the nation had failed to identify and separate from itself the devoted things and the perpetrator of the sin, God had regarded all of Israel as devoted things (*ḥērem*).[1] Once the identification occurred, this ban was restricted to the perpetrator with everything that could be considered as belonging to him. The sad inclusion of his sons and daughters in the punishment implies that God would not only take Achan's own life but also demand his *name*, here a reference to all future generations. They would all be given back to God as part of the devoted things. The salvation of Rahab and the preservation of her family and name contrasts with this judgment.[2] Joshua and Israel delivered Rahab and her family from a Jericho that perished among the devoted things. Achan would perish among the devoted things and thereby deliver Joshua and Israel from divine destruction.

The Valley of Achor has not been identified with certainty,

[1] Thus Achan and his household suffer the fate of holy war. See the discussion on the ban in the Introduction: 'Theology (a) Holy war and the ban' (pp. 42–46).

[2] See Ezekiel 18 and the promise that repentance from sin or from the intention to sin will have an effect upon the destiny of the person, regardless of what his or her earlier life might have been. A change from a holy life to the pursuit of sin will also have an effect.

although the suggestion that it is the Buqei'ah Valley could fit the boundary description of 15:7.[1] If it is the Buqei'ah, a valley beginning about 3 miles west-north-west of Khirbet Qumran and extending south-west into the Judean Desert for about 6 miles, the journey from Jericho would have been about 8 miles. Such a location would have led away as far as possible both from Gilgal and the eastward direction from which Israel had come as well as from Ai and the westward direction in which it appeared to be going. The location would emphasize the concern to remove the impurity from Israel's midst.

25. A wordplay associates the root 'to bring disaster' (Heb. '*kr*) with the identical root in the spelling of Achor. The punishment of burning with fire may have taken place after the victims were stoned to death. As with Jericho (6:24), this act was commanded in warfare as a means of 'devoting' the people and objects to divine judgment (Dt. 13:15–16). In Mesopotamia, the *asakku* corresponded to the Israelite devoted things. In Old Babylonian times, the punishment for its theft seems to have involved being burnt to death.[2] The stoning is mentioned twice in the MT, separated by the phrase describing the burning of Achan and all that belonged to him. The first act of stoning has a singular object: they *stoned him*. The second phrase uses a plural object and a different verb (Heb. *rgm*) for the stoning: *they had stoned*(?) the rest. It may be that the first refers to the putting to death of the victim(s) by stoning, while the second describes the covering of the charred remains with stones.

26. This would lead naturally to the monument that Israel builds over Achan's remains. The *large pile of rocks* uses the word 'circle' or *pile* (Heb. *gal*) to describe the structure, perhaps reminiscent of the site of the earlier monument, Gilgal (4:20). It may have been *large* in order to cover all the remains, or it may have served as a notice for travellers to see (and so to avoid) the site. The presence of stone mounds or cairns is attested throughout the Ancient Near East, especially in desert

---

[1] F. M. Cross, *Canaanite Myth and Hebrew Epic* (Cambridge, Massachusetts: Harvard University Press, 1973), pp. 109–110, n. 57.

[2] K. van der Toorn, *Sin and Sanction in Israel and Mesopotamia*, p. 26; M. Anbar, 'Le châtiment du crime de sacrilège d'après la Bible et un texte hépatoscopique paléo-babylonien', *Revue d'Assyriologie et d'archéologie orientale*, 68, 1974, pp. 172–173. This reference adds support to the MT's inclusion of the reference to burning with fire, omitted in the LXX. See Barthélemy, pp. 8–10, for additional arguments of homeoteleuton.

regions where semi-nomadic, pastoralist populations are found. Many of these were used as tombs. Indeed, tombs of venerated sheikhs in Palestine become associated with place names, either through the name of the sheikh's becoming attached to the place, or through the pre-existing place name becoming attached to the tomb site.[1] One of the most spectacular cairn tombs is Rogem Hiri in the Golan.[2] Although the radial walls were in use in the third millennium BC, the cairn with its tomb in the centre of the site was erected only in the latter part of the second millennium BC. This may be likened to the Valley of Achor, whose name may have been present long before it was used for the burial of Achan. However, the fate of Achan became permanently connected with the valley's name.

The *fierce anger* (Heb. *ḥᵃrôn 'ap̱*) of the LORD is used to describe his readiness to destroy the people due to gross covenant violations, *e.g.* the worship of the golden calf (Ex. 32:12), the idolatrous immorality at Baal-Peor (Nu. 25:4), and the warning to the tribes of the Transjordan if they refused to follow the LORD and Israel in the possession of Canaan (32:14–15). Its usage here recalls its one other appearance in the Pentateuch, the warning of God's fierce anger against Israel if it does not destroy all of the devoted things in battle (Dt. 13:18).

The story of Joshua 7 serves the literary purposes of the book by providing a necessary pause between the actions of the taking of Jericho and the capture of Ai. Joshua 1 – 9 portrays a series of scenes that oscillate between events where God deals with Israel inside their camp and events outside the camp. So far the reader has seen the choice of Joshua, the crossing of the Jordan and the circumcision, and the judgment of Achan, as events within the camp of Israel. Sandwiched between these have been the spies' visit to Jericho, the capture of Jericho, and the yet-to-come capture of Ai, all taking place as Israel ventures outside itself to take possession of the land. The literary effect of this variation is to focus the attention of the reader upon the events within the camp as a necessary preparation for what goes on outside it. In Joshua 7, Israel completes its task in relation to Jericho and prepares itself for further battles.

For Christians, the story of Ai has often been used as an illustration of sin in the life of a believer. Like Achan in Israel,

---

[1] A. F. Rainey, 'The Toponymics of Eretz-Israel', *BASOR*, 231, 1978, p. 10.
[2] Y. Mizrachi, 'Mystery Circles', *BAR*, 18/4, July/August 1992, pp. 46–57, 84.

as long as rebellion against God's will is tolerated there can be no success in life. Instead, it is necessary to eradicate the sin in order to grow in one's relationship with God and to receive the fullness of blessing. The sin of one member of a community has an effect upon the whole community and especially upon that person's family. The story of Achan is one that emphasizes the dangers to the people of God and the terrible consequences of sin for those involved. As already noted, it may be compared with the experience of Ananias and Sapphira and their fate in the young church of Acts 5:1–11 (p. 147).

Additional Note: The archaeology of Ai

The identification of Ai with et-Tell has created problems since its excavation revealed no occupation or destruction levels from 1550 to 1200 BC.[1] In the twelfth century, a village did exist on the tell. Archaeologists usually identify it as an Israelite village. The problem is that no-one can locate the Canaanite fort described in Joshua 7 – 8.[2] Scholars have suggested several solutions to resolve this tension:

(1) Et-Tell is not the site of biblical Ai. Et-Tell is the best site for Ai near Bethel (*cf.* 8:9, 17), however, if Bethel is Beitin. Some have proposed relocating Bethel away from Beitin,[3] but no adequate alternative has been found. Since Beitin best fits the available archaeological, biblical, and extrabiblical evidence, et-Tell remains the best choice for Ai.[4]

(2) The events of Joshua 8 originally applied to Bethel but later editors of Joshua confused the events with Ai.[5] This suggestion lacks textual evidence, as the single narrative of the capture of Bethel (Jdg. 1:22–26) bears no similarity to the

[1] L. Allen, 'Archaeology of Ai and the Accuracy of Joshua 7:1 – 8:29', *Restoration Quarterly*, 20, 1977, pp. 41–52; Z. Zevit, 'Archaeological and Literary Stratigraphy in Joshua 7 – 8', *BASOR*, 251, 1983, pp. 23–35; *idem*, 'The Problem of Ai', *BAR*, 11/2, 1985, pp. 58–69; E. A. Knauf, 'Beth Aven', *Bib*, 65, 1984, pp. 251–253; J. A. Callaway, 'Was My Excavation of Ai Worthwhile?', *BAR*, 11/2, 1985, pp. 68–69; B.-Z. Luria, 'The Location of Ai', *Dor le-Dor*, 17, 1988/9, pp. 153–158.

[2] J. A. Callaway, 'New Evidence on the Conquest of 'Ai', *JBL*, 87, 1968, pp. 312–320; *idem*, 'Ai' in *ABD*, I, pp. 125–130.

[3] D. Livingston, 'Location of Biblical Bethel and Ai Reconsidered', *WTJ*, 33, 1970, pp. 20–44.

[4] A. F. Rainey, 'Bethel is Still Beitin', *WTJ*, 33, 1970–1971, pp. 175–188.

[5] W. F. Albright, 'Ai and Beth-aven', *Annual of the ASOR*, 4, 1924, pp. 141–149.

accounts regarding Ai in Joshua 7 – 8. However, there seems to have been a fortified city at Beitin that was destroyed in the thirteenth century.[1] Since no Israelite destruction of Bethel is recorded in the Bible, it is possible that the events of Joshua 8 describe the capture of Bethel as well as Ai.[2] If so, it is not clear to what extent Bethel and Ai can be distinguished in the text. Could Ai have been an outpost of Bethel? If so, the absence of archaeological evidence at Ai continues to pose a problem.

(3) The narrative is an aetiology and therefore not historical. The entire narrative emerged as an attempt to explain the presence of the remains of one of the largest Early Bronze Age (third-millennium BC) sites in the hill country. The textual support in 8:29 is the phrase 'to this day', which is seen as a signal that what precedes it is an aetiology. For discussion of this assumption, see Additional Note: Aetiologies (pp. 110–111). There it is argued that the identification of a text as aetiological in terms of its form does not assist in answering the question: is it historical? The question of aetiology is a literary one, not a historical one.

(4) Ai in the Hebrew text means 'the ruin' (Heb. *hā'ay*). It had this name before the Israelites captured it because it was an unoccupied ruin. The walls, which were more than a thousand years old in the thirteenth century, would have provided a strategic fortress for the inhabitants of Bethel to establish a makeshift defence against Israelites coming westward on the road from the Jordan Valley.[3] The 'aetiological significance' for the narrator lay in the application of an already existing name of the site to the 'large pile of rocks' that remained after its destruction (8:28–29).[4] Such an explanation also allows the MT's association of Bethel with Ai, as well as the geographical association, to explain the reason for the absence of any mention of the destruction of the site of Bethel. Ai was more important to the narrator because of the wordplay on its name, the reversal of the defeat of Joshua 7, and perhaps because this

---

[1] A. Mazar, *Archaeology of the Holy Land 10,000–586 BCE* (Garden City, NY: Doubleday, 1990), pp. 333–334.

[2] This assumes that Jdg. 1:22–26 records the capture of Bethel and the slaughter of its inhabitants, but not the destruction of the city itself.

[3] A. R. Millard, *Treasures from Bible Times* (Tring: Lion, 1985), p. 99.

[4] For this rhetorical approach to aetiology, see P. J. van Dyk, 'The Function of So-Called Etiological Elements in Narratives', *ZAW*, 102, 1990, pp. 19–33.

was where the inhabitants of Bethel made their greatest defence.[1]

g. The second assault, part 2: the victory at Ai (8:1–29)

i. Then the LORD said to Joshua ... (8:1–2). Divine guidance was missing in the first attack on Ai (7:3–4). At Jericho, God had fought the battle (6:2–5) and Israel had participated ceremonially and by entry into Jericho after the battle had been won. The LORD's exhortation to Joshua begins with the command, *Do not be afraid; do not be discouraged.* The first part, *Do not be afraid,* occurs thirty-nine times in the MT. Sometimes, God reassures in the midst of a terrifying situation, for example by a divine visitation (Gn. 15:1; 26:24) or as part of a charge to venture forth into an unknown land (46:3). He also forbids fear when he commands battle (Nu. 21:34; Dt. 3:2). Examples of this are found later in the book (Jos. 10:8; 11:6). Normally, these occasions include a reference to the enemy and a promise of divine presence and support.[2] But the addition of *do not be discouraged* in 8:1 has only three parallels in the Hebrew Bible: Deuteronomy 1:21; 1 Chronicles 22:13; 28:20. The texts in 1 Chronicles form part of David's charge to Solomon to build the temple of the LORD. Deuteronomy 1:21 remembers God's exhortation to take the Promised Land and is addressed to Israel. This resembles Joshua 8:1 which forms one step in the fulfilment of that charge. All these passages share the common concern of accomplishing a great task commanded by God, the task being the fulfilment of a divinely ordained covenant, either in the promise of the land to Abram (Gn. 17) or in the promise of a dynasty for David (2 Sa. 7). Although the promise of the land is prominent in Joshua 8, another covenantal concern prompts the use of this phrase. The guilt of Achan's sin and of the devoted things has been removed. Once again Israel can progress in its occupation of the land.

---

[1] See the destruction of Shiloh, which archaeologically can be related to the Philistine defeat of Israel in 1 Sa. 4, but which is not mentioned in the text.

[2] See E. W. Conrad, *Fear Not, Warrior. A Study of 'al tîrā' Pericopes in the Hebrew Scriptures* (Scholars Press, 1985), pp. 6–17. However, his analysis of Jos. 8:1 is different from that proposed here. It does not consider the significance of the full phrase, *Do not be afraid; do not be discouraged.* It argues for an offensive action in ch. 8, while defensive actions are suggested for chs. 10 and 11.

The directives to Joshua differ from the recommendations of the spies in Joshua 7. All warriors must now participate, not just a few. Joshua will also be involved, as he takes the army with him to the battle. In language that parallels 6:2, the LORD promises Joshua possession of the land. The additional mention of the land of Ai may refer to the region that would form part of the Israelite settlement. Unlike Jericho, where no Israelite could settle without invoking the curse of Joshua, God would allow occupation by the Israelites of both Ai and its region. The king of Ai (6:2) was to be delivered to God, as was the town itself, but nothing else is mentioned as devoted things. *Plunder and livestock* of the defeated town (fort?) will belong to the Israelites. Although this was the custom for most battles, its specification signifies a break with the practice regarding the plunder of Jericho. There everything became devoted. This divine instruction signifies a flexibility on the meaning of the ban, which could be interpreted by God according to the particular needs of the people.[1] Since everything captured belonged to God, he could also choose to give some of it back to Israel.

Almost as an afterthought, the command to *Set an ambush behind the city* is added. The fulfilment of these injunctions would take place in reverse order to their presentation in verses 1–2. The ambush and victory would take place first; then Israel would carry off the plunder; and finally, the king would be killed. In this way Joshua will obey each of the divine instructions which become an outline (in reverse order) of the account.

The use of an ambush was part of Ancient Near Eastern warfare.[2] A tenth-century BC Assyrian king describes a strategy similar to the one used by Joshua:[3]

---

[1] This is preferable to an appeal to an *ad hoc* 'temporary suspension' of God's commands suggested by Polzin, p. 82; or to a contradiction suggested by Fritz, pp. 91–92.

[2] A. K. Grayson, 'Ambush and Animal Pit in Akkadian' in R. D. Biggs and J. A. Brinkman (eds.), *Studies Presented to A. Leo Oppenheim June 7, 1964* (Chicago: Oriental Institute of the University of Chicago, 1964), pp. 90–94. I thank Prof. D. J. Wiseman for this reference. Ambushes in Canaan are also mentioned in the thirteenth-century BC Egyptian Papyrus Anastasi I. See E. Wente, *Letters from Ancient Egypt*, SBL Writings from the Ancient World Series (Atlanta: Scholars Press, 1990), p. 108. Fritz, p. 90, cites a parallel strategy of drawing the enemy from the city and then burning it, used by Hamilcar in classical times.

[3] The passage occurs in the Annals of Ashurnasirpal. See A. K. Grayson, 'Ambush and Animal Pit in Akkadian', p. 91.

While I remained in front of (the city of) Parsindi I set the cavalry (and) pioneers in ambush (behind the city). I killed fifty troops, the fighting men of Ameka, in the open country.

Israel's ambush was initiated by God. Therefore, it was not challenged as an innovation by Joshua. Jesus also perceived the mission of his disciples as one of risk and danger. For this reason he counselled that they be as shrewd as snakes and as innocent as doves (Mt. 10:16).

ii. Battle instructions (8:3–8). The structure of this passage hinges on the divine instruction to Joshua regarding the javelin and on Joshua's response (v. 18). Joshua prepares for battle (vv. 3–13) and the armies of Bethel and Ai respond (vv. 14–17). Then the Israelites capture and destroy Ai (v. 19), defeating the Bethel-Ai army, its leader, and its defences (vv. 20–27). The story begins outside Ai and moves inside the fort. Then it moves back outside for the final defeat of the army. As before, the Israelite army moves westward from its camp at Jericho. When the Israelites lure the enemy away from Ai, they move eastward and the army of Bethel and Ai follows them. When the ambush enters Ai, they come from the west, going eastward. They continue the eastward movement when they confront the army of Ai in the vice-like movement that has Israelite contingents both east and west of the army of Ai, trapping it in the valley. In verse 18, Joshua signals from the point of the Israelite army's farthest eastern movement to their contingent farthest to the west, thereby uniting the two in their common strategy.

The account of the ambush resembles the Israelite ambush of Benjamin at Gibeah in Judges 20.[1] There are three similarities. (1) Israel suffers an initial defeat before God provides the necessary blessing. Unlike in Joshua, at Gibeah there is divine approval for two assaults that fail (vv. 18–23). (2) The Israelites lure the Benjaminites out of the town, at which point the men of the ambush enter from the west and set it ablaze. (3) The Israelites put to the sword all the enemy who fall into their hands. Unlike Joshua, they destroy animals as well

---

[1]See A. Malamat, 'Israelite Conduct of War in the Conquest of Canaan according to the Biblical Tradition' in F. M. Cross (ed.), *Symposia Celebrating the Seventy-Fifth Anniversary of the Founding of the ASOR (1900–1975)* (ASOR, 1979), pp. 49–51. Malamat cites additional examples of ambushes from Greco-Roman sources.

as people. Among Israel's wars, only the second point is unique to Joshua 8 and Judges 20. However, Israel does not lure the enemy outside its fortress by allowing itself to be chased. Instead, Benjamin is so occupied in its battle with Israel that it loses the sense of where it is positioned as it moves away from the town to continue the battle with the retreating Israelites. Perhaps the most significant parallel with the incident in Joshua is the opportunity for the ambush to hide nearby. This would be possible near both Ai and Gibeah due to the hilly nature of the terrain.

After an introductory summary statement (v. 3), there follow Joshua's charge to Israel (vv. 4–8), the preparations for battle (vv. 9–13), the reaction of Ai (vv. 14–17), the Israelite victory (vv. 18–22a), and the fulfilment of God's commands in verse 1 (vv. 22b–27).

3. Joshua obeys the divine instructions of verse 1. He and the whole army *moved out to attack Ai.* He *chose thirty thousand* (*i.e.* thirty military units: see comment at 7:3, p. 146) . . . *and sent them out at night.* The details of how this is done differ. Night warfare was rare in the Ancient Near East. It provided the possibility for deception and surprise, especially useful when the army was outnumbered. As this was often the case with Israel's army, there are several examples of night warfare in the Bible.[1] This verse repeats the verbs used in the divine commission of verse 1 in order to demonstrate the detailed and precise manner in which Joshua obeyed. The thirty units who are selected include both the force that will form the ambush and the main attack force. Verse 12 specifies that *five thousand men* were sent to support the ambush, leaving twenty-five units to form the main force. The mention of the *night* when Joshua sent the armies refers to the night or nights specified in verses 9 and 13. In fact, the final phrase of verse 3, *sent them out at night,* is repeated with a considerable expansion as the whole of verse 9. In this way, it forms something of a refrain that expands once more in verses 11–13, which describe the placement of the Israelite forces.

In verses 4–8, Joshua instructs Israel in the strategy. This section is delineated by the verbs 'to command' and 'to see', which occur together at the beginning and the end (obscured

---

[1] *Ibid.*, pp. 53–54. Malamat provides examples from Gn. 14:15; Jos. 10:9; Jdg. 7; 9:34; 1 Sa. 11:11; 14:36.

by NIV's *orders*). Joshua commands the warriors of Israel to do what God has commanded him. The command to 'see' frames the discourse where Joshua reveals the secret plan by which Israel will defeat the enemy. As verses 14 and 20 will demonstrate through the usage of the same verb, that which the enemy 'sees' will not be the true situation. Israel must 'see' what will actually happen in order that the enemy may not 'see' the truth and so may suffer destruction.

4–6. The ambush is to position itself west of Ai, but as close as possible to the fortress. The main force, commanded by Joshua, will approach Ai. The specifics are not provided until verse 11. Joshua's description of how the citizens of Ai will respond assumes that they will act *as they did before* and that they will calculate that Israel will act *as they did before* (vv. 5 and 6). Twice it is said that the enemy will *come out against* Israel. Three times Israel *will flee* from the army of Ai. The description employs the same verb as that found in Joshua 7:4, where Israel fled from Ai on the previous occasion. One may wonder why Joshua thought that the army of Ai would believe he would try the same strategy twice. The answer may lie in the increased size of the force he would employ, from the *three thousand* of chapter 7 to twenty-five 'thousand'. The army of Ai would think that Joshua sought to use the same tactics with a larger force. Whatever the explanation may be, Joshua was told that this was to be done, in the divine charge of verse 1.

7. When the ruse began to work and the army was drawn out from its defences, then the ambush could arise and occupy the fortress. Only here in chapter 8 does the verb 'to possess, dispossess' (Heb. *yrš*) appear. Its significance as part of God's covenantal promises for the acquisition of Canaan by Israel has already been noted (*cf.* 1:11). Its usage in the speech to the ambush party reminds them that this risky tactic will fulfil part of the divine mandate regarding Israel's possession of the land. In verse 1, God promised that he would give Ai into Joshua's *hand* or 'power'.

8. Joshua includes the ambush group and, by implication, all of Israel in this promise. The command to set the fortress ablaze recalls the fate of Jericho in 6:24. The whole passage forms an A–B–A' structure, beginning with the disposition of the Israelite forces (vv. 4b–5a), proceeding to the response of the army of Ai (vv. 5b–6), and returning to the responsibility of the Israelite forces (vv. 7–8a). *What the LORD has commanded* will be done (v. 8). The text is framed within Joshua's commands that the people are to *see*. As already noted, Israel is to *see* the secret plan. For this reason, the central phrase, around which the entire speech is constructed, is that of verse 6: *until we have lured them away from the city*. All of Joshua's instructions in verses 4–6a are designed to produce this effect upon the army of Ai. Everything that follows in verses 6b–8 assumes that this deception has worked. The verb 'to lure away' occurs in this form (Hiphil) only here and in Jeremiah 12:3, where it describes the movement of sheep to the slaughter. The passive form of the verb (Hophal) appears once, in Judges 20:31, in the episode already noted for its similarity with the narrative of Joshua 8. There, it describes how Benjamin was lured to follow Israel in the midst of battle. All cases of this verb describe the means by which the victim is positioned for destruction.

iii. The preparations (8:9–13). These verses describe the actual disposition of the Israelite forces, but it is not clear that they should be taken in chronological sequence. Like the descriptions of the spies at Jericho (ch. 2), of the crossing of the Jordan (chs. 3 – 4), and of the account of the Israelite war against Benjamin (Jdg. 20), the account here repeats key phrases, including temporal indicators (*e.g. that night* and *the next morning*) in order (1) to position each of several different groups and (2) to develop a theme through repetition and expansion.[1] The position of the ambush group is described twice, in verses 9 and 12. That of Joshua and the remaining Israelite forces is outlined in verses 10–11. Both are summarized in verse 13. The key thesis is that all the Israelite forces were placed exactly where Joshua intended. Verses 9 and 12 use nearly identical language to describe how the ambush group was situated between Bethel and Ai to the west of Ai. Verse 12 adds the information that about *five thousand* were selected by Joshua to make up this group.

Verses 10–11 describe how Joshua positioned the main force north of Ai and above the valley. The mention of *the leaders of Israel* may suggest the tribal leaders who would function as military officers in battle.

Two features are remarkable in the Hebrew text. Firstly, *Ai*

---

[1]Soggin, p. 103, and Fritz, pp. 87–92, use this literary technique as evidence for a composite text.

appears five times in verses 9–12, but becomes *the city* in the last phrase of verse 12 and twice in verse 13. Secondly, the last phrase of verse 9, *but Joshua spent that night with the people* is almost identical in the Hebrew to the last phrase of verse 13, *That night Joshua went into the valley,* despite their different translations into English. The only distinction is in the final words, *the people* and *the valley.* In both of these examples, the difference is a single letter of the Hebrew alphabet. *Ai* becomes *city* by adding a final *resh. The people* becomes *the valley* by adding a final *qoph.* The consistency of both changes suggests a deliberate alteration by the author, and not a scribal error. The intent is to juxtapose the two main forces according to their locations when the battle begins. The army of Ai is found in *the city* (or fortress; see the notes on Jericho and on Ai, pp. 137–138, 157–159). The army of Israel, which is called *the people* in verses 3, 10, 11 and 13, is situated in the *valley* to the north of Ai. It will be visible to the leader of Ai in the morning light.

iv. The reaction of Ai (8:14–17). The trap has been set. The response of the king and warriors of Ai indicates its effectiveness. *When the king of Ai saw this* contains the verb 'to see'. This verb appeared at the beginning and end of Joshua's instructions to the Israelites (vv. 4 and 8). It enjoined Israel to see truly what would happen if the plan were followed. In verse 14, the king of Ai *saw* the Israelites stationed outside his fortress, but he does not 'see' the ambush that lies in wait for him. Thus he sees what Joshua wants him to see. The note that the men of Ai *hurried out early in the morning to meet Israel* uses earlier phrases and thereby demonstrates the way in which the army of Ai responds exactly as Joshua had planned. Firstly, that they did this *early in the morning* contrasts with the identical description regarding Joshua in verse 10. Joshua had risen early the previous morning to deploy his armies where he wanted them. The king of Ai, plotting the same strategy as before, responds in a way for which Joshua is prepared. Secondly, the reference to marching out to meet Israel duplicates the language of verses 5 and 6, demonstrating that Joshua's predictions there were accurate. Verse 14 forms a summary of the action that will now be detailed in verses 15–17. It concludes with the key element that serves to inform the reader that Joshua's strategy has succeeded, *But he did not know that an ambush had been set against him behind the city.* While the second half of this sentence recalls the identical expression of verse 4 in which Joshua first describes the ambush, the first half focuses on the point of ignorance necessary for the ruse to succeed.

15–17. The expressions *they fled* (v. 15), *lured away from the city* (v. 16) and *went in pursuit of* (v. 17) continue to duplicate phrases from Joshua's plan in verses 5–6.[1] The threefold use of the verb 'to pursue' in verses 16 and 17 recalls the description of the failed first expedition in 7:5. Thus the direction towards the desert indicates the same eastward route as that along which the earlier Israelite army fled (see comment on 7:4–5, pp. 146–147). The emphasis of verses 16 and 17 is that no warrior was left at Ai, but that they all pursued Israel. So eager was the army to attack Israel that they *left the city open*. In 1:5, God had promised not to *forsake* Joshua, using the same verb. The abandonment of Ai implies that the army has disregarded its primary duty. The fortress is left open, the opposite of the 'shut up' fortifications of Jericho in chapters 2 and 6. The site is thus vulnerable.

The mention of Bethel in verse 17 as a participant in the attack, like its mention in verses 9 and 12, need not be understood as a later gloss or as a reference to a sanctuary within Ai itself.[2] Instead, it suggests the role of Ai as an outpost fort of Bethel (see Additional Note: The archaeology of Ai, pp. 157–159). In fact, the army of Bethel's participation in the pursuit of Israel is necessary to the story. If the army of Bethel had remained in its place, it would have observed the assault of the Israelite ambush upon Ai (et-Tell is visible from Beitin) and mounted a hasty attack against the Israelites. This would have prevented the Israelite ambush from destroying Ai and from cutting off the retreat of the enemy.

Verses 14–17 correspond to verses 9–13. In the earlier text, Joshua had completed his responsibilities of preparation for the ruse. In the latter text, the leader and army of Ai (and of Bethel) had fallen for the ruse. Careful preparations for war, such as those described here, were used as an illustration of discipleship by Jesus. He reminded his disciples of the need to count the cost of following him (Lk. 14:31–33).

---

[1] Boling and Wright, p. 240, observe how these verses increase suspense by pausing to repeat the action of v. 14.

[2] *Ibid.*, p. 240. LXX omits reference to Bethel.

v. The victory of Ai (8:18–29). Four events occur in the battle. Firstly, the ambush destroys Ai and then attacks the back of the army of Ai, effectively squeezing it from both the east and the west (v. 19). Secondly, the army of Ai, seeing its fortress in flames, realizes that the battle is lost and abandons hope (v. 20). Thirdly, the main Israelite army, witnessing this, destroys the army and citizenry of Ai and seizes the booty (vv. 21–27). Fourthly, Joshua directs the burning of the fortress and the execution of Ai's leader (vv. 28–29). Verse 18 forms the turning point in the battle and the narrative. Until this point, an observer would have determined that the army of Ai was once again defeating Israel. After this verse, the Israelite army is victorious.

18, 26. There are three points: (1) the word of God, and thus the LORD himself, is responsible for the Israelite victory; (2) Joshua's success is due to his faith in that word and his obedience to it; and (3) although the battle and its victory can be described in human terms and understood as the result of successful strategy, Israel's victory is no less a miracle than its earlier success at Jericho or the previous generation's defeat of Egypt at the Red Sea. There are four comparisons with the Red Sea crossing: (1) in Exodus 14:16 the same introduction is used as that in Jos. 8:18; (2) in both passages, the leader is instructed to *hold out* (Heb. *ntḥ*) an instrument in his hand; (3) as a result of his doing so Israel is saved and its enemy is defeated; and (4) there is an emphasis in both accounts upon strength or power, symbolized by references to the hand or arm. A difference exists in so far as Moses uses a staff (Heb. *mtḥ*) while Joshua uses a sickle sword (Heb. *kîdôn*, NIV *javelin*). The staff is the symbol of Moses' guidance through the desert, while Joshua's weapon is for battle. A careful study of the structure of the text reveals a word-for-word parallel between the divine charge, *Hold out towards Ai the javelin that is in your hand,* and Joshua's obedience, *So Joshua held out his javelin towards Ai.*[1] This literal execution of God's word is the key to the mission's success. Between these

---

[1] M. Anbar, 'La critique biblique à la lumière des Archives royales de Mari: Jos 8', *Bib*, 75, 1994, pp. 70–74, finds parallels with eighteenth century BC letters from Mari, especially J.-M. Durand, *Archives épistolaires de Mari I/1*, Archives royales de Mari xxvi (Paris: Éditions recherche sur les civilisations, 1988), text 169, lines 6–12. This text mentions the brandishing of a javelin in the context of armed revolt. It and the comparison with Moses are closer comparisons than attempts to identify Joshua's actions with that of a victorious Egyptian deity who

two phrases is the divine promise *for into your hand I will deliver the city*. The *hand* of Joshua is mentioned three times in these lines, representing his leadership over all that occurs.[1] Thus this leadership is divinely appointed before the defeat of Ai is completed.

19. If the army of Ai *hurried* when it saw its opportunity (v. 14), the Israelites waiting in ambush also acted *quickly* when they saw Joshua's signal (twice in v. 19).[2] The first and last lines of the description of their action correspond to the first and last lines of Joshua's instructions to them in verses 7–8a: *the men of the ambush rose quickly from their position* and they *set it on fire*. The verbs in between convey the sense of a rushed manoeuvre. Embedded in the midst of the Hebrew verse is the phrase *As soon as he did this, i.e.* when he stretched forth his hand.[3]

20–22. The armies of Ai and of Israel respond. The tables are turned. The same expressions that earlier described Ai's success and Israel's defeat are now used to enhance Joshua's leadership in reversing the apparent defeat. Also enhanced is the divine word which, through its revelation and through Israel's obedience to it, is powerful and effective in defeating Israel's enemy (see Is. 55:10–11).

The army of Ai once again *saw*, but whereas it had formerly perceived only part of the situation (v. 14), it now takes in the full reality of what has occurred (v. 20). The smoke of Ai is *rising against the sky*. Although the verb 'to rise' (Heb. '*lh*) was used in verse 3 of Joshua's movement 'up to Ai', its usage here is similar to the sacrifice of the whole burnt offering (Heb. '*ōlâ* from '*lh*) wherein the smoke of the offering rises into the sky. The

---

raises the sword. See O. Keel, *Wirkmächtige Siegeszeichen im Alten Testament*, (Freibourg: Universitätsverlag, 1974), p. 34.

[1] With the exception of the final *nun* in the consonantal text of the word for sword (*bkydwn* with inseparable preposition), the same letters are found in the expression *for into your hand* (*ky bydk*).

[2] O. Keel, *op. cit.*, pp. 11–83, especially 34, 51–76; Boling and Wright, pp. 240–241; Butler, p. 87; Fritz, p. 93, demonstrate that the *javelin* was a sickle sword. They argue that it represented divine sovereignty. Thus Joshua's action did not signal the ambush, who could not have seen him. Instead, it symbolized God's defeat of Ai. However, the structure of v. 19 assumes a connection between Joshua and the ambush. If Joshua was too far away for the ambush to see a signal from him, the rest of the Israelite army was not. When they saw Joshua brandishing the weapon, they would have halted and turned around on their pursuers. Aware of this, the ambush acted.

[3] In the NIV, this phrase appears at the beginning of the verse.

expression here and in verse 21 implies a dedication of this fortress to God in a manner reminiscent of sacrifice. The description of the army of Ai as having *no chance to escape* conceals yet another usage of the word for *hand* in this text. Here the strength of Ai has sapped away with the arousal of the strength given to Joshua and the Israelite army. The verb 'to escape' is identical to that used to describe how the Israelites would *flee from* the army of Ai (vv. 5–6). It appears in the next line of verse 20 to describe the Israelites *who had been fleeing.* They turned back upon their enemy. The army of Ai now sought to flee, but could not, as its strength was gone. The contrast with the former defeat of Israel is further heightened by the use of the same verb as in Joshua's earlier description of the defeat (7:8). Although Israel had *been routed* (Heb. *hpk*) by them, it now *turned round* (another form of *hpk*) against its enemies. Thus it began to pursue its pursuers.

If the army of Ai *saw* its defeat (v. 20), Joshua and the Israelite army *saw* victory (v. 21). The capture of and setting fire to Ai are repeated from the perspective of the Israelite army. With Ai destroyed, the ambush moves east and launches its attack upon the army of Ai. Just as the army of Ai had left the fortress to meet Israel in battle (vv. 6 and 14), identical language describes how the ambush now leaves the fortress to meet the army of Ai in battle (v. 22). In doing so, of course, the army of Ai is squeezed between the two parts of the Israelite army. The attack begins and will continue *leaving* (Heb. *š'r*) *neither survivors nor fugitives* of the army of Ai on the battlefield, just as *not a man remained* (*š'r*) of the army when it abandoned Ai (v. 17).

Verses 23–29 describe Israel's detailed fulfilment of the divine commands of verses 1–2. Israel does to the king of Ai, his people, his city and his land what it did to Jericho. They are consigned to the *ḥērem* (ban). As with Jericho, this requires setting them ablaze. This was done by the ambush with a description which suggests a sacrifice to God (see the comment on 6:6–25, pp. 132–135).

23. Although no mention is made of what was done to the leader of Jericho, he probably suffered the fate of everyone else. At Ai, the king is brought to Joshua, who puts him to death and erects a memorial over his burial site (v. 29).

24–25. Ai and all its inhabitants perish. The text mentions *men and women*, those who would be held responsible for their actions. On the possible significance of the *twelve thousand* or companies of inhabitants who were killed in the war, see the comment on 7:4–5 (pp. 146–147).

27. The Israelites acquired booty. Why here but not at Jericho? Perhaps the attack on Jericho, as the initial assault in Canaan, symbolized the dedication of all the land to God. Once this had taken place, booty was permitted. A second reason recalls Achan's sin. The first destruction and its plunder formed a divine test to determine whether or not Israel would obey God. The attackers of Ai passed this test. Therefore, it was not necessary to forbid them the spoils of battle. Furthermore, the mention of *livestock* recalls the precarious situation in which Israel now found itself. God no longer provided manna as he had done in the wilderness. Instead, Israel had to find its own food. Even here God provided: he gave his people the livestock, and so provided for their needs.

28. Joshua's destruction of Ai renders it a *permanent heap of ruins.* This phrase appears elsewhere only in Deuteronomy 13:16 (Heb. 17). Ai is punished in the same way as Jericho, by destruction (see comment on Jos. 6:26, p. 135). It failed to worship the God of Israel. The formula *to this day* applies the warnings of the story of Ai, both Israel's initial failure to destroy it and Ai's rejection of Israel's faith, to the author's own generation. (See Additional Note: Aetiologies, pp. 110–111).

29. The hanging of the king of Ai resembles Joshua 10:26–27 and the fate of the five Amorite kings. Younger has demonstrated that the Joshua 10 account, with its record of the hanging of the corpses of the slain kings (v. 26), is in language characteristic of Ancient Near Eastern conquest accounts. It is not an aetiology or a rewriting of the account in order to prove that Joshua fulfilled the Deuteronomic legislation of Deuteronomy 21:22–23.[1] The Assyrian king Sennacherib described how he executed the defeated rulers of Ekron, 'I hung their corpses on poles around the city' (Prism, Col. III 8–10). Joshua 8:28–29, where the bodies of defeated enemies are hung up for public display and humiliation, also should be understood as describing a practice of warfare and of propaganda. It is not based directly on Deuteronomy 21, which concerns criminal legisla-

---

[1]See Younger, pp. 222–223; M. Noth, 'Die Fünf Könige in der Höhle von Makkeda', *Palästina-Jahrbuch,* 33, 1937, pp. 22–36; M. Fishbane, *Biblical Interpretation in Ancient Israel* (Oxford: Clarendon, 1985), p. 148.

tion. However, the principle that a corpse should not remain exposed in such a way overnight is common to both criminal legislation (Dt. 21:23) and the practice of Israelite warfare. The city gate, where the conflict with Ai was first joined (Jos. 7:5), forms the final resting place for the leader of the opposition. As with Achan in Joshua 7:26, stones are erected as a memorial to Ai's former leader. (See comment on 7:26, pp. 155–156.) The final sentence brings to an end the account and ties it to the previous chapter's remedy for the failed assault on the fortress.

As literature, Joshua 8:1–29 relates to the preceding narratives in three ways. Firstly, its plot summaries, the repetition of actions and the shifting of the focus to different participants resemble the accounts of Rahab and the spies, of the crossing of the Jordan and of the assault on Jericho. Secondly, its verbal ties with Moses' actions at the Red Sea once again relate an event to the miraculous defeat of an earlier generation's enemy. Thirdly, the second assault on Ai and its success 'closes' the narrative of Joshua 7 with its failed assault. Although partially resolved in the identification and punishment of Achan, the concerns of Joshua 7:7–9 must be addressed with an Israelite success in battle. Chapter 8 provides the answer to this.

The strategic aspect of the battle moves Israel from the 'edge' of Canaan on the plains of Jericho to the centre of the hill country. From the strategic region of Bethel and Ai, Israel would be poised for the forthcoming events to the north (Jos. 8:30–35; 11) and to the south (Jos. 9 – 10).

For the Christian, the story of Ai illustrates God's forgiveness toward a repentant people and the manner in which continued obedience is rewarded with victory over the struggles and temptations of life. As Joshua discovered, obedience itself is a gracious gift of God. (See 1 Jn. 1:5–10; 2:1–17; 3:11–24.)

h. The covenant at Mount Ebal (8:30–35)

The text of 8:30–34 may be found before 5:2 in a Dead Sea Scroll fragment.[1]

In the sequence of Joshua's story, the external events, such as the attacks on Jericho and on Ai, alternate with the internal events, such as the Passover celebration, the punishment of Achan and the covenant celebration. The internal events

[1] See Introduction: 'Title and text' (pp. 19–20).

provide the spiritual centre for the external ones. This is nowhere more true than in the account of the covenant at Mount Ebal. Having introduced covenant concerns with the 'ban' and its violation in Joshua 7 – 8, this covenant-making ceremony re-establishes Israel's relationship with God.[1] Three theological themes dominate the text: the obedience of Joshua to the divine instruction, the participation of Israel, and the pre-eminent role of the Mosaic instruction in the ceremony.

Joshua appears at the beginning and the end. He built the altar[2] and omitted nothing of the Mosaic commands. He also *copied on stones the law of Moses* (v. 32) and *read all the words of the law* (v. 34). His first and last actions followed precisely the Mosaic instruction (Dt. 27:1–8). In verse 31a, Joshua does *as Moses* commanded and *according to what was written in the Book of the Law of Moses*. In verse 35a, a parallelism identifies the present function of Joshua with the former role of Moses:[3]

> *There was not a word*
> | | | |
> |---|---|---|
> | *of all that* | *Moses* | *had commanded* |
> | *that* | *Joshua* | *did not read.* |

33–35. The note of *all Israel,* as well as lists of the community members, indicates who was involved. The leadership includes *elders, officials and judges* as well as priests and Levites.[4] The reference to *aliens and citizens* includes common terms in the Pentateuch used to define all those living in Israel.[5] Verse 35 concludes with mention of those groups least able to defend their own rights, *the women and children, and the aliens.* The Mosaic legislation included everyone in its rights and responsibilities – civil, religious and social groups and their concerns.

30–33. The role of the Mosaic instruction (Heb. *tôrâ*) had its source in the LORD God. It was passed on to Israel in writing

---

[1] Butler, p. 91. Butler shows how these verses are a collection of texts from Deuteronomy (p. 90).

[2] On the past tense of the imperfect (prefix) conjugation following 'then' (*'āz*), as in v. 30, see B. K. Waltke and M. O'Connor, *An Introduction to Biblical Hebrew Syntax* (Winona Lake, Indiana: Eisenbrauns, 1990), pp. 514, 558.

[3] This is clear in the MT, where both lines are constructed with the same relative pronoun followed by a verb, and with the personal name appearing last on the line.

[4] The elders appear in Jos. 7:6. For the officials, see comment on Jos. 1:10–11, p. 74–76.

[5] See Ex. 12:19, 48, 49; Lv. 16:29; 17:15; 18:26; 19:34; 24:16, 22; 24:22; Nu. 9:14; 15:29, 30; Ezk. 47:22.

through the LORD's servant, Moses. Joshua 8:30–32 is a fulfilment of Deuteronomy 27:4–8, that which *Moses the servant of the LORD had formerly commanded* (Jos. 8:33). Thus Joshua builds *an altar of uncut stones* upon Mount Ebal. *Burnt offerings* and *fellowship offerings* are offered there. *Joshua copied on stones the law of Moses.*

There are parallels with Deuteronomy 27:12–13. In order to pronounce the curses and the blessings, half of Israel *stood in front of Mount Gerizim and half of them in front of Mount Ebal.* Deuteronomy adds details such as covering the stones with plaster in order to write upon them.[1] Thus the image is not that of cuneiform tablets in which the characters are impressed on the clay. Instead, it is similar to the plaster writings about Balaam that covered walls at Tell Deir 'Alla in the Jordan Valley.[2]

The covenant renewal takes place when Israel has entered the land (Dt. 27:2) and as it prepares to occupy it. Mount Gerizim lay to the south of Shechem and Mount Ebal to the north. Shechem is situated in the heart of the central hill country where Israel began its settlement. Shechem is nowhere mentioned as having been attacked by Israel, leaving open the possibility that it may have been occupied peacefully or joined Israel in alliance (note the mention of aliens twice in Jos. 8:30–35).[3] The patriarchs, especially Abram and Jacob, visited Shechem. The building of Abram's first altar (Gn. 12:6) and Jacob's first purchase of land for his tent (Gn. 33:19) took place here. It is the patriarchs' initial residence after their journeys from their families in Syria. Its location in the hill country may serve as a symbol of the habitation of the Canaanites in general. Like the Israelites in Joshua, the patriarchs have really entered Canaan when they reside at Shechem. Although its violent associations in Judges and Kings overshadow the accounts of Joshua, chapters 8 and 24 describe a place of unity before God. On the background and theological nature of the covenant, and the role of the curses

[1] Another detail in Deuteronomy is the division of Israel on the two mountains according to tribal groupings, six tribes (including Joseph) on Mt. Gerizim and six on Mt. Ebal.

[2] Boling and Wright, p. 248, also compare the writing at Kuntillet Ajrud in the northern Sinai.

[3] This interpretation does not consider the application of the events in Gn. 34 to the period of occupation of the land. Those who do apply it in some way to this time interpret it as a violent occupation of Shechem.

and blessings, see comment on Joshua 24 (pp. 299–309). For the Christian, the covenant renewal recalls the need to come together regularly and to renew commitment to God and obedience to God's will (see Heb. 10:25).

Additional Note: Joshua's altar on Mount Ebal?

When excavators at Tell Balatah, the site of ancient Shechem, first uncovered the sanctuary and found an altar and a standing stone from the time of Israel's appearance in Canaan, they identified these with texts such as Joshua 24:26–27. However, if these finds have any correlation with the biblical text, it is more likely that it is with the sanctuary of El-berith in Judges 9:46.[1] Surveys and excavations on Mount Ebal have revealed a site there, on the third highest peak, that the excavator suggests could be identified with Joshua's altar.[2] Several details have led to this proposal. Firstly, there is the date of occupation. Two levels were found at the site. On the basis of Egyptianized scarabs, a small decorated limestone 'seal' and the pottery, the earlier level extends to *c.* 1200 BC and the later level terminates *c.* 1150 BC. The site was then abandoned. Secondly, the excavator, Zertal, has interpreted the stone structure in the centre of the site as an altar. Constructed of uncut field stones, its later phase includes a ramp up to what he has identified as a veranda around the altar. In the centre, there is burnt ash. Thirdly, bones found at this structure indicate animals appropriate for Israelite sacrifice, such as sheep, goats and cattle. Fourthly, the absence of figurines at the site has led some archaeologists to doubt that it possessed a religious significance, and to suggest a house or tower. However, a faith that rejected images in its worship would not use images. Debate continues as to whether this discovery has associations with Joshua.[3] It remains the only thirteenth–twelfth-century BC structure found on Mount Ebal.

[1] See A. Mazar, *Archaeology and the Land of the Bible: 10,000–586 BCE*, The Anchor Bible Reference Library (Garden City, NY: Doubleday, 1990), p. 251.

[2] See A. Zertal, 'Has Joshua's Altar Been Found on Mt. Ebal?', *BAR*, 11/1, 1985, pp. 26–43; *idem*, 'How Can Kempinski Be So Wrong!', *BAR*, 12/1, 1986, pp. 43, 47, 49–53; *idem*, 'An Early Iron Age Cult Site on Mount Ebal: Excavation Seasons 1982–1987', *Tel Aviv*, 13–14, 1986–1987, pp. 105–165.

[3] See R. S. Hess, 'Early Israel in Canaan: A Survey of Recent Evidence and Interpretations', *PEQ*, 126, 1993, pp. 135–137.

i. Summary of the threat against Israel (9:1–2)

In the first eight chapters, Israel had chosen its military objectives and targets. At this point the situation changes. Others will define these objectives. The activity of nations 'hearing' appeared in Joshua 2:10 and 5:1. Joshua 5:1 begins with the identical words and grammar as 9:1. In 2:10, these record the reaction of Canaan to the crossing of the Red Sea and the defeat of the Transjordanian kings. In 5:1, it is the crossing of the Jordan River to which the kings of Canaan react. In both cases, the reaction is fear, bordering on paralysis. These features are not present in 9:1–2. Although similar wording evokes a comparison with the two earlier texts, this is done to stress a contrast. Three features are different. Firstly, there is no indication of an object for 'hear'. Although the NIV supplies *these things*, the text is silent about what it was that the kings of Canaan 'heard'. Secondly, there is a detailed list of the peoples represented in Canaan: 2:10 simply refers to how *we have heard* while 5:1 summarizes the leaders as Amorite and Canaanite. Thirdly, the text in 9:1–2 indicates an entirely different reaction to what is heard. No hearts melt. Instead, a coalition prepares to fight Israel.

The third difference contains the key to the explanation of the first two. No longer are the Canaanites cowed by the Israelites. What has changed? The texts between Joshua 5:1 and 9:1 relate the defeat of Jericho, the defeat of Ai and the covenant ceremony. It may be that these military victories were sufficient to arouse the inhabitants of the land to the threat of Israel. However, why would they not come together earlier, after the victory at Jericho? Further, the texts do not suggest that the Canaanites had ignored Israel before this. They had followed Israel's actions and knew of their victories from Egypt onwards. Indeed, the victory at Jericho enhances Joshua's fame throughout Canaan (Jos. 6:27). Earlier the Canaanites refused to attack Israel for fear of what would happen to them. They defended themselves only when attacked. Now they gather together, united for war against Israel. What has changed?

The answer lies in Israel's defeat at their first assault on Ai. Joshua predicted this consequence (Jos. 7:9). Until this point, Israel had been undefeated in battle. At Ai, Canaan learned that Israel could be defeated. Thus any belief in Israelite invincibility (always understood as based upon God's deliverance) evaporated with the sin of Achan. This is what the kings hear in 9:1. Although Bethel and Ai are ultimately defeated, the possibility now exists that Israel can lose battles. This is also the reason for the detailed list of peoples in the armies who gather against Israel. The stress is placed upon the numbers and the totality of the peoples represented. The armies will be large and the hostility of the land will be complete. For the peoples named in this list, see comment on 3:10 (p. 102).

Thus the passage underlines the awful effects of sin (see Rom. 3:9–20; 5:11–14). Because of one person's transgression, the occupation of the Promised Land is delayed indefinitely and many lives are lost in the process. Who can say what would have happened had Achan not sinned? Perhaps the battle at Ai could have been Israel's last. The other nations of Canaan would have responded like Rahab (and the Gibeonites) with belief in the one God of Israel, and Israel would have completely occupied the land. It is only with these verses that the reader of Joshua begins to realize the consequences of Achan's sin. The following chapters introduce the transition from a victorious people of God whose occupation of the land could have been the relatively simple matter of defeating those already discouraged to an unending history of battle, bloodshed, and idolatry that would haunt Israel throughout its history. As in the opening chapters of Genesis, so also in the opening chapters of Israel's dwelling in the Promised Land, a single transgression has cosmic ramifications.

Similar expressions of 'hearing' occur in Joshua 10:1 and 11:1. Both the southern and the northern kings form coalitions to fight Israel. Joshua 10:1 describes how the king of Jerusalem heard that Joshua had captured and destroyed other nearby towns. Joshua 11:1 does not relate what the king of Hazor heard. Both texts relate to Joshua 9:1–2 and form a literary refrain that unites all three chapters as part of a single sweep across the land of Canaan.[1]

j. The Gibeonite exception (9:3–27)

This story is an example of the operation of God's forgiveness

[1]Younger, pp. 197–198. This similarity of structure occurs only in the MT. The LXX places Jos. 9:1–2 before the covenant of 8:30–35.

and grace in the fallen world where Israel finds itself. The literary context parallels that of Rahab. Just as Rahab and her family escaped destruction through negotiations with representatives of Israel, so the Gibeonites do the same thing. Rahab's agreement precedes the account of the assault upon her town. The Gibeonites' treaty precedes the account of the war with the leaders of the surrounding towns in southern Canaan (ch. 10). In both cases, this deliverance occurs after the confession of God's deeds of salvation on behalf of Israel. The theological context parallels the account of Achan. Achan's sin followed the circumcision and special Passover celebration. The error with the Gibeonites occurs after the ceremony of covenant renewal. In both cases, Israel errs or sins without realizing it at the time. In both cases, a battle occurs after the fault is identified. The political context further describes the leadership of Joshua. As in Joshua 8:30–35, Joshua makes an agreement. Instead of a divine covenant, this is a treaty with neighbouring peoples. Joshua does not appear as personally responsible for the error of making a treaty with the Gibeonites. Instead, he is portrayed as the leader who acts to make the treaty on behalf of the leadership, pronounces judgment on the Gibeonites when their ruse is uncovered, and then delivers the Gibeonites from an angry Israel.

i. The Gibeonite deception (9:3–15). This text begins with a note, *when the people of Gibeon heard what Joshua had done to Jericho and Ai,* which includes the verb 'to hear' in verse 1. The verbal parallel contrasts the leaders of the towns, who make war, with the Gibeonites, who seek peace. Both the Gibeonites and Adoni-Zedek (Jos. 10:1) hear the same thing, the defeat of *Jericho and Ai.* The Gibeonites came from the region north of Jerusalem, the Palestinian town of el-Jîb.[1] The identification seems assured, based on later Israelite wine-jar handles found there with the name Gibeon stamped on them. Although this site has yielded no Late Bronze Age or Iron Age I remains of habitation, only a small part of the town has been excavated. Tombs from this period have been found.

4–5. The term for *ruse* has a meaning akin to 'wisdom,

---

[1] This is the traditional site of Gibeon. Its leadership of an alliance of four towns is suggested in v. 17. See Boling and Wright, p. 263.

understanding'. Used positively, as in Proverbs 1:4 and 8:5 and 12, it can denote prudence. Used negatively, as in Exodus 21:14, it implies treachery or malicious intent. Joshua 9:4 suggests a negative aspect, although not to the extent of murder as in Exodus 21. It is a prudent course for the Gibeonites, their sole means of self-preservation. Despite parallels with the same form of a verbal root in verse 12, *packed*, the MT of verse 4 uses the form of the particular root (Hithpael of *syr*) that can be translated as *They went as a delegation*.[1] There follows a lengthy explanation of how the emissaries prepared themselves so as to appear to come from a distant land. Bread and wine had to be brought along on the journey because they could not borrow from local Canaanite towns while seeking an alliance with enemies of the Canaanites. For the Christian, the Gibeonite deception recalls Jesus' commendation of the prudent steward (Lk. 16:1–9) who is able to *use worldly wealth to gain friends.*

6a. The Gibeonites met Israel at Gilgal. If this is the Gilgal of Joshua 4 – 5 then the story is out of sequence. It is unlikely that the main Israelite camp would have returned to the plains of Jordan after capturing a foothold in the hill country at Ai and after making a treaty at Shechem. It is more likely that the story is intended as chronologically sequential to these activities and that this Gilgal is near one of these hill-country places.[2]

6b–15. The style of verses 6b–11, with a rapid exchange between the two groups, parallels the exchange between Rahab and the two Israelites in chapter 2. In four verses the identity of the speakers changes four times: Gibeonites, Israelites, Gibeonites, Joshua, Gibeonites. The message of the Gibeonites contains three parts, two of which are summarized in verse 6. Firstly, they have come from a distant land. Secondly, they want a covenant with Israel. The third part of the message appears in verse 8, where the Gibeonites call themselves *your servants.* This term describes the willingness of

---

[1] See also the arguments of Barthélemy, pp. 13–14. Boling and Wright, pp. 255, 257, suggest that both verbs appeared here in the original text. The absence of any textual witness to support this conjecture renders it less likely.

[2] Recent proposals for sites of biblical Gilgals include Khirbet ed-Dawwara, south-east of et-Tell, and el 'Unuq, east of Shechem. See I. Finkelstein, 'Excavations at Khirbet ed-Dawwara: An Iron Age Site Northeast of Jerusalem', *Tel Aviv*, 17, 1990, pp. 163–208; A. Zertal, 'Israel Enters Canaan – Following the Pottery Trail', *BAR*, 17/5, September/October 1991, pp. 28–47.

the Gibeonites to become vassals of Israel. The scepticism of the Israelites (v. 7) and of Joshua (v. 8) leads to the confession by the Gibeonites of the power of the God of Israel (vv. 9–10) and of their mission (v. 11). The final phrases of verse 11 repeat the third and second parts of the message of the Gibeonites, their recognition of their 'servant' status and their request for a treaty. In verses 12–13, the Gibeonites provide further evidence of the first part of their message, that they have come from a distant land. The structure of these verses is that of a chiastic frame, composed of the three parts of the Gibeonite message, which encloses the descriptions of the scepticism of the Israelites and the Gibeonite response. Thus the Gibeonite confession of faith in the Israelite God lies at the centre of the structure.

The confession of faith resembles that of Rahab in Joshua 2:10–11. In both cases, they have heard of the victories in Egypt and Transjordan. The deeds of God in delivering his people form the basis for the belief of the Gibeonites, as they did in the case of Rahab. Also parallel is the manner in which the LORD God of Israel receives the credit. In fact, their explicit confession of the LORD contrasts with the absence of any confession on the part of the Israelites. The LORD is mentioned again in verse 14, where it is explicitly noted that Israel failed to enquire of their God. Both Rahab and the Gibeonites make similar confessions of faith, and both escape the destruction that God has decreed for the Canaanites.

7. Of special interest are the references to Hivites, elders, and the geographical details of the Transjordanian Israelite conquests. The Israelites are not aware of the nearby origin of the Gibeonites and they are said to address the Hivites. From this it may be concluded that the Gibeonites were part of a larger group of peoples called Hivites. But why is the detail mentioned here? It relates to Joshua 9:1 and the mention of the Hivites as one of the peoples of Canaan who would make war against Israel. Thus some of the peoples of Canaan did acknowledge the supremacy of Israel's God. It may also suggest an origin of this group in Anatolia (see comment on Jos. 3:10, p. 102). If so, this may explain the *elders* in verse 11. The local government of the Hittite empire in Anatolia was administered by elders.[1] This is uncommon among the Canaanites where the government

[1]O. R. Gurney, *The Hittites* (Harmondsworth: Penguin, 1952), p. 72.

tended to be led by a 'king' or single leader of some sort. As this is true for most towns in the book of Joshua, it is also the most common form of government in the Canaan of the fourteenth-century BC Amarna correspondence.[1] The northern origin of the Gibeonites would explain how Israel could know that they were Hivites, and their reference to elders involved in the rule of their country.

8–10. For the details of Sihon and Og in Joshua 9:10, see Deuteronomy 1:4. The Gibeonites had done their homework well, knowing enough about the Israelites to understand the gravity of their threat and to deceive them. Further, such a confession would tempt the Israelites to flatter themselves as invincible and thereby to set aside caution in the negotiations that followed.

12–15. The account of the Gibeonites convinces the Israelites. As in the defeat at Ai, no enquiry is made of the will of God. Here, however, the failure to do so is stated explicitly. As with Ai, the Israelites are deceived when they rely upon their own perceptions rather than upon divine direction. There, the deception concerned the military strength of Ai. Here, it concerns the origins of the people who sought a treaty. Verse 14 blames *the men of Israel* for not consulting the LORD. This excuses Joshua from the guilt of not consulting with God. Where Joshua was or what he was doing is not described, but he had been involved in the interrogation and therefore could not escape responsibility entirely.[2] No-one among Israel's spiritual leaders thought of the importance of making contact with God.

15. Joshua makes *peace* (Heb. *šālôm*) with the Gibeonites. The treaty's purpose is *to let them live*.[3] The preservation of life uses the same verb, 'to live' (Heb. *ḥyh*), as found in Joshua 2:13–14 and 6:25, where it describes the preservation of Rahab's family at the destruction of Jericho. The treaty that is made is to provide the same life for the Gibeonites. This treaty reflects an ideology similar to that of other Ancient Near Eastern countries. Especially in contemporary Egypt, this 'life' is

---

[1] Exceptions occurred, such as that of the citizens of Byblos who appear to overthrow their king, Rib-Addi, and to obtain some autonomy for themselves, in EA 139 and 140.

[2] Boling and Wright, p. 265, suggest that Joshua 'was not totally responsible' and was 'forced to ratify negotiations'. Butler, p. 103, is closer to the truth: 'Joshua stands condemned.'

[3] The NIV combines both lines, rendering the poetic parallelism as prose.

something that includes theological and economic aspects.[1] The Pharaoh bestows life upon his subjects; he is considered a god who gives the people the privilege of closeness to him and enjoyment of 'life' that his presence brings; and he is also the bestower of food upon the multitudes under his care, who would otherwise starve. By the treaty, the Gibeonites recognize the power of the Israelites to allow them to live (*cf.* vv. 24–25) and they confess the power of the God of Israel in defeating other enemies. Thus the Gibeonites accept a vassal status as Israel's servants.

The leaders of the assembly (Heb. *neśîʾē hāʿēdâ*) are mentioned eight times in Exodus, Numbers and Joshua. They serve alongside Moses, Joshua and the high priests in making reports and decisions about matters affecting the entire nation. In Joshua 22:30, they are involved with issues concerning the Transjordanian tribes (see Nu. 32:2). The acount of Korah's rebellion mentions 250 members of this group who joined Korah. It is not clear how many were involved with the Gibeonite treaty but the implication is that all of Israel was represented. Israel's deception in making this treaty recalls New Testament warnings against taking oaths which may place the Christian into positions of compromise (Mt. 5:33–37; Jas. 4:13–17).

ii. The Gibeonites exposed (9:16–27). This section has three parts that are summarized in verses 16–18 and then elaborated as follows: the Israelites learn of the deception (vv. 19–21), investigate the Gibeonites (vv. 22–25) and spare them (vv. 26–27). The summary in verses 16–18 omits the dialogue.

16. The *three days* (see the note at Jos. 2:22, p. 95) describe a passage of a few days. Like the other nations of verses 1 and 3, Israel also *heard* and acted. Verse 17 emphasizes what Israel hears by repeating it in two phrases. In both clauses, 'they' and a root meaning 'close by' (Heb. *qbr*) are mentioned, with these words placed in parallel order in the Hebrew text:

neighbours	were they [Gibeon]	to them [Israel]
near them	were they [Gibeon]	*living*

The second phrase resembles the Israelites' charge in verse 8, with a switch from the second person singular ('you') to the

[1] See Liverani, *Prestige and Interest*, pp. 230–239.

third person plural ('they'). Thus Israel learns that the very point that the Gibeonites expressly denied was true.

17. They *set out* for the towns of the Gibeonites and confirmed the story. The Gibeonite towns of verse 17 that the Israelites visited included Gibeon, Kephirah (Khirbet el-Kefireh, 5 miles west-south-west of Gibeon), Kiriath Jearim (Tell el-Azhar, about 8 miles north-west of Jerusalem) and Beeroth (el-Bîreh at Khirbet Raddana?). All sites lie in the territory of Benjamin.

18–19. Obedient to their treaty, the Israelite leadership did not put the Gibeonites to the sword but preserved them. This was based on the oath that they made by the LORD, the God of Israel. This particular expression of the name of God occurs in 119 verses in the Old Testament. It is found mainly in the historical books, with only three occurrences in the Pentateuch. There, it appears in Exodus 5:1 where Moses and Aaron identify God to Pharaoh, in Exodus 32:27 where God ordains punishment for worshipping the golden calf, and in Exodus 34:23 where Israelite males must appear before God three times a year. In addition to its appearance twice here, the phrase occurs twelve times in Joshua, including the accounts of Achan (7:13, 19, 20), the altar on Ebal (8:30), the defeat of the southern coalition (10:40, 42), the inheritance of Levi (13:14, 33), Caleb's faithfulness (14:14), the claim of the Transjordanian tribes to faithfulness towards God (22:24), and at the beginning and end of Joshua's description of God's covenant with Israel (24:2, 23). Elsewhere, it is associated with divine promises towards kings and dynasties (*e.g.* 1 Sa. 2:30) and especially towards the dynasty of David (1 Ki. 1:30; 8:15, 20, 25; 2 Ch. 6:4, 10, 16, 17). Thus the expression *the LORD, the God of Israel* has strong links with faithfulness and covenant. Its mention in reference to Achan echoed the seriousness of the covenant violation. Its usage here appeals to the faithful and covenant-keeping God for whom a violation of an oath could result only in the most terrible of consequences.

The oath given by the LORD, the God of Israel, is referred to twice. It frames the statement at the end of verse 18, *The whole assembly grumbled.* This verb (Heb. *lûn*) occurs elsewhere only to describe the wilderness wanderings in Exodus and Numbers (and possibly Ps. 59:15 [Heb. 16]). It characterizes the Israelites at their worst, in an attitude of complaint towards their leadership and towards God. Here, the people grumble against the leadership in general rather than Joshua in particular. Thus Joshua's leadership is not put in jeopardy. Neither is the grumbling directed against God or against any of his actions. In this account alone, nothing negative is said about the grumbling. The people render a judgment against the hasty and incorrect decision of their leadership, one that places them all in jeopardy with respect to God's command to destroy all inhabitants of the land.

20. The *wrath* (Heb. *qeṣep̄*) that the leaders wish to avoid occurs elsewhere in Joshua only in 22:20. There, it recalls the divine wrath that came upon Israel for the sin of Achan, presumably in the form of a military defeat. The leaders of Israel wish to avoid a repetition of the disaster of chapter 7. Therefore they must keep their word, whatever the cost. Apparently the oath that the Israelite leadership swore in alliance with the Gibeonites had no conditions regarding the truthfulness of the Gibeonites. Even though they may be found out as liars, the oath remains valid. The grumbling also anticipates the role of Joshua as deliverer of the Gibeonites. It is not only the treaty but Joshua's adherence to it that leads to their deliverance.

21. The proposal to make the Gibeonites *woodcutters and water-carriers* for Israel's sanctuary suggests the tasks that aliens living in the land are required to perform (Dt. 29:11 [Heb. 10]). Although axes to cut wood could be used as weapons (Je. 46:22), the description here suggests peaceful purposes. The drawing of water was a daily activity necessary for survival. It was particularly appropriate for inhabitants of Gibeon, where one of the largest cisterns in the hill country has been found. Mentioned in the Bible (2 Sa. 2:12–17 and Je. 41:12), it could have served as an important source of water for the surrounding area. An Israelite sanctuary at or near Gibeon (perhaps at neighbouring Nebi Samwil) achieved fame during the United Monarchy and may have been a site served by the Gibeonites.[1] Such servitude by the Gibeonites agrees with the description of those who surrender to Israel (Dt. 20:10–15; Jdg. 1:28). Their service could have extended beyond the sanctuary to include a larger segment of the Israelite population.

---

[1] See 1 Ki. 3:4–5; 1 Ch. 16:39; 21:29; 2 Ch. 1:3–13; J. Blenkinsopp, *Gibeon and Israel* (Cambridge: Cambridge University Press, 1972), p. 7; P. M. Arnold, 'Gibeon', *ABD*, II, pp. 1010–1013.

22–23. Joshua addresses the Gibeonites for the second time. The rest of the leadership disappears from the text. It is mentioned again with reference to matters within the community of Israel (Jos. 17:4; 22:14, 30, 32), not with regard to associations with non-Israelites. Joshua assumes the role of representative for the people of Israel. He again interrogates the Gibeonites with his question of verse 8 which the Gibeonites had answered untruthfully. He asks why the Gibeonites did not answer honestly. Throughout the discussions of verses 6–14 and verses 22–25 much detail is given, along with repetition. This demonstrates that Israel was innocent of intentional disobedience. It did not try to violate the command to destroy all the inhabitants of the land. Israel believed the Gibeonites, who lied. Although innocent of covenant violation, Israel is guilty of failing to consult with God about the matter (v. 14). It does not fall under God's curse, but Gibeon does. Joshua also spoke the other curse (Heb. *'ārûr*) in the book, that against Jericho's rebuilder (Jos. 6:26). The curse is against those who interfere with God's command to destroy the inhabitants of the land.

24–25. Like Rahab, the Gibeonites testify to knowledge of God's command to destroy all opposition. Acquisition of *the whole land* is promised to Israel in Exodus 32:13 and Deuteronomy 11:25 and 19:8. This anticipates acquisition of the whole land that is noted several times in Joshua (10:40; 11:16, 23; 21:43). Joshua had introduced the term *servant* to describe the Gibeonites. They now apply it to themselves. The conclusion of their speech reiterates this dependence upon Israel. In fact, the expression *servant* carries two implications: firstly, the Gibeonites are at Israel's mercy; and secondly, Israel is responsible for Gibeon. This will become fact in chapter 10. Here it provides a basis for the Gibeonites' appeal for Joshua's behaviour towards them to be *good and right.* Joshua should honour the treaty and preserve the Gibeonites alive. The same expression occurs in Jeremiah 26:14 where Jeremiah is threatened with death. He defends his message as from God and invites his accusers to *do with me whatever you think is good and right.* In both cases, there is an appeal to a superior power to act in accordance with justice and to spare the party making the appeal.[1]

---

[1]Jeremiah's comment in v. 15 could also be used by the Gibeonites, 'Be assured, however, that if you put me to death, you will bring the guilt of innocent blood on yourselves.'

26–27. Joshua's name refers to salvation. His deliverance of the Gibeonites is the only time when the text credits him with saving someone.[1] Joshua delivers the Gibeonites from the anger of the Israelites who sought their death. This remained a strong sentiment in certain quarters of Israel, as suggested by Saul's attempt to exterminate them and the reprisals taken by the Gibeonites against the sons of Saul (2 Sa. 21:1–9). Otherwise, the vow and promise of Joshua remained effective so that Gibeonites later returned among the exiles and rebult Jerusalem (Ne. 7:25). Although the altar that the text mentions may be associated with the cult site in Gibeon later visited by Solomon (see comment on v. 21), the reference to *the altar of the LORD at the place the LORD would choose* reminds the reader of the altar at Mount Ebal in chapter 8. This relates the covenant with God at Mount Ebal to the covenant between the Gibeonites and Israelites. As servants at the altar, the Gibeonites were not rejected by God. Instead, they joined the worshipping community before God. Their service at the altar at the place the LORD would choose recalls the same phrase in Deuteronomy 12:5, where it describes the appropriate procedure for worshipping Israel's God. Thus the Gibeonites become formally accepted into Israel's life and worship.

Younger demonstrates Egyptian, Assyrian and Hittite parallels in the form of accounts of a people who have heard of the fame of a conquering army and offer themselves in slavery in exchange for their lives.[2] This type of story was used by Ancient Near Eastern kings to magnify their glory, to demonstrate the wisdom of those who surrender without fighting, and to show their mercy as they allowed others to live. In the case of Joshua also, it could have served these purposes. The southern and northern coalitions which were gathering against Israel (9:1–2) could learn from the Gibeonites that they also could surrender to Israel and perhaps preserve their lives and their national identity. Their refusal to do this (11:19) further demonstrated their irredeemable nature. As with Pharaoh, their hard-hearted attitude of rebellion left Israel with no choice other

---

[1] However, the Hebrew root is different. For Joshua it is *yš'*. In v. 26 it is *nṣl.*

[2] Younger, pp. 200–204. Younger's comparisons, drawn from a variety of periods and nations and applied to the accounts of Jos. 9 – 12, considerably broaden the temporal and ethnic context beyond the Neo-Assyrian period suggested by J. van Seters, 'Joshua's Campaign of Canaan and Near Eastern Historiography', *SJOT*, 4, 1990, pp. 1–12.

than to fight them if it wished to obey God and to occupy the land.

From a literary perspective, this account focuses on the weaknesses of Israel's leadership and on the complaining attitude of the Israelite community toward that leadership. As with Achan and at Ai, Israel learned not to violate its covenants. It contrasts with the covenant at Mount Ebal by describing a covenant with an enemy. However, it connects both covenants and both peoples with the same place of worship. The text anticipates Gibeon's role in drawing Israel into conflict with the southern coalition. In the end, it serves Israelite purposes by advancing their divinely ordained task.

For the Christian, the inclusion of the Gibeonites in God's covenant community (like Rahab) challenges any attitude of self-righteousness. Instead, it teaches the importance of valuing all peoples and of representing to them the life of Christ (see Gal. 3:28).

k. Victory over the leader of Jerusalem and the coalition of southern Canaan (10:1–43)

This text continues the narrative style of the preceding chapters, with recollections of earlier events. Once again Joshua and God speak and they, along with the Israelite warriors, fight and have success. In chapter 10, the enemy speaks for the first time since chapter 2. Their strategy, its failure and their deaths are detailed. Despite these additions, the action of the narrative moves more quickly. The battle at Gibeon requires only twenty-seven verses to describe. There is no elaborate preparation on the part of Israel nor is there sin in the camp that leads to defeat. The narrative uses a series of 'panels' that describe contemporary actions from different perspectives, as with the crossing of the Jordan. As in that text, repeated words and phrases interlock the panels and provide clues as to the significance of each. Events progress even faster in the second half of the chapter. Seven towns are defeated in rapid succession. The repetition of each account, despite differences in detail, anticipates patterns that will dominate the second half of the book.

Theologically, the binding nature of a covenant agreement shifts in its demands from the avoidance of killing the Gibeonites (ch. 9) to the active participation in a war designed to rescue them (ch. 10). Holy war is a dominant theme here, with its distinctive vocabulary. As at Jericho and Ai, God fights for Israel and guarantees the victory. Joshua's leadership will be enhanced in actions in which God responds to Joshua's requests. Dramatic miracles accompany the obedience of Joshua and Israel. Here for the first time Israel does not initiate the aggression but responds to an ally's appeal.

Thus the attack of the Amorite leaders (vv. 1–5) stimulates the Gibeonite request for assistance (v. 6). The Israelite victory is first summarized (vv. 7–10) and then developed in three 'panels': God's assistance (vv. 11–15), Joshua and Israel's defeat of the enemy (vv. 16–27), and the systematic destruction of southern towns (vv. 28–39). A summary of the activities of the campaign concludes the account as Israel returns to where it began, at the worship centre of Gilgal (vv. 40–43).

i. The Amorite strategy (10:1–5).

1. The report that Adoni-Zedek hears compares Ai and Jericho as the two towns over which Israel not only had success but which she also devoted to the ban (*ḥrm*).[1] The focus is on the coalition's leader. As he is named so also the leaders of each of the towns are mentioned. The threat concerns Adoni-Zedek's person as well as his property. There is a contrast with Israel's attitude to Jericho and Ai and her treatment of Gibeon.[2] The Gibeonites *made a treaty of peace*, an expression that not only anticipates the same term in Adoni-Zedek's message to his allies, but also suggests an attitude of wellbeing that is the opposite of the devotion to the ban experienced by the other two towns. Thus the report to Adoni-Zedek captures the nature of the threat that Israel presents, a threat that demands a decision. Either Adoni-Zedek opposes Israel's divinely appointed advance and thereby faces the same judgment as Jericho and Ai, or he makes peace with Israel, joining Israel and Israel's God, and thereby finds a means of living in the midst of Israel, even if in a position of servitude.

2. Israel controlled the Benjaminite plateau, the crossroads between the hill country and the Judean wilderness. It

---

[1] On the ruler's name, see Introduction: 'Antiquity' (p. 29).

[2] E. Noort, 'Zwischen Mythos und Rationalität. Das Kriegshandeln Yhwhs in Josua 10, 1–11' in H. H. Schmid (ed.), *Mythos und Rationalität* (Gütersloh, 1988), pp. 149–161.

provided access to the coastal plain and lowlands to the west via the Beth Horon pass. Threatened with the loss of this strategic centre, the enemies of the south took counsel and made their attack upon Gibeon. The proximity of Gibeon to Jerusalem meant that the Israelite threat had now arrived at Adoni-Zedek's border. Further, the strategic position that the Gibeonites occupied, coupled with the defeat of Bethel and Ai, placed the crucial Benjaminite plateau under the complete control of Israel in the north and in the centre. Only the southern part of the region remained to the king of Jerusalem.[1] Gibeon, apparently a former ally, had deserted to the enemy. Four clauses describe Gibeon's strength. (1) *Gibeon was an important city* . . . It was a great city like Nineveh (Jon. 3:3). (2) It was *like one of the royal cities* . . . The term *royal city* describes Gath as the residence of the Philistine leader, Achish (1 Sa. 27:5). Thus it defines a centre secure against royal enemies. (3) *It was larger than Ai* . . . The security of Gibeon was greater than Ai, whose walls Israel did not breach. (4) *All its men were good fighters.* The term for males of age for military service appears here with the same meaning as in Joshua 7:14–18. The phrases magnify the value of this town for Israel even as they increase the extent of the threat present for Adoni-Zedek. Adoni-Zedek must regain control of the area of Gibeon for his own security.

3. These four phrases have a parallel in the four leaders and their armies for whom Adoni-Zedek sends. Like Adoni-Zedek, the names of the four leaders can be identified with similar names from texts and peoples in and around Palestine during the same period of time that the account in Joshua purports to describe, *i.e.* 1550–1100 BC.[2]

Hebron and Lachish are readily identified with Tell er-Rumeideh and Tell ed-Duweir. As with Jericho, archaeologists have not found evidence for habitation at Tell er-Rumeideh in

---

[1] The dominant status of Jerusalem in the Amarna letters of the fourteenth century BC and in Jos. 10 contrasts with the less significant role of Iron Age I Jerusalem as preserved in Jdg. 1:8 and 2 Sa. 5:6–9. Thus Jos. 10 preserves a distinct and authentic early memory of a city-state that controlled the Benjaminite plateau and influenced events in the towns of the Judean Shephelah. See Z. Kallai and H. Tadmor, 'Bīt Ninurta = Beth Horon – On the History of the Kingdom of Jerusalem in the Amarna Period', *EI*, 9, 1969, pp. 138–147, esp. p. 145, Hebrew; B. Margalit, 'The Day the Sun Did Not Stand Still: A New Look at Joshua X 8–15', *VT*, 42, 1992, pp. 466–491, esp. p. 486, n. 45.

[2] On the rulers' names, see Introduction: 'Antiquity' (pp. 29–30).

the Late Bronze Age (1550–1200 BC).[1] However, Late Bronze tombs were discovered and excavations did uncover pottery on the site that could be dated to the late thirteenth century.[2] Alternatively, the site of Joshua's Hebron may be located at a different place. A thirteenth-century BC itinerary of the Egyptian Pharaoh Ramses II may mention Hebron.[3] Late Bronze Age remains from Tell ed-Duweir attest to the presence of a Canaanite population at that site.[4] The site of Jarmuth has been identified with Khirbet el-Yarmuk = Tel Yarmut, 16 miles south-west from Jerusalem in the Shephelah (the low hill country east of the coastal plain of Philistia and west of the higher Judean hills). It was inhabited during the Late Bronze and Iron Ages.[5] Eglon is best identified with Tell 'Aitûn = Tel 'Eton, 'on the route from Lachish to Hebron via Wâdi el-Jizâ'ir (Naḥal Adorayim)'.[6]

These four sites formed a strategic choice for the king of Jerusalem.[7] Cut off from possible allies to the north, Adoni-Zedek chose Jarmuth, a site that straddled the Sorek and Elah valleys and thus provided a key defence for incursions to Jerusalem from the west. That is to say, Jarmuth was a western neighbour of Jerusalem. Lachish, Eglon, and Hebron formed a line of sites across the southern Shephelah and hill country. The road from Lachish to Hebron has been described as 'the most important ascent into the highlands in the entire region'.[8] Eglon linked Hebron with Gaza and Egypt. It also connected Lachish and the Mediterranean seaports with Arad and the

[1]A. Ofer, 'Excavations at Biblical Hebron', *Qadmoniot*, 22, 1989, pp. 88–93 (90), Hebrew.

[2]*Idem*, 'Tell Rumeideh (Hebron)', *Excavations and Surveys in Israel*, 6, 1987–1988, pp. 92–93.

[3]C. R. Krahmalkov, 'Exodus Itinerary Confirmed by Egyptian Evidence', *BAR*, 20/5, September/October 1994, pp. 60–61.

[4]D. Ussishkin, 'Lachish – Key to the Israelite Conquest of Canaan?', *BAR*, 13/1, January/February 1987, pp. 18–39.

[5]P. de Miroschedji, *ABD*, III, pp. 644–646.

[6]A. F. Rainey, 'The Biblical Shephelah of Judah', *BASOR*, 251, 1983, pp. 1–22 (10). Rainey discusses the earlier identifications of Tell el-Hesi and Tell Beit Mirsim, and shows how they do not conform to the geographic evidence of Jos. 10. For the original identification of Eglon with Tell 'Aitûn see Noth, p. 95.

[7]Their order in the list of vv. 3, 5, and 23 does not follow a geographical pattern as it does in vv. 31–37, where the order of attack follows a logical sequence. The order given here seems to be an alphabetical one.

[8]D. A. Dorsey, *The Roads and Highways of Ancient Israel* (Baltimore: Johns Hopkins University Press, 1991), p. 195.

Arabian trade routes.[1] All these centres benefited by trade with Jerusalem and its roads to the north. If Egypt still dominated the coastal plain, the Benjaminite plateau may have provided these towns with their primary access to all northern markets. With these cut off and with the survival of Jerusalem threatened, the rumours of Israel's successes would have brought the leaders of the southern towns to the aid of their ally. As the story goes on to relate, the 'domino theory' operated. If they could not stop Israel at Jerusalem, the leaders knew that their own towns faced destruction.

4. This is the only message in Joshua that one Canaanite leader sends another. In the fourteenth century BC, Jerusalem's leader wrote at least five letters to the Pharaoh regarding his town and its security. These letters, part of the collection known as the Amarna letters, are longer and more literate than contemporary missives of other Palestinian town leaders.[2] In many cases, they include a colophon addressed to the Pharaoh's scribe who would read the letter and speak to the leader. The leader of Jerusalem requests the scribe to use persuasive words. The elegant rhetoric of these letters is characterized by threefold repetition of important points.

Unlike the Amarna correspondence from Jerusalem, the message of verse 4 is surprisingly brief, composed of only thirteen words in the Hebrew text. This may be intended as a summary of the letter or it may reflect the actual text whose brevity was intended to stress the urgency. The request is styled in the form of two threefold repetitions, with three separate verbs describing what the readers must do (*come up, help me, attack*) and three nouns identifying the enemy (*Gibeon, Joshua, the Israelites*). The corresponding verb with the meaning 'to make peace with' (Heb. *šlm*) is also found in the Amarna letters.[3] It is used in this way twice by the leader of Jerusalem, and both times as a justification for going to war.[4]

---

[1] *Ibid.*, pp. 196–197.

[2] R. S. Hess, 'Hebrew Psalms and Amarna Correspondence from Jerusalem: Some Comparisons and Implications', *ZAW*, 101, 1989, 249–265.

[3] The noun is the familiar *shalom,* 'peace'. Strictly, this is not the same verb but the Akkadian cognate to the Hebrew verb formed from the root *šlm*. The Hebrew uses a causative Hiphil stem while the Akkadian uses the basic G stem, with a distinctive Amarna 'Canaanite' form.

[4] The texts are EA 287, line 12 and EA 288, line 27. See the translation of W. L. Moran, *The Amarna Letters* (Baltimore: Johns Hopkins University Press, 1992), p.

The same usage is found in verse 4.

5. Verse 4 ties in with the response of the leaders.[1] Verse 5 relates how they *moved up* against Gibeon. This is the same verb as the first one in the plea of Adoni-Zedek in verse 4. The leaders obeyed the request. The term *kings of the Amorites* appears in Joshua 5:1 and 9:10. Joshua 5:1 refers to the leaders west of the Jordan, who are the ones mentioned here. Joshua 9:10 refers to Sihon and Og, leaders of the Amorites east of the Jordan. With the exception of Joshua 5:1 and the account of chapter 10, all biblical references to *king(s) of the Amorites* describe these two Transjordanian rulers. Besides describing the location of the leaders in chapter 10, the term 'kings of the Amorites' connects these figures with Sihon and Og. It suggests their fate. The repetition of the names of the leaders emphasizes that all responded to Adoni-Zedek's request. The lists of verses 3 and 5 also frame the request in verse 4 and focus on the actions that are described there against Gibeon and Israel.

In these opening verses, the actions of the enemy have been outlined, as well as the reasons behind those actions. Three points summarize this account. Firstly, the focus is on the coalition of Adoni-Zedek and his plan to counter the expansion of Israel. This justifies the war that Israel fights. Secondly, the list of these leaders describes the strength of southern Palestine. The whole land has joined to fight. Israel's victory, when achieved, will acquire greater significance. Thirdly, the first object of the coalition is Gibeon. This ties together Joshua 9 and 10. If the treaty did not exist, the coalition would not wage war against Gibeon, nor would Gibeon draw Israel into that war.

ii. The Gibeonite response (10:6). Verse 6 parallels verses 3–4 using the same verbs: the Gibeonites *sent word* and said what

---

328, where the three cities are Gezer, Ashkelon and Lachish: May the [kin]g know (that) all the lands are [at] peace (with one another), but I am at war. May the king provide for his land. Consider the lands of Gazru, Ašqaluna, and L[akis]i. They have given them food, oil, and any other requirement. So may the king provide for archers and send the archers against men that commit crimes against the king, my lord.' During the Amarna period of the fourteenth century, Lachish was hostile towards Jerusalem, rather than its ally as in the book of Joshua.

[1]It also has literary connections with v. 6, for which see below.

they needed. However, the contrast is marked between the list of leaders and towns to which Adoni-Zedek appeals and the single name, Joshua, to which the Gibeonites appeal. Thus Joshua is set over against all the powers of the south. His location, *in the camp at Gilgal,* parallels the town names in verse 3. This expression also introduces the Israelites. When they finish their war with the south, the same expression appears (vv. 15 and 43) as the destination of their return home. This is the same site as the Gilgal where the Gibeonites met with Israel (9:6).

The request of the Gibeonites begins, *Do not abandon* (literally 'take away your hand from') *your servants.* The 'hand' symbolizes the military might of Israel, just as it did when Joshua stretched out his hand against Ai in Joshua 8:18. The verb 'to take away' (Heb. *rph*) occurred in Joshua 1:5, where God promised Joshua that there would always be divine support for him. It is given in the context of a declaration of loyalty, just as here Gibeon expects Joshua to be loyal to their treaty. The reference to *your servants* indicates that in this treaty relationship the Gibeonites are the vassals. The entreaty *Come up to us quickly . . . Help us* uses verbs identical to those of Adoni-Zedek (v. 4), emphasizing the confrontation. Unlike Adoni-Zedek, however, Gibeon inserts the phrase *save us* between the commands for Israel to come to their aid. In fact, this seems to replace Adoni-Zedek's *help me attack,* contrasting the two intents. One comes to attack and destroy Gibeon. The other comes to deliver it.

The Gibeonites complain that they are besieged by *all the Amorite kings from the hill country.* The term *all the kings* may suggest: (1) hyperbole on the part of the Gibeonites to express the dire nature of their plight;[1] (2) that these were the major political centres in southern Palestine; or (3) that the Amorites were a special group of people located at these five places but not elsewhere. There is no evidence for (3). (2) is possible but unlikely insofar as verses 28–39 indicate a strategy that includes towns other than these. (1) is most likely. It serves to heighten the significance of the conflict. The whole of the Amorite peoples had gathered at Gibeon, as represented by the finest of their leaders and warriors who could be mustered for the fight.

For the Christian, these verses recall the psalms of lamenta-

---

[1]Note the earlier request for Israel to 'hurry'.

tion in which the psalmist is threatened by the enemy round about and calls upon the psalmist's covenant God to give salvation.[1] Through Christ, the Christian claims a covenant relationship with God. Prayer becomes the means to petition the Father in times of need, just as this message formed the means by which the Gibeonites sought help (Mt. 6:9; 26:41; Mk. 14:38; Lk. 11:2; 22:40; 2 Cor. 13:7; Eph. 6:18; Col. 1:9; Jas. 5:13–16; Rev. 5:8; 8:4).

iii. Victory (10:7–43). The remainder of the chapter details Israel's victory. The account is presented in a series of 'panels' or pictures that overlap in time but focus on different aspects of the victory. This technique was used in the stories of Rahab, of the crossing of the Jordan River and of the defeat of Jericho and Ai. The first panel (vv. 7–10) summarizes the victory. Then the details of the LORD's work in the victory are considered (vv. 11–15). This is followed by details of Israel's battles with the leaders (vv. 16–27) and with the towns (vv. 28–40). A summary reviews the success and returns the victors to camp (vv. 41–43).

a. Summary (10:7–10).
7. As the southern coalition obeyed Adoni-Zedek's plea to *come up,* so Joshua responds to the same entreaty from the Gibeonites. Although the verb 'to ascend' (Heb. '*lh*) may simply describe an appearance on the scene, the location of Gibeon and nearby Nebi Samwel as the highest point in that region of the hill country implies that an ascent was probably necessary for both antagonists. As in verse 5, the respondents are first identified with a general statement (*the five kings of the Amorites*) and then with a specific description of each member of the coalition, so in verse 7 there is a general statement of the respondent, *Joshua,* which is followed by a specific description of who is involved, *i.e.* Joshua and his army. Joshua represents Israel's army. This designation anticipates the *Joshua and all Israel with him* that occurs seven times in the chapter. It introduces each battle and concludes the whole account in verse 43, which, with verse 7, frames the participation of Israel. Thus verse 7 defines *all Israel* as used later in the chapter. It

---

[1] S. Mowinckel, *The Psalms in Israel's Worship,* 1, tr. D. R. Ap-Thomas (Oxford: Blackwell, 1962), p. 194, identifies Psalms 12, 14, 44, 58, 60, 74, 79, 80, 83, 89 and 144 with these.

means the whole army under Joshua's command. That they were *the best fighting men* recalls the *good fighters* of Gibeon (v. 2). This description foreshadows their victory over the southern coalition, the quality of whose forces is never so described. A theme common elsewhere in the Ancient Near East is one where many opponents fight against a single, unified army.[1] In Joshua as well, the unity and order of a single nation worshipping a single God with a united army under one person's leadership is an advantage. Likewise, the unity of the church as the body of Christ under his leadership (Eph. 1:22; Col. 1:18) is emphasized both by Jesus (Jn. 17) and his disciples (Acts 15; 1 Cor. 3).

8. The command 'do not fear' recalls Joshua 8:1. Here also there follows a reference to the enemy and a promise of divine presence and support. The Gibeonites requested a *hand* (Heb. *yad*) in verse 6 (literally 'Do not withdraw your hand'; NIV, *Do not abandon*). Joshua repeats it to his army at the rout of the enemy in verse 19. It refers to Israel's military power to destroy their enemies and to preserve their allies. Behind this lies the gracious empowerment of God, who enables Israel to achieve success. The promise that no-one *will be able to withstand you* uses a verb, 'to stand' (Heb. *'md*), that recurs in two important places: when the sun and moon 'stand' in verse 13 and again when Joshua addresses his army in verse 19, telling them not to stand still but to chase the enemy. With different subjects in each case, the verb relates the activities of God, of Joshua and of the enemy.

9–10. The strategy of an all-night march responded to the Gibeonite request for haste and facilitated the divinely ordained confusion of the enemy when they saw Israel appear out of the morning mists. Divine confusion of the enemy is described elsewhere in the Old Testament using the same verb (Heb. *hmm*).[2] It is found in other battle accounts throughout the Ancient Near East in the form of the terror and panic that overtake the enemy.[3] Here it forms a summary statement anticipating verse 11, at the beginning of the second 'panel'.

---

[1] M. Liverani, 'The Ideology of the Assyrian Empire,' in *Power*, pp. 297–317, especially p. 31.

[2] Ex. 14:24; 23:27; Dt. 7:23; Jdg. 4:15; 1 Sa. 7:10. H.-P. Müller, *TDOT*, III, p. 419, identifies it as a technical term for describing holy war.

[3] See Younger, pp. 73–74 and 133–134, for examples from Assyrian and Hittite accounts. Often the Ancient Near Eastern materials refer to the king rather

The *great victory* summarizes the results of the battle for Joshua. It anticipates the same expression that introduces the defeat of the armies in the third 'panel' (v. 20, NIV *destroyed them completely*). Corresponding to verse 20 and to the following phrase in verse 10, it is Joshua who wins the great victory. Thus both God and Joshua are involved in the success of the battle.

Four place names appear. Gibeon is where the battle begins. Perhaps Israel marched from the east and cut off the coalition so that they could not return via Jerusalem. Israel drove the coalition westward to Beth Horon, the major pass in the area that provides access between the hill country and the Shephelah and plain to the west. The chase continued southward in the Shephelah to Azekah. As this site is close to Jarmuth, the armies could seek refuge there. The best identification of Makkedah is Khirbet el-Qom, which lies in the Shephelah.[1] This would allow the remnants of the coalition to retreat eastward into the Elah Valley and then southward from Succoth to Adullam, where they joined one of two major north-south routes through the Shephelah which passed through Makkedah.[2] Located at Khirbet el-Qom, Makkedah lies midway between Lachish, Eglon and Hebron. It allowed coalition survivors to seek refuge in these, their home towns. The names Azekah and Makkedah summarize the battle and anticipate the two following 'panels' that describe the events in greater detail (vv. 11 and 16).[3]

---

than to a deity as the agent that directly causes the fear. This is not the case in Joshua, where God alone is the subject.

[1]D. Dorsey, 'The Location of Biblical Makkedah', *Tel Aviv*, 7, 1980, pp. 185–193.

[2]*Idem, The Roads and Highways of Ancient Israel*, pp. 152–153.

[3]A cautious appreciation of the structure of the narrative eliminates the supposed problems in the text as identified by B. Margalit, 'The Day the Sun Did Not Stand Still: A New Look at Joshua X 8–15', p. 470: 'One could describe at considerable length the exegetical acrobatics of commentators ancient and modern in their attempt to make sense of these verses, be it in literary, historical, or astronomical terms. For if, as we learn from vv. 10–11, the scene of battle had already shifted to the Lachish area, what is the point of arresting the sun over Gibeon? To be sure, Noth and others would excise the references to Azeqah and Maqqedah in these verses, but only because the narrative is otherwise reduced to geographical nonsense.' Neither these nor problems with the return to Gilgal in v. 15 require a two-source literary solution as Margalit proposes. Rather, presented here is a series of 'panels' or scenes that each present an account of the battle from their own perspectives and with their own distinctive emphases.

b. God's role in the battle (10:11–15).

11. At the Beth Horon descent, God aided Israel by casting *hailstones* from heaven against the enemy. In second-millennium BC Hittite and first-millennium BC Assyrian sources, 'stones from heaven' are used by deities in similar contexts of battling with the enemy.[1] As here, it is often an explanation of how the enemy was thrown into confusion. Hailstones can occur during the spring.[2] The *hailstones* anticipate the *large rocks* (same words in the Hebrew) that seal the leaders of the coalition in caves (v. 18).

12. Verses 12a and 14 frame the central concern of the passage, the miracle of the standing sun and moon. Both refer to the special day when God fought for Israel. The pass of Beth Horon descends westward into the Valley of Aijalon. There the battle raged as Joshua called out for the sun to stand still (Heb. *dôm*) at Gibeon in the east and the moon at the Valley of Aijalon to the west.[3] The locations of these heavenly bodies suggest that the time of the occurrence was early enough in the morning for both sun and moon to be visible.

13. Verse 12 is fulfilled. The reliability of its record is attested in the *Book of Jashar*, as noted in the second half of verse 13. Finally, verse 14 comments on the significance of the event. What actually happened? The request for the sun and moon to be affected so that they *stand still* is a translation of the verb in verse 12 (*dôm*). In verse 13, the identical verb is used to describe

[1] M. Weinfeld, 'Divine Intervention in War in Ancient Israel and in the Ancient Near East' in *HHI*, pp. 140–141; Younger, pp. 208–211. For example, Younger translates a relevant passage in Sargon's Letter to the God about an enemy coalition: 'I filled ascents and descents with the bodies of (their) fighters. Over 6 'double-hours' of ground from Mt. Uauš to Mt. Zimur, the jasper mountain, I pursued them at the point of the javelin. The rest of the people, who had fled to save their lives, whom he had abandoned that the glorious might of Aššur, my lord, might be magnified, Adad, the violent, the son of Anu, the valiant, uttered his loud cry against them; and with the flood cloud and hailstones (lit. 'the stone of heaven', NA₄ AN-e), he totally annihilated the remainder.'

[2] R. B. Y. Scott, 'Meteorological Phenomena and Terminology in the Old Testament', *ZAW*, 64, 1952, pp. 19–20; Butler, p. 116.

[3] J. G. Taylor, *Yahweh and the Sun. Biblical and Archaeological Evidence for Sun Worship in Ancient Israel*, JSOT Supplement 111 (Sheffield: JSOT Press, 1993), pp. 114–118, identifies the LORD with the sun in Gibeon. In Joshua, the sun is a symbol of the LORD God, not a separate deity. Joshua speaks to the LORD (v. 12) by addressing the sun in Gibeon. In the same way, the LORD listens to the voice of a man (v. 14).

what happened to the sun. The next line describes what happened to the moon. Both lines form a chiastic structure (A–B–B'–A'):

A. *stood still*   B. *the sun*
B'. *and the moon*   A'. *stopped*

Thus the two verbs parallel one another, as do the two nouns.

Interpretations of what happened fall into three categories. In the first, traditional, view the sun and moon simply stayed where they were in the sky until the battle ended and light was no longer necessary. This has support in the context of Joshua's night march from Gilgal to Gibeon. If it was a full moon, the moonlight could have enabled a safe march. It would also anticipate the miraculous provision for both moonlight and sunlight. There are parallels to this request in the *Iliad* and classical Greek literature.[1] However, the position of the sun to the east (or even overhead) implies that Joshua made the request before the afternoon, which would be very early in the day for a general to foresee the need for additional hours of sunlight.

A second alternative has been to find in the prayer a request for a solar eclipse. This darkening of the sky would bring about fear among the enemy and make their slaughter easier. This meaning occurs in Habakkuk 3:11 where a similar verb is used.[2] However, the first verb is subject to a number of possible interpretations, and darkness is only one. Further, the confusion has already been created. If an eclipse or some other astronomical darkness were intended, it would have only hindered the pursuit of the battle. So it seems unlikely that Joshua would call for such a sign, especially when the fearful casting down of stones from heaven had already achieved this purpose.

---

[1] M. Weinfeld, 'Divine Intervention in War in Ancient Israel and in the Ancient Near East', p. 147. In *Iliad* II lines 413–415, Agamemnon entreats Zeus, 'Let not the sun go down and the darkness come, until I cast down headlong the citadel of Priam . . . ' See W. H. D. Rouse (tr.), *Homer, The Iliad* (Edinburgh: Thomas Nelson, 1938), p. 30.

[2] B. Margalit, 'The Day the Sun Did Not Stand Still: A New Look at Joshua X 8–15', pp. 480–481. If this option is followed and an eclipse is intended, then it can be dated to 30 September 1131 BC. See J. F. A. Sawyer, 'Joshua 10:12–14 and the Solar Eclipse of 30 September 1131 BC', *PEQ*, 104, 1972, pp. 139–146; F. R. Stephenson, 'Astronomical Verification and Dating of Old Testament Passages Referring to Solar Eclipses', *PEQ*, 107, 1975, pp. 117–120.

The third suggestion considers Neo-Assyrian astrology. It argues that these texts indicate that a bad omen occurs when the sun and moon are seen at the same time on days other than the fourteenth of the month.[1] Thus Joshua was requesting either a favourable omen for himself and his army, or, if one wishes to separate Joshua from astrological beliefs, he could have been requesting an unfavourable omen to confound the Canaanites who might have believed in astrology.[2] By itself, this does not make sense of the phrase *till the nation avenged itself on its enemies.* The remainder of the chapter implies that the vengeance took many hours, perhaps days, to complete. The Neo-Assyrian omens do not remain on exhibition until what they imply about events on earth takes place. Why should the omen remain in the sky in Joshua? The interpretation of the *Book of Jashar* also suggests that the sun remained in the sky for an unusually long period. This has led some commentators to conclude that the comment from the *Book of Jashar* reflects a later source that did not understand the earlier statement about the sun and moon remaining stationary.[3]

Thus none of the explanations is entirely satisfactory. Perhaps the mystery remains because not enough is known about astrological practices in the second millennium BC. Certainly the use of an omen or the demonstration of divine power superior to the omen could explain some of the text.[4] It may be that the retention of the same position of the sun and moon served to accomplish this. Like the large stones, this miracle demonstrated God's special participation in the defeat

[1] See H. Hunger, *Astrological Reports to Assyrian Kings*, State Archives of Assyria 8 (Helsinki: Helsinki University Press, 1992). Numerous texts illustrate this belief. An example may be quoted from no. 25, lines 6–10: 'If on the 16th day the moon and sun [are seen] together: one king [will send hostile messages] to another; the king [will be shut up] in his palace; [the step of] the enemy [will be set towards his land]; the enemy [will march around] victorious[ly in his land].' The reconstructions are certain because of the repetitious nature of this message.

[2] J. S. Holladay, Jr., 'The Day(s) the Moon Stood Still', *JBL*, 87, 1968, pp. 166–178.

[3] *Ibid.*; P. D. Miller, *The Divine Warrior in Early Israel* (Cambridge, Massachusetts: Harvard University Press, 1973), p. 126; B. Halpern, 'Doctrine by Misadventure: Between the Israelite Source and the Biblical Historian' in R. E. Friedman (ed.) *The Poet and the Historian. Essays in Literary and Historical Biblical Criticism* (Chico, California: Scholars Press, 1983), pp. 41–73 (55).

[4] This is suggested by J. H. Walton, 'Joshua 10:12–15 and Mesopotamian Celestial Omen Texts', *FTH*, pp. 181–190.

of Israel's enemies. The record in the *Book of Jashar* may suggest a special significance to the miracle. Nothing more is known about this source, which seems to have preserved nationalistic songs such as 2 Samuel 1:19–27 and possibly 1 Kings 8:12–13.[1]

14. As with verse 12, there is an A–B–B'–A' chiasm:

A. *The LORD gave the Amorites over to Israel* (v. 12)
  B. *Joshua said to the LORD* (v. 12)
  B'. *the LORD listened to a man* (v. 14)
A'. *the LORD was fighting for Israel* (v. 14).

As with the miracle of the casting down of the hailstones, the emphasis in this story is God's assistance to Israel. This is the background to the fight on the ground. It was God's will that Joshua should win.

15. The same statement will recur in verse 43, where it will signal the end of the next 'panel'. Like verse 6, at the beginning of the battle account, this statement suggests that Israel begins and ends each campaign in the presence of God at the sanctuary of Gilgal.[2] As in verse 43, *Joshua returned with all Israel* implies that there was no loss to Israel in the battle, nor did any disunity result.

For the Christian, the repeated mention of God's miraculous intervention in Israel's wars recalls the spiritual warfare with sin that forms a daily struggle. This too involves spiritual forces. Although they may not always manifest themselves in the overtly miraculous, they are no less real (Eph. 6:12).

c. Israel's role in the battle (10:16–43).

16–17. Like the previous 'panel', this one begins with the verb 'to flee' (Heb. *nûs*). Here it is not the whole army but the five leaders who flee. The mention of Makkedah recalls verse 10, where the three locations summarized the battle. Two of these appeared in the 'panel' of verses 11–15. Now the

---

[1] The latter is identified in the LXX as from the 'Book of Song'. 'Song' and 'Jashar' are spelled with the same three consonants but in different order, *šyr* instead of *yšr.*

[2] For Mitchell, p. 99, the references to the camp form part of the composition structure of Jos. 1 – 12. For Y. Kaufmann, *The Biblical Account of the Conquest of Palestine*, p. 92, this return to the camp prevents battle weary Israelites from settling in the land prematurely. However, the emphasis upon the unity of the people ordered before God is the most powerful image conveyed by these references of returning to and setting out from the camp at Gilgal.

remaining place name occurs at verse 16. The same phrase, *hidden/hiding in the cave at Makkedah,* occurs twice. The verb 'to hide' (Heb. *ḥbʾ*) recurs in the last verse of the section and frames the whole story. The reference to the five leaders is also repeated in verses 16 and 17. It anticipates verses 28–40 in so far as the execution of the leaders is associated with the conquest of their towns. The leaders who had appeared at the head of their armies disappear into hiding. Such is the power of God in aiding the Israelite army.

18. For *the large rocks,* see verse 11 (p. 196). Under Joshua's direction, Israel imitates the action of God in its use of these boulders. Again, the *large rocks* at *the mouth of the cave* anticipates the same expression in verse 27. The rock-sealed cave becomes the prison and then the tomb of the leaders.

19. This passage serves three purposes. Firstly, it relates a similar action to that in verses 11–15, portraying it from Israel's perspective rather than God's. Joshua's command to Israel, *Don't stop* (Heb. *ʿmd*), uses the same verb as the divine promise to Joshua in verse 8 that *Not one of them will be able to withstand* Israel. It also ties in with the sun and moon that 'stand' in the heavens (v. 13). The same verb (Heb. *lābôʾ*) that describes how the sun *delayed going down* also defines how Israel is not to allow the enemy to *reach their cities.* Both the signs in the heavens and the army on earth follow Joshua's instructions. Behind both is the divine promise that God has given the enemy to Israel (vv. 8, 19). Thus Israel believes God's promise and receives the benefit of victory. That Israel *defeated them in a great victory* (v. 10) is repeated in verse 20 (NIV, *destroyed them completely*).

20. Secondly, in verses 19–21, Joshua used a strategy that maximized Israel's victory. The battle that fanned out from Makkedah left no Canaanite survivors except those who escaped to the towns. Scattered and isolated, the leaders and each of the towns were conquered the more easily.

Thirdly, the text foreshadows the second half of this 'panel' (vv. 28–40) that describes Israel's role from the perspective of each town conquered. The reader understands that Israel has moved to the southern Shephelah, where *the few who were left* (Heb. *haśśĕrîdîm*) *reached their fortified cities.* The negative of this, *They left no survivors* (*śārîd*), occurs five times in verses 28–40, making clear that the destruction of the towns was a continuation of this earlier battle. The elimination of *survivors* occurs in battles against Sihon and Og as well as at Ai.[1] It attests to the obedience of Israel in carrying out God's instructions regarding such wars (Dt. 20:10–18).

21. These verses complete one phase of a larger battle in the south, so the army returned to Makkedah, rather than to Gilgal, where they go at the end of the battle (vv. 15, 43). Their success enhanced Israel's unity. The absence of complaint in verse 21 contrasts with the grumbling of the people when they discovered that their leaders had made a treaty with the Gibeonites (9:18).[2]

22–27. This section completes notes on the rebellion of the coalition leaders (vv. 3–5) and their fate (vv. 16–18). The list of the leaders repeats the lists of verses 3 and 5. Those who began the revolt are brought before Joshua and executed. The army's obedience to Joshua is demonstrated by the commands given by him in verses 22 and 24 and the word-for-word detail in which they are followed in verses 23 and 25. The obedience of Joshua towards God is demonstrated by his execution of the leaders of the Canaanites, which is witnessed by the Israelite leaders and by the army. It is performed by Joshua although the leaders place their feet upon the necks of each of the captives.[3] The ceremony does not end with the execution. It also entails the hanging of the corpses on wooden poles. Hanging upon a wooden pole or tree was also the treatment given to the corpse of the ruler of Ai.[4] In both accounts, the corpses are buried later. This public spectacle of Israelite victory also served to frighten Canaanite onlookers, perhaps in the nearby town of Makkedah.

25. In the centre of this section is Joshua's instruction to the leaders and his confession that God will defeat all Israel's enemies. The initial *Do not be afraid* resembles verse 8 and God's

---

[1]Nu. 21:35; Dt. 2:34; 3:3; Jos. 8:22.

[2]This assumes that the Israelites are the subject of the verb, *i.e.* that they do the complaining rather than being the recipients of the complaints. See Ex. 11:7 for the same idiom and a similar syntax.

[3]For placing one's foot on top of an enemy as an image of defeat both in the Bible and in the Ancient Near East, see H. W. Lay and R. W. Vunderinck, 'Foot', *ISBE*, I, pp. 332–333.

[4]See comment on Jos. 8:29. There is one Hebrew word for both 'wood' and 'tree', *'ēṣ*. As a plural, it includes the same consonants as the word, 'very' (*'ṣm*), in the final phrase of v. 27, *which are there to this day*. Concerning the use of this phrase as a testimony of the author's experience, see the note on aetiologies in ch. 3, pp.110–111.

charge to Joshua at the beginning of the campaign. Joshua passes on the responsibility of war to the army. Joshua 1:9 closely resembles Joshua's instructions here: *Be strong and courageous. Do not be terrified; do not be discouraged.* In chapter 10, Joshua passes on this divine charge to his generals. The context is the execution of the Canaanite leaders. He argues for the divine election of Israel and its leaders and also implies God's rejection of all who oppose Israel, symbolically cursing them by his treatment of the coalition leaders' corpses.

27. The conclusion notes the caves in which the kings had formerly hidden and where their bodies are now placed. The phrase *At the mouth of the cave they placed large rocks* is a near duplicate of the beginning of the account (v. 18). This framing technique exhibits a concern for order and cohesion in the story, something that corresponds to the order and unity in the Israelite army.

For the Christian, these brutal scenes seem far removed from the worship of the *Prince of Peace* (Is. 9:6). Yet Jesus counselled his own followers that discipleship would bring warfare (Mt. 10:34–39; Lk. 22:36) and persecution (Mt. 24). The horrors of warfare are not alien to the Christian, nor has the Bible ever denied that the one who came in peace and suffered for it will return with a sword (Rev. 19 – 20).

28–39. Israel conquers seven towns in the region where the Canaanite leaders are put to death: Makkedah, Libnah, Lachish, Gezer, Eglon, Hebron, Debir. Actually, the fourth town, Gezer, is not described as captured. Instead, its king, Horam, and his army fight against Joshua and are defeated. Indeed, this account deviates from what is otherwise an observable pattern for each of the towns. Similar phrases are repeated to describe operations at each town. Table 1 summarizes the phrases (singular and plural verbs are not distinguished) and their occurrences in the accounts of the conquest.

Joshua 11:13 implies that none of these major southern towns was put to the torch. According to Joshua 15:13–16, inhabitants still remained in Hebron and Debir. Perhaps either (1) the texts date from different periods and sources and so the contradiction is not real; or (2) Joshua 15:13–16 occurred as a result of a repopulation after Israel's initial conquest of the towns; or (3) Joshua 15:13–16 is identical with the account of chapter 10. However, (1) is special pleading since any redactor would have seen the problem and could easily have omitted

Table 1: Phrases used to describe the conquests listed in 10:28–39

Phrases	M	Li	La	G	E	H	D
he *took* it	×		×		×	×	×
he *took up positions against it*			×		×		
he *attacked* it		×	×		×	×	×
the LORD *gave that city*		×	×				
its king	×	×				×	×
its villages						×	×
he *put to the sword*	×	×	×		×	×	×
he *totally destroyed it*	×				×		×
everyone in it	×	×	×		×	×	×
he left no survivors	×	×				×	×
he did to Y as he had done to Z	×	×	×		×	×	×

Key: M = Makkedah; Li = Libnah; La = Lachish; G = Gezer; E = Eglon; H = Hebron; D = Debir.

mention of Hebron and Debir in chapter 10; (2) has no textual support; and (3) is possible although the position of chapter 15 suggests that it occurred during the allotment, while chapter 10 took place before it. Younger has shown that similar expressions are used in Ancient Near Eastern texts. He gives examples from the Merneptah stele, where 'Israel is wasted, his seed is not', and from the ninth-century BC Moabite stele, where King Mesha states, 'Israel has utterly perished forever.'[1] In neither case did these phrases describe the total elimination of Israel, however, as they are sweeping statements of victory that create an impression of complete conquest.

Although some symmetry can be observed in the accounts of these battles, there is no consistent pattern. This is perhaps intentional. It suggests that while the campaign enjoyed success at each stage, different tactics were used. It also implies that this is not the repetition of a formula with different towns inserted to create a fictional account. Such an annalistic style is well known in the recording of Hittite and Assyrian campaigns, where the overall pattern is repeated but specifics are altered

[1]Younger, p. 227.

according to the unique elements involved in capturing each town. That the same effect was achieved everywhere is indicated by the note at the end of each conquest, in which it is compared with earlier accounts. This literary style served two purposes. Firstly, it demonstrated the consistent success of Israel's army and the hopeless state of all who resisted them. It drives home a point that the God of Israel's army does win. Secondly, the annalistic form corresponds as closely as any Ancient Near Eastern conquest account can to the recitation of what we know of as history. It is more regular than the free-flowing narratives of the preceding chapters but more individualized than the list of towns captured in chapter 12. Thus it preserves the form of an official account without losing the details specific to each event described.

Notes such as *that* (same) *day* at Makkedah and Eglon and *on the second day* at Lachish refer to the length of time spent in conquering the towns. Lachish, the most massive of the sites, may have taken the longest. At many of the sites, there is no evidence that they were surrounded by Late Bronze Age fortifications, a fact that may have made their capture easier.

The mention of the leader of Gezer in the centre of the conquests emphasizes his importance. Although the town was not conquered by Israel (Jos. 16:10), the defeat of its leader and his army was considered a major event. Gezer is Tell Jezer, a site that guards the western entrance to the Aijalon Valley that leads to Jerusalem. Perhaps Israel bypassed the site in its chase. It is mentioned in the Amarna letters and in the Merneptah stele. The stele records the conquest by Pharaoh Merneptah of Ashkelon, Gezer and Yenoam (*c.* 1207 BC). Thus it was considered a strategic site and was one with its own Late Bronze Age fortification wall.[1] The name of its king, Horam, is West Semitic, just as is the name of the king of Gezer in the Amarna letters.[2] Perhaps, under Egyptian control, a town such as Gezer would not have had any responsibility to defend Jerusalem. However, it was not in the interest of the Egyptian garrison to allow an army such as that of Israel to wander

[1] W. G. Dever, 'Gezer', *ABD*, II, pp. 998–1003. The Outer Wall at Gezer remains 'the only defense system *originally* constructed in the LB [Late Bronze Age] and not reused from an earlier period' (p. 1001). See *idem*, 'Further Evidence on the Date of the Outer Wall at Gezer', *BASOR*, 289, 1993, 35–54.

[2] R. S. Hess, 'Non-Israelite Personal Names in the Narratives of the Book of Joshua', *CBQ*, forthcoming.

through the region at will. For Joshua, this army's defeat constituted a high point in the southern military successes.

There is a geographical sequence to the towns, beginning with Makkedah, located in the midst of the others. The armies sweep in an arc from Libnah (Tell Bornât = Tel Burna)[1] at the north-west corner, south through Lachish and Eglon, and then north to Hebron which lies in the north-east corner of the arc. From this point, the army turned south along the watershed of the hill country and reached Debir, identified with Khirbet Rabûd, the most important Late Bronze Age site in the hill country south of Hebron.[2]

40. This lengthy account concludes with a threefold summary: by region (v. 40), by boundaries (v. 41) and by the length of time taken (v. 42). The regions begin with the hill country that includes the towns of Jerusalem, Hebron and Debir. The Negev, or southern country, is not included among the towns listed, but the capture of Eglon brought Israel control of the trade routes to the Negev. In addition, the summary of towns acquired in chapter 12 includes Hormah and Arad, both centres in the Negev. The Shephelah or *western foothills* is the location of the remaining towns. *The mountain slopes* seem to be connected with the Shephelah and may describe the valleys and passes from the coastal plain to the hill country. This summary ends with phrases characteristic of those used in the previous section: *He left no survivors*, and *He totally destroyed all who breathed.* For the end of the verse, see Joshua 9:18–19, where the Israelites were faithful to their vow to God. Here as well the war becomes an expression of obedience to God.

41. The southern region coincides with the southern part of the border in Joshua 1:4. Kadesh Barnea marks the boundary with the wilderness of Sinai. It represents the point from which

---

[1] W. F. Albright, 'Researches of the School in Western Judaea', *BASOR*, 15, 1924, pp. 2–11, esp. p. 9; A. F. Rainey, 'The Biblical Shephelah of Judah', p. 11.

[2] A. F. Rainey, 'Debir', *ISBE*, I, pp. 901–904. Accepting these identifications, there is no reason to suggest that Joshua followed a 'zigzag track'. See J. Barr, 'Mythical Monarch Unmasked? Mysterious Doings of Debir King of Eglon', *JSOT*, 48, 1990, pp. 33–49, esp. p. 60. If any writer, whether writing history or merely pretending to write it, had displayed an ignorance about the geography of the readers' native land, that writer would have been rejected. The burden of proof lies with the modern critic to establish inaccuracies in geography. Barr is aware of some modern identifications of sites such as Eglon (*ibid.*, p. 67, n. 7). However, he prefers the discredited identifications that support a less coherent account.

the Israelites first attempted to enter the land but were driven back (Nu. 14). Gaza represents the border with Egypt to the west. Gaza was historically understood as the first Canaanite town one encountered when departing from Egypt.[1] Goshen does not describe the land where the Israelites lived before leaving Egypt but the Goshen of Joshua 11:16 attached to the site in 15:51. If this describes any border, it would be the south-eastern one towards the Dead Sea and the Negev. The final site, Gibeon, defines the area in the hill country where the battle began.

42. *Joshua conquered* (Heb. *lākad,* a verb that appeared in Joshua 10:1 to describe the conquest of Ai), closes off the account of chapter 10 by linking it with the previous military victory. The syntax of the first half of the verse and its structure resembles the description of Joshua's capture of Makkedah (v. 28). There, the conquest takes place *that day;* here it occurs *in one campaign.* This emphasizes how quickly it was completed because God fought on behalf of Israel. The same phrase in verse 14 comments on the miracle of the sun and moon. Thus verse 42 ties in the defeat of all the towns in the south with the miraculous work of God, demonstrated by the overt wonders in the heavens as well as by the aid given in capturing each town.

43. The last 'panel' ends with the phrase *Joshua . . . with all Israel,* as in verse 15, where it signalled the end of a panel. As Israel set out from Gilgal (v. 6), so it now returns to the sanctuary site. This completes the tour of the south and seals the victory with the appearance of the nation and its leader before God at the sanctuary.

Chapter 10 serves four literary purposes: firstly, it moves Israel out of the central hill country; secondly, it surveys the conquest of the south in the same way that the preceding chapters had focussed on the central hill country; thirdly, the panels enable the author to shift back and forth between the work of God and that of Israel; and finally, the structure of the account increases the speed of the action. Fewer verses than before are devoted to the conquest of a whole region with many towns. This more highly paced action will continue in chapter 11 and reach a climax in chapter 12, where it will move so quickly that only the place names will be given.

---

[1]C. J. Bergoffen, 'Overland Trade in Northern Sinai: The Evidence of the Late Cypriot Pottery', *BASOR,* 284, 1991, pp. 59–76, esp. p. 61.

For Christians, this text and the following story of the northern battle symbolize the life of the disciple. Faced with daily pressures and struggles, the decision whether to follow Christ in humility and love forms part of the spiritual warfare described in Ephesians 6. The warrior cannot succeed without divine help, and this is available through constant walking in the will of God as illuminated by a knowledge of God's Word and as strengthened by prayerful communion with him.

1. Victory over the northern coalition (11:1–11)

This passage is connected with chapter 10 and the conquest of the south. Similar verbs and expressions occur, as well as larger blocks of material whose organization resembles that of chapter 10. There is another coalition of town leaders led by a single named ruler. They are defeated; their armies are destroyed; and their towns and territories are captured by Israel. Finally, there is a similar theological pattern: God promises Joshua victory and instructs him; Joshua obeys and leads Israel; and they also obey and are victorious.

There are also distinctive features. This account is shorter than that in chapter 10. Only one town is described in detail and there are no lengthy descriptions of a chase or of miracles. This suggests an acceleration in the narrative. Moving ever more quickly, the text completes the description of the conquest. Although the information must be noted, there is no lingering over gory details of destruction. Perhaps because this section is shorter, its literary structure is simplified. There is not a series of 'panels' as in chapter 10. Instead, there are three parts: the threat of the northern coalition, their defeat and Hazor's destruction. In each part, concentric structures frame the key elements: the regions and groups that made up the coalition, the role of God in giving Israel victory and the importance of Hazor. There is no concept of an egalitarian coalition; rather there is one leader and the remainder follow. This is a different region from the hill country of chapter 10. The battle moves to the lowlands and the valleys, where horses and chariots are effective. Finally, the account anticipates the division of the land by bringing to an end the main conquest.

i. The threat of the northern coalition (11:1–5).
1. The chapter opens in the same way as chapters 5 and 10,

with the ominous *When X heard . . .* As in the previous chapter, this refers to the preceding military victories of Israel. The subject of the clause (X) becomes the chief opponent of Joshua and Israel. Thus there will be another battle and another opportunity for God to work in the development of Israel's faith. Jabin, king of Hazor, opposes Israel. Jabin is a West Semitic name, not unknown in Hazor in the second millennium BC.[1] On the size and importance of Hazor, see commentary on 11:10–11 (pp. 212–213). The next major action of Jabin after hearing is that *he sent word* to his allies or vassals, just as Adoni-Zedek had done (Jos. 10:3).

The only ally named is Jobab. This is another West Semitic name, though less frequently attested.[2] The question of Madon, Jobab's town, has perplexed scholars. It is mentioned elsewhere only in Joshua 12:19. Some important textual witnesses read an 'r' instead of a 'd', *i.e.* Maron, which could be identical with Merom.[3] Merom is attested in extrabiblical sources as well as in the Bible. The text portrays the site as the most important vassal of Hazor, since it is mentioned first and its leader is named. Since Madon is otherwise unknown and Merom is known from a variety of sources, it is best to regard Madon in verse 1 as a reference to Merom.[4]

The kings of Shimron and Acshaph are also mentioned. Shimron is Khirbet Sammuniya (= Tel Shimron), 5 miles due

---

[1] This name may relate to the Hebrew root *byn*, 'to discern', or to the root *bny*, 'to build'. Although the former is grammatically more likely, it has fewer attestations in personal names. Derived from the root *bny*, 'to build', Jabin has been compared with Yabni-Addu, the king of a Hazor known in the Mari texts. It also has its counterpart with *ib-ni*, part of a name which appears in the Old Babylonian cuneiform tablet found at Hazor. See R. S. Hess, 'Non-Israelite Personal Names in the Narratives of the Book of Joshua', *CBQ,* forthcoming. Its occurrence again in Jdg. 4:2 suggests it may have been a dynastic name at Hazor. C. R. Krahmalkov, 'Exodus Itinerary Confirmed by Egyptian Evidence', *BAR,* 20/5, September/October 1994, p. 61, argues that Qishon of Jabin (Ybn) on an itinerary of Ramses II refers to the biblical Jabin of Jdg. 4 – 5. If it is the same name, it may suggest the influence of the dynasty across the Galilee.

[2] R. S. Hess, 'Non-Israelite Personal Names in the Narratives of the Book of Joshua'.

[3] The LXX and the Syriac read an 'r'. However, the LXX also reads 'Marron' in vv. 5 and 7, in place of Merom. See Barthélemy, p. 18. The alteration between the '-on' and the '-om' suffixes in place names of Galilee is not uncommon. See Na'aman, *Borders,* p. 121, n.6.

[4] Note that this conclusion does not necessarily require a textual alteration, as it is possible for both names to refer to the same site.

west of Nazareth in the hills north of the western end of the Jezreel Valley.[1] Acshaph lies further north-west in the Acco plain, perhaps at Tell Keisan.[2] Both are mentioned in Late Bronze Age sources.[3] With these two sites located, the site of Madon/Merom can be suggested. The best location that agrees with the biblical and extrabiblical evidence is that of Tel Qarnei Hittin, about 5 miles west of modern Tiberias.[4] Atop a summit overlooking the main route from the Jezreel Valley to Hazor and the north, this site was fortified in the Late Bronze Age and destroyed in the mid-thirteenth century BC about the same time as Hazor.[5] Madon/Merom thus bordered the kingdom of Shimron to the west and that of Hazor to the north and east. These were the major forces located in the north, who could bring along the remaining leaders of smaller towns and villages, as detailed in verse 2.

2. The general regions may be compared with those of the south in Joshua 10:40. In both cases, the whole country is summarized in four terms, beginning with a reference to the hill country. This included the territories later occupied by

[1] Grid number 170234. On this name and its relation to the identical Shimon in other sources, see A. F. Rainey, 'Toponymic Problems: Shim'on – Shimron', *Tel Aviv*, 3, 1976, pp. 57–69; Kallai, p. 417. For the Late Bronze occupational evidence, see G. E. B. Caessens, *A History of Northwest Palestine in the Middle Bronze II – Late Bronze I Period* (PhD thesis, University of Cambridge, 1990), p. 276. The author thanks Dr Caessens for permission to refer to her important study.

[2] Grid number 164253, about 4½ miles south of ancient Acco on the eastern side of the Acco plain. See Na'aman, *Borders*, p. 123. The site's large size and evidence of Late Bronze Age occupation favour it. However, Aharoni, *Land*, p. 429, suggests Khirbet el-Rabaj = Tel Regev (grid number 159240) at the foot of Mount Carmel and the entrance to the Jokneam Pass to the Jezreel Valley. Occupational remains from the Late Bronze Age have been discovered at both sites. See G. E. B. Caessens, *op. cit.*, pp. 274–275.

[3] For their place in the itinerary of Thutmose III, see Aharoni, *Land*, p. 160. In the fourteenth century BC the leaders of both corresponded with the Pharaoh, as attested by El Amarna letters 225 and 367.

[4] Grid number 193245. For the Late Bronze Age occupational evidence, see G. E. B. Caessens, *op. cit.*, p. 294. The location, associated with the name of the nearby Khirbet Madin, has been proposed by Garstang, p. 189. Although a site in Upper Galilee has been proposed (see Aharoni, *Land*, pp. 224–227), it seems an unsuitable place for chariot warfare. See H. Rösel, 'Studien zur Topographie der Kriege in den Büchen Josua und Richter', *ZDPV*, 91, 1975, pp. 159–190, especially pp. 179–180.

[5] Z. Gal, 'Tel Rekesh and Tel Qarney Hittin', *Eretz-Israel*, 15, 1981, pp. 213–221, Hebrew; *idem, Lower Galilee During the Iron Age*, ASOR Dissertation Series 8 (Winona Lake, Indiana: Eisenbrauns, 1992), pp. 44–45, 89; Na'aman, *Borders*, pp. 120–127.

Ephraim and Manasseh, to the south of the Jezreel Valley, and the Galilean highlands to the north. The term *Negev* which appears in Joshua 10:40 is used as a common noun, meaning *south* in 11:2, *i.e.* the *Arabah south of Kinnereth*. The site of Kinnereth, Khirbet el-'Ureima (= Tel Kinrot), overlooks the north-west shore of the Sea of Galilee. South is the el-Ghuwayer Plain which may be the area intended.[1] However, it is more likely that the entire region of the northern Jordan Valley, south of the Sea of Galilee (= Sea of Kinnereth), is intended. As in the southern description of Joshua 10:40, the third place mentioned is the Shephelah, the lower hill country west of the Samarian hills. In the southern description, the last region is defined with a term that sounds like one of the sea-coast sites, Ashdod. The same is true here in verse 2. No one knows to what Naphoth in Naphoth Dor refers, but presumably it has some association with the town of Dor on the coast.[2] Thus the text emphasizes the totality of the northern region that came to oppose Joshua, like that of the southern region as described in chapter 10.

3. Unlike the southern coalition, which is described as Amorite, the northern one is composed of diverse groups.[3] These groups appeared in Joshua 3:10. The last two groups are specified by additional geographical terms. The Jebusites here are those in the hill country. No further information is available. For the Hivites *below Hermon in the region of Mizpah* see *the Valley of Mizpah on the east* (v. 8) and *the Valley of Lebanon below Mount Hermon* (v. 17). These refer to one of the valleys on the western slopes of Mount Hermon.[4] However, Hermon may include the Ante-Lebanon range stretching north of what is today Mount Hermon.[5] Therefore, Mizpah should include the

---

[1] Grid no. 200252. For the Late Bronze Age occupation evidence, see G. E. B. Caessens, *op. cit.*, p. 281; V. Fritz, 'Chinnereth' in *ABD*, I, pp. 909–910.

[2] The translation 'heights of Dor', is a guess. Na'aman, *Borders*, pp. 184–185 and n. 26, suggests that it represents the coastal strip from Mt. Carmel south to the Yarkon River.

[3] This anticipates the more cosmopolitan nature of the Northern Kingdom in the first millennium BC. With the Jezreel Valley bisecting the region, it formed an international corridor for armies and trade throughout recorded history.

[4] Aharoni, *Land*, p. 239, suggests Marj 'Ayyun or the valley of the Ḥesbani River.

[5] This is based on the equation of Hermon with Sirion and Senir in Dt. 3:9 and its identification with the Ante-Lebanon in Egyptian sources as early as the nineteenth century BC. See Mazar, pp. 194–195, n. 27.

eastern part of the Litani River,[1] whose flow from the southern end of the Beqa Valley along the Marj'Ayyun Valley passes close to the northern end of the Huleh Basin before turning west towards Tyre.

4. With all their forces, this coalition was *a huge army.* Equally large was the number of *horses and chariots.* This expression occurs in eight other places in the Hebrew text.[2] It describes the most fearful fighting machinery available. For example, Egypt pursues Israel into the sea with horses and chariots (Ex. 15:1, 21). In Deuteronomy 20:1, it points to God's protection of Israel in the same sort of situation.

5. The northern coalition encamps at the Waters of Merom. North of Tel Qarnei Hittin lies Wadi el-Hamam, the likely location of the Waters of Merom.[3] The forces met on the road north to Hazor. The structural similarities with the beginning of chapter 10 demonstrate that the battle with Hazor was not just another skirmish such as those against the towns at the end of chapter 10. It was on a scale parallel to the whole southern coalition. Like that coalition, the leaders of the north met Israel as a united group but this group was even more fearsome, possessing horses and chariots.

ii. Victory over the northern coalition (11:6–9).

6. God addresses Joshua. The exhortation not to fear occurs here as it did before Ai and before the southern coalition. The victory will occur within a single day. The divine instructions are clear about every element of the threat. Hamstringing the horses ensured that nothing survived that would be usable in a future war.

7–9. These commands are fulfilled in the same detail in verses 8b–9. In fact, the command and the fulfilment form the outer envelope of a concentric structure that describes the battle. The inner core is Joshua's arrival and attack in verse 7, which corresponds to the verbs *defeated* and *pursued* in verse 8. The outer envelope describes events before and after the battle. The core explains how Joshua confronted the enemy

[1]Na'aman, *Borders*, p. 43.
[2]Ex. 15:1, 21; Dt. 20:1; 1 Ki. 20:1, 25; 2 Ki. 6:15; Je. 51:21; Ezk. 39:20. Reference to chariots and horse riders also appears in the ninth century BC Aramaic stele from Dan. A. Biran and J. Naveh, 'An Aramaic Stele Fragment from Tel Dan' *IEJ*, 43, 1993, pp. 81–98.
[3]Na'aman, *Borders*, p. 126.

and how he had success. At the centre of this lies the key to Israel's victory, *the LORD gave them into the hand of Israel.* As always, the victory depended upon God. The only miracle is the defeat of a mighty coalition by a less well armed army.

8. The pursuit appears to have taken the Israelite army on a tour clockwise around the borders of Galilee.[1] Assuming that Greater Sidon (= Sidon) forms the north-western border of the tribal allotments and Misrephoth Maim the north-eastern border (located along the Litani River), it is possible to see a pursuit that moved westward initially into the Jezreel Valley and then through the pass (perhaps at Tel Hannathon) north along the Acco plain and around the 'Ladder of Tyre' past Tyre and north to Sidon. Then, turning south-eastward, the army crossed over to the Marij 'Ayyun Valley passing Misrephoth Maim, and southward along the Litani River (= *Valley of Mizpah*) until it was able to enter the Huleh Valley and continue south to Hazor. All the kingdoms of the coalition were invaded and the territory that would become Israel's northern allotment was toured.

iii. Victory over Hazor (11:10–11). Geographically, the above outline explains how Joshua and his army *turned back* (v. 10) to arrive at Hazor. *At that time* indicates that the conquest of Hazor occurred as part of the same campaign. A sequence of actions similar to that of Joshua 10:28–39 is described: he *captured* it; everyone in it they *put to the sword,* he *totally destroyed* it, *not sparing anything that breathed* (he left no survivors). This pattern indicates that Hazor was conquered just like the towns of the south, under divine direction. Several additional notes appear in the Hazor account which do not occur in the earlier conquests: the importance of Hazor, the repetition of the verb *destroyed* and the burning of Hazor.

Hazor (Tell el-Qedah) is one of the largest Bronze Age tells in Palestine, measuring some 26 acres at its base.[2] The description of Hazor as *the head of all these kingdoms* is attested

[1] *Ibid.,* pp. 47–51, 126.
[2] Grid no. 203269. See G. E. B. Caessens, *A History of Northwest Palestine in the Middle Bronze II – Late Bronze I Period,* p. 288; Y. Yadin, *Hazor. The Head of All Those Kingdoms* (Oxford: Oxford University Press, 1972), pp. 13–17; *idem,* 'Biblical Archaeology Today: The Archaeological Aspect' in J. Amitai *et al.* (eds.), *Biblical Archaeology Today. Proceedings of the International Congress on Biblical Archaeology, Jerusalem, April 1984* (Jerusalem: IES, 1985), pp. 21–27.

by its size and also by its prominence in second-millennium BC written records from Pella, Tyre, Egypt, Mari and Hazor itself.[1] It is further suggested by its key position along the main south-north route from the Jezreel Valley to the Lebanese Beqa Valley and on to the great cities of Syria and Mesopotamia. The archaeological evidence of a well-fortified city with international contacts confirms its leading status during the second millennium.

The repetition of the verb *destroyed*[2] emphasizes Hazor's fate. The same is true of the repetition of the noun *sword*. Both occurrences of these two words are divided by the note on the supremacy of Hazor among cities in Galilee. Thus they frame this note and serve to suggest the importance of Joshua's victory over the strongest and most important of northern strongholds.

The final note, as to how Joshua burnt the city, emphasizes the total destruction of Hazor. It also anticipates the references to this act as a unique aspect of the conquest in verse 13. Finally, this note brings to an end the detailed description of the conquest that began with Jericho and Ai. As Jericho experienced a total destruction that was described vividly, so Hazor experiences the same with a description of burning, used only

---

[1]The evidence from Pella and Tyre is found in fourteenth-century BC Amarna letters EA 148 and 364, which originated at these two sites. Both Tyre to the west and Pella to the south describe Hazor as a threat. See the translations of W. L. Moran, *The Amarna Letters* (Baltimore: Johns Hopkins University Press, 1992), pp. 235, 362. For the evidence from Mari, see A. Malamat, *Mari and the Early Israelite Experience*, pp. 56–68. Concerning the identification of Palestinian Hazor with Mari's Hazor, see the scepticism of M. C. Astour, 'The Location of Ḥaṣurā of the Mari Texts', *Maarav*, 7, 1991, pp. 51–65. Hazor itself preserves a variety of cuneiform evidence, including a liver-model omen text, a legal document, a lexical fragment, an administrative text, and a fragment of a letter. See B. Landsberger and H. Tadmor, 'Fragments of Clay Liver Models from Hazor', *IEJ*, 14, 1964, pp. 201–217; W. W. Hallo and H. Tadmor, 'A Lawsuit from Hazor', *IEJ*, 27, 1977, pp. 1–11; H. Tadmor, 'A Lexicographical Text from Hazor', *IEJ*, 27, 1977, pp. 98–102; W. Horowitz and A. Shaffer, 'An Administrative Tablet from Hazor: A Preliminary Edition', *IEJ*, 42, 1992, pp. 21–33, 167; *idem*, 'A Fragment of a Letter from Hazor', *IEJ*, 42, 1992, pp. 165–166. From the Amarna texts, two letters, EA 227 and 228, were written by the 'king' of Hazor. See W. L. Moran, *The Amarna Letters*, pp. 288–290. See also Y. Yadin, *Hazor. The Head of All Those Kingdoms*, pp. 7–9, who observes that the use of the title of honour, translated 'king', by a town leader in Palestine is unique to the ruler of Hazor. Of course, Hazor is also mentioned in Egyptian sources throughout the second millennium. See *ibid.*, pp. 1–2, 6–7.

[2]Hiphil of *nkh*.

of these three fortified centres (Jos. 6:24; 8:8, 19). These descriptions frame the conquest narrative and imply a general destruction of all those towns that resisted Israelite occupation. The destruction of Hazor correlates with the burn layer of the Upper Tell in Stratum 13, as identified by the excavator Y. Yadin.[1] The Late Bronze Age city occupied the entire tell. Its destruction was complete and is dated to the mid-thirteenth century BC.

This account concludes the detailed conquest narrative by describing Israel's victory in the north. It continues to demonstrate the order of successful leadership, in which God reveals the divine will to Joshua, who obeys in detail. The people follow Joshua in corresponding obedience and this leads to success in achieving the goal of Israel's occupation of the land. These verses anticipate the summary of the conquest that is to follow in chapter 12. They also prepare for the allotments of chapters 13 – 19, especially those in the northern areas that Israel conquered.

For the Christian, the destruction of Hazor, like that of Jericho, represents a sign of God's displeasure with resistance to his will. Jesus taught his disciples to pray, 'Your kingdom come, your will be done on earth' (Mt. 6:10; Lk. 11:2). The terrible consequences of violating God's will may not be so apparent to modern readers, but they are there all the same. The wars, famine and disease that continue to plague humanity have their origins in sin and rebellion (Rom. 1 – 5). Christianity provides no facile solution but it does insist that the extension of God's kingdom remains the best context in which to address the needs of society.

---

[1] Y. Yadin, *op. cit.*, pp. 126–128, 198–200. This destruction fits well with a thirteenth-century date for the Israelite conquest. However, such a conclusion begs the question of the evidence of the subsequent stratum, 12, without city walls or substantial public buildings, and its relationship to Jdg. 4 – 5, where Hazor appears again as a strongly fortified centre. Yadin suggests that the references to Hazor in Jdg. 4 are late and unhistorical (pp. 129–132). Waltke sees stratum 12 as evidence against the thirteenth-century date (*e.g.* B. K. Waltke, 'The Date of the Conquest', *WTJ*, 52, 1990, pp. 199–200). Note that stratum 12, however poor, apparently covered the entire tell. The present excavations at Hazor have been undertaken by Ben-Tor to check Yadin's stratigraphy and to enlarge the excavated areas. These may yield new data to help to resolve this question. See A. Ben-Tor, 'The Hazor Tablet: Foreword', *IEJ*, 42, 1992, p. 17.

m. By divine command: a summary of the whole conquest (11:12–23)

i. Title: Joshua did all that God told him (11:12). The summary nature of verses 12–23 is demonstrated by its distinctive form. In the previous verses the customary Hebrew word order dominates: the verb begins each sentence and the subject and subordinate clauses follow. In verses 12–23, however, the subordinate clauses regularly precede the main verb in the sentence. This structure emphasizes the initial clauses and allows two or more verbs to cluster together for a repetitive emphasis. This is illustrated by verse 12. Although not clear in the English translations, the Hebrew text begins with *all these royal cities and their kings.* The actions of Joshua, that he *took, put to the sword* and *totally destroyed* follow in a rapid succession. This gives the impression of the speed and effectiveness with which everything was conquered. The reference to Moses recalls the opening chapters and the concern there to establish Joshua as legitimate successor to Moses. All of Joshua's successes contributed to this recognition. The secret of Joshua's victories was his obedience to God.

ii. Towns conquered (11:13–17a). This section divides into a discussion of how Israel treated the conquered towns and a list of the regions represented. In between these two lies the focus of the section, the repeated emphasis upon Joshua's obedience (v. 15).

13. Only Hazor was set ablaze by Joshua. No other town upon its mound experienced burning. In chapter 10, the expression that the towns were set on fire does not appear. Jericho and Ai were both burnt. The text assumes that the reader knows of these. The focus is on the unusual treatment of Hazor in comparison with other towns in Joshua 10 – 11.[1]

14. Other towns were plundered of their booty. As with Jericho and Ai, all the citizens were killed. Three verbs are used to describe this action, as if to make clear (as in v. 12) that the destruction was complete.

15. Why were the towns destroyed? Moses faithfully passed on

---

[1]See the discussion on the ban in the Introduction: 'Theology (a) Holy war and the ban' (pp. 42–46).

to Joshua God's command to take the land. Compare Deuteronomy 31:7–8, where Moses commands Joshua to occupy the land and to distribute it to Israel. The five phrases of verse 15 form a simple A–B–B'–A' pattern:

A. *As the LORD commanded his servant Moses, so Moses commanded Joshua,*
  B. *and Joshua did it;*
  B'. *he left nothing undone*
A'. *of all that the LORD commanded Moses.*

The A and A' elements are parallel in their content, demonstrating that what Joshua did he did as the divinely appointed successor to Moses. Joshua's obedience is complete. It lies at the centre of the literary form.

16–17a. The completeness of Joshua's obedience is illustrated by the totality of regions conquered in the south (see Jos. 10:40–41) and north (see Jos. 11:2–3). Joshua then turns to the boundaries, from Mount Halak in the south to Baal Gad in the north. Mount Halak appears in Joshua 12:7, where it divides Israel and Edom. It may be identified with Jebel Halaq, midway between Kadesh Barnea and the southern tip of the Dead Sea.[1] Baal Gad is the northern boundary. Located in the Valley of Lebanon and also below Mount Hermon (Jos. 12:7; 13:5), no certain identification has been made. The Valley of Lebanon is usually equated with the Beqa Valley, but it may also include the valley of the Litani River to the south. This is the Valley of Mizpeh of verses 3 and 8. In this region, Baal Gad is to be sought.[2] As with Joshua 10:40–41, the regions are

[1] The root, *ḥlq*, means 'smooth', and describes a bare or bald mountain. See Har Haluqim at grid no. 133035.

[2] This seems more realistic than suggestions to move it farther north into the Beqa and even to Baalbek (Eissfeldt), or to move the town eastward to Banias (Wright and Boling). The former elongates the campaign against the northern coalition (11:7–8, in so far as Mizpah and Baal Gad are close to one another since they are both 'below Mt. Hermon'), correlates less well with the boundaries in the passage of Jdg. 3:3 where Mt. Baal Hermon substitutes for Baal Gad, and would include a great deal of territory that was not alloted in chs. 13 – 19. The suggestion of Banias should be balanced by the earlier observations concerning the possibility that Mt. Hermon refers to the Ante-Lebanon range and not only to Jebel esh-Sheikh. Excavations at Banias have yet to reveal evidence for occupation in the Late Bronze or Iron I periods. On the other hand, the region of the Beqa Valley, and possibly the Litani valley to the south of the Beqa, attests occupation throughout these periods and includes a number of sites which played important roles in the fourteenth-century BC

described and then the boundaries (Jos. 11:21–22). This style anticipates the tribal allotments of chapters 13 – 19, where for many tribes specific places (towns rather than regions) within the tribal territory will be described as well as the boundaries of that tribe.

iii. Kings conquered (11:17b–22). As with the previous section, this one has three parts: the kings' fate (vv. 17b–19), God's will and its transformation into battle (v. 20), and a geographical outline of regions and boundaries (vv. 21–22).

17b. As with the summary statement of verse 12, the object is followed by a sequence of verbs. The first two are identical in both texts: Joshua *captured* (Heb. *lkd*) and *put to the sword* (verbal root *nkh*). The third verb is different. In verse 12, Joshua *totally destroyed them*, from the verb meaning to commit to the ban (*ḥrm*). Verse 17b changes this to *putting them to death* (*Heb. mwt*). The more general verb in verse 12 can apply to both towns and leaders; that used in verse 17 specifies what happened to the leaders. In both texts, the threefold verb sequence stresses the aggressive and destructive nature of the action.

18. In contrast to the fast-paced action before, all the battles here took *a long time*. The implication is that there were additional battles to the ones already described. This is explicit in chapter 12 where the list of rulers conquered includes some not mentioned in the battles of Joshua. The stress is upon the leadership, the *kings*, and not the towns. The ruling élite were opposed to Joshua. Nothing is said of the citizenry of these towns and their attitude.[1]

19. Only the Gibeonite leadership *made a treaty of peace*. This verb has appeared before in Joshua only in the report to Adoni-Zedek about the Gibeonites making peace with Israel (10:1). As noted in the comments on chapter 9 (pp. 179–180), the Gibeonites may not have been ruled by a king. How widespread this type of government was is not known. The emphasis is on the long and comprehensive nature of the struggle that Israel

Amarna letters. See R. S. Hess, 'Cultural Aspects of Onomastic Distribution in the Amarna Texts', *UF*, 21, 1989, pp. 209–216.

[1]See Gottwald, pp. 512–534; Mitchell, p. 123, who observe that the inhabitants (Heb. *yōš^ebîm*) of the land were the leaders. This is suggested in 12:2–3, where this term is used to describe Sihon and Og.

and Joshua experienced in their attempt to gain control of the land that was given to them by God.

20. *It was the LORD himself* also occurs in Psalm 118:23. In both texts God does a special work for Israel. *Hardened their hearts* occurs in Exodus 4 – 14 to describe how Pharaoh's heart was hardened (both by God and by Pharaoh himself) along with those of his subjects. The *hearts* of the Canaanites *sank* before the Israelites and their victories (see comment on Jos. 2:11; 5:1, pp. 90, 118). Thus the hearts of the Canaanites, sunk with fear, need to be hardened so that their inclination can become a firm resolve to fight the Israelites. This is the cause of the destruction of the Canaanites, a destruction that did not require mercy since there was no submission on the part of the enemy. For Israel, this was all a process of obedience to the word of God given by Moses. Thus the obedience of Israel is contrasted with the rebellion and disobedience of the Canaanites. This text demonstrates how for Joshua the reason for the destruction of the Canaanites was neither their wickedness nor their cursed origins (Gn. 9). Instead, it was their rebellion against the will of God for Israel, a rebellion that led to armed resistance.[1]

21–22. One of the battles not previously recorded was that with the Anakites. The promise of Deuteronomy 9:1–3, which specifically predicts the defeat of the fearsome Anakites, is fulfilled.[2] The association of the sons of Anak with the Nephilim (Nu. 13:33), who elsewhere are themselves associated with the Rephaim (Dt. 2:11), suggests that they were mighty warriors slain by Israel.[3] Hebron and Debir anticipate Caleb's acquisition of Hebron (Jos. 14:6–15) and Othniel's conquest of Debir (Jos. 15:13–19), the only narratives of individual conquests among the allotments of chapters 13 – 19. Anab is probably Khirbet 'Unnâb eṣ-Ṣeghîr, about 15 miles south-west of

---

[1] See L. G. Stone, 'Ethical and Apologetic Tendencies in the Redaction of the Book of Joshua', *CBQ*, 53, 1991, pp. 25–36.

[2] Butler, p. 130, observes how the Anakites were associated with the major enemies who discouraged the spies from recommending conquest in Nu. 13:28, 33; Dt. 1:28.

[3] R. S. Hess, 'Nephilim' in *ABD*, IV, pp. 1072–1073. The thirteenth-century BC Egyptian Papyrus Anastasi I describes bedouin in Canaan, 'some of whom are of four cubits or five cubits (from) their nose to foot and have fierce faces'. See E. Wente, *Letters from Ancient Egypt*, SBL Writings from the Ancient World Series (Atlanta: Scholars Press, 1990), p. 108. Five Egyptian cubits would be 2.7 metres.

Hebron.[1] For the early-second-millennium BC origins of Anak, see Introduction: 'Antiquity' (p. 30). Some think that these earlier Anakites lived along the southern coast of Palestine.[2] In Joshua, they inhabited coastal towns of southern Palestine such as Gaza and Ashdod.

Verses 17b–22 have a similar structure to verses 13–17a. The conquest of towns or kings includes an exception to their general treatment, either Hazor or the Gibeonites. Then the obedience of Joshua and Israel to God and Moses is noted. Finally, regions and boundaries related to the conquest are described. This style continues the repetitive emphasis that the preceding accounts of the conquest of the different towns had begun. It emphasizes the completeness of Israel's conquest and of their obedience to God's word through Moses.

However, the incompleteness of the occupation is also noted. Verses 21–22 focus on one of the groups to be conquered, the Anakites. The description of the regions where Israel defeated the Anakites (v. 21) parallels the description of the regions where Israel had victory over its enemies (v. 16). What is missing in both is the coast and the Jezreel Valley. On the one hand, *Israelite territory* became free of Anakites; on the other hand, they remained in Gaza, Gath and Ashdod. These three towns would become Philistine. Gaza lies at the site of modern Gaza.[3] Gath is best located in the Shephelah at Tell eṣ-Ṣâfi, 10 miles south-east from Ekron.[4] Ashdod is identified with a site along the coast south of modern Tel Aviv and about $2\frac{1}{2}$ miles inland from the Mediterranean Sea.[5] The section concludes with a statement anticipating the description of the incompleteness of the conquest in Joshua 13:1–7 and Judges 1. It makes this clear before describing the distribution of the allotments so that no one will assume that Israel possessed all the land west of the Jordan. It makes no moral judgment on this fact. Therefore,

[2]D. B. Redford, *Egypt, Canaan, and Israel in Ancient Times* (Princeton: Princeton University Press, 1992), pp. 90–91.

[3]Tell Ḥarube, grid no. 099101.

[4]Grid no. 135123. A. F. Rainey, 'The Identification of Philistine Gath', *Eretz Israel*, 12, 1975, pp. 63*–76*.

[5]Tel Ashdod, grid no. 117129.

the term *Israelite territory* does not imply the unconquered land. The book of Joshua does not portray a conquest of every square metre of land west of the Jordan.[1]

iv. Summary and transition (11:23). Verse 23 repeats the opening verse and frames the section with the twin themes: the completeness of the conquest and the obedience to God's word given through Moses. In the context of verse 22, *the entire land* cannot imply that every region west of the Jordan was conquered. Verse 23 moves on to describe the allotment that would occur in the following chapters. The transition is effected by the same subject, Joshua, and two different verbs.[2] At first, Joshua *took the entire land* and then he *gave* the land to Israel. The first phrase occurs in Joshua 11:16, where the text describes which parts of *the entire land* were conquered. The second phrase echoes Joshua 10:8 and 11:8, where the LORD promises and gives the coalition armies into Israel's hand. Here, however, it is the land itself that is a gift.

The effect of this is to anticipate the distribution of the land. Along with the word for *an inheritance* (Heb. *nah^{a}lâ*), it provides a transition to the following chapters. *Inheritance* is first used here in Joshua, but it will recur forty-two times. It describes that which has been divinely given to the families of Israel for their possession. This could not become an inheritance until God gave it to Israel in the conquest. Now that the conquest has occurred, it will form the concrete expression of the promised blessings of God's covenant with Abram and his descendants.[3]

The *rest from war* that the land enjoyed suggests that the conquest part of Israel's work was finished for the moment. Land remained to be possessed, but there were to be no more wars from this point. This phrase recurs in Joshua 14:15, where it concludes Caleb's campaign to conquer Hebron. There too it signals that the wars are ended. The prophetic promise of a land at peace is here realized, however briefly, while the

---

[1] See Additional Note: 'A partial or complete conquest?', at 21:43–45 (pp. 284–286).

[2] The roots are *took* (Heb. *lqh̩*) and *gave* (Heb. *ntn*).

[3] Gn. 12:1–3, 7; 13:14–17; 15:18–21; 17:8; 26:3–4; 28:13–15; 35:11–12. See E. W. Davies, 'Land: Its Rights and Privileges' in *World of Ancient Israel*, pp. 349–369; C. J. H. Wright, *God's People in God's Land. Family, Land, and Property in the Old Testament* (Grand Rapids, Michigan: Eerdmans; Exeter: Paternoster, 1990).

Israelites receive their allotments and reaffirm their covenant.[1] For the Christian, the 'battle' against the powers of darkness has been won by Christ. At best the 'rest' for the Israelites of Joshua was temporary (Heb. 4:8). In Christ, eternal rest is promised. This rest comes through justification (Heb. 4:10). It is described as the Sabbath rest of God's people (Heb. 4:9), who will enjoy their inheritance for ever (1 Pet. 1:4–5).

n. An outline of the conquest (12:1–24)

Continuing with the theme of the defeated leaders (Jos. 11:17b–22), this section describes their territories, in Transjordan under Moses' leadership (12:1–6) and west of the Jordan under Joshua (12:7–24). The phrase *these are the kings of the land* (v. 1) introduces the names of the kings. Their peoples are defined and their land is described, including capitals and regions. Verse 6 concludes the section by noting how Moses allocated the land to the tribes of Reuben, Gad and the half tribe of Manasseh. The second section has similar elements but in reverse order as a mirror image. *These are the kings of the land* (v. 7) introduces the leadership of Joshua and his allocation of the lands for tribal possessions. Regions and boundaries are summarized in verses 7 and 8. Then a list of the various peoples of the region appears, including names found in Joshua 3:10 and 11:3. This introduces the list of the towns and their leaders.

This literary structure incorporates the conquests of Joshua 1 – 12 into the larger picture of all the conquests of Israel. As Joshua 11:12–23 summarizes the whole of Joshua 1 – 11, so chapter 12 provides a summary of all the conquests, those of Moses as well as those of Joshua. Thus Joshua's work fits into a greater picture, one that is reviewed before moving on to the description of the allotments. Joshua is the true successor of Moses, who could complete the work that Moses had begun. Moses, as servant of the LORD, and Joshua, as obedient to all that Moses said, are obedient to God. The covenanted blessings of inheritance become Israel's (chs. 13 – 19) because of their faithfulness to God through all the battles and because of the faithfulness of Moses and Joshua.

---

[1] The verb 'to rest' (Heb. *šāqaṭ*), is found primarily in the prophetic books. The expectation of a land at peace forms a significant aspect of prophetic teaching. See *e.g.* Is. 2:4.

i. Kings defeated east of the Jordan River (12:1–6).

1. In contrast to those west of the Jordan, these leaders controlled regions rather than only towns. These areas are outlined in the sequence of Israel's victory over them. The Arnon Gorge is the southern border of Sihon's Amorite kingdom.[1] South of this gorge was the land of Moab. Mount Hermon is the northern extent of the region where Israel was victorious. This south-north extent compares with that west of the Jordan (Jos. 11:17; 12:7).

2. Sihon's defeat is described in Numbers and Deuteronomy.[2] Sihon and Og appeared in Joshua 2:10 and 9:10 as part of the confessions of Rahab and of the Gibeonites regarding God's mighty works on behalf of Israel. Table 2(a–c) provides a summary of the sites named in verses 2 and 3.

Table 2: Sites associated with Sihon (12:2–3)

2(a): Town names

Verse	Town (NIV)	Arabic name	LB[a]	Iron[b]	Grid no.[c]
2	Heshbon[3]				
	Aroer	'Ara'ir	Yes	Yes	228097
	Beth Jeshimoth	Tell'Azeimeh			208132

Note:
[a]LB – Late Bronze Age (1550–1220 BC) – shows whether or not there is extrabiblical archaeological or textual evidence for occupation of the site.
[b]Iron – Iron Age (1200–586 BC) – shows whether or not there is extrabiblical archaeological or textual evidence for occupation of the site.
[c]The grid-number system pinpoints a site according to its west-east location in the first three numbers, and then according to its south-north location in the second group of three numbers. The large numbers indicate sites farther east, for the first three digits, and farther north for the second three digits.

---

[1]R. G. Boling and G. E. Wright, *Joshua*, p. 322, describe the Arnon: 'The immense Wadi el-Mujib, descending some 1.06 km through the Transjordan plateau in a distance of 48 km . . . '
[2]Nu. 21:21–30; Dt. 1:4; 2:24–37; 29:6–7.
[3]See Additional Note: The location of Heshbon (pp. 225–226).

2(b): *Geographical features*

Verse	Geographical feature	Arabic name
2	Arnon Gorge	Wadi el-Mujib
	Jabbok River	Wadi ez-Zerqa (*cf.* 3:16)
3	Sea of Kinnereth	Sea of Galilee (*cf.* 11:2)
	Sea of the Arabah	Dead Sea (*cf.* 3:16)
	Salt Sea	Dead Sea

2(c): *Regions*

Verse	Region	Boundaries/description
3	Gilead	S. – Arnon River; W. – Jordan River; N. – Unclear, perhaps Yarmuk River; E. – desert
	Arabah	Jordan Valley (*cf.* 11:2)
	slopes of Pisgah	north-western edge of the Moabite tableland
	Pisgah	1.5 miles west-north-west of Mt. Nebo at Ras es-Siyagha, grid no. 218130

4. Og's defeat is also found in Numbers and Deuteronomy.[1] He controlled a region north of that of Sihon, known as Bashan. As *one of the last of the Rephaites,* he may be associated with Rapi'u, who may appear in Late Bronze Age Ugaritic texts as (1) a ruler of Ashtaroth and Edrei, (2) a title for kings who had died and (3) a deity who was able to grant requests.[2] Like the Rapi'u, Og was from this region and was dead by the time this text was written. The Rephaites or Rephaim appear elsewhere in the Bible as a general designation for the dead (Ps. 88:10 [Heb. 11]) and as giants or mighty warriors (Gn.

[1]Nu. 21:33–35; 32:33; Dt. 1:4; 3:1–10; 4:47; 29:7[6]; 31:4.

[2]The key text is RS 24.252 (= KTU 1.108). For this text and Rapi'u's identification with place names in Bashan, see B. Margulis, 'A Ugaritic Psalm (RŠ 24.252)', *JBL,* 89, 1970, pp. 292–304; R. M. Good, 'On RS 24.252', *UF,* 23, 1991, pp. 155–160, and the bibliography there, as well as translations in J. C. de Moor, *An Anthology of Religious Texts from Ugarit* (Nisaba; Leiden: Brill 1987). On archaeological evidence for the question of an ancestor cult in Palestine, see E. Bloch-Smith, *Judahite Burial Practices and Beliefs about the Dead,* JSOT Supplement 123 (Sheffield: Sheffield Academic Press, 1992). Because of debate associated with many aspects of translation of the Ugaritic mythological texts, two recent translations of the first four lines of KTU 1.108 are provided. De Moor, p. 187, renders '[Look!] Let the Saviour, the eternal king, drink! And let [the god] Gathru-and-Yaqaru drink, the god who is dwelling in Athtartu, the god who is judging in Haddura'iyu.' J. Day, 'Ashtoreth' in *ABD,* I, p. 491, rejects this translation and the association of Rapi'u with these place names. He translates lines 3–4, 'El (or the god) sits next to Astarte, El (or the god) the judge next to Hadad the shepherd.'

14:5).[1] The Rephaim recall the Anakites mentioned in chapter 11. (See comment on Jos. 11:21.) They were mighty warriors, most of whom had been slain long before. Some were defeated by Israel.[2] The name *Sihon* begins and ends verses 2–5.

Table 3(a–c) provides a summary of the place names listed in verses 4 and 5.

Table 3: Sites associated with Og (12:4–5)

3(a): Town names

Verse	Town (NIV)	Arabic name	LB	Iron	Grid no.
4	Ashtaroth	Tell 'Ashtarah	Yes	Yes	243244
	Edrei	Der 'ā	Yes		253224
5	Salecah	Salkhad			311212

3(b): Geographical features

Verse	Geographical feature	Arabic name
5	Mount Hermon	Ante-lebanon range[3]

3(c): Regions

Verse	Region	Boundaries/description
4	Bashan	S. – Yarmuk River; W. – Nahal Raqqad; N. – Mt. Hermon; E. – Jebel Druze; comprising the southern Hauran with centres at Ashtaroth and Edrei.
5	Geshur	S. – Yarmuk River; W. – Sea of Galilee; N. – Nahal Samakh; E. – Nahal Raqqad; comprising the fertile southern part of the Golan Heights.[4]
	Maacah	S. – Nahal Samakh; W. – Huleh Basin; N. – Mt. Hermon; E. – Bashan; comprising the Upper Golan, less fertile and less populated than the area of Golan occupied by Geshur.
	Gilead	S. – Arnon Gorge; W. – Jordan Valley; N. – Yarmuk River; E. – desert.[5]

---

[1]M. S. Smith, 'Rephaim', *ABD*, V, p. 674–676; *idem, The Early History of God. Yahweh and the Other Deities in Ancient Israel* (San Francisco: Harper & Row, 1990), pp. 128–130.

[2]R. S. Hess, 'Nephilim' in *ABD*, IV, pp. 1072–1073.

[3]Not merely Jebel esh-Sheikh. See discussion of 11:1–5, p. 210.

[4]Z. U. Ma'oz, 'Geshur' in *ABD*, II, p. 996; Mazar, pp. 113–125; M. Kochavi *et al.*, 'Rediscovered! The Land of Geshur', *BAR*, 18/4, July/August 1992, pp. 30–44, 84–85.

[5]G. L. Mattingly, 'Gilead' in W. E. Mills *et. al.* (eds.), *Mercer Dictionary of the Bible* (Macon, Georgia: Mercer University Press, 1990), pp. 331–332; M. Ottosson, 'Gilead (Place)' in *ABD*, II, pp. 1020–1022.

6. See similar statements at Joshua 13:8 and 32.

Additional Note: The location of Heshbon

Although identified with Tell Hesban, 14 miles south-west of modern Amman,[1] the absence of any Late Bronze Age remains at the site has led some to conclude that the accounts of Sihon's kingdom should be dated later, in the Iron Age.[2] Others, noting the numerous attestations of Heshbon in the Pentateuch, have suggested that the name of the site shifted to Tell Hesban from an earlier Heshbon at a different location.[3] The phenomenon of site shift is attested for other biblical place names.[4] A name can shift several miles from one site to another.[5] Possible locations for the earlier Heshbon include Tell Jalul or Tell el-Umeiri (West), both of which were tells of significant size with occupational evidence for the Late Bronze Age and the Iron Age I.[6] Heshbon is not the only Transjordanian site mentioned in ancient sources for which archaeological evidence has not been identified at the expected site. The example of Dibon,

[1] Palestine grid no. 226134. L. T. Geraty, 'Heshbon' in *ABD*, III, pp. 181–184.

[2] See the summary of A. Lemaire, 'Heshbôn = Hisbân', *Eretz-Israel*, 23, 1992, pp. 64*–70*.

[3] G. J. Wenham, *Numbers. An Introduction and Commentary* (Leicester and Downers Grove: IVP, 1981), pp. 160–161, n. 4.

[4] A. F. Rainey, 'The Toponymics of Eretz-Israel', *BASOR*, 231, 1978, p. 10; *idem*, 'Historical Geography' in J. F. Drinkard, Jr, G. L. Mattingly and J. M. Miller (eds.), *Benchmarks in Time and Culture. Essays in Honor of Joseph A. Callaway*, Archaeology and Biblical Studies 1 (Atlanta: Scholars Press, 1988), p. 362; Aharoni, *Land*, pp. 123–124.

[5] Aharoni, *Land*, p. 124, cites the example of Ekron's movement to the village, 'Aqir, six miles away from the ancient site at Khirbet Muqanneh. This would be a similar distance as that between Tell Hesban and Tell Jalul, one of the possible locations for a Late Bronze Age Heshbon. Thus the objection of J. M. Miller, 'Site Identification: A Problem Area in Contemporary Biblical Scholarship', *ZDPV*, 99, 1983, pp. 124–125, (see A. Lemaire, 'Heshbôn = Hisbân', p. 68*), that the migration of such a distance 'is difficult to imagine' carries no cogency.

[6] L. G. Herr, 'The Search for Biblical Heshbon', *BAR*, 19/6, November/December 1993, pp. 36–37, 68. For Tell Jalul, see R. D. Ibach, Jr., 'An Intensive Surface Survey at Jalul', *Andrews University Seminary Studies*, 16, 1978, pp. 201–213; R. G. Boling, *The Early Biblical Community in Transjordan*, The SWBA Series 6 (Sheffield: Almond, 1988), pp. 32, 47. For Tell el-Umeiri (Palestinian grid no. 235142), see L. G. Herr *et al.*, 'Madaba Plains Project: A Preliminary Report of the 1987 Season at Tell El-'Umeiri and Vicinity' in W. E. Rast (ed.), *Preliminary Reports of ASOR–Sponsored Excavations 1983–1987*, BASOR Supplement 26 (Baltimore: Johns Hopkins University Press, 1990), pp. 59–88. The latter site has also been identified with Abel-Keramim of Jdg. 11:33. See *ibid.*, p. 85.

mentioned in Egyptian sources of the Late Bronze Age, may be compared.[1]

ii. Kings defeated west of the Jordan River (12:7–24).

7–8. On the mirror-image literary structure of verses 1–6 see above (p. 221). The boundaries of Joshua 11:17 are repeated, followed by the regions, which are a selection of those listed in Joshua 10:40; 11:2, 16, and 21.

9–24. Conquest lists of Ancient Near Eastern kings have been compared.[2] Close comparisons exist between this list and those composed for Pharaohs who campaigned in Palestine. These lists often date to the New Kingdom period (*i.e. c.* 1550–1200 BC). They often suggest a summary of the coalition forces that met the Pharaoh on the battlefield and were defeated there. These lists can be selective and need not include all the areas that were actually conquered.[3] Chapter 12 is clear that the leaders of the named towns were defeated, not necessarily that every town was destroyed. Thus this list is not useful for attempting to correlate the names with destruction levels at the named sites. The mention of a number, here always *one*, associated with each leader seems to reflect the number of rulers at each town. This may contrast with the Gibeonites, who had no single ruler over them. The total of *thirty-one kings* agrees with the actual number in verses 9–24. Note that Bethel is not actually identified as having a leader who was conquered. Perhaps this is because Bethel and Ai were both ruled by the same leadership. Alternatively, Ai, meaning 'ruin', may have been applied to a variety of places, and the reference *near Bethel* may provide a means of distinguishing it from the others.

---

[1] See above under 'Additional Note: The date of the entrance into Canaan' (pp.139–143).

[2] Younger, pp. 230–232, notes examples from the thirteenth-century BC Pharaoh Ramses II and from the Assyrian king Sennacherib (705–681 BC).

[3] Thus one of the most famous such lists, that of Thutmose III from the fifteenth century BC, may reflect a Canaanite coalition met by Egyptians composed of a main force as well as 'flying columns' that attacked Canaanite forces represented by groups of towns named. See K. A. Kitchen, *The Third Intermediate Period in Egypt (1100–650 BC)* (Warminster: Aris & Philips, 1973), p. 445.

Table 4: Sites of southern cities conquered, showing Arab and Israeli names where appropriate (12:9–24)

Verse	Name (NIV)	Arab	Israeli	Grid no.
9	Jericho (2:1; 6)	T es-Sultan		192142
	Ai (near Bethel) (7)			
10	Jerusalem (10:1)	el-Quds	Jerusalem	172131
	Hebron (10:3)	T er-Rumeideh		160104
11	Jarmuth (10:3)	Kh el-Yarmuk	Yarmut	147124
	Lachish (10:3)	T ed-Duweir	T Lachish	135108
12	Eglon (10:3)	T 'Aiṭûn	T 'Eton	143100
	Gezer (10:33)	T Jezer	T Gezer	142140
13	Debir (10:38)	Kh Rabûd		151093
	Geder[1]	Kh Jedûr		158115
14	Hormah (Nu. 14:45)	Kh el-Meshâsh	T Masos	146069
	Arad (Nu. 21:1–3)	T el-Milḥ	T Malhata	152069
15	Libnah (10:29)	T Bornâṭ	T Burna	138115
	Adullam	T esh-Sheikh Madhkûr	Kh 'Adullam	150117
16	Makkedah (10:10)	Kh el-Qôm		146104
	Bethel (8:9)	Beitîn		172148
17	Tappuah	Sheikh Abū Zarad		172168
	Hepher	T el-Muḥafar[2]		171205
18	Aphek	Râs el-'Ain	T Afeq	143168
	Lasharon		Sharon Plain	
19	Madon (11:1)	Qarn Ḥaṭṭîn	T Qarnei Hittin	193245
	Hazor (11:1)	T el-Qedah	T Hazor	203269
20	Shimron Meron (11:1)	Kh Sammuniya	T Shimron	170234
	Acshaph (11:1)	T Keisan	T Kison	164253
21	Taanach	T Ti'innik	T Ta'anakh	171214
	Megiddo	T el-Mutesellim	T Megiddo	167221
22	Kedesh[3]	T Abu Qudeis	T Qedesh	170218
	Jokneam in Carmel	T Qeimûn	T Yoqneam	160230

[1] S. Ben-Arieh, 'Tell Jedur', *Eretz Israel*, 15, 1981, pp. 115–128, Hebrew.

[2] A. Zertal, *Arruboth, Hepher, and the Third Solomonic District* (Tel Aviv: Hakibutz Hmeuchad, 1984), pp. 70–72, 98–99, Hebrew.

[3] V. Fritz, 'Die sogenannte Liste der besiegten Könige in Josua 12', *ZDPV*, 85, 1969, pp. 136–161 (152–153), observes that there are various possible locations for Kedesh. T Abu Qudeis fits this list, however, as it is located between Taanach and Megiddo and as it preserves evidence of occupation at least between the

Verse	Name (NIV)	Arab	Israeli	Grid no.
23	Dor in Naphoth Dor (11:2)	Kh el-Burj	T Dor	142224
	Goyim in Gilgal[1]		Galilee?	
24	Tirzah	Kh T el-Fâr'ah north		182188

The order in which the towns are listed generally follows that of the sequence of conquests in chapters 6 – 11. It begins with Jericho and Ai. Then the list includes the southern coalition, picking up Hormah and Arad from farther south, which appeared in Numbers. Turning north, Bethel and the next four names appear out of place as there is no mention of the conquest of this region. Major sites such as Shechem and Dothan are not mentioned. Here is evidence that the conquests of the hill country are not recorded in the narratives of Joshua. The reasons for this remain speculative. The next ten sites include a summary of the northern campaign, adding many prominent sites that were not mentioned in chapter 11. The return to the hill country with the final site, Tirzah, signals

---

twelfth and ninth centuries BC. See R. Arav, 'Kedesh, 2' in *ABD*, IV, p. 11; Boling and Wright, p. 329.

[1] The Septuagint reads 'Galilee' in place of 'Gilgal'. This reading has been accepted by most because: (1) there is no other evidence of a Gilgal in the region under consideration; (2) Galilee would then allow a comparison with Harosheth Haggoyim, which also includes 'goyim' and is located in or near the Galilee in Jdg. 4:13, 16; and (3) the preceding locations of Jokneam and Dor are both followed by a *lamed* plus a region just as Goyim is followed by a *lamed* plus a region. Galilee is a region, but Gilgal is not. See Barthélemy, p. 27; Aharoni, *Land*, p. 223. However, Galilee and Gilgal may be variations of the same name. Both names may derive from the same root, related to *gal*, 'mound, circle of stones' (Gn. 31:46; Jos. 7:26; 8:29; 18:17). See Hos. 12:11 (Heb. 12), where Galilee may refer to the cult site of Gilgal. See G. B. Martínez, 'Origen y significación primera del nombre Galilea', *Estudios Bíblicos*, 40, 1982, pp. 119–126 (123–124); G. Münderlein, 'גלל *gll*' in *TDOT*, III, pp. 20–23. If comparable, then Goyim in Gilgal may also refer to a region in the north. As a shortened form of Harosheth Haggoyim, it designates a region of royal estates maintained for Pharaohs in the Late Bronze Age in the Jezreel Valley near Megiddo and Taanach. See A. F. Rainey, 'The Military Camp Ground at Taanach by the Waters of Megiddo', *Eretz Israel*, 15, 1981, pp. 61*–66*; *idem*, 'Toponymic Problems (cont.)', *Tel Aviv*, 10, 1983, pp. 46–48. Goyim in Gilgal is a shortened form of Harosheth Haggoyim in Gilgal/Galilee. It is a region and not a single site. However, its leader may have ruled from a single site, perhaps preserved in Jiljuliyey (grid no. 145173), 3 miles north of Aphek. See F. M. Abel, *Géographie de la Palestine*, 2 vols. (Paris, 1933), p. 327; W. R. Kotter, 'Gilgal, 4' in *ABD*, II, p. 1023.

completion of the list and a return of the people to their heartland. From there, the allocation of the land would take place. This list ties together the conquest accounts in the book of Joshua with those of Hormah and Arad mentioned in the book of Numbers. From a historical perspective, the list suggests that the narratives of Joshua 6 – 11 are partial and therefore serve a purpose other than to chronicle the adventures of the Israelites under Joshua. That purpose is theological. Like the previous narratives, this text shows how most regions of the Promised Land were conquered by the Israelites in obedience to God. While the sites dot many parts of the land, the careful reader will notice that some regions are not mentioned. Thus the text prepares for the description of the land not yet conquered.

For the Christian, these military successes represent the inheritance of God's people in their covenant blessings. Thus the battle is not against military forces but spiritual ones. As God gave victory to Israel, so victory in the daily struggle against sin is assured through the death and resurrection of Jesus Christ. As Israel recorded its successes, so the Christian is exhorted to remember this victory and to celebrate it as part of a life of faith, *cf.* 1 Cor. 15:1–11.

II. THE ISRAELITE TRIBAL ALLOTMENTS (13:1 – 21:45)

a. The remaining land (13:1–7)

1. Joshua's advanced age is consistent with the Pentateuch's picture of his first appearance on the way to Mount Sinai (Ex. 18:7–13; Jos. 23:1). There, he is already a warrior who is a leader among the people. Add to this the forty years of wandering in the wilderness and the long time (Jos. 11:18) during which Joshua waged war, and the note signals the end of Joshua's participation in wars of conquest at an age approaching his death at 110 (Jos. 24:29). It introduces a new section of the book.

2. The remaining land describes those towns and regions that lie within the borders of Canaan (Nu. 34:1–12) but are not possessed by Israel. Its appearance in verses 2–7 serves as an introduction to what follows (*cf.* Jdg. 1), in the case of Joshua 13 – 21 the allotments of the land. In Joshua 1:2–4, the account of

Israel's entrance and conquest of the land is also begun by an introduction of Joshua followed by an explicit word from God to him. In chapter 1, the message was an encouragement to conquer the land; in chapter 13, the emphasis is on the land not yet conquered.

For lands of the Philistines and Geshurites, see Joshua 11:22; 12:5. The former dwelt along the sea-coast and the latter were found east of the sea of Galilee.

3. The land of the Philistines is described by a town list composed of their traditional five towns that is summarized in Table 5.

Table 5: List of Philistine towns (13:3)

Verse	Name (NIV)	Arab	Israeli	Grid no.
3	Gaza (11:22)	T Ḥarube		099101
	Ashdod (11:22)	Esdûd	T Ashdod	117129
	Ashkelon	'Asqalân	T Ashqelon	107118
	Gath (11:22)	T eṣ-Ṣâfi	T Zafit	135123
	Ekron	K el-Muqanna'	T Miqne	136131

Like the list of chapter 12, this one is identified in terms of the leaders of the towns named. Here, however, the word for 'leader' is not the one customarily translated as 'king' (Heb. *melek*), but the distinctive word for *Philistine rulers* (Heb. *seren*), occurring for the first time in the Old Testament. Although disputed, the possibility remains that this term should be related to the early Greek word for leader, *tyrannos*.[1] If so, this is one more piece of evidence that traces Philistine origins to the Aegean.[2] The *Avvites* is a gentilic, *i.e.* a name of a population group rather than a place. The same is true of the Philistine towns. They are all gentilics. The Avvim are identified (Dt. 2:23) with the region to the south of Philistia.[3]

4. Canaan is defined according to those boundaries as found elsewhere in the Old Testament and in the New Kingdom

[1] See L. Koehler W. Baumgartner and J. J. Stamm, *Hebräisches und Aramäisches Lexikon zum Alten Testament*, 3rd edition, 5 vols. (Leiden: Brill, 1967–1995), p. 727. The correspondence between the initial letters, Hebrew *samekh* and Greek *tau*, is possible.

[2] G. W. Ahlström, *The History of Ancient Palestine from the Palaeolithic Period to Alexander's Conquest*, ed. D. Edelman, *JSOT* Supplement 146 (Sheffield: JSOT Press, 1993), pp. 306–333.

[3] S. E. McGarry, 'Avvim' in *ABD*, I, pp. 531–532.

Egyptian sources (see Jos. 1:4). The whole region north of Baal Gad (Jos. 11:17) was not conquered, nor was the coastal region. This is divided into four parts according to the inhabitants: Sidonians, Amorites, Gebalites. *The Sidonians* include the entire coastal region that borders Philistia at Aphek in the south and extends north to the border of the Gebalites. Arah is not otherwise known.[1]

The region of the Amorites represents a unique use of the term 'Amorite' in the Bible. Elsewhere it is a general term for the people of Canaan, perhaps especially those of the hill country. Here it represents the kingdom of Amurru, known to have existed only in the Late Bronze Age (1550–1200 BC) when it formed a state situated between the region controlled by Egypt to the south and that controlled by the Hittites to the north. This region is north of the Nahr el-Kalb River.[2]

5. Gebal is the city-state of Byblos, whose control included the coastal region from the border of the Sidonians north to the northern border of Canaan along the coast.

6a. The Lebanon constitutes the range of mountains that extends from south to north throughout the midst of the modern country by the same name. For Baal Gad, see comment on Joshua 11:17 (pp. 216–217).

The divine promise to drive out the inhabitants of the area controlled by the city state of Sidon (v. 6), and extending eastward to include the regions of Lebanon and Misrephoth Maim, was not realized before the period of the United Monarchy. David controlled this region at that time, but it was soon lost by Solomon (1 Ki. 11:23–25). If Rainey is correct in identifying the 'way of the sea' of Isaiah 9:1 with the valley north of Galilee, then this region may again find reference in prophecy of days to come.[3] It formed part of the Promised Land.

---

[1]This interpretation (*mē'ārâ*) best explains developments to the MT's 'cave' (*mᵉ'ārâ*) and to the LXX's 'from Gaza' (*mē'azzâ*). See Barthélemy, pp. 27–28; Na'aman, *Borders*, p. 52, n. 23.

[2]M. Liverani, 'The Amorites' in *POTT*, pp. 100–133 (123–124); Aharoni, *Land*, pp. 237–239.

[3]A. F. Rainey, 'Toponymic Problems (cont.)', *Tel Aviv*, 8, 1981, pp. 146–151.

Table 6: Towns of the Lebanon area (13:4–6)

Verse	Name (NIV)	Arab	Grid no.
4	Sidon (11:7)	Ṣaidā	184329
	Aphek[1]	Afqa	231382
5	Gebal (Byblos)	Jebeil	210391
	Lebo Hamath	Lebweh	277397
6	Misrephoth Maim (11:7)	Serifah?[2]	187298

6b–7. The division of the land was idealistic at the time of the allotment. The territory of Canaan, which constituted the Promised Land, lay to the west of the Jordan. To the east was land allocated to Reuben, Gad and the half tribe of Manasseh. However, it was not part of the Promised Land, *i.e.* Canaan. The remaining land describes only unconquered areas in Canaan, not east of the Jordan. The tribes east of the Jordan had already received their allotment from Moses (Nu. 32). These are now reviewed before the new allotments are described.

Polzin observes that verse 1 contains reported speech from God to Joshua.[3] He compares this with the other instances of reported speech in Joshua 13 – 21. These other examples illustrate the truth of Joshua 13:1. Thus the unconquered parts of the land are described in the dialogue between Joshua and the Joseph tribes and between Joshua and the seven remaining tribes (Jos. 17:14–18; 18:3–8). Caleb's words to Joshua described the region he will conquer (Jos. 14:12). The same is true of the words of God regarding the towns of refuge (see comment on Jos. 20:1–6, pp. 277–279). Polzin also locates notes that illustrate God's words about the unconquered parts of the land: Joshua 15:63 (Jerusalem), 16:10 (Gezer), 17:11–13 (six Canaanite towns in Manasseh), 18:2 (the allocations for seven of the tribes) and 19:47 (Dan's loss of territory). As Polzin notes, the outsiders of the book of Joshua either are destroyed or are brought into the covenant community.[4] This

[1] Not the Aphek of the Sharon Plain, but the one which lay on the border between Sidon and Byblos. It lay near the sources of the Nahr Ibrahim, a river south-east of Byblos. See Aharoni, *Land*, p. 238.

[2] This possibility is suggested cautiously by Na'aman, *Borders*, p. 49, 12 miles east of Tyre and just over 1 mile south of the Litani River.

[3] Polzin, pp. 127–131.

[4] Polzin, pp. 130–134.

was true for Rahab and the Gibeonites. It will also be true for Caleb the Kenizzite, for the daughters of Zelophehad and for Acsah and for the Canaanite enclaves that remain. As these groups were allowed to live and given a share in the inheritance, Israel would be reminded of its present failure to fulfil completely those commands. These observations in Joshua 13 – 21 contrast with the allotment of all the land described in the same chapters. The full sense of this contrast reaches its climax at the end (see comment on Jos. 21:43–45, pp. 284–286).

For the Christian, Israel's failure to conquer the land fully anticipates the inability to enjoy the full favour of God's blessing in this life (1 Cor. 10:1–13). Christians are not perfect, though they are called to perfect holiness. They live in a tension between the rewards of a life lived fully in the Holy Spirit, which are available here and now, and their own failure, which prevents the appropriation of those gifts. This paradox has no resolution in this life but it does have the promise of God's continual presence with believers to enable them to receive forgiveness and to live a life of obedience (1 Jn. 1:5–10).

b. The allotment east of the Jordan River (13:8–33)

Verses 8–13 describe the whole area according to its topographical features. A concluding note anticipates the Levitic towns of chapter 21. The territory reached from the Arnon Gorge in the south to Bashan and Mount Hermon in the north. From the Jordan River, it extended eastward to the desert as far as the upper reaches of the Jabbok and other rivers. This matches the extent of the combined kingdoms of Sihon and Og as described in 12:1. Beginning in the south and proceeding north, towns allotted to Reuben (vv. 15–23), to Gad (vv. 24–28) and to the half-tribe of Manasseh (vv. 29–31) are detailed.

Table 7: Sites allotted to Reuben and Gad (13:9)

Verse	Name (NIV)	MT	LXX	Arab	Grid no.
9	Aroer (12:2)	Yes	Yes	ʿAraʿir	228097
	Arnon Gorge (12:2)	Yes	Yes	Wadi el-Mujib	
	town in middle of the Gorge	Yes	Yes	Kh el-Medeineh?[1]	240092
	Medeba	Yes	No	Mâdebā	225124
	Dibon	Yes	Yes	T Dhibân?[2]	

For the kingdoms of Sihon and Og, and all the proper names in verses 10–13, *cf.* comment at 12:2–5 (pp. 222–225).

15–23. In addition to the sites already noted, the allotment for Reuben includes the places listed in Table 8.

Table 8: Sites allotted to Reuben (13:17–20)

Verse	Name (NIV)	MT	LXX	Arab	Grid no.
17	Bamoth Baal	Yes	Yes	Kh el-Quweiqiyeh? or Kh Libb?[3]	220126 222113
	Beth Baal Meon	Yes	Yes	Māʿîn	219120
18	Jahaz	Yes	Yes	Kh el-Medeineh[4]	236111
	Kedemoth	Yes	Yes	ʿAleiyân or Saliyah	233104

[1] It could be a small outpost that disappeared without leaving a trace. See D. N. Pienaar, 'Die stad aan die rivier (Jos 13:16)', *Nederduits Gereformeerde Teologiese Tydskrif*, 30, 1989, pp. 376–382. Others have suggested the Khirbet el-Medeineh at the juncture of Wadi Sālīyeh and the Wadi Saʿīdeh. See J. M. Miller, 'Six Khirbet el-Medeinehs in the Region East of the Dead Sea', *BASOR*, 276, 1989, pp. 25–28.

[2] On problems with the identification of this site as Dibon, and yet on clear attestations for it from Egyptian records of the New Kingdom, see the Additional Notes: 'The Location of Heshbon' (pp. 225–226) and 'The date of the entrance into Canaan' (pp. 139–143). See also R. S. Hess, 'Fallacies in the Study of Early Israel', *TynB*, 45, 1994, pp. 342–344.

[3] Quweiqiyeh is the traditional identification. See G. L. Mattingly, 'Bamoth-Baal' in *ABD*, I, pp. 574–575. If Bamoth Baal can be connected with Beth Bamoth, Dearman proposes Libb. See J. A. Dearman, 'Historical Reconstruction and the Mesha Inscription' in *Moab*, pp. 185–186. J. M. Miller, 'The Israelite Journey through (around) Moab and Moabite Toponymy', *JBL*, 108, 1989, pp. 577–595 [589–590] rejects Libb but does so by disputing the claims of Nu. 21 and Jdg. 11 regarding Israel's claim that they travelled around Moab. Miller identifies Jahaz with Libb.

[4] J. M. Miller, 'Six Khirbet el-Medeinehs in the Region East of the Dead Sea', p. 25; J. A. Dearman, 'The Levitical Cities of Reuben and Moabite Toponymy', *BASOR*, 276, 1989, pp. 55–66 (61–63); *idem*, 'The Location of Jahaz', *ZDPV*, 100, 1984, pp. 122–126.

Verse	Name (NIV)	MT	LXX	Arab	Grid no.
	Mephaath	Yes	Yes	Umm er-Raṣaṣ[1]	237101
19	Kiriathaim	Yes	Yes	Qaryat el-Mekhaiyeṭ? or Kh el-Qereiyât?	220128 216124
	Sibmah	Yes	Yes	Kh el-Qibsh?[2]	
	Zereth Shahar	Yes	Yes	ez-Zārât?	203111
	hill in the valley	Yes	Yes	Mt. 'Aṭṭarus	
20	Beth Peor	Yes	Yes		
	slopes of Pisgah (12:3)	Yes	Yes	north-western edge of the Moabite tableland	
	Beth Jeshimoth (12:3)	Yes	Yes	T el-'Aẓeimeh	208132

On the death of Balaam see Numbers 31:8.

24–28. In addition to the sites already noted, the allotment for Gad includes the names listed in Table 9.[3]

Table 9: Sites allotted to Gad (13:25–28)

Verse	Name (NIV)	MT	LXX	Arab	Grid no.
25	Jazer	Yes	Yes	Kh Jazzir[4]	219156
	Rabbah	Yes	Yes	'Ammân	238151
26	Ramath Mizpah	Yes	Yes	Kh Jel'ad	223169
	Betonim	Yes	Yes	Kh Baṭneh	217154
	Mahanaim	Yes	Yes	Kh ed-Dhahab el-Garbi[5]	214177

[1]A. Niccacci, 'Scoperto l'antico nome di Um Er-Rasas: Mefaa', *Rivista Bib*, 35, 1987, pp. 83–84; Y Elitzur, 'The Identification of Mefa'at in View of the Discoveries from Kh. Umm er-Raṣāṣ', *IEJ*, 39, 1989, pp. 267–277; R. W. Younker and P. M. Daviau, 'Is Mefa'at to be Found at Tell Jawa (South)?', *IEJ*, 43, 1993, pp. 23–28; Z. Kallai, 'A Note on "Is Mefa'at to be Found at Tell Jawa (South)?"', *IEJ*, 43, 1993, pp. 249–251. Kallai continues to prefer the identification of Mephaath with Tell Jawa. Although this is possible, the Byzantine mosaic excavated at Kh. Umm er-Raṣāṣ would appear to argue convincingly for this latter identification.

[2]This identification is doubtful because there have been no Iron Age remains found there. See Kallai, p. 441. Wüst suggests a site closer to Beth Baal Meon. See M. Wüst, *Untersuchungen zu den siedlungsgeographischen Texten des Alten Testaments. I Östjordanland* (Weisbaden: Harrassowitz, 1975), p. 160; P. N. Franklyn, 'Sibmah' in *ABD*, VI, pp. 1–2.

[3]For Gilead, see 13:11. For Ammonites, see 13:10. For Aroer, see 12:2 and 13:9. For Heshbon, see 12:2 and 13:10.

[4]J. L. Peterson, 'Jazer' in *ABD*, III, pp. 650–651.

[5]D. V. Edelman, 'Mahaniam' in *ABD*, IV, pp. 472–473, describes the location: '. . . located on the N side of the Zerqa, in an extension of land that projects S to form the W side of a sharp, S-shaped bend in the river. It has a smaller companion site, Teld ed-Dhahab es-Sharqia, located on the S bank of the river,

Verse	Name (NIV)	MT	LXX	Arab	Grid no.
	Debir (= Lo-debar)	Yes	Yes	T Dober[1]	209232
27	Beth Haram	Yes	Yes	T Iktanu	214136
	Beth Nimrah	Yes	Yes	T el-Bleibil	210146
	Succoth	Yes	Yes	T Deir 'Allā	208178
	Zaphon	Yes	Yes	T el-Qôs[2]	208182

29–31. The territorial description of the half tribe of Manasseh contains place names that have already been discussed, with the exception of *the settlements of Jair*[3]. Jair was a son of Manasseh whose territory east of the Sea of Galilee (= Sea of Kinnereth) included sixty population centres.[4] If he is identified with the judge by that name, his thirty sons ruled thirty of these.[5] By the time of the writing of 1 Chronicles, the number of towns or villages was twenty-three.[6] Although translation of the word *towns* is uncertain, this provides an example of the tendency to name sites and regions according to family inheritances.[7] The same is true of the reference to the allotment given to the descendants of Makir.[8]

32–33. The reference to the inheritance of the Levites in verse 33 resembles that in verse 14. It concludes the allotments east of the Jordan, *i.e.* the general description of the land east of the Jordan River, verses 8–13, and the specific divisions by tribe, verses 14–33. It introduces the allotments west of the Jordan in 14:3–4, where it is repeated. The Levites were chosen as a tribe dedicated to the service of the LORD (Ex. 32:26–29). They were a replacement for the first-born of Israel, which God claimed from every family (Nu. 8:15–22; Dt. 10:8–9). Several points are significant. Firstly, the mention of the Levites in connection with the allotments east of the Jordan River recalls that both groups

---

which forms the E side of the S-curve. The latter is a strong candidate for PENUEL.'

[1] D. V. Edelman, 'Lo-debar' in *ABD*, IV, pp. 345–346, who describes it as 'strategically situated below the southwesternmost tip of the Golan, N of the Yarmuk, facing the Jordan Valley plain lying S and SE of the Sea of Galilee'.

[2] P. N. Franklyn, 'Zaphon' in *ADB*, VI, p. 1040. For Tell es-Sa'idiyeh, a site sometimes identified with Zaphon, as Zarethan, see comment on 3:16 (p. 105).

[3] For the others, see 13:11, 12, and 30.

[4] Nu. 32:41; Dt. 3:13–14; 1 Ki. 4:13.

[5] Jdg. 10:4. This Jair is identified as a Gileadite.

[6] 1 Ch. 2:22–23.

[7] Na'aman, *Borders*, p. 190.

[8] See comment on Jos. 17:1–6 (pp. 258–259).

were given their inheritance under the leadership of Moses. Neither owed it to Joshua. Secondly, their mention in connection with allotments on both sides of the Jordan recalls their role as representatives of the first-born of all families from all tribes. Thus they are the tribe that links all the inheritances together. Thirdly, their service to the LORD provides a theological theme for the inheritances on both sides of the Jordan. All tribes worship God with the help of the Levites, who assist in the sacrifices and blessings. This point anticipates the allotment of the towns of the Levites in chapter 21, already mentioned in 14:4. By scattering throughout the land, they would also represent the unity of the people who worshipped the God of Israel.

c. Introduction to the allotment west of the Jordan River (14:1–5)

Nine and a half tribes remained to receive their allotments. The allotments of the previous chapter are summarized and the division of the land west of the Jordan is described.

1. *The land of Canaan* recalls the designation of Canaan as the land west of the Jordan.[1] Eleazar the priest appears here for the first time in the book of Joshua. He is both a son and successor of Aaron[2] and also the leader of the Levites.[3] Involved in the commissioning of Joshua, he was to determine God's will from the Urim in order to guide Joshua (Nu. 27:19–22). With Aaron, Eleazar is commanded to allot the land in Numbers 34:17. As already noted, *the son of Nun* is applied to Joshua to identify him with his earlier appearances in the Pentateuch and in Joshua.[4] Thus the same Joshua who led Israel in the conquest of the land here prepares to apportion that land.

2. For the first time in Joshua the *lot* (Heb. *gôrāl*) is mentioned. Although the techniques behind the use of this instrument are never fully explained, it is apparent that its proper use is not only allowed as a means of enquiry to learn the divine will, but is also on occasion commanded. Thus the choice of the scapegoat on the Day of Atonement is

[1] See comment on 1:4 (pp. 69–70).
[2] Ex. 6:23–25; 28:1; Nu. 3:2; 20:25–28; 26:60; Dt. 10:6; 1 Ch. 6:3; 24:1–2.
[3] Nu. 3:32. 1 Ch. 24:3–4 attributes to Eleazar the line of Zadok, the pre-eminent priestly family during the Monarchy.
[4] Jos. 1:1; 2:1; 2:23; 6:6; 14:1; 17:4; 19:49, 51; 21:1; 24:29.

determined by casting lots (Lv. 16:8–10). Repeatedly, it is commanded that the land is to be distributed by lot.[1] Although instructions provide for some choice according to the size of the tribe (Nu. 33:54), the lot is to determine the divine will as to the tribal and clan possessions. The text of Joshua testifies that all the tribal lands are determined by this system, as well as the Levitical towns for the Kohathites, the Gershonites and the Merarites.[2] With Joshua and the tribal leaders, Eleazar the priest apportions the inheritances by lot (Jos. 19:51).

For the Christian, the example of casting lots raises the issue of discovering God's will for one's life. Although the lots may have seemed a matter of chance, this is not true. They were cast at God's direction and their decision was an expression of divine will (Pr. 16:33). The discovery of God's will is not a matter of chance for the Christian. As with Israel, it requires obedience to what we have already received of God's direction in his Word, regular approach towards him in prayer, and consideration of the advice of mature Christians (*cf.* Acts 15:6, 12, 15, 28).

4. The *pasture-lands* of the Levites occur in Leviticus 25:34 and Numbers 32:1–5.[3] In the first case, the lands are adjacent to Levitical towns and belong to the Levites. In Numbers, they are lands in Transjordan. The term occurs another thirty-two times in Joshua, all in chapter 21.

d. The allotment for Judah (14:6 – 15:63)

This allotment appears first among those west of the Jordan. Its sequence is best explained on the basis of the following.

(1) The general order of the conquest in Joshua 1 – 12 was from south to north.

(2) Accounts relating to both the Judah and the Joseph tribes contain narratives in which claimants for land refer to promises or decisions that Moses gave. Like the Transjordanian tribes, therefore, these allotments have already been determined, at least in part, by Moses.

(3) There is a favourable attitude toward Judah. This was

[1] Nu. 26:55, 56; 33:54; 34:13; 36:2.
[2] Jos. 15:1; 16:1; 17:1, 14; 18:6, 8, 10, 11; 19:1, 10, 17, 24, 32, 40, 51; 21:4–10, 20, 40. See also 1 Ch. 6:54, 61, 63, 65.
[3] *migrāš.* See D. C. Hopkins, *The Highlands of Canaan*, SWBA Series 3 (Sheffield: JSOT Press, 1985), pp. 236–237, and the further discussion at Jos. 21 (pp. 282–284).

suggested in Joshua 10, where the conquest of the south (= Judah) includes divine intervention not apparent elsewhere. There is also the positive narrative of Caleb's conquest (he does not complain like the tribes of Joseph in 17:14–18, and he succeeds in his conquest), the large number of towns named in Judah (more than any other tribe or region) and the complete description of Judean boundaries and town lists (more than for any other tribe).[1]

i. Caleb's allotment, part 1 (14:6–15). The account relating to Caleb is divided into two parts: the first half appears in 14:6–15 and the second half in 15:13–19. Caleb represents one among many families of Judah who received allotments. The first part of the narrative matches the first part of the account of the allotment to Judah (14:6–15) and describes the general tribal allotment. The second half describes the later acquisition of specific towns by members of Caleb's family and is similar to the second half of the allotment given to Judah (15:21–63). It describes the later acquisition of specific areas in the tribal region through the naming of towns and villages in this allotment. Caleb represents all of Israel as one who receives an allotment and takes the land for himself.

6. Caleb's words and deeds are recorded only here and in Numbers 13 – 14. Caleb was one of the two spies sent to explore Canaan who encouraged the people to enter the land. After Numbers 14, Caleb recedes into the background. He does not act or speak again until Joshua 15. He patiently waited forty years until God's promise came true and he could possess the land.

The men of Judah approached Joshua just as the Levites do in Joshua 21:1, where the same verb is used.[2] In both cases, it describes a formal request to receive their allotment of land. Gilgal is the headquarters of Joshua and centre for the priestly service to the LORD. In Numbers 13 and 14, Caleb was described as a representative of the tribe of Judah sent to spy out the land; he and Joshua were the only two who returned a favourable report. At Kadesh Barnea, where the spies reported and where divine punishment was decreed for Israel's unwillingness to enter the land, God rewarded Caleb and Joshua with

---

[1] Ottosson; Hawk, pp. 102–113; Mitchell, p. 108.

[2] *ngš*. This verb also appears in the *waw*-consecutive 'narrative' form in 8:11, where it describes how the Israelite force with Joshua approached Ai.

the promise that they would both enter the land and receive an allotment. *Kenizzite* is associated only with Caleb and is not otherwise known. Along with Jerahmeelites and Cherethites, Calebites and Kenizzites occupied the area of Hebron and the southern hill country, the Negev of Caleb.[1]

8. Caleb recounts his experience, one that Joshua already knew. He recalls how the other spies brought a discouraging report. They *made the hearts of the people melt with fear*. This theme is used of the enemies of God whose heart melts when they learn of the mighty works of divine redemption done on behalf of Israel.[2] In contrast, Caleb *followed the LORD my God wholeheartedly*. This expression, 'follow after the LORD', is used of Caleb and Joshua (Nu. 32:12; Dt. 1:36) in contrast with the rest of Israel who refused to follow after the LORD (Nu. 14:43). Elsewhere, the term refers to serving the covenant of the God of Israel alone and not following other deities.[3]

9–12. Caleb refers to Moses' promise and the faithfulness of God in maintaining him alive for forty-five years.[4] This temporal reference bridges the gap between the past promise and its present fulfilment. Joshua, as Moses' successor, is the appropriate representative for fulfilling the promise. The mention of the strength and vigour of Caleb emphasizes both that (1) he is the same person who received earlier promises, and that (2) he is physically capable of acquiring the allotment that was promised to him. Indeed, the confession that God has kept Caleb alive (v. 10) suggests that Caleb's present certainty of his prowess is divinely guaranteed.

13–15. Therefore there is no reason to refuse the promise. On the contrary, Joshua the faithful servant of the LORD must carry it out. The Anakites represented the fearsome enemy that caused the Israel of Numbers 13 to refuse to enter the land. On the background of these Anakites see the comment on Joshua 11:21–22 (also 15:13–14) (pp. 218–220, 244), where the conquest of the Anakites is anticipated and summarized as

---

[1]1 Sa. 30:14. See A. F. Rainey, 'Early Historical Geography of the Negeb', pp. 88–104. If Kenizzites are related to Kenites, then they should be located in the region around Arad. See Jdg. 1:16.
[2]See Rahab's confession at 2:9.
[3]Dt. 13:4; Jos. 22:16, 18, 23, 29; 1 Sa. 7:2; 12:20; 1 Ki. 11:6; 2 Ki. 17:21; 2 Ch. 25:27; 34:31; 34:33; Ho. 1:2; 11:10; Ze. 1:6.
[4]Butler, p. 174, observes that, given forty years of wandering in the wilderness, this statement suggests that the conquest occurred over a period of five years.

part of the conquest of the southern coalition. The account of Caleb is intended as a detailed development of the campaign in chapter 11 and is signalled by both accounts' ending with the phrase *Then the land had rest from war.* Thus this account is part of the overall conquest of the south.

Joshua's response is consistent with his role as the successor of Moses. All the promises that Moses made are kept. The gift of Hebron is reaffirmed,[1] suggesting that this text serves the theological purpose of demonstrating the blessing of God for those who, like Caleb, remain committed to God in spite of unpopularity. The note on Hebron's earlier name of Kiriath Arba is designed to relate its founder, Arba, to the Anakites.[2] This association demonstrates that Hebron was originally possessed by the Anakites, the point made by Caleb in verse 12. Thus Caleb's words are shown to be true and the reader is reminded how a faithful servant of God can have success against the greatest of enemies.

For the Christian, as for Israel, Caleb represents the ideal of the believer who courageously acts upon the promises of God (Heb. 11). In Numbers, Caleb took an unpopular stand, based solely on the divine promise that Israel would receive the land. Although the unbelief of others prevented its realization at that time, Caleb did not abandon God's people. Instead, he remained with them, patiently and faithfully awaiting the

[1]For vv. 13–14 as a perpetual land grant, like those of Abraham and David, and for similar grants to warriors both within the Bible (1 Sa. 27:6) and elsewhere in the Ancient Near East, see Weinfeld, *Promise*, pp. 261–262.

[2]Hebrew Kiriath Arba means 'city of four', which may relate it to three neighbouring settlements, Aner, Eshcol, and Mamre (Gn. 14:13, 24). So B. Mazar, *Archaeology*, Israel Pocket Library (Jerusalem: Keter, 1974), p. 100. Alternatively, E. Lipiński, ''Anaq-Kiryat'Arba' – Hébron et ses sanctuaires tribaux', pp. 41–44, 47–48, suggests that Anak was the ancient name of Hebron and that the three 'sons of Anak' were three clan chiefs. Kiriath Arba would then represent the centre of four sanctuaries, three of which should be associated with the three 'sons'. The fourth sanctuary would be associated with Caleb. A third suggestion is that the word 'Arba' may have originated to the north of Palestine, either as the name of a Hurrian deity (Boling and Wright, p. 358) or as a Hittite word. Y. L. Arbeitman, 'The Hittite is Thy Mother: An Anatolian Approach to Genesis 23 (Ex Indo-Europea Lux)' in Y. L. Arbeitman and A. R. Bomhard (eds.), *Bono Homini Donum: Essays in Historical Linguistics in Memory of J. Alexander Kerns*, Amsterdam Studies in the Theory and History of Linguistic Science, Series IV: Current Issues in Linguistic Theory 16 (Amsterdam: John Benjamins, 1981), pp. 889–1018, argues a Hittite origin for 'Arba' so that 'Kiriath Arba' means 'Place of the Treaty-Friend', the same meaning as the Hebrew etymology of Hebron.

fulfilment of the promise (Hab. 2:3–4). This came to pass in Caleb's old age. Being one old man against the mighty Anakites did not daunt Caleb's faith. Instead, he spoke and acted boldly with the sort of faith that can move mountains (Mt. 17:20; Lk. 17:6). In this way, he receives his inheritance as a sign of God's blessing. If the term 'Kenizzite' suggests that Caleb's ancestry was originally non-Israelite (despite his later incorporation into the tribe of Judah, *cf.* Nu. 13:6), then this text also illustrates the incorporation of outsiders into God's people, outsiders such as Rahab and the Gibeonites (see Eph. 2:11–13).

ii. Judah's boundary (15:1–12). Along with Benjamin, Judah has the most extensive boundary description in chapters 13 – 19. It begins in the southern desert and moves counter-clockwise. Although the eastern border saw no change, the southern and northern borders changed from time to time during the history of ancient Israel. Westward as the boundary moves into the Shephelah (low hill country) and especially along the plain, fewer points are designated, testifying that it remained unconquered before this area fell under the control of David.[1] Judah's boundaries are listed in tables 10(a–d).

Table 10: Judah's boundaries (15:1–12)

10(a): Judah's southern boundary (15:1–4)

Verse	Name (NIV)	MT	LXX	Arab	Israeli	Grid no.
1	Edom	Yes	Yes			
	Desert of Zin	Yes	Yes			
	Kadesh (Kadesh Barnea)	No	Yes			
	the Crest	No	Yes			
2	the bay at the southern end of the Salt Sea	Yes	No	Lisan		
3	Scorpion Pass	Yes	Yes	Naqb eṣ-Ṣafā		
	Zin[2]	Yes	Yes			
	Kadesh Barnea	Yes	Yes	'Aim el-Qudeirât		096006
	Hezron (Addar)	Yes	Yes	'Ain Qedeis		100999

[1] K. Elliger, 'Tribes, Territories of', p. 704.
[2] This is the Wilderness of Zin, for which see previous note.

Verse	Name (NIV)	MT	LXX	Arab	Israeli	Grid no.
	Karka[1]	Yes	No	'Ain Qoṣeimeh		089007
4	Azmon	Yes	Yes	'Ain Muweiliḥ		085010
	Wadi of Egypt	Yes	Yes	Wadi el-'Arîsh		

10(b): Judah's eastern boundary (15:5a)

Verse	Name (NIV)	MT	LXX	Arab	Israeli	Grid no.
5	Salt Sea	Yes	Yes			
	Jordan	Yes	Yes			

10(c): Judah's northern boundary (15:5b–11)

Verse	Name (NIV)	MT	LXX	Arab	Israeli	Grid no.
5	the bay of the sea at the mouth of the Jordan	Yes	Yes			
6	Beth Hoglah	Yes	Yes	Deir Ḥajlah		197136
	Beth Arabah	Yes	Yes	'Ain el-Gharabeh		197139
	Stone of Bohan son of Reuben	Yes	Yes			
7	Valley of Achor (7:24)	Yes	Yes	Buqei'ah Valley?[2]		
	Debir	Yes	No	Khan et Ḥatrur?[3]		184136
	Gilgal[4]	Yes	Yes	Araq ed-Deir		180133
	Pass of Adummim	Yes	Yes	Tal 'at ed-Damm	Ma'alê 'adum-mîm	178132
	the gorge	Yes	No	Wâdi el-Ḥavd		178133
	waters of En Shemesh	Yes	Yes	'Ain el-Hôd		175131
	En Rogel	Yes	Yes	Bir Ayyûb	En Rogel	173130
8	Valley of Ben Hinnom	Yes	Yes	Wâdi er-Rabâbeh		
	Jerusalem	Yes	Yes	el-Quds	'îr Dawîd	172131

[1]LXX, Kadesh.

[2]Kallai, pp. 119–120, suggests that this location is too far south and prefers a wadi in the Jordan Valley. He identifies Gilgal here with the Gilgal of Jos. 1 – 12, located near Jericho.

[3]R. Boling, 'Where Were Debir 2 and Gilgal 3?' *ASOR Newsletter*, July–August 1976, pp. 7–8.

[4]*Ibid.* Probably to be distinguished from the Gilgal(s) of Jos. 1 – 12. It is identical with Geliloth of 18:17.

Verse	Name (NIV)	MT	LXX	Arab	Israeli	Grid no.
	Valley of Rephaim	Yes	Yes	Wâdī el-Ward		
9	waters of Nephtoah[1]	Yes	Yes	Liftā	Mê Neftoaḥ	168133
	Mount Ephron	Yes	Yes	el-Qastel?	Mevasseret Ṣiyyon	165134
	Baalah (Kiriath Jearim)	Yes	Yes	T el-Azhar	T Qiryat Yeʿarim	159135
10	Mount Seir	Yes	Yes	Sārîs	Šōreš Beth-Meir	157134
	Mount Jearim (Kesalon)	Yes	Yes	Keslā	Kesalon	154132
	Beth Shemesh	Yes	Yes	T er-Rumeileh	T Bet Shemesh	147128
	Timnah	Yes	No	T Baṭashi	T Baṭash	141132
11	Ekron	Yes	Yes	Kh el-Muqannaʿ	T Miqne	136131
	Shikkeron	Yes	Yes	T el-Fûl		132137
	Mount Baalah	Yes	Yes	Mughâr		130139
	Jabneel	Yes	Yes	Yebnā	Yavne	126141

10(d): Judah's western boundary (15:12)

Verse	Name (NIV)	MT	LXX	Arab	Israeli	Grid no.
12	Great Sea	Yes	Yes			

iii. Caleb's allotment, part 2 (15:13–19). This text, also in Judges 1:9–15, continues the account of Joshua 14:6–15. See the comments there on Caleb, Arba, Anak, and Qiryath-Arba (pp. 239–242). Joshua gave Caleb, a Judahite, an inheritance in the midst of his tribal allotment. The names of the *Anakites* whom Caleb evicted are Sheshai, Ahiman, and Talmai.[2]

15. The reference to a second, earlier name for Debir (= Kiriath Sepher) is not unique. A second name for towns occurs in early accounts of the capture of noteworthy places in the Promised Land. This is true of Hebron (Kiriath Arba), Bethel (Luz), Dan (Laish) and Jerusalem (Jebus). The double name may serve two purposes. (1) It reflects the mixed population of these fortified centres, attested by earlier names (in the case of Jebus, Luz and perhaps Kiriath Arba) that are northern or Hurrian in origin. Thus the double name indicates the

---

[1] The Hebrew consonants may also be read as 'Waters of Merneptah'. Merneptah was the Pharaoh of Egypt at the end of the thirteenth century BC. See Additional Note: 'The date of the entrance into Canaan' (p. 139).

[2] On the background of these names, see Introduction: 'Antiquity' (p. 30).

presence of Canaanites as well as some of the other groups (*e.g.* Perizzites, Jebusites, *etc.*) who probably possessed northern origins. (2) It serves to focus on the importance of these conquests, for these towns are often strategic ones. This is parallel to the double names given to key founders of Israel (Abram/Abraham; Jacob/Israel; Sarai/Sarah).

16–17. The story of the gift of Debir in exchange for its conquest anticipates the story of David's conquest of Jerusalem in 2 Samuel 5:6–15. In both cases, the army commander promises a special reward to the warrior who captures the town. In 2 Samuel 5, David is based in Hebron and moves to Jerusalem. Debir is close to Hebron. This may suggest an intent on David's part to duplicate the Joshua 15 account by describing the capture of another town from a base at Hebron. In both cases, the captured town becomes the inheritance of those involved in its capture.

18–19. Acsah's request for the springs is reminiscent of Rebekah's meeting with Isaac (Gn. 24:61–67) in which she also (1) approaches riding on an animal; (2) descends;[1] (3) makes a request;[2] and (4) receives the desired result from the person whom she approaches. Both accounts involve an inheritance of the blessing that God had promised to Abraham. This is probably the reason for the inclusion of this particular note. It demonstrates that the claim of the descendants of Othniel to these water sources (important in the desert of the Negev, see

---

[1]The root, *ṣnḥ*, appears only here, in the parallel Jdg. 1:14 and in Jdg. 4:21. No translation is certain but this is as likely as any. See the discussion of Butler, pp. 180–181.

[2]Before the request to Caleb in v. 19, there is a statement in v. 18 (NIV), 'she urged him to ask her father for a field'. I follow the MT rather than the LXX, where Othniel urged Acsah to make the request. Acsah urged Caleb in one of two possible ways. Perhaps she 'beguiled' him at a propitious moment, at the capture of Debir. See P. G. Mosca, 'Who Seduced Whom? A Note on Joshua 15:18//Judges 1:14', *CBQ*, 46, 1984, pp. 18–22. Alternatively, R. Westbrook uses the story of Acsah as an example of his claim that a wife in ancient Israel retained some potential rights over her dowry but that it also became part of the husband's property. The text here is an example of this ambiguity. Acsah persuaded her husband to request her dowry from Caleb, her father. However, she requested the additional water sources directly from her father. Westbrook's argument is bolstered by parallel practices elsewhere in Ancient Near Eastern laws and marriage contracts. See R. Westbrook, *Property and the Family in Biblical Law, JSOT* Supplement 113 (Sheffield: Sheffield Academic Press, 1991), pp. 152–153.

Ps. 126:4) was based upon a legal bequest by the original recipient of the territory.

For the Christian, Acsah represents a woman who would not be denied her full inheritance. She is a model resembling the women of the gospels who sought out Jesus and refused to be turned back by the crowds and by Jesus' own disciples. As a result, they found salvation, healing and blessing for themselves and their families. (See Mt. 9:20–22; 15:21–28; 26:7–13; Mk. 7:24–30; 14:3–9; Lk. 2:36–38; 7:11–15, 36–50; 8:43–48; 13:10–17; 18:1–5.

iv. Judah's town list (15:20–63). Caleb's conquest and allotment prepare for the remaining regions and their allotments. However, the detail is reduced to the names of the towns in the regions. Previous study of the Judean lists has emphasized the districts into which the towns are organized and the date and number of these districts. The southern district (vv. 21–32) corresponds with some of the list of Simeon (19:2–8). Alt related the three districts of the western hill country, the Shephelah (vv. 33–44), to the territory controlled by the city-states of Adullam, Lachish, and Keilah.[1] Rainey noted that these districts are organized according to the east-west valleys that penetrate the hill country.[2] Thus the northern district contains the Soreq and Elah Valleys, the Soreq River providing the northern boundary for Judah. The middle district extends from the watershed south of the Elah Valley to the watershed north of the Naḥal Lakhish. The southern district extends across the Lakhish Valley southwards towards the Negev. An additional district lies farther west, along the Mediterranean (vv. 45–47). This could not have been occupied by Israel before the period of the United Monarchy. Three districts are found in the southern mountain region (vv. 48–51, 52–54, 55–57). These include the districts where Debir and Hebron are located. A region to the north appears in verses 58–59. The LXX preserves an additional twelfth district (including Bethlehem) at this point, one that is not found in the MT. The wilderness district along the Dead Sea is found in verses 61–62. On the basis of survey work and excavations, the

---

[1] A. Alt, 'Judas Gaue unter Josia', *KS*, II, pp. 276–288 (286).
[2] A. F. Rainey, 'The Biblical Shephelah of Judah', *BASOR*, 251, 1983, p. 7.

settlement of this region does not predate the eighth century BC.[1]

Scholars have argued that Benjamin or Dan originally preserved a tribal district that was part of Judah. They note that both Judah and Benjamin contain the towns of Kiriath Jearim and Beth Arabah, and both Judah and Dan contain Eshtaol and Zorah.[2] Alt included both Benjamin and Dan among the Judean lists, and dated them to the time of Josiah.[3] Cross and Wright argued that the Danite list was not historical, but an artificial collection of border descriptions and town lists designed to fill the gap left where Judah, Benjamin and Ephraim meet.[4] They preserved Benjamin's list as part of Judah, dividing it into two districts and dating it to the time of Jehoshaphat.

Kallai suggested that the Benjaminite list belonged to the time of Abijah and that of Judah to the period of Hezekiah.[5] Aharoni also dated the whole composition to Hezekiah's time.[6] By correlating the omission of Beth Shemesh from the lists with the archaeological data from the site, both Aharoni and Kallai arrived at the Hezekiah date.[7] Kallai notes that in the period before Hezekiah's revolt against Sennacherib, *i.e.* 705–701 BC, Ashkelon was an ally with Hezekiah. Ekron, Ashdod and Gaza were not. These three towns are mentioned in the list because they came under Hezekiah's dominion. Beth Shemesh is not mentioned because it (likewise Aijalon, Gederoth, Socoh, Timnah and Gimzo) had been captured by Ekron during the previous generation and was now part of Ekron's territory. The weakness of this argument is the assumption that Ekron would not be mentioned even though Hezekiah maintained political control over it. In the Bible and Ancient Near East, the recapture of a city that earlier was claimed by the conqueror would always be mentioned as part of the latter's territory and

---

[1]Z. Greenhut, 'The City of Salt', *BAR*, 19/4, July/August 1993, pp. 32–35, 38–43.

[2]15:33, 60–61; 18:22; 19:41.

[3]A. Alt, 'Judas Gaue unter Josia'.

[4]F. M. Cross and G. E. Wright, 'The Boundary and Province Lists of the Kingdom of Judah'; Fritz, p. 164.

[5]Z. Kallai-Kleinmann, 'The Town Lists of Judah, Simeon, Benjamin and Dan', *VT*, 8, 1958, pp. 134–160.

[6]Y. Aharoni, 'The Province Lists of Judah', *VT*, 9, 1959, pp. 225–246.

[7]See also Kallai, pp. 374–375; Svensson, p. 43.

would not remain part of the territory of the newly conquered city-state (*i.e.* Ekron). It would be restored to its 'original' position as part of Jerusalem.

Na'aman disputes an eighth-century date.[1] He prefers dating the town lists of Judah a century later, during the time of Josiah. For Na'aman, Joshua's author incorporated the town lists at a time when Judah and Benjamin were no longer separate. This distinction between the two tribes is artificial and reflects a concern to match later town lists to ancient tribal boundary descriptions. The town lists do not reflect family allotments, because the Calebites inhabit three districts separate from Hebron (1 Ch. 2:44–45). The lists derive from general geographical administrative descriptions that divide Judah into the Negev, the Shephelah (low hill country bordering Philistia), the hill country and the wilderness, with Benjamin and Jerusalem as two separate administrative districts.[2] Na'aman rejects Kallai's suggestion of a date in Hezekiah's time, noting that the *lmlk* jar seal impressions at both Beth Shemesh and Timnah suggest that these towns were under direct administrative control just before Sennacherib's invasion and that there is no historical evidence for Hezekiah's annexation of Philistine towns.[3] Na'aman observes how little correlation exists between the town lists of Joshua 15 and contemporary references to the area by eighth-century prophets (Isaiah and Micah) and archaeology (*lmlk* sites). He notes the correspondence with seventh-century Arad and Lachish archives as well as sites where the seventh-century 'rosette seal' impression jars are found. Sites such as Jericho are included in Simeon's town list, but Jericho was part of the Northern Kingdom and incorporated into Assyria. Only with the Assyrian retreat in the seventh century could Josiah incorporate it into his kingdom. Finally, Beth Shemesh was not inhabited in the seventh century, which explains its lack of mention in the town lists.

Several points should be noted. Firstly, the development of the town lists from family allotments to administrative docu-

---

[1]N. Na'aman, 'The Kingdom of Judah under Josiah', *Tel Aviv*, 18, 1991, pp. 3–72, esp. pp. 5–33.

[2]Jos. 15:21, 33, 48, 61; 18:21. Na'aman compares Jos. 10:40; 11:2, 16; 12:8; Dt. 1:7; Je. 17:26; 32:44; 33:13.

[3]The *lmlk* seals have been dated to Hezekiah's era. They may represent commodities rationed by the palace to different administrative centres throughout the kingdom for purposes of withstanding an Assyrian siege.

ments, as found in the covenant context of Joshua 12 – 24, does not preclude the possible change in family locations, especially in the later periods of the Monarchy. Secondly, if these documents were regularly consulted and used as part of the established legal order of the kingdom, there is no question as to the development and specification of their texts as new towns emerged. This would continue until the end of their use at the close of the Monarchy. Therefore, the observations of Alt and Na'aman pointing to features of the late Monarchy in the texts demonstrate their continued use but do not establish the origins of these texts. Thus a distinction should be made between the process of settlement and the town lists themselves. The origins of these lists are connected with the allotments. They were used for administrative purposes, as their forms suggest.[1] However, the origins of the divisions and allotments themselves should not be tied exclusively to the dating of the archaeological remains at the sites that can be identified. The founding of these sites may represent the later process of occupation of the land. Table 11(a–l) provides summaries of the lists.

Table 11. Town lists for Judah (15:21–62)

Note that the town lists for Joshua 15:21–62 are different in the LXX Alexandrinus and the LXX Vaticanus. Under the LXX column, A will indicate attestation in Alexandrinus, B will indicate attestation in Vaticanus, AB will indicate both, and No will indicate neither. LXX Vaticanus deviates more than LXX Alexandrinus from both the vocalized and the consonantal form of the MT.

11(a): Southern Negev (15:21–32)

Verse	Name (NIV)	MT	LXX	Arab	Israeli	Grid no.
21	Kabzeel	Yes	AB			
	Eder (Arad)[2]	Yes	AB	T 'Arâd	T 'Arad	162076
	Jagur	Yes	AB	Kh el-Gharrah?		148071
22	Kinah	Yes	AB	Kh Gazze?	Kh 'Uza	165068

[1] R. S. Hess, 'A Typology of West Semitic Place Name Lists with Special Reference to Joshua 13 – 19', forthcoming.

[2] The LXX reads 'Arad'. Note that the location here is that of the Israelite Arad, distinct from the Canaanite Arad of the Late Bronze Age, in 12:14.

Verse	Name (NIV)	MT	LXX	Arab	Israeli	Grid no.
	Dimonah	Yes	A B	Kh edh-Dheiba?	Kh Taiyib	164079
	Adadah (Aroer?)	Yes	A B	Kh Aroer?[1]	Kh Aroer	148062
23	Kedesh (Kadesh Barnea)	Yes	A B	'Ain el-Qudeirât		096006
	Hazor	Yes	B			
	Ithnan[2]	Yes	A B			
24	Ziph	Yes	A	Kh Kusēfe?[3]		
	Telem	Yes	A B			
	Bealoth	Yes	A B			
25	Hazor Hadattah	Yes	No			
	Kerioth Hezron (Hazor)	Yes	A B	Kh el-Qaryatein?	T Qeriyot	161083
26	Amam	Yes	A B	Bīr el-Ḥamām?[4]	Be'er Nevatim	141070
	Shema	Yes	A B			
	Moladah	Yes	A B	Kh el-Waṭen?	Kh Yittan	142074
27	Hazar Gaddah	Yes	A B			
	Heshmon	Yes	No			
	Beth Pelet	Yes	A B			
28	Hazar Shual	Yes	A B			
	Beersheba	Yes	A B	T es-Seba' or Bir es-Seba'[5]	T Beer Sheva ' or Be'er Sheva'	134072 or 130072
	Biziothiah[6]	Yes	A			
29	Baalah	Yes	A B			

[1] See Fritz, p. 165. L. E. Axelsson, *The Lord Rose up from Seir. Studies in the History and Traditions of the Negev and Southern Judah*, CBOTS 25 (Stockholm: Almqvist and Wiksell, 1987), p. 19, notes, however, that no remains predating the eighth century have been found here.

[2] With LXX, combine Hazor and Ithnan into a single place name. See Fritz, pp. 156, 166.

[3] N. Na'aman, 'The Inheritance of the Sons of Simeon', *ZDPV*, 96, 1980, pp. 136–152 (145, n. 38). He does not accept the identification with a site in Kurnub (Mampsis) as this would be south of the Beer Sheba Valley and this district does not extend so far. L. Axelsson, *The Lord Rose up from Seir*, pp. 76–77, follows earlier geographers in identifying this site with Kh. ez-Zeife, 19 miles south of Arad. See Svensson, p. 32.

[4] N. Na'aman, 'The Inheritance of the Sons of Simeon', p. 146.

[5] *Ibid.*, pp. 149–151, proposes Bīr es-Seba', beneath the modern town of Beer-Sheva.

[6] On the basis of the parallel with Ne. 11:27, G. A. Herion, 'Biziothiah' in *ABD*, I, p. 753, suggests that this reading is incorrect and should read, instead, 'Beersheba and its daughters' (*bᵉnōteyhā*).

Verse	Name (NIV)	MT	LXX	Arab	Israeli	Grid no.
	Iim	Yes	AB			
	Ezem	Yes	AB	Umm el-'Azām?[1]		148051
30	Eltolad	Yes	AB			
	Kesil	Yes	AB[2]	T Umm Bētīn		138076
	Hormah	Yes	AB	Kh el-Meshâsh or T Khuweilfeh	T Masos or T Halif[3]	146069 or 137087
31	Ziklag	Yes	AB	T esh-Shāri'ah or T es-Seba'[4]	T Sera' or T Beer Sheva'	119088 or 134072
	Madmannah	Yes	AB	Kh Tatrît		143084
	Sansannah	Yes	AB	Kh esh-Shamsaniyat		140083
32	Lebaoth	Yes	AB			
	Shilhim (Sharuhen)	Yes	AB	T el-Fâr'ah S. or T el-'Ajjul	T Sharuhen	100076 or 094097
	Ain[5]	Yes	No			
	Rimmon	Yes	AB	Kh Khu-welifeh?	T Halif	137087

11(b): Western foothills: district 1 (15:33–36)

Verse	Name (NIV)	MT	LXX	Arab	Israeli	Grid no.
33	Eshtaol	Yes	AB	Deir Abū Qābûs		151132
	Zorah	Yes	AB	Sar'ah	T Zor'a	148131
	Ashnah	Yes	AB			
	Ramen	No	AB			
34	Zanoah	Yes	AB	Kh Zanû'	Kh Zanoah	150125

[1]Fritz, p. 165, suggests this possibility following Albright, *JPOS*, 4, 1924, pp. 146, 154.

[2]B, βαιθηλ. A Bethel of the region is mentioned in 1 Sa. 30:27 and identified with T Umm Bētīn, by N. Na'aman, 'The Inheritance of the Sons of Simeon', p. 147; Fritz, p. 165.

[3]Na'aman, 'The Inheritance of the Sons of Simeon', pp. 142–143, suggests this possibility, noting that Masos was abandoned from the tenth century until the seventh. See also Fritz, p. 165.

[4]V. Fritz, 'Where is David's Ziklag?', *BAR*, 19/3, May/June 1993, pp. 58–61, 76.

[5]On the basis of the reading Ashan in 1 Ch. 6:59 (English 59), W. F. Albright, 'The List of Levitic Cities' in Louis Ginzberg, *Jubilee Volume on the Occasion of His Seventieth Birthday* (New York, 1945), pp. 49–73 (61), proposed that Ashan should be read.

JOSHUA 14:6 – 15:63

Verse	Name (NIV)	MT	LXX	Arab	Israeli	Grid no.
	En Gannim	Yes	No	Kh Ummedh-Dhiyâd?[1]		
	Tappuah	Yes	No	Kh Shumeila?		
	Enam	Yes	AB	Kh en-Nebī Būlus?		
35	Jarmuth	Yes	AB	Kh Yarmûk	T Yarmut	148124
	Adullam	Yes	AB	Kh esh-Sheikh Madhkûr	Kh 'Adullam	150117
	Socoh	Yes	AB	Kh 'Abbâd	Kh Sokho	147121
	Azekah	Yes	AB	Kh T Zakarîyeh	T 'Azeqa	144123
36	Shaaraim	Yes	AB			
	Adithaim	Yes	AB[2]			
	Gederah (Gederothaim)	Yes	AB	Kh Judraya[3]		149121

11(c): Western foothills: district 2[4] (15:37–41)

Verse	Name (NIV)	MT	LXX	Arab	Israeli	Grid no.
37	Zenan	Yes	AB			
	Hadashah	Yes	AB			
	Migdal Gad	Yes	AB	Kh el-Mejdeleh	Kh Migdal Gad	140105
38	Dilean	Yes	AB			
	Mizpah	Yes	AB			
	Joktheel	Yes	AB			
39	Lachish	Yes	AB	T ed-Duweir	T Lachish	135108
	Bozkath	Yes	AB			
	Eglon	Yes	AB	T'Aiṭûn	T 'Eton	143100
40	Cabbon	Yes	AB			
	Lahmas	Yes	AB			
	Kitlish	Yes	AB			
41	Gederoth	Yes	AB			
	Beth Dagon	Yes	AB			
	Naamah	Yes	AB			
	Makkedah	Yes	AB	Kh el-Qôm		146104

[1]This and the next two sites are found along the Naḥal Yarmut. Fritz, pp. 175–176.
[2]Precedes Enam.
[3]Svensson, p. 38; Fritz, p. 166.
[4]Fritz, p. 166, locates these between Wadi Qubebe to the north and Kh Khuwelifeh to the south.

11(d): Western foothills: district 3 (15:42–44)

Verse	Name (NIV)	MT	LXX	Arab	Israeli	Grid no.
42	Libnah	Yes	AB	T Bornât	T Burna	138115
	Ether	Yes	AB	Kh el-'Ater	T 'Eter	138113
	Ashan	Yes	No	T Beit Mirsim?	T Bet Mirsham	142096
43	Iphtah	Yes	AB			
	Ashnah	Yes	AB	Idnā		148107
	Nezib	Yes	AB	Kh Beit Neṣîb esh-Sharqîyeh		151110
44	Keilah	Yes	AB	Kh Qîlā		150113
	Aczib	Yes	AB	Kh T el-Beidā?	Kh Lavnin	145116
	Mareshah	Yes	A	T Sandaḥannah	T Maresha	140111
	Edom	No	A			
	Kezib	No	B			
	Bathesar	No	B			
	Ailon	No	B			

11(e): Western foothills: district 4 (coastal plain) (15:45–47)

Verse	Name (NIV)	MT	LXX	Arab	Israeli	Grid no.
45	Ekron	Yes	AB	Kh el-Muqanna'	T Miqne	136131
46	Ashdod	Yes	AB	Esdûd	T Ashdod	117129
47	Gaza	Yes	AB	Ghazzeh		099101
	Wadi of Egypt	Yes	AB	Wadi el-'Arish		

11(f): Hill country: district 1 (15:48–51)

Verse	Name (NIV)	MT	LXX	Arab	Israeli	Grid no.
48	Shamir	Yes	AB			
	Jattir	Yes	AB	Kh 'Attîr	Kh Yatir	151084
	Socoh	Yes	AB	Kh Shuweikeh		150090
49	Dannah	Yes	AB[1]			
	Kiriath Sannah (Debir)	Yes	AB	Kh Rabûd		151093
50	Anab	Yes	AB	Kh 'Anâb eṣ-Ṣeghîreh		145091
	Eshtemoh	Yes	AB	es-Semû'		156089
	Anim	Yes	AB	Kh Ghuwein et-Taḥtā	Kh 'Anim	156084
51	Goshen	Yes	AB			
	Holon	Yes	AB	Kh 'Alîn		152118
	Giloh	Yes	AB			

[1]LXX A reads Rennah; LXX B reads Rannah.

11(g): Hill country: district 2[1] (15:52–54)

Verse	Name (NIV)	MT	LXX	Arab	Israeli	Grid no.
52	Arab	Yes	AB	Kh er-Rabiyeh?		153093
	Dumah[2]	Yes	AB	Kh ed-Deir Dômeh		148093
	Eshan	Yes	AB			
53	Janim	Yes	AB			
	Beth Tappuah	Yes	AB	Taffûḥ		154105
	Aphekah	Yes	AB	Kh Marajim?		152099
54	Humtah	Yes	AB			
	Kiriath Arba (Hebron)	Yes	AB	T er-Rumeideh		160104
	Zior	Yes	AB			

11(h): Hill country: district 3 (15:55–57)

Verse	Name (NIV)	MT	LXX	Arab	Israeli	Grid no.
55	Maon	Yes	AB	Kh Ma'în		162090
	Carmel	Yes	AB	Kh el-Kirmil		162092
	Ziph	Yes	AB	T Zif		162098
	Juttah	Yes	AB	Yaṭṭā		158095
56	Jezreel	Yes	AB			
	Jokdeam	Yes	AB	Kh er-Raqqa?		160096
	Zanoah	Yes	AB	Kh Beit Amra?		155095
57	Kain	Yes	AB[3]	en-Nebī Yaqîn?		165100
	Gibeah	Yes	AB			
	Timnah	Yes	AB			

11(i): Hill country: district 4 (15:58–59)

Verse	Name (NIV)	MT	LXX	Arab	Israeli	Grid no.
58	Halhul	Yes	AB	Ḥalḥûl		160109
	Beth Zur	Yes	AB	Kh et-Tubeiqeh		159110
	Gedor	Yes	AB	Kh Jedûr		158115

[1] C. R. Krahmalkov, 'Exodus Itinerary Confirmed by Egyptian Evidence', *BAR,* 20/5, September/October 1994, pp. 60–61, argues that Hebron, Janim and Aphekah all appear on a contemporary list of sites conquered by Ramses II, Pharaoh of Egypt in the thirteenth century BC.

[2] MT reads Rumah. LXX A reads Roumah; LXX B reads Remnah. The order of Dumah and Eshan are reversed in LXX A and LXX B.

[3] Both LXX witnesses combine Zanoah and Kain; LXX A has Zanōakim; LXX B has Zakanaim.

Verse	Name (NIV)	MT	LXX	Arab	Israeli	Grid no.
59	Maarath	Yes	AB	Kh Qufin?[1]		160114
	Beth Anoth	Yes	AB	Kh Beit 'Anûn		162107
	Eltekon	Yes	AB	Kh ed-Deir?		160122

11(j): Hill country: towns listed in the LXX only (15:59a)

Verse	Name (NIV)	MT	LXX	Arab	Israeli	Grid no.
59	Thekō	No	AB			
	Ephratha (Bethlehem)	No	AB	Beit Laḥm		169123
	Phagōr	No	AB			
	Aitam	No	AB			
	Koulon	No	AB			
	Tatami	No	AB			
	Sōrēs	No	AB			
	Karem	No	AB			
	Gallim	No	AB			
	Baithēr	No	AB			
	Manochō	No	AB			

11 (k): Hill country: district 5 (15:60)

Verse	Name (NIV)	MT	LXX	Arab	Israeli	Grid no.
60	Kiriath Baal (Kiriath Jearim)	Yes	AB	Deir el-'Âzar	T Qiryat Ye'arim	159135
	Rabbah	Yes	AB	Kh Ḥamîdeh?		149137

11(l): Desert (Judean Wilderness) (15:61–62)

Verse	Name (NIV)	MT	LXX	Arab	Israeli	Grid no.
61	Beth Arabah	Yes	AB	'Ain el-Gharabeh		197139
	Middin	Yes	AB	Kh Mazin		193120
	Secacah	Yes	AB	Kh Qumran		194128
62	Nibshan	Yes	AB	Ein el-Ghuweir		189115
	City of Salt	Yes	AB	Ein el-Turaba or Maṣad Gozal[2]		189113 184062
	En Gedi	Yes	AB	'Ain Jidī (T Jurn)	'En Gedi (Goren)	187097

---

[1] V. R. Gold, 'Maarath' in *IDB*, III, p. 196.
[2] H. Eshel, 'A Note on Joshua 15:61–62 and the Identification of the City of Salt', *IEJ*, 45, 1995, pp. 37–40.

The observation that the Jebusites of Jerusalem were not dislodged (Jos. 15:63) appears as a note attached to the end of the allotment, just as the observation concerning the Canaanite towns that Manasseh was unable to occupy appears after the allotment of the Joseph tribes (Jos. 17:11–13).

e. The allotment for the tribes of Joseph (16:1 – 17:18)

Ephraim and Manasseh were the two sons of Joseph. To each tribe was allotted a part of the central hill country, north of the allotments of Dan and Benjamin and south of the Jezreel Valley. Ephraim was the southern of the two. Thus its southern boundary (Jos. 16:5) matches that of Joseph (16:1–3). Ephraim's northern boundary parallels Manasseh's southern border. This follows the Wadi Qanah in the west and the Wadi Far'ah in the east.[1] Manasseh's northern boundary borders Asher and Issachar (17:10). Preceding both Asher and Issachar in Joshua 17:11 is a *beth* preposition, meaning 'beside' or 'near'. It thus defines areas outside the tribal boundary of Manasseh but belonging to that tribe.

16:2–3. Two population groups appear for the first time in the book of Joshua, the Arkites and the Japhletites. Both groups are in the hill country on the southern border of Ephraim. Like other groups in this region, they may represent northerners who migrated south.[2] Except for Hushai, David's diplomat who was an Arkite, the two groups are not otherwise attested.[3] The remaining place names are listed in order in Tables 12 and 13.

Table 12: Southern boundary of Ephraim (16:1–3)

Verse	Name (NIV)	MT	LXX	Arab	Israeli	Grid no.
1	Jordan of Jericho (= Jordan River)	Yes	Yes			
	waters of Jericho (=Jordan River)[4]	Yes	Yes			

---

[1] Na'aman, *Borders*, pp. 145–166.

[2] See comment on the groups named in 3:10, p. 102.

[3] The group here should be distinguished from the Arkite of Gn. 10:17, which is spelled differently; *'rky* instead of *'rqy*. An Asherite, son of Heber, named Japhlet, is mentioned in 1 Ch. 7:32–33.

[4] S. Mittmann, 'Josua 16, 1 und die Präposition l^e', *Biblische Notizen*, 70, 1993, pp. 14–20, argues that the preposition before 'waters of Jericho' is one of

Verse	Name (NIV)	MT	LXX	Arab	Israeli	Grid no.
2	Bethel (Luz)	Yes	Yes	Beitîn		173148
	Ataroth	Yes	Yes	T el-Mazar (eṣ-Ṣimadi)		196171
3	Lower Beth Horon	Yes	Yes	Beit Ûr et-Taḥtā		158144
	Gezer	Yes	No	T Jezer	T Gezer	142140

Table 13: Northern boundary of Ephraim (16:5–10)

Verse	Name (NIV)	MT	LXX	Arab	Israeli	Grid no.
5	Ataroth Addar	Yes	Yes	T el-Mazar (eṣ-Ṣimadi)		196171
	Upper Beth Horon	Yes	Yes	Beit 'Ûr el-Fôqā		160143
6	the sea (= Mediterranean)					
	Micmethath	Yes	No	Jebel el-Kabîr[1]		181183
	Taanath Shiloh	Yes	Yes	Kh Ta'na el-Fôqā?		185175
7	Janoah[2]	Yes	Yes	Kh Marāḥ el 'Inab or Bab en-Naqb or T Miske?		193179 or 190182 or 187183
	Ataroth	Yes	Yes	T el-Mazar (eṣ-Ṣimadi)		196171
	Naarah	Yes	No	Kh el-Mifğir[3]		193193
	Jericho	Yes	Yes	T es-Sulṭân		192142
	Jordan (= Jordan River)					
8	Tappuah	Yes	Yes	Sheikh Abū Zarad		172168
	Kanah Ravine (= Wâdi Qânah)	Yes	Yes			

relationship and does not describe direction. He rejects Noth's suggestion that 'the waters of Jericho' refers to 'Ain ed-Duq or 'Ain en-Nu'eimeh (grid 190145) because they both lie north-west of Jericho and thus make nonsense of the eastward direction in the second half of the verse.

[1] Na'aman, *Borders*, pp. 151–153. It is not necessary to posit a textual omission, as Na'aman does, in order to accept that this is the name of a natural feature such as a mountain.

[2] *Ibid.*, pp. 157–158, locates it among one of three possible Iron Age II sites along the Wadi Tirzah.

[3] Kallai, p. 164.

16:10. As with Judah, the unconquered towns are appended to Ephraim (Jos. 16:10) and Manasseh (17:11–12). The use of forced labour among Canaanite towns in the Jezreel Valley was a known practice. The *forced labour* in Joshua 17:13 is *mas*, which appears in a fourteenth-century BC Amarna letter from the leader of Megiddo. He describes a corvée that is cultivating the fields of the Pharaoh in the region of Shunem (Šunama).[1] Such practice forms a background to the type of work implied here and anticipates Solomon's use of it (1 Ki. 4:6; 9:21). Canaanite subjection may have occurred as a result of the battle of Judges 4 – 5.

17:1–13. Chapter 16 began with a boundary description of the Joseph tribes as a whole. Verse 4 introduced the remaining detail about Ephraim's southern boundary (vv. 5–6a) and the Ephraim/Manasseh boundary (vv. 6b–8). There are two reasons for the absence of town lists within the territories of the Joseph tribes: (1) it emphasizes the difficulty of settlement beyond the major towns due to the forested land described in Joshua 17:12–18; and (2) they do occur for Manasseh in the male and female descendants as described in Joshua 17:2–6. As the family of Makir represented the major inheritor of the allotment to the east of the Jordan, so that of the clans of Abiezer, Helek, Asriel, Shechem, Hepher and Shemida formed the inheritance west of the Jordan.[2] Except for Hepher, all are identified with sites that are attested on the Samaria ostraca. Hepher is the father of Zelophehad and grandfather of the five daughters who received an inheritance from Moses.[3] The five

---

[1] EA 365, lines 8–14. A. F. Rainey, *El Amarna Tablets 359–379. Supplement to J. A. Knudtzon Die El-Amarna-Tafeln*, AOAT 8 (Kevelaer: Butzon & Bercker; Neukirchen-Vluyn: Neukirchener, [2]1978), p. 29; *idem*, 'Compulsory Labor Gangs in Ancient Israel', *IEJ*, 20, 1970, pp. 194–195.

[2] Nu. 26:30–33; 27:1–11.

[3] Nu. 27:1–11. For the biblical background to the custom of the inheritance of daughters, see the discussion of G. J. Wenham, *Numbers. An Introduction and Commentary*, (Leicester and Downers Grove: IVP, 1981), pp. 191–194. For the Ancient Near Eastern practice of designating daughters as 'sons' who would then be able to inherit family property in the Late Bronze Age Syrian cities of Emar and Nuzi, see Z. Ben-Barak, 'Inheritance by Daughters in the Ancient Near East', *Journal of Semitic Studies*, 25, 1980, pp. 22–33; R. S. Hess, 'Milcah' in *ABD*, IV, pp. 824–825; J. Huehnergard, 'Biblical Notes on Some New Akkadian Texts from Emar (Syria)', *CBQ*, 47, 1985, pp. 428–434 (429–430); J. Paradise, 'A Daughter and Her Father's Property at Nuzi', *Journal of Cuneiform Studies*, 32, 1980, pp. 189–207; *idem*, 'Daughters as "Sons" at Nuzi', in D. I. Owen and M. A.

sons inherited districts in the southern and western parts of Manasseh's hill country, while the five daughters of Zelophehad possessed districts in the northern and eastern parts of the allotment.[1] Tables 14 to 17 summarize the allotments to Manasseh.

Table 14: the allotment for Makir's 'sons'[2] (17:2)

Verse	Name (NIV)	MT	LXX	Arab	Israeli	Grid no.
2	Abiezer	Yes	Yes			
	Helek	Yes	Yes			
	Asriel	Yes	Yes			
	Shechem	Yes	Yes	T Balâṭah		176179
	Hepher	Yes				
	Shemida	Yes	Yes			

Table 15: The allotment for Zelophehad's 'daughters'[3] (17:3)

Verse	Name (NIV)	MT	LXX	Arab	Israeli	Grid no.
3	Mahlah	Yes	Yes			
	Noah	Yes	Yes			
	Hoglah	Yes	Yes	Yaṣîd		176189
	Milcah	Yes	Yes	?[4]		
	Tirzah	Yes	Yes	T el-Far'a North		182188

Morrison (eds.), *Studies on the Civilization and Culture of Nuzi and the Hurrians*, 2 (Winona Lake, Indiana: Eisenbrauns, 1987), pp. 203–213.

[1] A. Lemaire, 'Le "pays de Hepher" et les "filles de Zelophehad" à la lumière des ostraca de Samarie', *Semitica*, 22, 1972, pp. 13–20; Na'aman, *Borders*, pp. 160–162.

[2] These are clan names that describe districts rather than names of towns. See A. Lamaire, *Inscriptions hébraïques. Tome I: Les ostraca*, Littératures anciennes du proche-orient 9 (Paris: Cerf, 1977), pp. 59–65. Lemaire locates the region of Abiezer south-west of Shechem and Asriel south of Abiezer. Helek is north-west of Shechem and Shemida is west of Helek.

[3] *Ibid.* Lemaire locates Hoglah north of Shechem and Tirzah north-east of Shechem. The region of Mahlah is north-east of Tirzah where the Wadi Mâliḥ enters the Jordan Valley. Noah lies north of Hoglah.

[4] *Ibid.* Lemaire places it immediately west of Noah. However, A. Demsky, 'The Genealogies of Manasseh and the Location of the Territory of Milcah Daughter of Zelophehad', *Eretz Israel*, 16, 1982, pp. 70–75, associates Milcah with Hammolecheth of 1 Ch. 7:18 and places it near Tell el-Far'a North.

Table 16: Manasseh's boundary (17:7–10)

Verse	Name (NIV)	MT	LXX	Arab	Israeli	Grid no.
7	Micmethath	Yes	No	Jebel el-Kabîr		181183
	Shechem	Yes	No	T Balâṭah		176179
	Jashib	No	Yes	Yāsûf?		172168
	En Tappuah	Yes	Yes	Sheikh Abū Zarad		172168
9	Kanah Ravine (= Wâdī Qânah)	Yes	Yes			

Table 17: Towns within Issachar and Asher (17:11)

Verse	Name (NIV)	MT	LXX	Arab	Israeli	Grid no.
11	Beth Shan	Yes	Yes	T el-Ḥuṣn	T Bet Shean	197212
	Ibleam	Yes	No	T Bel'ameh		177205
	Dor (Naphoth Dor)	Yes	Yes	Kh el-Burj	T Dor	142224
	Endor	Yes	No	Kh Ṣafṣâfeh	Kh Ṣafṣafot	187227
	Taanach	Yes	Yes	T Ti'innik		171214
	Megiddo	Yes	Yes	T el-Mutesellim	T Megiddo	167221
	Naphoth (= Dor)	Yes	Yes			

14–18. The use of iron chariots by the Canaanites of the Jezreel and Beth Shan valleys prevented Manasseh from expanding into this region. Its repetition in Joshua 17:16 and 18 stresses the importance of this factor in Israel's settlement. Iron chariots, understood as chariots reinforced with some iron fittings, are envisaged.[1] Their use, like that of all chariotry of the period, would be confined to the flat plains and valleys. The settlement evidence from the twelfth century BC suggests that the earliest and most significant settlement was in the hill country of Manasseh (and Ephraim). Hundreds of small

---

[1] On the presence of iron, see A. R. Millard, 'King Og's Bed and Other Ancient Ironmongery', in L. Eslinger and G. Taylor (eds.), *Ascribe to the Lord. Biblical and Other Studies in Memory of Peter C. Craigie, JSOT* Supplement 67 (Sheffield: JSOT Press, 1988), pp. 481–492. For a response to the objections of R. Drews, 'The "Chariots of Iron" of Joshua and Judges', *JSOT*, 45, 1989, pp. 15–23, that iron would be too heavy and collapse lightweight Late Bronze Age chariots, see A. R. Millard, 'Back to the Iron Bed: Og's or Procrustes'?' pp. 194–195. Millard argues that a small amount of iron could be carried and used defensively by such a chariot.

villages appear here.[1] As with many other forested regions of the Middle East, the third and second millennia saw a gradual process of deforestation. The twelfth century BC saw the intensification of this process, the intention of which was the systematic construction of terraces for agricultural purposes. Although terraces existed much earlier in this region and although the earliest village settlements in the hill country were not in regions requiring terraces, their development on a widespread scale at this period attests to the occupation of the hill country in an unprecedented manner.[2] Terraces are difficult to date, but examples from the hill-country sites of Ai and Raddana date from this time. Thus a variety of textual and archaeological evidence combines to date this account into the early Iron Age (*c.* twelfth century BC) and to illuminate its description in its Ancient Near Eastern context.[3]

[1] I. Finkelstein, *The Archaeology of the Israelite Settlement* (Jerusalem: IES, 1988); R. S. Hess, 'Tribes, Territories of' in G. W. Bromiley *et al* (eds.), *The International Standard Bible Encyclopedia*, Revised edition, 4 vols. (Grand Rapids: Eerdmans, 1979–1988), IV, pp. 907–913. This has been challenged by T. L. Thompson, *Early History of the Israelite People from the Written and Archaeological Sources*, Studies in the History of the Ancient Near East 4 (Leiden: Brill, 1992), p. 259. He objects that early Iron Age settlements in the Galilee preserve a culture distinct from those of the hill country and exhibit a continuation of the culture associated with Late Bronze Age Lower Galilee sites. This interpretation is challenged by Z. Gal, *Lower Galilee during the Iron Age*, ASOR Dissertation Series 8 (Winona Lake, Indiana: Eisenbrauns, 1992), pp. 88–93. He argues that, although some settlement in the valleys may support the interpretation of Canaanites from the Late Bronze Age towns resettling in villages, the new settlement patterns in the hill country of Galilee and the chronological gap between the destruction of the Late Bronze Age Canaanite towns and the settlement of villages, 'suggests a new type of settler who did not have a direct connection to the Canaanite culture which preceded them' (p. 88). A. Zertal, 'The Trek of the Tribes as They Settled in Canaan', *BAR*, 17/5, September–October 1991, pp. 48–49, 75, argues that the Israelites entered Canaan in the thirteenth and twelfth centuries BC and first settled in the territory of Manasseh where at least six of the Israelite tribes are mentioned in the Bible (especially in Jos. 13 – 19 and Jdg. 4 – 5) as passing through or having contact with Manasseh.
[2] On terraces see L. E. Stager, 'The Archaeology of the East Slope of Jerusalem and the Terraces of the Kidron', *Journal of Near Eastern Studies*, 41, 1982, pp. 111–121; *idem*, 'The Family in Ancient Israel', *BASOR*, 260, 1985, pp. 5–10; D. C. Hopkins, *The Highlands of Canaan*, pp. 173–186; and the discussion between I. Finkelstein and W. Dever in H. Shanks *et al.*, *The Rise of Ancient Israel* (Washington, D.C.: Biblical Archaeology Society, 1992), pp. 64–65, 79.
[3] On the Perizzites of v. 15, see the comment on 3:10 (p. 102). On the Rephaites, see comment on 11:21–22 (pp. 218–219). The Rephaites seem to correspond to the Anakites in Joshua, but whereas the Anakites are located in southern Judah, the Rephaites are found farther north, as in the central hill

f. The allotments of the remaining tribes (18:1 – 19:51)

i. Introduction (18:1–10). The scene shifts from Gilgal to Shiloh. The tribes meet with Joshua. The speaker changes from the third person to the second person as Joshua addresses the whole assembly (vv. 3–7) and then the map-makers themselves (v. 8). There is a return to the third person in the final two verses as these 'scouts' carry out their work and Joshua begins the allotment procedure. Thus this section changes from the allotments of the earlier tribes, which had already been approved by Moses, to those of the remaining seven tribes. In so doing, there is a change of place, of map-making method, and of the persons involved. Its literary location is at the centre of the tribal allotments, and therefore it is theologically significant for understanding the allotments.[1]

1. Shiloh remains a cult centre until the time of Eli (1 Sa. 1 – 4). Here it represents the fulfilment of God's promise to dwell with Israel (Lv. 26:11–12; Dt. 12).[2] Shiloh is identified with Khirbet Seilûn. Excavations have revealed a Middle Bronze Age (2000–1550 BC) shrine and a Late Bronze Age (1550–1200 BC) centre for nomadic peoples. Its occupation in the Iron Age (1200–586 BC) and its size suggest that it could have served as a centre for the tribes of Israel.[3] The *Tent of Meeting* appears in parallel with Shiloh. The tent was the place where Israel and God met; through it, the divine will was made known. Its presence here in Joshua and again at the end of the allotments (Jos. 19:51) provides a literary inclusion for all the remaining allotments. This emphasizes that all was done according to God's will. It is an important component as nowhere is there specific mention that God was consulted in the map-making

---

country of Manasseh. See Z. Kallai, 'The Land of the Perizzites and the Rephaim (Joshua 17, 14–18)', in C. Brekelmans and J. Lust (eds.), *Pentateuchal and Deuteronomistic Studies. Papers Read at the XIIIth IOSOT Congress. Leuven 1989*, BETL 94 (Leuven: Peeters and Leuven University Press, 1990), pp. 197–205.

[1] Koorevaar, pp. 183, 193–195; J. G. McConville, *Grace in the End. A Study in Deuteronomic Theology*, Studies in Old Testament Biblical Theology (Carlisle, Paternoster, 1993), pp. 101–102.

[2] Koorevaar, pp. 289–293. Koorevaar identifies an elaborate chiastic arrangement for chs. 13 – 22, and he locates this text at the centre of that chiasm.

[3] I. Finkelstein, 'Excavations at Shiloh: 1981–1984: Preliminary Report', *Tel Aviv*, 12, 1985, pp. 123–180 (131–138, 169–170); R. S. Hess, 'Early Israel in Canaan: A Survey of Recent Evidence and Interpretations', *PEQ*, 126, 1993, pp. 125–142.

process. The reason, of course, is that Israel had long been promised an inheritance in the land, so no further divine direction was necessary. It only remained to define the specific inheritances, a procedure that would enlist the divine will in the form of the lot.

In Joshua 11:23 and 14:15, notes indicate that the land has rest from war.[1] Here the note emphasizes the completion of the conquest through the observation that *the country was brought under their control.* This does not require conquest of every fortification in the land; verse 2 observes that this has not occurred. It means only that the wars had met with success and that map-makers could now be sent out. The allotment was an orderly process. As Joshua and Israel followed God's will in the conquest, so that will would now be obeyed in the allotment process.

2. The second verse prepares the reader for the allotment process that is to follow. It specifies that seven tribes remain to receive their allotment. This prepares for the three sections that follow and that deal with this need: Joshua's address to the assembly (vv. 4–7), Joshua's charge to the scouts (v. 8) and a description of how these map-makers carried out their task and what happened (vv. 9–10). Three points should be considered: the repetition of the instructions, the nature of the cartography, and the mention of the remaining tribes.

5–7. All the previous allotments are specifically named in this passage: Judah and the 'house of Joseph' (*i.e.* Ephraim and Manasseh, v. 5) and the Transjordanian tribes (v. 7). As a literary device, these references connect the previous chapters with chapter 19. The seven tribes received their allotments and map-making after the other tribes. This is a continuation of the previous allotments, but it is no less the will of God.

6–10. Everything is recorded in a book. Joshua writes the covenant in *the Book of the Law of God* (24:26; see also 8:32, 34). Just as the law guides the people in their life, the map book will guide the people in their possession of God's blessing of the land. The towns form the basis for the tribal boundaries and town lists that comprise the allotments. On this correspondence see the general discussion of Joshua 13 – 21

[1]Mitchell, pp. 101–109, regards the cessation of warfare as 'the overwhelming impression' created by the land allocation.

in the Introduction (pp. 53–60). The repetition of these instructions emphasizes their importance. Despite the success of the conquest, the land is not yet possessed, as Joshua observes (v. 3). It must be mapped and allotted. The repetition of the instructions also exemplifies the leadership of Joshua. He explains the procedure and the map-makers follow it step by step. Theirs is complete obedience to God's chosen leader. Regarding the casting of lots as an act of obedience to God's will, see the comment on Joshua 14:1–5 (pp. 237–238).

8–10. Corresponding to the three divisions (comment at v. 2), there is a threefold repetition of the instructions for these scouts. The focus of the instructions is the series of verbs: *go* (Heb. *hlk*), *make a survey* (Heb. *hlk*), *write* (Heb. *ktb*), *return* (Heb. *šwb* or *bw'*) and *cast* (*šlk*, Hiphil). In verse 9, the map-makers execute these instructions, the verbs corresponding to those in verse 8. The last verb describes Joshua's own act of casting lots (v. 10). Otherwise, the scouts do the work. Unlike the spies of Numbers 13 and Joshua 2, the purpose of the map-makers is not to study the opposition but to provide information about the land. In verse 9, they 'map' the towns so that they can be divided into seven regions.

For the Christian, the establishment of a sanctuary and centre at Shiloh testifies to how God fulfils his promises. God has given his people the blessing of his presence among them. They must respond in obedience by occupying the land and living according to the divine covenant. The fundamental importance of the sanctuary is illustrated by its central position among the tribes (in the central hill country) and by its position in the midst of the allotments of Joshua 13 – 21. Christians are also called upon to see the worship of God as central to their lives. As with the gatherings at the Shiloh sanctuary so regular meetings for worship are a chief means to provide unity and common encouragement for faithful living (Heb. 10:25).

ii. The allotment of Benjamin (18:11–28). The territory of this tribe bordered the Jordan River on the east, Ephraim on the north, Dan on the west, and Judah on the south. Its town list included an eastern (vv. 21–24) and a western (vv. 25–28) district. A third district has been posited, consisting of Anathoth, Azmaveth, and Alemuth, as these towns elsewhere belong to Benjamin but do not seem to be listed here.[1] Table 18(a–e) provides summaries for the allotments for Benjamin.

Table 18: The allotments for Benjamin (18:12–28)

18(a): Northern boundary (18:12–13)

Verse	Name (NIV)	MT	LXX	Arab	Israeli	Grid no.
12	Jordan River	Yes	Yes			
	Jericho	Yes	Yes	T es-Sulṭân		192142
	Beth Aven	Yes	Yes	T Maryam?		175141
13	Luz (Bethel)	Yes	Yes	Beitîn		173148
	Ataroth Addar	Yes	Yes	T el-Mazar (eṣ-Ṣimadi)		196171
	Lower Beth Horon	Yes	Yes	Beit 'Ûr et-Taḥtā		158144

18(b): Western boundary (18:14)

Verse	Name (NIV)	MT	LXX	Arab	Israeli	Grid no.
14	Kiriath Baal (Kiriath Jearim)	Yes	Yes	T el-Azhar	T Qiryat Ye'arim	159135

18(c): Southern boundary (18:15–17)

Verse	Name (NIV)	MT	LXX	Arab	Israeli	Grid no.
15	waters of Nephtoah	Yes	Yes	Liftā	Mê Neftoaḥ	168133
16	Valley of Ben Hinnom	Yes	Yes	Wâdī er-Rabâbeh		
	Valley of Rephaim	Yes	Yes	Wâdī el-Ward		
	Jebusite City (= Jerusalem)	Yes	Yes	el-Quds	'îr Dawîd	172131
	En Rogel	Yes	Yes	Bir Ayyûb	En Rogel	173130
17	En Shemesh	Yes	Yes	'Ain el-Hôd		175131
	Geliloth (= Gilgal)	Yes	Yes	Araq ed-Deir[2]		180133
	Pass of Adummim	Yes	Yes	Tal 'at ed-Damm	Ma'alê 'adum-mîm	178132
	Stone of Bohan son of Reuben	Yes	Yes			

[1] Z. Kallai-Kleinmann, 'The Town Lists of Judah, Simeon, Benjamin and Dan', p. 139. He also suggests including Gibeah in this district. However, this does not seem to be attested.
[2] W. R. Kotter, 'Gilgal' in *ABD*, II, pp. 1022–1024.

JOSHUA 18:1 – 19:51

Verse	Name (NIV)	MT	LXX	Arab	Israeli	Grid no.
	Beth Arabah	Yes	Yes	'Ain el-Gharabeh		197139
	Beth Hoglah	Yes	Yes	Deir Ḥajlah		197136
	northern bay of the Salt Sea	Yes	Yes			
	Jordan River	Yes	Yes			

18(d): Eastern towns (18:21–24)

Verse	Name (NIV)	MT	LXX	Arab	Israeli	Grid no.
21	Jericho	Yes	Yes	T es-Sulṭân		192142
	Beth Hoglah	Yes	Yes	Deir Ḥajlah		197136
	Emek Keziz	Yes	Yes			
22	Beth Arabah	Yes	Yes	'Ain el-Gharabeh		197139
	Zemaraim	Yes	Yes	Râs eṭ-Ṭâḥûneh?		170147
	Bethel	Yes	Yes	Beitîn		173148
23	Avvim[1]	Yes	Yes			
	Parah	Yes	Yes	Kh 'Ain Farah?		179138
	Ophrah	Yes	Yes	eṭ-Ṭaiyibeh		178151
24	Kephar Ammoni[2]	Yes	Yes			
	Ophni[3]	Yes	Yes			
	Geba	Yes	Yes	Kh et-Tell[4]		174158

Table 18(e): Western towns (18:25–28)

Verse	Name (NIV)	MT	LXX	Arab	Israeli	Grid no.
25	Gibeon	Yes	Yes	el-Jîb		167139
	Ramah	Yes	Yes	er-Râm		172140

[1]Probably a gentilic, connected with inhabitants of Ai or Aiatha. Kallai, pp. 400–401. N. Na'aman and R. Zadok, 'Sargon II's Deportations to Israel and Philistia', *Journal of Cuneiform Studies*, 40, 1988, pp. 36–46 (45), argue that this name comes from the inhabitants of Avva whom Sargon II resettled in the region in the late eighth century BC. However, see Jos. 13:3 and the comment on Avvim which occurs there. Na'aman assumes that this is a homonym.

[2]Probably a gentilic, connected with Ammonites. Kallai, pp. 400–401.

[3]Probably a gentilic. See *ibid.*

[4]G. Galil, 'Geba'-Ephraim and the Northern Boundary of Judah in the Days of Judah', *RB*, 100, 1993, pp. 358–367. The alternative site, Jaba' (grid no. 175140), is proposed by Boling and Wright, p. 431. Boling observes that Peterson found no sherds earlier than the eighth century in a surface survey of this site.

Verse	Name (NIV)	MT	LXX	Arab	Israeli	Grid no.
	Beeroth	Yes	Yes	el-Bireh?[1]		170146
26	Mizpah	Yes	Yes	T en-Naṣbeh		170143
	Kephirah	Yes	Yes	Kh el-Kefireh		160138
	Mozah	Yes	Yes	Qâlunyah	Mevasseret Ṣiyyon	165134
27	Rekem	Yes	Yes			
	Irpeel	Yes	Yes[2]			
	Taralah	Yes	Yes			
28	Zelah	Yes	Yes[3]			
	Haeleph	Yes	Yes			
	Jebusite city (Jerusalem)	Yes	Yes	el-Quds	'îr Dawîd	172131
	Gibeah[4]	Yes	Yes	T el-Fûl[5]		172136
	Kiriath (= Jearim)	Yes	Yes[6]	T el-Azhar	T Qiryat Ye'arim	159135

iii. The allotment of Simeon (19:1–9).

Simeon has no boundary description. The towns of Simeon lie within the southern borders of Judah. The southern (15:26–32) and central Shephelah (15:42) districts of Judah contain these towns.[7] There are two districts, eastern and western. The towns in this region would serve Israel's defensive network along its southern border where the Edomi s threatened the nation. The variety of peoples in this region, noted in the introduction, would create a need for a group such as Simeon to provide

[1] D. A. Dorsey, 'Beeroth' in *ABD*, I, pp. 646–647.

[2] LXX B reads here Kaphan and Nakan.

[3] LXX B places Zelah before Taralah. Both LXX A and LXX B combine Zelah and Haeleph in one name. This is preferred by Boling and Wright, p. 431, who translate it as 'rib (slope) of the 'eleph', where 'eleph' is the military muster unit of the clan or village. See also D. V. Edelman, 'Zela' in *ABD*, VI, p. 1072, who also combines the names with the translation, 'ox-rib'. Although some names have been suggested, the absence of evidence does not allow for any certain or likely identification.

[4] The MT includes a final *taw*, *i.e.* Gibeath. However, the name is generally identified with Gibeah.

[5] For identification with Jaba' see J. M. Miller, 'Geba/Gibeah of Benjamin', *VT*, 25, 1975, pp. 1–22; P. M. Arnold, 'Hosea and the Sin of Gibeah', *CBQ*, 51, 1989, pp. 447–460 (455). For possible problems with such an identification, see the note on Geba, p. 266, n. 4.

[6] LXX B combines Gibeah and Kiriath in one name. This is followed by Aharoni, *Land*, p. 435, who identifies the site as Abū Ghôsh (grid no. 160134).

[7] See 1 Ch. 4:28–33, where the same list appears.

tribal and national identity and to represent the official theology. Thus the Simeonite towns resemble those of the Levites in terms of their function. Table 19(a–b) lists the towns alloted to Simeon.

Table 19: The allotment of Simeon (19:1–9)

19(a): Eastern towns of Simeon (19:2–6)

Verse	Name (NIV)	MT	LXX	Arab	Israeli	Grid no.
2	Beersheba	Yes	AB	T es-Seba' or Bīr es-Seba'[1]	T Beer Sheva' or Be'er Sheva'	134072 or 130072
	Sheba (= Shema)	Yes	AB			
	Moladah	Yes	AB	Kh el-Waten?	Kh Yittan	142074
3	Hazar Shual	Yes	AB			
	Balah	Yes	AB			
	Ezem	Yes	AB			
4	Eltolad	Yes	AB			
	Bethul (= Kesil)	Yes	B	T Umm Bētēn		138076
	Hormah	Yes	AB	Kh el-Me-shâsh or T Khuwelifeh	T Masos or T Halif[2]	146069 or 137087
5	Ziklag	Yes	AB	T esh-Shārî'ah or T es-Seba'	T Sera' or T Beer Sheva'	119088 or 134072
	Beth Marcaboth (= Madmannah)	Yes	AB	Kh Tatrît		143084
	Hazar Susah (= Sansannah)	Yes	AB	Kh esh-Shamsaniyat		140083
6	Beth Lebaoth	Yes	AB			
	Sharuhen	Yes	AB	T el-Fâr'ah S. or T el-'Ajjul	T Sharuhen	100076 or 094097

19(b): Western towns of Simeon (19:7–8)

Verse	Name (NIV)	MT	LXX	Arab	Israeli	Grid no.
7	Ain	Yes	AB			
	Rimmon	Yes	AB	Kh Khuweilfeh?	T Halif	137087

[1]N. Na'aman, 'The Inheritance of the Sons of Simeon', pp. 149–151, proposes Bīr es-Seba', beneath the modern town of Beer-Sheva.

[2]Na'aman, 'The Inheritance of the Sons of Simeon', pp. 142–143, suggests this possibility, noting that Masos was abandoned from the eighth century until the seventh. See also Fritz, p. 165.

Verse	Name (NIV)	MT	LXX	Arab	Israeli	Grid no.
	Tochan	No	B			
	Ether	Yes	AB	Kh el-'Ater	T 'Eter	138113
	Ashan	Yes	AB	T Beit Mirsim?	T Bet Mirsham	142096
8	Baalath Beer (Ramah in the Negev) = Kinah?	Yes	AB	Kh Ghazzah?[1]	Kh 'Uzza	165068

iv. The allotment of Zebulun (19:10–16). This allotment appears in the western area of the Lower Galilee. Most of it lies between the Jezreel and the Bet Netofa (Sahl el-Battof) valleys. The border description begins in the south and travels east before turning north.[2] Verse 15 lists fewer than the twelve towns that are counted. This may suggest that the text originally included more towns than it does now. The western border of Zebulun formed the eastern boundary of Asher (19:27–28). Table 20(a–c) lists the allotments to Zebulun.

Table 20. The allotment of Zebulun (19:10–11)

20(a): Southern boundary (19:10–11)

Verse	Name (NIV)	MT	LXX	Arab	Israeli	Grid no.
10	Sarid	Yes	AB	T Shadûd		172229
	Gola	No	B			
11	Maralah	Yes	AB			
	Dabbesheth	Yes	A			
	Jokneam Ravine	Yes	AB			

20(b): Eastern boundary (19:12–13)

Verse	Name (NIV)	MT	LXX	Arab	Israeli	Grid no.
12	Kisloth Tabor	Yes	AB	Iksâl		180232
	Daberath	Yes	AB	Dabûriyeh		185233
	Japhia	Yes	AB	Yâfâ or Mishad[3]		176232 or 181238
13	Gath Hepher	Yes	AB	Kh ez-Zurrâ'	T Gat Ḥefer	180238

[1] Y. Beit-Aryeh, 'Horvat 'Uzzah – A Border Fortress in the Eastern Negev', *Qadmoniot*, 19, 1986, pp. 31–40, Hebrew. Others suggest Kh el-Garra, north-east of Masos. See Fritz, p. 187.

[2] However the poetry of Gn. 49:13 is understood, the boundary of Zebulun fits best in Lower Galilee rather than along the coast.

[3] Boling and Wright, p. 445.

Verse	Name (NIV)	MT	LXX	Arab	Israeli	Grid no.
	Eth Kazin	Yes	AB	Lubiyeh?[1]		192244
	Rimmon (= Merom)	Yes	AB	Qarn Ḥaṭṭîn[2]	Kh Qarnei Ḥiṭṭin	193245
	Amathar	No	AB			
	Neah	Yes	A	Bet Netofa Valley	Sahl el-Baṭṭof Valley	

20(c): Northern boundary (19:14–15)

Verse	Name (NIV)	MT	LXX	Arab	Israeli	Grid no.
14	Hannathon	Yes	AB	T el-Bedei-wîyeh	T Ḥannaton	174243
	Valley of Iphtah El	Yes	AB	Wâdī el-Malik		
15	Kattah (= Kitron)	Yes	AB			
	Nahalal	Yes	AB	Ma'lul[3]		173234
	Shimron	Yes	AB	Kh Sammûniyeh	T Shimron	170234
	Idalah	Yes	A			
	Bethlehem	Yes	AB	Beit Laḥm	Bet Leḥem Hagelilit	168238

v. The allotment of Issachar (19:17–23). This allotment is limited to a town list, though some would identify part of a northern boundary line in verse 22. The north-eastern part of Manasseh is not distinct from southern Issachar's inheritance (11:16; 17:10–11) in the Beth Shan plain. Issachar's northern section extended to the Valley of Yiptah-el. Thus it consisted of much of eastern Lower Galilee. The town list comprises three topographical regions: Jezreel Valley (first four places), basalt heights (the next five places), edge of the cliffs (last four places).[4] Unless Tabor is identified as a village (rather than a mountain), the Hebrew text preserves fifteen names. To achieve the number sixteen (v. 22), Shahazumah may be divided into two names, or Beeroth, found in the Septuagint, may be added. Issachar means 'hireling'. Some have found here evidence that the tribe originated among corvée workers for Canaanite cities in the Jezreel Valley. However, Gal finds a

---

[1] Na'aman, *Borders*, p. 135.
[2] *Ibid*, p. 137.
[3] Z. Gal, *Lower Galilee during the Iron Age*, p. 102.
[4] Z. Gal, 'The Settlement of Issachar: Some New Observations', *Tel Aviv*, 9, 1982, pp. 79–86; Kallai, pp. 421–426.

chronological gap between the dates of the destruction of Canaanite cities and the settlement of villages in Issachar (tenth century BC). Table 21 lists the allotment of Issachar.

Table 21: The allotment of Issachar (19:17–23)

Verse	Name (NIV)	MT	LXX	Arab	Israeli	Grid no.
18	Jezreel	Yes	AB	Zar'in	T Yizre'el	181218
	Kesulloth	Yes	AB	Iksál		180232
	Shunem	Yes	AB	Sulem	Shunem	181223
19	Hapharaim	Yes	A	'Affuleh?		177224
	Shion	Yes	AB			
	Beeroth	No	AB	En Beera		197224
	Anaharath	Yes	AB	T el-Mu-kharkhash	T Rekhesh	194228
20	Rabbith (Daberath)	Yes	AB	Dabûriyeh		185233
	Kishion	Yes	AB	Kh Qasyûn	T Qishyon	187229
	Ebez	Yes	A	En Hayadid	T Remet	199221
21	Remeth = Jarmuth	Yes	AB	Kh ed-Dir		200229
	En Gannim	Yes	B	el-Hadetheh	T 'En Hadda	195232
	En Haddah	Yes	B			
	Beth Pazzez	Yes	AB			
22	Tabor	Yes	AB			
	Shahazumah	Yes	AB	Kh Sheikh esh-Shamsāwi?	Kh Shemesh	199232
	Beth Shemesh	Yes	AB	el- 'Abeidîyeh?		202232

vi. The allotment of Asher (19:24–31). There may be an early reference to Asher in a place name Gath-Asher that appears in an Egyptian inscription of Ramses II from the thirteenth century BC.[1] This territory is defined by a boundary description that moves from the southern to the eastern border, and then goes on to the western coastal border.[2] Part of this region,

---

[1]See Aharoni, *Land*, p. 181. Aharoni identifies it with modern Jett in Western Galilee.

[2]Lipiński argues that the allotment of Asher is a town list rather than a boundary description. He dates the town list to the Persian period (*c.* 400 BC) on the basis of literary critical conclusions about the Deuteronomic and Priestly redactions. With Gal, the text is a boundary description. Lemaire dates Asher's list to the end of David's reign on the basis of the period of occupation of sites such as that identified with Cabul (eleventh and tenth centuries BC). See Z. Gal,

especially Cabul, was given by Solomon to Hiram of Tyre (1 Kg. 9:11–13). Its southern boundary was Carmel. The territory encompasses the Acco Plain to the north. Table 22(a–c) lists the allotment of Asher.

Table 22: The allotment of Asher (19:24–31)

22(a): Southern boundary[1] (19:25–26)

Verse	Name (NIV)	MT	LXX	Arab	Israeli	Grid no.
25	Helkath	Yes	AB		T 'Amar	159237
	Hali	Yes	AB	Kh Râs 'Âli	T 'Alil Hamma'arabi?	164242
	Beten	Yes	AB	T el-Far		160242
	Acshaph	Yes	AB	T Kīsân	T Keisan	164253
26	Allammelech	Yes	B			
	Amad	Yes	AB			
	Mishal	Yes	AB	T el-Naḥal?		157245
	Carmel	Yes	AB			
	Shihor Libnath	Yes	AB	T Abū Huwâm?		152245

22(b): Eastern boundary (19:27–28)

Verse	Name (NIV)	MT	LXX	Arab	Israeli	Grid no.
27	Beth Dagon	Yes	AB		Beth She'arim or Kh Buṣṣin	162234 or 163238
	Valley of Iphtah El	Yes	AB		Naḥal 'I 'blin[2]	
	Beth Emek	Yes	AB	Kh Abu Mudawer Tamra		170247
	Neiel	Yes	AB	Kh Ya'nîn	Kh Ya'anin	171255
	Cabul	Yes	AB		Kh Ro'sh Zayit[3]	172254

Lower Galilee during the Iron Age, pp. 102–104; A. Lemaire, 'Asher et le royaume de Tyr' in E. Lipiński (ed.), *Phoenicia and the Bible. Proceedings of the Conference Held at the University of Leuven on the 15th and 16th of March 1990,* Orientalia Lovaniensia Analecta 44, Studia Phoenicia 11 (Louvain: Peeters, 1991), pp. 135–152; E. Lipiński, 'The Territory of Tyre and the Tribe of Asher' in E. Lipiński (ed.) *op. cit.,* pp. 153–166.

[1]For the southern and eastern boundaries, see Z. Gal, *Lower Galilee during the Iron Age,* pp. 102–104.

[2]Z. Gal, 'Cabul, Jiphthah-El and the Boundary between Asher and Zebulun in the Light of Archaeological Evidence', *ZDPV,* 101, 1985, pp. 114–127.

[3]Z. Gal, 'Khorvat Rosh Zayit – A Phoenician Fort in the Lower Galilee', *Qadmoniot,* 17, 1984, pp. 56–69.

Verse	Name (NIV)	MT	LXX	Arab	Israeli	Grid no.
28	Abdon[1]	Yes	AB	Kh 'Abdeh	T 'Avdon	165272
	Rehob	Yes	AB	T el-Gharbī?	T Bira	166256
	Hammon	Yes	AB	Umm el 'Awāmîd		164281
	Kanah	Yes	AB	Qânā		178290
	Greater Sidon	Yes	AB	Ṣaidā		184329

22(c): Western boundary (19:29–30)

Verse	Name (NIV)	MT	LXX	Arab	Israeli	Grid no.
29	Ramah	Yes	AB			
	fortified city of Tyre	Yes	AB	eṣ-Ṣûr		168297
	Hosah (= Usu)	Yes	AB	T Rashīdîyeh		170293
	Ahlab (= Mahalab)	No	B	Ras el-Abyad?[2]		166285
	Aczib	Yes	AB	ez-Zîb	T Akhziv	159272
30	Ummah	Yes	AB			
	Aphek	Yes	AB	T Kurdâneh	T Afeq	160250
	Rehob	Yes	AB	T el-Gharbī?	T Bira	166256

vii. The allotment of Naphtali (19:32–39). This territory is described by a boundary description (vv. 33–34) and a town list (vv. 35–38). The towns of verse 33 form the southern boundary of the tribe.[3] The borders and town list predate David's incorporation of Ijon and Abel Beth Maacah into the territory of Israel. These two towns are not listed here, but they would have formed part of Naphtali's territory when they were added. Naphtali included Upper Galilee and the eastern portion of Lower Galilee. As verse 34 observes, it bordered Asher on the west, Zebulun (and Issachar) on the south, and the Jordan River (north of the Sea of Galilee) on the east. Table 23(a–b) lists the allotment of Naphtali.

[1] Most Hebrew manuscripts read 'Ebron'.

[2] See Na'aman, *Borders*, p. 60.

[3] Some have attempted to associate this verse with the northern border of Naphtali. However, if the large tree in Zaanannim is near Kadesh (Jdg. 4:11) and if Barak came from Kadesh, then Kadesh cannot be the north Galilean Canaanite town but must be another place. This allows for a southern location for this boundary description. See R. S. Hess, 'Tribes, Territories of' in G W. Bromiley *et al*, *The International Standard Bible Encyclopedia*, Revised edition, 4 vols. (Grand Rapids: Eerdmans,1979–1988), IV p. 910.

Table 23: The allotment of Naphtali (19:33–38)

23(a): Southern boundary[1] (19:33–34)

Verse	Name (NIV)	MT	LXX	Arab	Israeli	Grid no.
33	Heleph	Yes	A	Kh 'Irbâdeh?	Kh 'Arpad	189236
	large tree in Zaanannim[2]	Yes	No			
	Adami Nekeb	Yes	AB	Kh Dâmiyeh	T Adami	193239
	Jabneel	Yes	AB	T en-Na'am	T Yin'am	198235
	Lakkum	Yes	A	Kh el-Man-sûrah?		202233
34	Aznoth Tabor	Yes	AB	Kh el-Jebeil?	T Gobel	186237
	Hukkok	Yes	AB	Yaquq? or Kh el-Jemeijmeh?	Kh Gamom?	195254 or 175252

Table 23(b): Town list (19:35–38)

Verse	Name (NIV)	MT	LXX	Arab	Israeli	Grid no.
35	Ziddim and Zer	Yes	AB[3]			
	Hammath	Yes	AB	Hammâm Ṭabariyeh	Hame Ṭeveriya	201241
	Rakkath	Yes	AB	Kh el-Qu-neiṭireh	T Raqqat	199245
	Kinnereth	Yes	AB	Kh el-'Oreimeh	T Kinrot[4]	200252
36	Adamah	Yes	AB			
	Ramah	Yes	A	Kh Zeitûn	er-Râmah	187259
	Hazor	Yes	AB	T el-Qedaḥ	T Haṣor	203269
37	Kedesh	Yes	AB	T Qades	T Qedesh	199279
	Edrei	Yes	AB			
	En Hazor	Yes	AB	'Ainatha		191281
38	Iron	Yes	AB	Yārûn?		189276
	Migdal El	Yes	AB	Majdel Islim? or Kh el-Meğdel[5]		194292 or 184293

[1] See Z. Gal, *Lower Galilee during the Iron Age*, pp. 104–105; Na'aman, *Borders*, pp. 121–143.

[2] Z. Gal. *op. cit.*, p. 105, places it in the Tabor area.

[3] Following the LXX here, read, 'and the fortified towns of the Tyrians, Tyre and . . . '

[4] V. Fritz, 'Kinneret: A Biblical City on the Sea of Galilee', *Archaeology*, 40/4, 1987, pp. 42–49.

[5] D. Kellerman, 'Migdal-El – Magdiel', *ZDPV*, 98, 1982, pp. 63–69.

Verse	Name (NIV)	MT	LXX	Arab	Israeli	Grid no.
	Horem	Yes	A B	Ḥaris?		185286
	Beth Anath	Yes	A B	Ṣafed el-Baṭṭikh?		190289
	Beth Shemesh	Yes	A B	Kh T er-Ruweisī?	T Rosh	181271

viii. The allotment of Dan (19:40–48). This territory contains only a town list, with no boundary description. As with its eastern neighbour, Benjamin, this town list also has eastern (vv. 42–44) and western (vv. 45–46) sections. Alt argued that Dan's allotment should be located within Judah because the boundaries of Ephraim and Judah left no space in between.[1] Kaufmann suggested that Dan and Judah shared a common border point at Ekron but that the tribal allotments were otherwise separate.[2] Gevirtz suggested that the Danite territory was later possessed by Judah and that this event was evoked in Jacob's blessing on Judah.[3] The text describes the allotment of Dan as separate from its neighbouring tribes. The town list should be dated to the time of Dan's conquest of the town of Dan, north of the Sea of Galilee (Jdg. 18:11). Table 24(a–b) lists the allotment of Dan.

Table 24: The allotment of Dan (19:41–47)

24(a): Eastern towns of Dan (19:41–44)

Verse	Name (NIV)	MT	LXX	Arab	Israeli	Grid no.
41	Zorah	Yes	A B	Ṣar'ah	T Ṣor'a	148131
	Eshtaol	Yes	A	Deir Abū Qābûs		151132
	Ir Shemesh (Beth Shemesh)	Yes	A B	T er-Rumeileh	T Bet Shemesh	147128
42	Shaalabbin	Yes	A B	Selbît	T Sha'alevim	148141
	Aijalon (= Ammon)	Yes	A B	Yālō		152138
	Ithlah	Yes	A B			
43	Elon	Yes	A B			
	Timnah	Yes	A B	T el-Baṭâshi		141132
	Ekron	Yes	A B	Kh el-Muqanna'	T Miqne	136131

---

[1] A. Alt, 'Die Landnahme der Israeliten in Palästina', *Reformationsprogramm der Universität Leipzig* (1925), p. 33.

[2] Y. Kaufmann, *The Biblical Account of the Conquest of Canaan*.

[3] Gn. 49:8–12. S. Gevirtz, 'Adumbrations of Dan in Jacob's Blessing on Judah', *ZAW*, 93, 1981, pp. 21–37.

Verse	Name (NIV)	MT	LXX	Arab	Israeli	Grid no.
44	Eltekeh	Yes	AB	T esh-Shallaf? or T Melât[1]	T Shalaf	128144 or 137140
	Gibbethon	Yes	AB	T Melât or Ras Abu Hamid[2]		137140 or 139145
	Baalath	Yes	AB	el-Mughâr?		129138

24(b): Western towns of Dan and Leshem (19:45–47)

Verse	Name (NIV)	MT	LXX	Arab	Israeli	Grid no.
45	Jehud	Yes	A	el-Yehudîyeh	Yehud	139159
	Bene Berak	Yes	AB	Ibn-ibrâq	Kh Bene-beraq	133160
	Gath Rimmon	Yes	AB	T el-Jerîsheh or T Abu Zeitun	T Gerisa	132166 or 134167
46	Me Yarkon	Yes	AB	Nahr el-Auja (river) or T Qasile[3]		131168
	Rakkon	Yes	No	Nahr el-Barîdeh (river)[4] or T er- Reqqeit		129168
	Joppa	Yes	AB	Yâfâ	Yafo	126162
47	Leshem (= Dan)	Yes	AB	T el-Qâdī	T Dan	211294

ix. The allotment of Joshua (19:49–51). The two spies who returned a good report in Numbers 13 are rewarded with their own inheritance. That of Caleb, in the south of the central hill country (at Hebron) is described at the beginning of the allotment for the tribes west of the Jordan (Jos. 14:6–15; 15:13–19). The inheritance of Joshua is described at the end of the allotments. It is in the central hill country of Ephraim (Joshua's tribe) at Timnath Serah[5] and is identified with Khirbet Tibnah, 16 miles south-west of Shechem.[6] From a literary perspective, the two individual inheritances begin and end the allotments. Joshua waits until all the other inheritances are assigned before taking any for himself. Thus he

[1] Na'aman, *Borders*, p. 108, n. 49.
[2] *Ibid.*
[3] J. J. Simons, *The Geographical and Topographical Texts of the Old Testament,* Francisci Scholten memoriae dedicata 2 (Leiden: Brill, 1959), p. 201.
[4] Kallai, p. 370.
[5] This is Timnath Heres in Jdg. 2:9.
[6] Grid no. 160157.

preserves his right to a share of the land without any suggestion of an abuse of his leadership responsibilities. The allotment was done according to God's will, with Eleazar the priest presiding 'before the Lord' at Shiloh's sanctuary. The land is God's blessing upon Israel and forms a testimony of the divine presence among them.

For the Christian, this account of Joshua's inheritance provides several lessons about Christian ministry. Firstly, the leader seeks to proclaim and follow God's Word through to its conclusion, without compromising or changing things midway (1 Tim. 4:11–16; Tit. 1:9). Joshua and Eleazar obeyed God throughout the allotment. Secondly, the leader exhibits courtesy and humility (Gal. 5:22–26). Although Joshua could have rightly claimed his portion at the beginning of the allotment or during the allotment to Ephraim, the text places it as the last of all the portions allotted to Israel. Joshua receives his land, as God promised, but he does so only after everyone else has received theirs. Thirdly, Joshua as God's appointed leader does indeed receive an allotment. He is given a fair share in Israel's inheritance (1 Tim. 5:17–18).

g. Towns of refuge (20:1–9)

Commentators who focus on the land conclude the allotments with chapter 19, the fundamental concern of these chapters being the tribes and their inheritance. Basic to this argument is the division of chapters 13 – 19 by tribe and the naming of towns in the central hill country according to the family that inherits the area in which the town is located.[1] Chapters 20 – 21 appear after the tribal allotments because they represent a second phase in the land grants. Firstly, God gave the Promised Land to Israel (chs. 13 – 19). Secondly, Israel gave back some of this land, setting it aside for specific purposes. In Joshua 20, towns are set aside for the inadvertent killer to find safety from blood vengeance.

This had been described already in Exodus 21:12–14, as well as Numbers 35 and Deuteronomy 4 and 19. Exodus 21 places the law of asylum at the head of its discussion of capital offences. It describes how God will designate a place for the unintentional

---

[1] See the discussion on the town lists in the introductory material to chs. 13 – 21, pp. 56–60.

killer to flee for safety.[1] Numbers 35:9–15 defines six places as towns of asylum, three east of the Jordan and three to the west. Verses 22–28 go on to state that the town must guarantee protection for the person who is found not guilty of murder, but if the person wanders from the town he may be killed by the avenger of blood. Deuteronomy 4:41–43 describes the three towns of asylum east of the Jordan which Moses designated in that area.

2. Deuteronomy 19:1–10 affirms the instruction to set aside three towns in addition to the three already set aside west of the Jordan: 'If the LORD your God enlarges your territory, as he promised on oath to your forefathers, and gives you the whole land he promised them, because you carefully follow all these laws I command you today – to love the LORD your God and to walk always in his ways – then you are to set aside three more cities' (vv. 8–9). Polzin observes how the failure to achieve a complete conquest, noted in Joshua 13:1, is confirmed by the allotment of only three towns west of the Jordan, rather than six.[2]

3. The law distinguishes between intentional killing, with premeditation, and unintentional killing. The former is liable to the death penalty, whether inflicted by the society or by *the avenger of blood.* Unintentional killing is not liable to the death penalty, but *the avenger of blood* must seek compensation for the loss incurred by the death of someone from his clan.[3] In this case, putting the killer to death would spill innocent blood and

[1]The place suggested is the town of refuge as developed in the other passages. See J. M. Sprinkle, *The Book of the Covenant. A Literary Approach, JSOT* Supplement 174 (Sheffield: Sheffield Academic Press, 1994), pp. 81–84.

[2]Polzin, pp. 129–130. For a comparison of the towns of asylum with towns serving a similar purpose in Ancient Near Eastern treaty clauses, see M. Löhr, *Das Asylwesen im Alten Testament* (Halle: Max Niemeyer, 1930); Butler, p. 214. In Jos. 20, however, the town list forms part of a land grant. Nevertheless, the treaty context allows for an antiquity to this law and the towns named. This antiquity is supported by the absence of reference to towns of asylum (as well as the Levitical towns) in Samuel, Kings, Chronicles and all of the post-exilic books. See Boling and Wright, p. 473. It is challenged by A. Rofé, who argues that the towns form a type of exile, a concept not supported by the language of Jos. 20 (compared with biblical accounts of exile). See A. Rofé, 'Joshua 20: Historico-Literary Criticism Illustrated' in J. H. Tigay (ed.), *Empirical Models for Biblical Criticism* (Philadelphia: University of Pennsylvania Press, 1985), pp. 131–147; *idem,* 'The History of the Cities of Refuge in Biblical Law' in S. Japhet (ed.), *Studies in the Bible 1986,* Scripta Hierosolymitana Volume 31 (Jerusalem: Magnes, 1986), pp. 205–239.

[3]R. L. Hubbard, Jr., 'The Go'el in Ancient Israel: Theological Reflections on an Israelite Institution, *Bulletin for Biblical Research,* 1, 1991, pp. 3–19.

pollute the land. The law seeks to prevent this by establishing asylum centres.

4–6. Joshua 20 adds that the unintentional killer must *stand in the entrance of the city gate and state his case.* Then the elders are *to admit him.* His safety is guaranteed until the time of his trial in his home village (Nu. 35:22–28). Even if he is acquitted of premeditated murder, the threat from *the avenger of blood* remains. In order to escape this, he may live in the town of asylum *until the death of the high priest.* The high priest represents the nation, especially in terms of its guilt and its sacrifice (Lv. 16).[1] The death of the priest symbolically terminates the guilt incurred by the killer's act.[2] Presumably, the avenger of blood would accept this death as a substitute for the death of the killer. The compensation had been paid. Nothing further was required.

The asylum towns are located throughout the regions occupied by early Israel. They include well-known strategic centres (*e.g.* Shechem and Hebron) that would allow the asylum seekers a convenient and easily located refuge and would provide maximum security from any avenger of blood. Table 25 lists the towns of asylum.[3]

Table 25: Towns of asylum (20:7–8)

Verse	Name (NIV)	MT	LXX	Arab	Israeli	Grid no.
7	Kedesh Naphtali	Yes	Yes	T Qades	T Qedesh	199279
	Shechem	Yes	Yes	T Balâtah		176179
	Hebron[4]	Yes	Yes	T er-Rumeideh		160104
8	Bezer	Yes	Yes	Umm el-'Amad?		235132
	Ramoth	Yes	Yes	T Ramith[5]		244210
	Golan	Yes	Yes	Sahem el-Joulan?		238243

---

[1] M. Greenberg, 'The Biblical Conception of Asylum', *JBL*, 78, 1959, pp. 125–132.

[2] Fritz, p. 204, notes that the word 'unintentionally' (*šggh*) in v. 3 occurs elsewhere only in the context of priestly and cultic activities.

[3] The suggestion of A. G. Auld, 'Cities of Refuge in Israelite Tradition', *JSOT*, 10, 1978, pp. 26–40, that these towns are drawn directly from the Levitical list of Jos. 21 is challenged by Butler, p. 216, who finds in these towns evidence for ancient holy places in Israel.

[4] On Hebron as Kiriath Arba, see the discussion at Jos. 14:6–15, pp. 239–241.

[5] Fritz, p. 205, disputes this identification, citing P. Lapp's discovery here of only a fortress during the period of Israel's wars with Aram. However, this is the very reason that Boling and Wright, p. 475, accept it.

On the system of towns of asylum, R. E. Boling and G. E. Wright comment:

> For a couple of hundred years, in any case, the ideology and system of asylum-towns must have been highly effective, for we know exceedingly few cases of attempts to execute private vengeance in the Hebrew Bible. Classic examples are seen in the stories of Gideon in Judges 8 and the anonymous Levite in Judges 19 – 20, both of whom are presented as scathing caricatures, probably for this very reason.

For the Christian, the relation of the high priest to the practice of asylum, as much as any of the high priest's roles, anticipates the sacrifice of Jesus Christ. His death is explicitly tied with the removal of sin and guilt once for all (Heb. 9:11 – 10:18). Joshua 20:9 allows anyone, Israelite or alien, the right to take advantage of these havens. The forgiveness of Christianity is also open to anyone, without regard to their background (Gal. 5:6).

h. Towns for the Levites (21:1–42)

This text concludes the apportioning of the land. Like Joshua 20, it describes places scattered throughout the whole allotment. Also like its preceding chapter, it is a gift of towns from Israel for the service of God. It fulfils the divine command of Numbers 35:1–8, where neither the number nor the location of the towns is specified. Numbers 35 provides detailed measurements for the land surrounding the towns that would belong to the Levites. The description of their size suggests that these towns were often small hamlets of a few houses each.[1]

1 Chronicles 6:54–81 (Heb. 39–66) repeats the town list, suggesting that it remained an important part of the life of Israel.[2] This passage also implies the interest it held in the post-exilic period, when occupation by the Levites of most of the towns was unrealized.[3] Albright concluded that the lists in

[1]G. J. Wenham, *Numbers. An Introduction and Commentary*, pp. 234–235. On the significance of the Levitical towns for Israel, see comment on Jos. 13:32–33, pp. 236–237.

[2]M. J. Selman, *1 and 2 Chronicles. An Introduction and Commentary*, (Leicester and Downers Grove: IVP, 1994), p. 112.

[3]S. Japhet, *1 and 2 Chronicles. A Commentary*, OTL (Louisville: Westminster/John Knox, 1993), pp. 164–165.

Joshua and Chronicles have a common origin.[1] Although some recent studies have denied a historical reality to the list, many of the sites do have an identification that places them in the period of the Monarchy.[2]

Mazar suggested that the Levitical towns could be compared to Egyptian priestly towns.[3] These also preserve lists but their form is different from that of Joshua 21. A closer parallel lies with land grants and the sale of properties, found in Ancient Near Eastern texts from Alalakh. One text describes towns that are given 'with their districts', just as in Joshua 21 the towns are given with their pasture-lands.[4] Many of the Levitical towns were previously Canaanite and lay on the borders of the tribal lands. This suggests that they were designed to allow the Levites centres for the preservation and dissemination of the faith and culture of Israel.[5]

For Christians, the allotment of Levitical towns from each tribe illustrates the principle of returning to God a portion of what has been given to them. These gifts are then used to support others in need and to encourage the proclamation of the faith (*cf.* Acts 2:44–47; Rom. 15:26–27; Phil. 4:10–18).

[1]W. F. Albright, 'The List of Levitic Cities', *Louis Ginzberg Jubilee Volume I* (New York: The American Academy for Jewish Research, 1945) pp. 49–73.

[2]Na'aman, *Borders*, pp. 203–236, interprets the list as a late-seventh-century fictitious creation drawn from the tribal place name lists of Jos. 13 – 19. See also E. Ben Zvi, 'The List of the Levitical Cities', *JSOT*, 54, 1992, pp. 77–106; Fritz, p. 212. None of these studies addresses the work of J. Peterson, *A Topographical Surface Survey of the Levitical 'Cities' of Joshua and 1 Chronicles 6*, PhD dissertation (Chicago Institute of Advanced Theological Studies; Evanston: Seabury-Western, 1977). Peterson has found evidence for Iron Age II pottery at the Levitical towns that he identified.

[3]B. Mazar, 'The Cities of the Priests and Levites', *Supplements to VT*, 7, 1960, pp. 204–205; reprinted in Sh. Aḥituv (ed.) *Biblical Israel: State and People* (Jerusalem: Magnes, 1992), p. 145; R. G. Boling, 'Levitical Cities: Archaeology and Texts' in A. Kort and S. Morschauser (eds.), *Biblical and Related Studies Presented to Samuel Iwry* (Winona Lake, Indiana: Eisenbrauns, 1985), p. 28; Boling and Wright, p. 495. Mazar cites the earlier work of A. Alt, 'Aegyptische Tempel in Palaestina und die Landnahme der Philister', *Kleine Schriften zur Geschichte des Volkes Israel*, 1 (Munich: C. H. Beck, 1953), pp. 216ff.

[4]The text is AT 56. See the discussion of R. S. Hess, 'A Typology of West Semitic Place Name Lists with Special Reference to Joshua 13 – 19', forthcoming. For the translation of the biblical term for *pasture-lands* as 'districts', see J. Barr, '*migrāš* in the Old Testament', *Journal of Semitic Studies*, 29, 1984, pp. 15–31.

[5]J. Peterson, *A Topographical Surface Survey of the Levitical 'Cities' of Joshua 21 and 1 Chronicles 6*, uses the term 'Yahweh teaching centers'. See Aharoni, *Land*, p. 305; R. S. Hess, 'Tribes, Territories of the', pp. 911–912.

i. Introduction to the Levitical towns (21:1–8). *The family heads of the Levites approached* Joshua, Eleazar and other tribal heads with a request for their allotment just as Judah had done (Jos. 14:6). The location of Shiloh was the site of the sanctuary and the place whence the map-makers went to map the allotments for the northern tribes (Jos. 18:1–10). On *pasture-lands* see the discussion of Joshua 14:1–5 (pp. 237–238).

3–8. The allotment was done *as the LORD had commanded.* Appearing in verses 3 and 8, this statement frames the proceedings and emphasizes the fulfilment of the divine instructions of Numbers 35:1–5.

4. Verses 4–7 explain how towns from each tribe are to be allotted to four groups of Levites. The *descendants of Aaron* had a special role among the Levites (Nu. 18:1–6), a role that would naturally place them near the temple at Jerusalem. Thus their allotment of towns comes from the southern tribes.

5. The Kohathites claimed descent from the second son of Levi (Gn. 46:11). They transported the ark and other tabernacle furniture through the wilderness (Nu. 3:1; 4:15–20; 7:9). They received Levitical towns from the central hill country, the heartland of early Israel and the first centre of its worship (18:1–10).

6. The Gershonites claimed descent from Levi's first son. They transported the tabernacle's textiles and coverings through the wilderness (Nu. 3:25–26; 4:24–26). They received Levitical towns in the Galilee and Bashan areas.

7. The Merarites claimed descent from Levi's third son. They guarded the tabernacle and transported its structural components through the wilderness (Nu. 1:47–53; 3:33–37; 4:29–33). They received Levitical towns in the Transjordanian and Zebulun areas.

ii. The Levitical towns (21:9–42). The forty-eight towns of the Levites are carefully organized and listed. There are headings and summaries at the beginning and end of each subsection as there are for the whole list. The numbers of towns allocated are included with each summary. Specific notes remind the reader of those towns that are towns of refuge and of the two names of Hebron/Kiriath Arba and its occupation by Caleb (see the discussion at 14:6–15). In many ways, the organization of this list is similar to administrative documents found in the palace archives of West Semitic cities such as Alalakh and Ugarit.[1] Like them, copies of this document may have served the purpose of keeping track of the Levites and thus ensuring that their important roles as priests, teachers and spiritual leaders of the people of Israel were fulfilled.

Since the great majority of these towns have appeared before in Joshua, they will not be discussed again. Only a note as to their location earlier in the book will be made. In the case of a town's first occurrence in Joshua, a site identification is proposed.

10–19. The Aaronites received Hebron (Jos. 10:3–5; 10:36–39; 14:13–15; 15:13), Libnah (10:29–32), Jattir (15:48), Eshtemoa (15:50), Holon (15:51), Debir (10:38–39), Ain (15:32), Juttah (15:55), Beth Shemesh (15:10), Gibeon (9:3, 17), Geba (Jaba', grid no. 175140), Anathoth (Ras el Karrubeh, grid no. 175135) and Almon (Kh 'Almit, grid no. 176136).

20–26. The Kohathites received Shechem (Jos. 17:7), Gezer (10:33; 16:3, 10), Kibzaim (not certain), Beth Horon (10:10–11), Eltekeh (19:44), Gibbethon (19:44), Aijalon (19:42), Gath Rimmon (19:45), Taanach (12:21, 17:11) and Ibleam (17:11).[2]

27–33. The Gershonites received Golan in Bashan (Jos. 20:8), Be Eshtarah (= Ashtaroth) (12:4; 13:31), Kishion (19:20), Daberath (19:12), Jarmuth (10:3, 5, 23), En Gannim (19:21), Mishal (19:26), Abdon (19:28), Helkath (19:25), Rehob (19:28, 30), Kedesh in Galilee (20:7), Hammoth Dor (= Hammath) (19:35) and Kartan (Kh el-Qureiyeh, grid no. 194280).

34–40. The Merarites received Jokneam (Jos. 12:22; 19:11), Kartah[3] (*cf.* [Kisloth] Tabor of Jos. 19:12, 1 Ch. 6:77); Dimnah (= Rimmon of Jos. 19:13, 1 Ch. 6:77), Nahalal (19:15), Bezer (20:8), Jahaz (13:18), Kedemoth (13:18), Mephaath (13:18), Ramoth in Gilead (20:8), Mahanaim (13:26, 30), Heshbon (9:10; 12:2, 5; 13:10–27) and Jazer (13:25).[4]

---

[1]R. S. Hess, 'A Typology of West Semitic Place Name Lists with Special Reference to Joshua 13 – 19', forthcoming.

[2]MT, Gath Rimmon. LXX and all versions of the parallel text, 1 Ch. 6:55, read Ibleam.

[3]The parallel 1 Ch. 6:76–77 (Heb. 61–62) passage preserves no similar name but does include Tabor.

[4]At the end of v. 42, the LXX adds the following : 'So Joshua finished assigning their allotments. According to the command of the LORD, the Israelites gave

iii. **Conclusion to the allotments (21:43–45).** This text emphasizes the fulfilment of God's promises and the completeness of the victory. God's promises to the patriarchs,[1] that the land would belong to their descendants, has appeared throughout Joshua.[2] He had also promised *rest* from their enemies (Dt. 12:9–10; Jos. 1:13, 15; 22:4; 23:1). Three times an emphasis is placed upon God's promises coming true. Six times in the MT the Hebrew for *all* (*kol*) is used in a chiastic fashion:[3]

> *all the land*
> > *just as he had sworn to give their forefathers.*
> > *Not one of their enemies withstood them,*
> > *The LORD handed all their enemies,*
> *all the LORD's good promises*
> *every one was fulfilled.*

The emphasis is on the defeat of all Israel's enemies. This is accomplished because God swore it. As a result of this victory, Israel has all the land, and all that God has promised has occurred.

Additional Note: A partial or complete conquest?

This concludes the section on the allotments that began with chapter 13. However, there is a problem. Already in Joshua 13:1–7 (see also 12:22) God highlights the incomplete conquest of the land. Except for the conquests of Caleb at Hebron (Jos. 14 – 15), there is no indication that any of the areas mentioned in chapter 13 were occupied by Israel. How then can the text claim that the whole of the land was taken? Commentators have traditionally stressed the difference between God's faithfulness and the people's lack of faithfulness. Thus Keil and Delitzsch quote Calvin.[4]

Joshua the town that he wanted; they gave him Timnath Serah in Mount Ephraim. Joshua built the town and lived there. He took the flint knives, with which he had circumcised the Israelites when they came out of the desert, and he put them in Timnath Serah.'
  [1]Gn. 12:1–3; 15:18–21; 22:17–18; 24:7; 26:3; 50:24; Nu. 11:12; 14:16, 23; Dt. 1:8, 35; 6:10.
  [2]Jos. 1:2–3, 6, 11, 13, 15; 2:9, 24; 5:6; 6:2, 16; 8:1, 7; 10:8. See Woudstra, p. 314.
  [3]Mitchell, p. 104.
  [4]Keil and Delitzsch, p. 216.

... it is right to distinguish well between the clear, un-wavering, and certain fidelity of God in the fulfilment of His promises, and the weakness and indolence of the people, which caused the blessings of God to slip from their hands ... Consequently, although they did not destroy them all, so as to empty the land for their own possession, the truth of God stood out as distinctly as if they had; for there would have been no difficulty in their accomplishment of all that remained to be done, if they had only been disposed to grasp the victories that were ready to their hand.

Thus the tendency has been to understand here a process of dispossession. Israel had begun it under God but the nation's failure to complete it was a failure in its obedience to complete the process.[1]

However, the absolute nature of these verses has led recent literary studies to question traditional analyses. For Polzin, 'if one is to understand and accept the ideology that controls all of 13:1 – 21:40, the ideology that supports the phraseology of 21:41–43 must be categorically rejected'.[2] The solution is to find in verses 41–43 an irony that describes an ideal. This ideal was not achieved by Israel, a fact already suggested within chapters 13 – 21. Polzin compares these chapters to the laws of Deuteronomy, observing that as these mapped out the territory of Israel's life, so Joshua 14 – 21 describe the 'legal limits' of the land that God promised.[3] To make this apparent, he reviews the reported speeches of the chapters and identifies the sources with alien Kenizzites (Caleb and Othniel), women (Acsah and the daughters of Zelophehad) and dependants (Levites). In each case, Joshua makes room for them to live in Israel. As with Rahab and the Gibeonites who came into Israel in the first half of the book, so these other groups are brought 'within Israel's midst territorially or cultically'.[4]

Hawk also observes the tension created by the absence of fulfilment of what is described in these verses.[5] For him, it is part of the book's style to juxtapose descriptions of disintegration and destruction with claims of control and mastery. These

---

[1]Blaikie, pp. 356–357.
[2]Polzin, p. 132.
[3]*Ibid.*, p. 128.
[4]*Ibid.*, p. 134.
[5]Hawk, pp. 115–116.

conflicting plots move the reader on to the end and an ambiguous conclusion that points to a future judgment.

Mitchell observes how the references to *rest* in 1:13 and 15, as well as 22:4 and 23:1, tie this section in with the opening verses of the book and anticipate the next two chapters.[1] He finds similarities between 21:43–45 and promises in Joshua 1. Most important is the contrast that he finds between the description of the other nations in 13:1 – 21:42 and their description elsewhere.[2] In 13:1 – 21:42, the nations are isolated individuals and groups that must still be uprooted but from 21:43 on the nations are once again (as in chs. 1 – 12) a combined force. Understood in this way, the statements of verses 43–45 do not contradict what precedes them. Instead, they assert that Israel had realized God's promises concerning the destruction of the nations. No longer would these appear as a unified force as they had in Joshua 1 – 12. The coalitions were defeated. Instead, the challenge of chapters 13 – 19 would remain. Israel must defend itself against and drive out the isolated pockets of resistance that remain.

Thus each of these studies contributes to unravelling the difficulties of a text that appears to claim something that did not happen. The idealistic nature of the statements invites comparison with the unrealized ideals of the Deuteronomic laws, and thereby unites both Deuteronomy and Joshua as two dimensions of a single covenant between God and his people. The emphasis on conflicting plots moves the reader forward, but also anticipates the terrible truth that God's judgment for Israel's failure is coming. Finally, an understanding of how the references to Israel's enemies are used in the book of Joshua resolves the contradiction of 21:43–45 into a contrast with chapters 13 – 21, and attaches these three verses to the remaining three chapters in the book.

For the Christian, this text illustrates the tension between two opposites. On the one hand, there is the power of God's word to effect his will and to bring about a good end to his plan of redemption (Is. 55:10–11). On the other hand, sin and suffering remain in the world. These two contrasting 'plots' of world history await resolution in the final victory of Christ and his eternal rule of salvation, health and peace (Is. 2:1–4; Rev. 19 – 21).

[1] Mitchell, pp. 103–104.
[2] *Ibid.*, pp. 133–141.

III. THE CONCLUSION: PROPER WORSHIP OF GOD
(22:1 – 24:33)

Each of the final three chapters describes a single event. At first glance, these events seem to be a random collection of leftovers: a dispute between the tribes about an altar, a farewell address, and another covenant ceremony. However, upon closer examination it becomes apparent that they all focus on a single matter, the proper worship of Israel's God – how to offer it and what will happen if Israel does not do so. Thus the altar law teaches how community worship should unify the tribes, not divide them. Joshua's farewell address recalls his role and authority as Moses' successor and warns the people against violation of God's commands. The covenant renewal at Shechem brings together all the people for a final time. United under a single political and religious leadership, the tribes confess their allegiance to God and accept his covenant. The deaths and burials of Joshua and Eleazar, as well as the reburial of Joseph, signify the living symbols of Israel's unity.

a. The disputed altar (22:1–34)

This account moves the reader from the affirmation that God's will was accomplished in all that Israel did (21:43–45) to the resolution of the first challenge to that statement. Joshua releases and rewards the Transjordanian tribes (vv. 1–8) who return to their homes and build an altar on their border with Israel proper (vv. 9–10). This arouses the anger of the rest of Israel who prepare for war but send representatives to attempt to avoid conflict (vv. 11–14). The representatives remind the Transjordanian tribes of the consequences of past acts of disobedience in Israel (vv. 15–20) and the Transjordanian tribes respond with assurances that the altar is a symbol of their unity with Israel, and not for separate sacrifices (vv. 21–29). This satisfies the representatives who return home (vv. 30–33). The Transjordanian tribes name their altar according to its purpose (v. 34). The chiastic structure of verses 10–34 has been identified by Jobling:[1]

[1] D. Jobling, *The Sense of Biblical Narrative: Structural Analyses in the Hebrew Bible II, JSOT* Supplement 39 (Sheffield: JSOT Press, 1986), pp. 98–99.

Transjordanians build an altar (v. 10)
  Cisjordanians threaten war (v. 12)
    Cisjordanians send an embassy (vv. 13–15a)
      Embassy accuses Transjordanians (vv. 15b–20)
        Transjordanians swear innocence (vv. 22–23)
          Transjordanians explain the altar (vv. 24–27a)
          Transjordanians explain the altar (vv. 27b–28)
        Transjordanians swear innocence (vv. 29)
      Embassy accepts Transjordanian explanation (vv. 30–31)
    Cisjordanian embassy returns home (v. 32)
  Cisjordanians withdraw their threat (v. 33)
Transjordanians name the altar (v. 34)

Some have identified priestly sources that sought to preserve the unity of the cult in a single location, whether Gilgal, Shiloh or Jerusalem (*cf.* Dt. 12).[1] Butler has pointed out the relevance of this account for the exiles in Babylonia. They would learn of the dangers of duplicating the Jerusalem worship, but at the same time recognize the necessity of remaining faithful in exile.[2]

Literary studies have emphasized the crucial importance of Joshua 22 to the question of Israel's identity. Polzin, in particular, finds in the term used to describe *Israel* and in the invitation *come over* a distinction between *the LORD's land* (v. 19) west of the Jordan and the ten tribes who live there, and everyone east of the Jordan.[3] Thus the group represented by Phinehas west of the Jordan includes *the whole assembly of the LORD* (v. 16), *the whole community of Israel* (vv. 18 and 20) and *each of the tribes of Israel* (v. 14). However, these ten tribes are merely called *the Israelites* (vv. 30–32) after the tribes east of the Jordan satisfy them that they are loyal Israelites who worship God faithfully. The implication is that the eastern tribes are now also part of Israel.

The verb *come over* (= *cross over*) (Heb. '*br*), so characteristic of the first five chapters of Joshua, never describes the return of the Transjordanian tribes to their homes east of the Jordan. It is used only in Phinehas' exhortation to them to return to *the*

---

[1] For example J. S. Kloppenberg, 'Joshua 22: The Priestly Editing of an Ancient Tradition', *Bib*, 62, 1981, pp. 347–371; N. H. Snaith, 'The Altar at Gilgal: Joshua xxii 23–29', *VT*, 28, 1978, pp. 330–335.
[2] Butler, pp. 243–244.
[3] Polzin, pp. 134–138.

LORD's land west of the Jordan. Polzin also observes the shift in tenses in the speeches of both Phinehas and the Transjordanian tribes. There are references to the present, *i.e. today, this day* (Heb. *hayyôm*), and to the future, *i.e. tomorrow, in the future* (Heb. *māhār*).[1] The Transjordanian tribes, already seen in chapters 1, 4, 6 and 13, as well as 14:3 and 18:7, represent the abiding presence in Israel of those who are fully Israelite and who completely fulfil the laws and promises although their inheritance is outside the land of promise. Like Rahab, the Gibeonites, Caleb and others, the Transjordanian tribes represent the 'aliens' who can become Israelites. They also represent all Israel in their failure to take the land completely and thus to obey the ideal of God's promises. The promises remain and they are fulfilled, but only by God's grace in spite of the failure of those called to obey.

For the Christian, one reading of Joshua 22 recalls Jesus' instructions on church discipline (Mt. 18:15–20). In order to preserve unity among the people of God, there is a procedure for reconciling disputes that provides for representatives to approach the offending party before the whole community participates. In Joshua 22, representatives of the people of God successfully resolve the issue. On a deeper level, this chapter questions the identity of God's people. There is a tension between the concern for unity (Jn. 17) and the need to preserve a people holy before a holy God (2 Cor. 6:14–18). In the end, Israel is able to discern between what is essential (proper worship of God) and what is peripheral (possession of a piece of the Promised Land) to membership in the people of God. In recognizing and holding fellowship with other believers, Christians are also called to discern between the essential elements of the faith (2 Jn. 7–11) and those that allow for disagreement (1 Cor. 3 and 8).

i. Joshua's charge to the Transjordanians (22:1–8).

1–4. Joshua addresses the Transjordanian tribes of *the Reubenites, the Gadites and the half-tribe of Manasseh.* He recalls their faithfulness in words that repeat the instructions that he gave to them in 1:12–15. Thus as Joshua charged them, they did

---

[1] *Ibid.*, pp. 139–141. See D. Jobling, *The Sense of Biblical Narrative: Structural Analyses in the Hebrew Bible II, JSOT* Supplement 39 (Sheffield: JSOT Press, 1986), pp. 103–106.

everything that *Moses the servant of the* LORD *commanded* (as in 1:13). Joshua observes how *you have obeyed me in everything I commanded*, using the same language as that of the Transjordanian tribes' promise to obey in 1:18. *That the* LORD *your God has given your brothers rest* not only continues the fulfilment of 21:44 but also recalls the same language of Joshua in 1:13 and 15. Joshua now fulfils the promise that he made then, that Israel's achievement of rest from their enemies would allow the Transjordanian tribes to return to their homes. In this way, both the promises of God (21:43–45) and the promises of Joshua (22:1–8), made at the beginning of Joshua's leadership, come true.

5–8. Joshua's exhortation in verse 5 repeats the exhortations of Moses to Israel in the first eleven chapters of Deuteronomy. The concern *to love the* LORD *your God . . . with all your heart and all your soul* forms part of the central confession of Deuteronomy 6:5.[1] Along with Joshua's blessing on these tribes and his gift of the booty, this signifies his recognition that they are fully part of the covenant community of Israel. However, the note of the division of Manasseh, half east and half west of the Jordan, symbolizes the problem of potential disunity in Israel as a whole.[2] It foreshadows the division that is to come.

ii. The Transjordanians return home (22:9). The narrative begins the account of how the Transjordanian tribes *left . . . to return*, using the same verb as when Joshua commanded them to *return* (v. 8). This demonstrates that their return was itself part of their obedience to Joshua. There is an emphasis on their departure from the nation of Israel (*left the Israelites*), from the cult of Israel (*at Shiloh*) and from the land given to Israel (*in Canaan*). This foreshadows the divisions that appear in the following verses.

iii. The altar (22:10–11). *Geliloth* is mentioned as part of the border of Benjamin in Joshua 18:17. It may also be a general term describing the regions of the Jordan. Verse 10 suggests

[1] Woudstra, p. 317, adds Dt. 4:4, 29; 10:12; 11:13, *etc.* See Boling and Wright, pp. 509–510.

[2] Hawk, p. 120. See the speculation of Fritz, p. 226, that this is inserted because an older literary source behind Jos. 22 had included only Reuben and Gad as the Transjordanian territories.

that the altar was constructed in the land of Canaan and that it was *an imposing altar*. Practically, this would render it visible to the Transjordanians in their homeland. The phrase used to describe the altar (Heb. *gāḏôl lᵉmar'eh*) is similar to that used to describe the burning bush of Exodus 3:3. Thus it would arrest the attention of passers-by. The establishment of a sanctuary on the border of the land was not unknown in later Israel, when Jeroboam I created sanctuaries with altars at Dan and Bethel on the borders of the Northern Kingdom of Israel (1 Ki. 12:28–29).

iv. The Cisjordanians threaten war (22:12–20). Verses 12–15 describe the reaction of the tribes and the selection of a delegation. The ten tribes return to a 'war footing' as they prepare to execute a holy war against any violation of their unity in worshipping a single deity at a single sanctuary (Dt. 12:5).

13–15. As the matter concerns proper worship, the Israelites choose a priest to represent them. Although Eleazar had been involved with the allotments (*cf.* 14:1), his son Phinehas leads the delegation. Although this may be due to Eleazar's age, Phinehas had already risen to prominence as the priest who stopped Israel's worship at Baal Peor in Transjordan (Nu. 25:6–18). Thus he was competent to deal with any challenges from deviant religious practices east of the Jordan. Since the matter also concerns the unity of Israel, a representative of each of the ten remaining tribes goes along.[1]

16–20. The sin of Baal Peor and that of Achan (Joshua 7) are mentioned as precedents. In both cases, a shadow fell over Israel's future. God's judgment threatened to destroy the whole nation. The terms *break faith* and *acted unfaithfully* use the same root as that used to describe unfaithfulness in Israel, including the sin of Achan in Joshua 7.[2] Between these two accounts lay two warnings against rebellion against God (vv. 18–19). In verse 18, the delegation reaffirms its concern for the preservation of the nation as a whole in the face of God's anger. In verse 19, a solution is proposed. Let the tribes east of

[1] On the terms for *family division* and *clan*, see the discussion of Jos. 7:14–18, pp. 150–151.
[2] See the discussion there on *mᶜl* (p. 143). See also the use of the term in Lv. 5:15 and 21; Nu. 5:6, 11 – 31; and Ezk. 14:13–30; Woudstra, p. 324; Fritz, p. 223.

the Jordan take a share in the land west of the Jordan. There the Transjordanian tribes would find the true Israel worshipping the true God in its divinely appointed land. The ten tribes fear that the Transjordanian tribes have made a rival altar to sacrifice to other deities.[1] Israel's earlier sins of rebellion come to mind as they seek to dissuade the Transjordanians from this course of action.

v. The Transjordanians explain the altar (22:21–29).

21–22. The confession with which the Transjordanians begin their response bears witness to their faith in the God of Israel. The repeated confession *The Mighty One, God, the LORD!* can also be translated by the superlative 'The LORD is the greatest God'. With the strongest of oaths, they confirm that they have no intention to worship any other deity at the altar.

23–26. The list of *burnt offerings, grain offerings* and *fellowship offerings* includes the first three sacrifices mentioned in the list of Leviticus 1 – 7 (*cf.* 1:3; 2:1; 3:1). Together they symbolize all the offerings that could be made on the altar. By mentioning these, the Transjordanians deny that they intended to use the altar for sacrifice.

27–29. Instead, the altar is a *witness* (Heb. '*ēḏ*) and a *replica* (Heb. *tabnît*). The *witness* is the same word for human witnesses in a law court (Lv. 5:1; Dt. 17:15) and for a memorial erected at a boundary between two parties (Gn. 31:48–52). In Joshua, it is erected at a boundary between the two tribal groups (east and west of the Jordan) to remind the western group of their identity with the eastern group. The worship of a *replica* of any creature on earth is forbidden to Israel (Dt. 4:15–20). However, God shows a *replica* (NIV *pattern*) of the tabernacle that Israel is to build (Ex. 25:9, 40). The altar at Geliloth Jordan is a replica of the true altar of worship for all of Israel, which itself is built according to the divine pattern (Ex. 27:1–8). Thus the altar reminds all Israel of its identity and also of its unity in worship. The establishment of these reminders has already occurred in Joshua (Jos. 4:8–9; 7:26; 8:29). In the wilderness through which Israel passed, ancient

---

[1] Hawk, p. 126. The key words, *m‘l* ('unfaithfulness') and *mrd* ('rebellion') occur throughout vv. 12–20 and describe the attitude of the ten tribes toward the Transjordanians. See Mitchell, p. 110.

peoples used standing stones and other markers to signify religious monuments.[1]

vi. The embassy accepts the explanation and returns home (22:30–33). Lengthy and repeated identifications of each of the parties involved characterize this section. They suggest a formal and legal pronouncement, with careful identification of each participant. The pleasure of the embassy anticipates that of the ten tribes. Phinehas' pronouncement exonerates the accused by negating the charge of verse 16 in the words *you have not acted unfaithfully towards the LORD in this matter.* The recognition that *you have rescued the Israelites* recalls the only other occurrence of the identical verbal form in Joshua, the request of Rahab in 2:13 *that you will save us from death.* In both cases, divine judgment threatens death, and those who are addressed provide deliverance from destruction. Moses commands Israel to praise God for their good land in Deuteronomy 8:10. In Joshua 22:33, Israel praises God that there is peace in the land of the Reubenites and Gadites. For all the destruction that takes place in the book of Joshua, it is surprising that the common verb *to devastate* appears only here.

vii. The Transjordanians name the altar (22:34). The naming of an object normally follows its creation. The two tribes built this altar in verse 10. The intervening account provides the background for the name *A Witness Between Us that the LORD is God.* This is a confession of the faith of Israel. For the Christian, as noted above, the altar recalls the need to retain a true faith without making that confession a source of division and strife.

b. The farewell address (23:1–16)

This chapter recounts a sermon that Joshua gives to assembled Israel at the end of his life. In its purpose, it resembles the deathbed testaments of other leaders of Israel: Jacob (Gn. 48 – 49), Joseph (Gn. 50:22–26), Moses and David (1 Ki. 2:1–9).[2] For Moses, the whole of the book of Deuteronomy serves as his

---

[1] U. Avner, 'Ancient Cult Sites in the Negev and Sinai Deserts', *Tel Aviv*, 11, 1984, pp. 115–131; *idem*, 'Ancient Agricultural Settlement and Religion in the Uvda Valley in Southern Israel', *BA*, 53, 1990, pp. 125–141.
[2] Butler, p. 253.

final address. All of these occasions allow the leader to describe the future of Israel. Only in the cases of Moses and Joshua is there a choice as to what that fate will be. In both cases, it depends on the decision of the people. Like Moses, Joshua reminds the people of all that God has given to them. He calls them to faithfulness. Indeed, 'his address consists entirely of reminiscences from the Pentateuch, more especially from Deuteronomy, as he had nothing fresh to announce to the people, but could only impress the old truths upon their minds once more'.[1]

Verses 2–11 describe God's past works of conquest on behalf of Israel and exhort Israel to remain faithful to God so that the remaining land may be conquered. Verses 12–16 contain warnings of what will happen if Israel fails to keep God's covenant and goes after foreign gods. The themes of history, exhortation, blessing and cursing are interwoven. The repetition emphasizes the importance of the message.

i. God's deeds for Israel (23:1–5). For the Christian, the message of God's work of redemption and blessing on behalf of his people resembles God's work of redemption in Christ and the blessings of the Christian life. While Christians may enjoy these, they are called to lives which are faithful to the teachings of their master. It is only through faithfulness that Christians can continue to enjoy the divine blessings (Eph. 2:8–10).

1–2. Joshua is *old and well advanced in years*, as in Joshua 13:1. In both chapters 13 and 23, a description of land not yet occupied by Israel follows this introductory note. Joshua's death does not end Israel's responsibilities to occupy the land. This is true despite the note that *the LORD had given Israel rest from all their enemies around them*. The promise of rest is found in Deuteronomy (3:20; 12:10; 25:19) and occurs in the exhortation of Joshua 1 (vv. 13 and 15) and amid the summaries of chapters 21:42 and 22:4. In Deuteronomy and in Joshua 1, it is part of God's promise to the people and to Joshua in reward for their faithfulness. In Joshua 22 – 24, it is the result of God's

---

[1]Keil and Delitzsch, pp. 223–224. Much of the information regarding Deuteronomic phrases in this chapter can be found in M. Weinfeld, *Deuteronomy and the Deuteronomic School*, (Oxford: Clarendon, 1972), pp. 320–365. On the poetic structure, see W. T. Koopmans, 'The Poetic Prose of Joshua 23' in W. van der Meer and J. C. de Moor (eds.), *The Structural Analysis of Biblical and Canaanite Poetry, JSOT* Supplement 74 (Sheffield: JSOT Press, 1988), pp. 83–118.

blessing upon Israel and a reward for the nation's faithfulness.

The *elders, leaders, judges and officials* represent all of Israel because they teach and exercise authority over all the tribes and their subgroups.[1] Three of these also appear in Deuteronomy 29:10 (Heb. 9) where they represent the entire nation at a covenant ceremony.[2] The 'officials' appeared in Joshua 1:10. Joshua's acknowledgment of his age closes the introduction by repeating the statement of verse 1. With verse 14a, this heads the first of two major sections to Joshua's address and reaffirms what God had said in 13:1. Joshua reminds Israel that his review of their history is based on firsthand experience, travelling from Egypt to Shechem. For the Christian, this confirms the important role of the elder Christian in instructing the community of the faithful and in exhorting them to faith and obedience (1 Tim. 5:17–19; 1 Pet. 5:1–4).

3. Joshua reminds the leaders that *You yourselves have seen* what God did. The same verb is used in verse 4 as a command to bear witness again to the present condition. In the past, the God of Israel fought on behalf of Israel. God will continue to fight to drive out the remaining nations. The expression *it was the LORD your God who fought for you* is repeated word for word in the Hebrew text of verse 10. This is a key theme of Joshua's address. Israel did not win the battles through its own skill. God won Israel's battles. He would go on doing so only if Israel remained faithful.

4. *The nations that remain* occurs in verses 4, 7 and 12. It also represents a key theme of this address. Joshua looks forward to the work that will remain to be done after his death. Like the nations that God defeated (v. 3), the remaining nations must also be expelled. God has given Israel *an inheritance* (Jos. 11:23) from the River Jordan to the Mediterranean Sea. Israel must occupy it. In verse 4, Joshua reminds the people that he conquered many of these nations. Thus he knows that it can be done.

5. It is God who gives the victory but the future Israel, like the past generation, must lay claim to what God has promised.

---

[1] For the leadership role of the judges and the antiquity of the term, see Koopmans, *Joshua 24*, p. 278. For the elders, see the comments at Jos. 7:6, p. 148.

[2] The judges (Heb. *špt*) *do not appear in Deuteronomy. Instead, the 'chief men' (Heb. šbt*) are named. The two groups are spelled in a similar manner. The LXX includes 'judges'.

Verse 5's A–B–A structure focuses on divine action and human responsibility:

> *He will push them out before you,*
> *and you will take possession of their land,*
> *as the LORD your God promised you.*

The verbs *He will push them out* and *you will take possession* are from the same root in Hebrew meaning 'to possess, dispossess' (*yrš*). This suggests a complementary response by the people to the faithful act of God's deliverance.

ii. A challenge to obedience (23:6–11). Verses 6–8 and 11 describe the responsibility of Israel in the strategy of victory. As verse 8 makes clear, it is no new strategy, only *to hold fast to the LORD your God, as you have until now.* The concern to *be very careful* begins and ends this section, suggesting that this is the key to victory. The care exercised is one of (1) precise obedience, (2) avoidance of other gods, and (3) *to love the LORD your God.*

6. The *Book of the Law of Moses* was mentioned in Joshua 8:31, where it described the construction of the altar according to Exodus 20:22–26. It refers to the Book of the Covenant of Exodus 24:7, the divine instruction that Moses received from God. Joshua 1:7–8 also refers to the Book of the Law, from which God warns Joshua not to turn either to the right or to the left. This warning Joshua now passes on to Israel.

7. God's people must avoid association with the other nations so that they do not worship their gods. This fundamental command against idolatry (Ex. 20:3–6; Dt. 5:7–10) becomes the chief test of obedience. The expression *nations that remain* appeared in verse 4 where Joshua gives their territories to Israel. It will occur again in verse 12 where Joshua warns against association with this group or worship of their gods. In a series of four prohibitions, Joshua warns Israel to avoid other deities. These prohibitions are as strong as possible.[1]

9–11. Finally, verse 11 summarizes this command with the positive instruction *to love the LORD your God.* As in Deuteronomy 6:4–9, the love described is a covenantal commitment to God and his word. Verses 9–10 describe the victory that Israel

---

[1] Negative *lô'* plus the imperfect. The same form occurs in commands 6–8 of the Decalogue (Ex. 20:13–16).

has experienced for its faithfulness *until now*. Again the A–B–B'–A' structure provides a clue to the point of this recollection:

A. *The LORD has driven out before you this day great and powerful nations;*

  B. *to this day no-one has been able to withstand you.*

  B'. *One of you routs a thousand*[1]

A'. *because the LORD your God fights for you . . .*

God wins the victories (A/A' elements): he enables Israel to win (B/B' elements). Without faithfulness to God, Israel cannot hope to enjoy its successes. For the Christian, the avoidance of idolatry and its promise of victory is a theme to which Paul alludes when he asks for whole-hearted dedication to Christ (Rom. 12:1), just as Jesus himself demanded such total and loving commitment in his teaching on discipleship (Mt. 16:24; Lk. 9:62; 14:26, 33).

iii. Warnings for the future (23:12–16). With the blessings for faithfulness described, Joshua now considers the curses for disobedience. Blessings and cursings form a part of God's covenant and reflect Ancient Near Eastern treaty structure.[2] Joshua's speech naturally concludes with warnings for disobedience. They motivate the listener with three descriptions of covenant violation and its consequences: (1) association and intermarriage with the inhabitants of the land (vv. 12–13), (2) the certainty of God's judgment (vv. 14–15), and (3) idolatry (v. 16).

12. As in verse 8, there is a conditional clause.[3] However, whereas verse 8 envisaged that Israel would *hold fast to the LORD your God*, verse 12 describes Israelites who *turn away and ally yourselves with the survivors of these nations that remain among you.* The expressions *hold fast* and *ally* use the same root word (*dbq*). These similarities between the two clauses suggest an intentional contrast between those who remain faithful and their reward (vv. 8–11) and those who prove faithless and the result (vv. 12–16). The Israelites would demonstrate their lack of faithfulness by

[1]See Dt. 32:30 for the same phrase in a context that challenges Israel's unbelief in the light of such miracles.

[2]See Dt. 28. K. A. Kitchen, 'The Fall and Rise of Covenant, Law and Treaty', *TynB*, 40, 1989, pp. 124–135; *idem*, 'The Patriarchal Age. Myth or History?', *BAR*, 21/2, March/April 1995, pp. 52–56.

[3]Heb. *kî'îm*.

intermarrying with the remaining inhabitants of the land. This would be a direct violation of Deuteronomy 7:3.

13. Emphatic verbs[1] open both verse 12 which sets the condition (*if you turn away*) and verse 13 which describes the consequences (*then you may be sure*). The sin of faithlessness and intermarriage with unbelievers voids God's promise of verse 5: he will not *drive* the nations out of Israel's way. The descriptions of *snares* and *whips* portray the nations as conquerors and enslavers of Israel, and finally as destroyers of this people.[2] Thus the nations act out Israel's role of conqueror on Israel itself. The expression *until you perish from this good land, which the* LORD *your God has given you* also appears at the end of verses 15 and 16. It marks the end of each description of covenant violation and its consequences. For the Christian, this is an example of the warning not to associate with those who do not repent of their sin (1 Cor. 6).

14–15. The second part of the section focuses on the consequences of covenant violation. If Israel sins, God will punish the nation. Joshua wants the people to know that God will continue to treat Israel with the same justice, despite his imminent departure.[3] Joshua may die but God will not change. Israel has experienced God's faithfulness to his promises and knows this *with all* its *heart and soul*. This resembles Deuteronomy 6:5 and the command to love God with all one's heart and soul, *i.e.* to give an uncompromising and total loving commitment to God. Joshua repeats the fact that every word has come true. However, his purpose is not to praise God for his faithfulness but to warn Israel that God will apply this same faithfulness to his judgments upon the sinful nation: he will destroy it. The certainty of God's judgment is a central theme in the Bible. The psalmist (*e.g.* Ps. 73) and the prophets proclaim it repeatedly. Their purpose is not to condemn the people, but to bring them to repentance (Jon. 3 – 4). Here as well, Joshua wishes Israel to remain faithful and uses these warnings to emphasize the point.

16. The message repeats its central concern: do not give in to worshipping other deities. The key word in the opening

---

[1] Infinitive absolute followed by the imperfect form of the verb.

[2] The expression 'thorns in your sides' occurs in Nu. 33:55, also as a consequence of failing to drive out the inhabitants of the land.

[3] For a similar expression to *the way of all the earth*, see David in 1 Ki. 2:2.

chapters of Joshua described how the nation 'crossed over' (Heb. '*br*) to the Promised Land. Now this same verb warns Israel not to *violate* God's covenant. In phrases that resemble verse 7's list of things not to do with other gods, Joshua summarizes the chief cause for God's wrath and his punishment against Israel. The loss of their land would mean that God took back what was his all along. Although the entire book of Joshua describes the occupation and allocation of the land, it will be lost if Israel does not remain faithful to God and worship him alone. Hebrews 6 warns the Christian of the dangers of not remaining faithful to God's covenant in Christ.

c. The covenant at Shechem (24:1–27)

Source criticism, which divides the text of the Pentateuch into four major literary documents or sources, has undergone a revolution in recent years. Some of its underlying presuppositions have been challenged. Perhaps this explains the tendency to attribute diverse sources to Joshua 24:1–27. Nineteenth-century scholarship decided that the E (Elohist) source was the origin of chapter 24. Within the past few decades, however, various views have emerged. These identify Joshua 24 as a ninth–eighth-century northern text (Sperling), as a seventh-century Deuteronomistic document (Perlitt), or as the work of a sixth-century exilic Jahwist (Van Seters).[1]

As noted in the Introduction (p. 49), Joshua 24:25 designates this chapter as a covenant-making ceremony. Scholars have identified a similar form between biblical covenants and ancient Near Eastern treaty texts, especially those from before 1200 BC preserved by the Hittites. The following items are found in Hittite vassal treaty texts and in biblical covenants from the Pentateuch and Joshua: introduction, historical prologue, set of stipulations, deposit in the temple and public reading, list of divine witnesses, and curses for disobedience and blessings for obedience. Kitchen's structural identification of Joshua 24 with the Hittite treaty texts will serve as a useful

[1] L. Perlitt, *Bundestheologie im Alten Testament* (Neukirchen-Vluyn: Neukirchener, 1969); S. D. Sperling, 'Joshua 24 Re-examined', *Hebrew Union College Annual*, 58, 1987, pp. 119–136; J. Van Seters, 'Joshua 24 and the Problem of Tradition in the Old Testament' in W. B. Barrick and J. R. Spencer (eds.), *In the Shelter of Elyon. Essays on Ancient Palestinian Life and Literature in Honor of G. W. Ahlström, JSOT* Supplement 31 (Sheffield: JSOT Press, 1984), pp. 139–158.

outline of the text.¹ He finds here 'a highly abbreviated account'.² There is an introduction (v. 2b), a historical prologue (vv. 2c–13), a set of stipulations (vv. 14–24), a deposit of the text (v. 26) and a witness (vv. 26–27). The curses and blessings are implicit in verse 20.

i. A new assembly at Shechem (24:1). The list of leaders that Joshua summons corresponds to the list in 23:2 and connects the two chapters. The address of chapter 23 did not end Joshua's relationship with Israel. Something had to be done in order to make concrete the vision that Joshua had for the people he had served. Joshua 24 relates the ratification of God's covenant. As in a treaty ceremony, the whole nation (or its legal representatives) gather before their Lord to make the agreement. As in Joshua 8:30–35, Shechem is the place of covenant-making.

That the people *presented themselves before God* implies two things: (1) God was going to make a covenant with them; and (2) it was a time of transition in the leadership. Once before in the Bible does the verb *presented themselves* and the name of God appear as here.³ In Exodus 19:17, the people presented themselves before God in order to hear the covenant, to agree to it and to ratify it in a covenant ceremony. The same events will take place here. This special verb also occurs in Deuteronomy 31:14 where Moses and Joshua appear before God and Joshua is commissioned to lead the people after Moses' imminent death. In Joshua 24, Joshua will die and his 'successor' will be the representatives of the people (v. 31).

For the Christian, regular presentation before God in worship is an essential feature of a life of faith (Heb. 10:25). In gatherings for worship, Christ provides the opportunity to receive the new covenant as represented by his blood shed upon the cross (Mt. 26:28; Mk. 14:24; Lk. 22:10; 1 Cor. 11:25).

ii. God's redemptive work for Israel (24:2–13). In a treaty document, the text would begin with a prologue in which the lord identifies himself to the vassals. Here Joshua identifies the

---

¹K. A. Kitchen, 'The Patriarchal Age. Myth or History?', pp. 52–56.
²*Ibid.*, p. 56 note.
³The Hebrew verb is *yityaṣṣĕbû*. The name of God has a definite article before it, *i.e.* 'the God'. This also occurs repeatedly in Ex. 19 and 24.

lord as *the* LORD, *the God of Israel.* These words introduce God's explanation that there is sin in Israel at the time of the defeat of Ai (Jos. 7:13). They now emphasize the importance of the occasion. Israel's future life depends on listening.

The historical prologue of a treaty text reviewed the benefits and good relations that the lord had with the vassal in the past. It demonstrated that the vassal's faithfulness to the lord brought protection and success. Acts of past disloyalty led only to danger and misery. This prologue formed the argument for faithfulness on the part of the vassal to the present treaty. The same happens in verses 2–13. God reviews Israel's history and his dealings with the nation from its beginnings. The purpose of this review is to show the people how their faithfulness in the past has brought about God's blessings. Further, God initiated his gracious acts of salvation for Israel and has continued them without abatement up to the present generation.

For the Christian as well, God's redemptive acts on behalf of his people are an essential component of the Christian faith (Jn. 20:31; 1 Cor. 15:1–11; Heb. 11).

God summarizes Israel's history in four parts: the patriarchs (vv. 2–4), the exodus (vv. 5–7), the Transjordanian victories (vv. 8–10), the conquests in the Promised Land (vv. 11–13). Every section contains a repeated emphasis upon God as the actor. He always describes the actions of deliverance as his own, *i.e.* 'I did . . .' Neither Joshua nor Israel (nor even their ancestors) brought about their birth and success as a nation. God alone has done this. Israel must recognize what God has done in order to appreciate the covenant that he offers them.

2. The ancestors of the patriarchs *worshipped other gods.* The gods of Nahor and Terah are mentioned in Genesis 31:53 where Laban swears by them to guarantee that he and Jacob do not encroach upon each other's domain. The deities may refer to ancestors and have to do with inheritance and property rights.[1] If so, it may be significant that *beyond the River* is mentioned twice. This is the Euphrates River and refers to the original homeland of Abram's ancestors.

3. When God took Abram from this land, he also removed

---

[1]R. S. Hess, 'Nahor (Person)' in *ABD*, IV, pp. 996–997. Koopmans, *Joshua 24,* p. 313, notes that many treaties begin with a reference to the 'fathers' of the present generation. In Hebrew, the words for 'father' and 'ancestor' are identical.

him from ties with ancestral deities. Laban, having remained *beyond the River* in Haran, had continued these ties. God's work with Israel began by enabling Abram to worship God alone. This historical recitation would end with a challenge to Joshua's generation to worship God alone (v. 14). In addition to taking Abraham, God *led him* and *gave him descendants.*

4. God states that he was responsible for each generation of the patriarchs. Therefore, the patriarchs are not ancestor deities to be worshipped or venerated. Nor are other deities responsible for the fruitfulness of the patriarchs. God was in control from the beginning and everything went according to his plan, even the descent into Egypt.

5–7. God delivered Israel from Egypt through his mighty wonders.[1] Thus Joshua describes the plagues by which God *afflicted the Egyptians* and his protection of Israel from the Egyptian army when *he brought the sea over them and covered them.*[2] Unlike Rahab's confession (2:10), no mention is made of God's act of drying up the *Red Sea* so that Israel could cross. Rahab wished to emphasize that no obstacle, natural or human, could oppose Israel's advance. In Joshua 24, the stress falls on divine deliverance from enemy peoples, beginning with Egypt.[3] Israel must understand that its God can grant victory for all the enemies that remain in the land. For this reason, neither the miracles of the Red Sea crossing nor the provision of manna in the wilderness receive attention. Instead, the Israelites *saw with their own eyes* what God did to their enemies. In verse 4, the section on the patriarchs concluded with a note on Egypt. This prepared for the account of the exodus. This account concludes with the mention of the *desert*, which prepares for the discussion of Israel in Transjordan.

8–10. The events of Numbers 21 – 24 are recounted. In Joshua 10:5, Amorites occupied the southern hill country west

[1] See similar expressions in Ex. 3:20; 10:1; Nu. 14:11; Ps. 78:4.

[2] The shift from first-person ('I') to third-person ('he') references to God are a customary feature of Hebrew prose and of West Semitic rhetoric in general. See S. Gevirtz, 'On Canaanite Rhetoric: The Evidence of the Amarna Letters from Tyre', *Or*, 42, 1973, pp. 170–171.

[3] The *darkness* that God brings is a word that occurs only here. However, it describes the cloud of protection in Ex. 14:19–20. The divine use of a cloud for this purpose is also found in Hittite and Homeric accounts. See M. Weinfeld, 'Divine Intervention in War in Ancient Israel and in the Ancient Near East', pp. 144–145.

of the Dead Sea and Jordan River. As in Numbers 21, here the Amorites also populate the region to the east of the Dead Sea.[1] The description that Israel *took possession* of the land of the defeated Amorites uses the same verb as the descriptions in Joshua of taking possession of the land west of the Jordan. These two territories form Israel's tribal lands. As chapter 22 has demonstrated, Israel, whether east or west of the Jordan, all serve a single God.

9. The story of Balak and Balaam is recounted from Numbers 22 – 24. Jephthah refers to it in Judges 11:25. There he denies that Balak ever did *fight against Israel*. This is an apparent contradiction to Joshua 24:9. Perhaps this is an ironic reference that describes Balak as having 'exhausted' his fighting strength through the employment of Balaam to pronounce curses.[2]

10. God's power 'rescued' Abram from *other gods*. He delivered Israel from the mighty army of the Egyptians. In the case of Balaam, God overcame the power of a prophet and his curse and transformed it into a blessing for his people, and so rescued them.[3]

11–13. The conquest of the land west of the Jordan is described. As with the account of events in Transjordan, the enemies initiate the battle: *they fought against you*. As in verse 8 the scene changes when God says, *I gave them into your hands*. So again the achievement of victory belongs to God alone (v. 12); the people merely enter and occupy the land and receive its riches (v. 13).

11. The first conquest, that of Jericho, was symbolic of the subsequent victories. The list of nations is the same as in Joshua 3:10 where God promises victory to Israel. The *citizens of Jericho* are probably the chief leaders of the town.[4]

12. The identity of *the hornet* has been disputed. Is it (1)

[1] See E. C. Hostetter, 'Geographic Distribution of the Pre-Israelite Peoples of Ancient Palestine', *BZ*, 38, 1994, pp. 81–86. The term can include other groups. See Jos. 13:4.

[2] Boling and Wright, p. 536. See also Keil and Delitzsch, p. 299.

[3] For the Ancient Near Eastern context of expressions such as *I gave them into your hands* and *I delivered you out of his hand*, see Koopmans, *Joshua 24*, pp. 329–330. In both expressions, the hands represent power or control.

[4] The expression appears in Jdg. 9:2 and 1 Sa. 23:11–12. In both cases, it describes a group or assembly that makes decisions for Shechem and Keilah. The expression occurs at Amarna and Ugarit, where it refers to a group distinguished from the king or chief leader. W. L. Moran, *The Amarna Letters*, p. 175, n. 5.

Egypt, (2) insects in warfare, or (3) terror?[1] Egypt is unlikely since it is nowhere mentioned and this identification does not exist in the Bible. Insects may have been used in warfare, but their presence in this text is unlikely, since only one hornet is mentioned and there is no account of their use in Joshua or anywhere else in the Bible. The alternative translation of this word as 'terror' or the use of the picture of a hornet to symbolize such terror seems to satisfy the descriptions of the enemies in Exodus 15:14–16; Joshua 2:9–11, 24; 5:1; 6:27.

The *hornet* appears as part of God's promised blessings at the end of the Book of the Covenant (Ex. 23:27–28, where it is used in parallel with *terror*). The *two kings of the Amorites* are Sihon and Og, as mentioned in Joshua 2:10; 9:10; *etc.* The reference to the sword and the bow not winning Israel's victories also occurs in Jacob's gift of the hill country to Joseph in Genesis 48:21–22; there Jacob claims he took it with his sword and bow. Joshua 24:12 joins together a selection of texts from throughout the Pentateuch which promise Israel victory. It thus demonstrates that the God who spoke of these promises has also fulfilled them for Israel; he will continue to win battles for Israel so long as it remains faithful to him.

13. God's grace gave Israel the land and its riches. Like Deuteronomy 6:10–11, this verse describes the fulfilment of all God's promises in the wealth and blessing that Israel received freely from God. For the Christian, it is difficult to read these passages and not reflect upon Ephesians 2:8–10 and the free gift of God's grace in the person and work of Christ.

iii. The covenant agreement (24:14–24). Verses 14–24 correspond to stipulations in a treaty document. Having established the basis for loyalty in the historical summary of past events, a treaty would then explain how that loyalty should be manifested in specific laws. In Deuteronomy, also a covenant document, these stipulations are found in the laws of chapters 12 – 26. In Joshua 24, they take the form of a dialogue between

[1] For (1) see O. Borowski, 'The Identity of the Biblical *ṣir'â*' in E. L. Meyers and M. O'Connor (eds), *The Word of the Lord Shall Go Forth. Essays in Honor of David Noel Freedman in Celebration of His Sixtieth Birthday* (Philadelphia: ASOR; Winona Lake, Indiana: Eisenbrauns, 1983), pp. 315–319. For (2) see E. Neufeld, 'Insects as Warfare Agents in the Ancient Near East (Ex. 23:28; Dt. 7:20; Jos. 24:12; Is. 7:18–20)', *Orientalia*, 49, 1980, pp. 30–57. For (3) see L. Köhler, 'Hebräische Vokabeln I', *ZAW*, 54, 1936, p. 291.

Joshua and the people regarding their loyalty to God: Joshua challenges the people to decide for or against exclusive devotion to God (vv. 14–15) and the people recall God's gracious salvation and preservation of their nation (vv. 16–18). They agree to serve the LORD. Joshua warns the people of the difficulties that their choice will involve but Israel insists upon it (vv. 19–21). They take an oath of loyalty (vv. 22–24).

14–15. The 'service' (Heb. *'bd*) of the LORD is repeated seven times. Four times it refers to the present generation of Israel. Twice Joshua commands them to serve the God of Israel; twice he challenges Israel to choose whom they will serve; twice he refers to *the gods your forefathers worshipped beyond the River* as in verse 2. Joshua concludes with a commitment of himself and his *household.*[1] The *gods of the Amorites* represent those of the nations surrounding Israel. After Joshua's death, the people chose to worship these deities (Jdg. 2:11–13; 6:10) despite Joshua's warnings and Israel's confession in Joshua 24. Joshua and his household represent the minority who would remain faithful. For the Christian, Joshua's testimony is a model of bearing witness to one's faith even when it means standing out from the majority. In the New Testament, Stephen (Acts 7) and Paul (Acts 9:20–25) represent Christians who confessed their faith despite its unpopularity.

16–18. The people recount God's work of creating and delivering their nation. They repeat their recent experience of God's victorious acts both as a confession demonstrating that they believe in the God of Israel and to show their agreement with Joshua's covenant speech in verses 5–13. The people refuse *to forsake the LORD*, insisting they will not *serve other gods.*[2] The expressions *to serve other gods* and *serve the LORD* (vv. 16, 18) use the same root word (*'bd*) as is found in *that land of slavery* from which God delivered the people.

17. This forms the basis for the people's confession.[3] They were slaves to another nation, to Egypt. God delivered them from that slavery, so it is only right that they should serve him.

[1]See comments on 7:14–18 (pp. 150–151) for family units and on 2:13 (pp. 91) for their leadership.

[2]On *forsake*, see comment on 1:5, p. 71.

[3]*Land of slavery* occurs thirteen times in the Bible, always with reference to Egypt and to the event of the exodus. It is part of God's self identification at the beginning of the ten commandments (Ex. 20:2; Dt. 5:6). See also Ex. 13:3; 13:14; Dt. 6:12; 7:8; 8:14; 13:6, 11; Jdg. 6:8; Je. 34:13; Mi. 6:4.

God has brought them from an imposed servitude to a service of thanksgiving and appreciation. The Christian has also been delivered from slavery to a kingdom of darkness and brought into God's kingdom of light, with the opportunity of a similar response of worship and service toward Christ (Gal. 4:1–20; Eph. 2:11–22; 5:8–21). For the *great signs* that God performed, compare 2:12 where *sign* (Heb. *'ôt*) refers to the oath that the spies give to Rahab to guarantee their promise to her, and 4:6 where Joshua uses it to identify the stones in the Jordan River as a sign to mark Israel's crossing. In Joshua 24, however, it describes the miracles of the exodus and occupation (vv. 5–13).

18. With their confession, Israel takes to heart the historical summary as proof of God's redemption and right to demand their exclusive loyalty. The LORD *drove out . . . all the nations* for Israel because only the God of Israel is in control of all nations of the world and thus able to move peoples from one land to another.[1]

19–20. Joshua challenges the people. No longer content with giving them a choice as in verses 14–15, he charges the people with a lack of ability to follow the true God. The structure of Joshua's reasoning is an A–B–B'–A' chiasm:

A. *He is a holy God; he is a jealous God.*
   B. *He will not forgive your rebellion and your sins.*
   B'. *If you forsake the LORD and serve foreign gods,*
A'. *he will turn and bring disaster on you and make and end of you.*

The outer 'envelope' describes the holy nature of God and the bearing that this will have on Israel's sin. The inner two lines focus on the foremost sin that Joshua fears that Israel will commit, that of the worship of foreign gods. Joshua wishes Israel to address this particular issue, which, as Judges 2:11–13 demonstrates, the people were prone to transgress. Joshua's warning that God will not forgive Israel's sins has been described as 'perhaps the most shocking statement in the OT'.[2] The plural pronoun suffixes attached to *your rebellion and your sins* suggest that all Israel is intended. As with the Canaanites, God will not overlook the sins of a nation. Judgment will come to a sinning nation, despite the repentance

---

[1] Hertzberg, pp. 136–137.
[2] Butler, p. 274. Butler suggests that this is a feature of God's holiness and inability to tolerate any sin.

of some (Is. 6:9–13). God *is a jealous God.* The word for jealous (Heb. *qannô*, v. 19), as a description of *God* (Heb. *'ēl*), occurs in the Ten Commandments in a similar form (*qannō*). There it also refers to God's intolerance of the worship of other deities (Ex. 20:5; Dt. 5:9).[1]

21. The people respond with a direct and forceful *No!* They deny Joshua's charge and freely choose to remain loyal to the LORD God. For the Christian, Israel represents those who confess their faith (Mt. 10:32; Lk. 12:8; Rom. 10:9). This is the first step of Christianity, however much the true strength of that faith remains to be tested.

22–24. The people accept themselves and their testimony as a witness that their promise to serve the LORD is true.[2] Joshua's charge to the people to *throw away the foreign gods* and to *yield your hearts* meets a response in which the people promise to *serve* and to *obey* (literally 'hear, listen to') God. In other texts, obedience to a command is demonstrated by an explicit note (4:8, *the Israelites did as Joshua commanded them*) or by a narrative that describes the commanded action as being done (5:2–3, *'Make flint knives'* . . . *Joshua made flint knives*).

24. The people do not respond to any of the specifics that Joshua has commanded. They only repeat their earlier promise to *serve the LORD*. The omission of an explicit note of obedience is ominous. It is not like the response of Jacob's family who buried all their images and cultic items at Shechem (Gn. 35:2–4). It suggests that, whatever loyalty the people swore, they kept their images and symbols of other deities. Deeds, in addition to words, were essential to demonstrate their faith. The people did nothing. For the Christian, there is also the expectation that service must accompany pronouncements of faith (Jas. 2:14–16).

iv. The ratification of the covenant (24:25–27). As in the treaty document structure, verses 25–27 include the deposit of the text and the witnesses.[3] The mention of Shechem,

---

[1]The same phrase *jealous God* appears in Na. 1:2 in the context of descriptions of God as an avenger.

[2]Biblical Hebrew has a word for 'no' (*lō*) but no word for 'yes' in the Bible. Instead, the people agree with Joshua in v. 22 by repeating the term *witnesses.*

[3]M. Weinfeld, 'The Loyalty Oath in the Ancient Near East', *UF*, 8, 1976, pp. 379–414, designates this as a loyalty oath (p. 405). However, the elements of the

appearing in verse 1 as well, brings to an end the account of the covenant making ceremony.[1]

26. Joshua's writing of the words of the covenant corresponds to the clauses in treaties that describe the text's having been written and deposited in a temple. The covenant that Joshua writes forms part of *the Book of the Law of God. A holy place of the LORD* is mentioned in Joshua 24:26. This implies that the covenant was kept there and that it was part of a larger, older work. The intention is to tie what has been written in with the law of Moses. However, Moses is no longer mentioned. Unlike the early chapters of Joshua, where Moses' name occurs to support Joshua's work, in this chapter an older Joshua writes the covenant without the need to appeal to Moses' authority. What was the covenant? The text does not make this clear. It may have been the earlier words in chapter 24 or something similar. Joshua's writing of the covenant gave it a permanent and fixed authority. It would be available for study and consultation. For ancient Israel, the writing and preservation of the covenant made it accessible to as many people as possible. For the Christian, the Word of God is the written covenant. Its accessibility is essential to its use as a guide for faith and life. (See 2 Tim. 3:16–17; 1 Pet. 1:10–12.)

27. The stone of witness continues the tradition of using stones for memorials, already seen in the crossing of the Jordan (4:1–9). However, as a witness of a vow, the stone resembles the one set up by Jacob at Bethel (Gn. 28:16–22) and that set up in negotiation with Laban (Gn. 31:43–54). In both cases, Jacob made a vow and the stone was connected with that vow. Witnesses of treaties were usually the deities of the nations involved. Since Joshua and the people recognized no gods but the LORD, they could not invoke other deities as witnesses. The stone served as a lasting memorial that would remind future generations of the covenant made at Shechem and its importance.[2] Jacob's connection with a stone and with

---

loyalty oath that Weinfeld lists are diverse, and Jos. 24:24–26 contains only a few of them. Therefore, the covenant/treaty structure, with fewer elements in number and with greater correspondence of each element, is a better form for comparison.

[1] On the role of Shechem in the Old Testament, see comment on 8:30–35, pp. 171–174.

[2] On the question of the identity of the stone, see the Additional Note: 'Joshua's altar on Mount Ebal?' after the comment on 8:30–35, p. 174.

Shechem is especially significant for this passage.

At Shechem, Jacob buried all the foreign gods that his wives and concubines brought from their family home in Haran (Gn. 35:2–4). The erection of a stone witness at this same spot confirms that the people do not intend to worship these deities. However, it may also identify the place where the images were buried. Thus the ambiguity of the place remains. Will Israel worship the LORD alone, as symbolized by the stone of witness, or will it return to this spot in order to worship other deities, as symbolized by the buried images? Israel's choice to betray its promise (Jdg. 2:11–13) was signalled by its omission of any reference to foreign deities in response to Joshua's challenge (24:23–24). This also contrasts with Jacob whose command to his family to put away their deities met with a positive response (Gn. 35:2–4).

d. The settlement in the land (24:28–33)

28. Although the allotment of the land has already been described, the settlement in the land comes only after the covenant has been formalized. Four events are described: the death of Joshua, the loyalty of Israel, the burial of Joseph and the death of Eleazar. These events are introduced with Joshua's dismissal of Israel to return to their *inheritance.* The fact that *Joshua sent* someone has occurred three times previously in this book: 2:1, where he sent two spies to examine Canaan; 7:2, where he sends spies to investigate Ai; and 7:22, where messengers discover Achan's plunder in his tent. In every case, this act marks the beginning of a mission. In verse 28, Joshua sends the nation to occupy their *inheritance.* Having completed the covenant with God, there now begins the work of living faithfully in the land.

29–31. In the MT of Joshua, the leader's death precedes the notice about Israel's faithfulness. In the LXX of Joshua, as well as the parallel passage in Judges 2:6–9, this order is reversed. A chronological order favours Judges because the people's faithfulness during Joshua's lifetime would necessarily precede his death, but the order in Joshua follows logically from the mention of Joshua in verses 1–28. As the chief human character, his fate is considered first. Then reference is made to the people, who also played a key role in chapter 24 and throughout the whole book. Finally, notes appear that develop the importance of Shechem, as Joseph's final resting place, and of Eleazar who was involved in the allotment process.

29. Like Moses (see comment on 1:1, pp. 67–68), at death Joshua receives the special title *servant of the LORD*. Joshua's lifespan of 110 years is longer than most (Ps. 90:10) but shorter than that of Moses (120 years, Dt. 34:7).[1] It indicates a life blessed by God and one with a special calling to perform all that God has commanded. Joseph also died at the age of 110 (Gn. 50:26). This number associates Joshua, who brought Israel into Canaan, with the patriarchal figure who took Israel into Egypt. It anticipates the mention of Joseph in verse 32.

30. Joshua is buried on the 'border' (Heb. *gᵉbûl*) of Timnath Serah.[2] This word occurs more than fifty times in the allocations of Joshua 12 – 19. With *the land of his inheritance*, it not only brings to a close the life of Joshua but also closes the era of tribal allotments. Joshua's inheritance had been the last one to be designated among the tribes receiving an inheritance. He was also the last to 'go to his inheritance', doing so only after he had sent all Israel to theirs (v. 28).[3]

31. This verse resembles Judges 2:7, where it introduces the death of Joshua and the subsequent apostasy of Israel. In Joshua, verse 30 closes the story of the leader of Israel and verse 31 completes the account of Israel in the generation of Joshua but nothing is said about the future. Instead, there is a pause to reflect upon the generation that had witnessed *everything the LORD had done for Israel*. This generation knew God in a special way and remained faithful on the basis of that knowledge. For the Christian, this passage may be compared with John's testimony of having witnessed Jesus Christ and his teaching, miracles, death and resurrection (1 Jn. 1:1). As a result, the testimony of John and the other apostles carries a special importance and authority (Acts 21:22; 1 Cor. 15:8–11).

32. Both the mention of Joseph's bones (Gn. 50:24–26) and the reminiscence of Jacob's purchase of the burial ground (Gn.

---

[1] Fritz, p. 250. See also the comment on Jos. 24:23–27.

[2] See comment on 19:49–50. *Mount Gaash* is otherwise unknown. The *ravines of Gaash* occur in 2 Sa. 23:30 (= 1 Ch. 11:32).

[3] The LXX adds: 'In the tomb where they buried him they placed alongside him the flint knives with which he circumcised the Israelites after he brought them from Egypt just as the LORD commanded them. They are there to this day.' *Cf.* 5:1–9 and the LXX addition to 21:42.

33:18–20) tie together the book of Joshua with Genesis and provide a conclusion to the great epic of the formation of the family, tribes, and national identity of God's people as begun in Genesis and concluded in Joshua.[1]

33. The high priest Eleazar, who had been instrumental in helping with the tribal allocations (see Jos. 14:1), also died. The reference to his son, Phinehas (see comment on 22:14, p. 291), prepares for the next generation and the book of Judges.[2] As in the case of Joseph, mention is made of the descendant(s) of Eleazar. This contrasts with Joshua whose family is never mentioned. He has no offspring or successor in contrast to Moses and Eleazar. There are two reasons for this. The first is that Joshua's leadership was never intended to continue. This was not the age of kings but of leaders raised up by God for a specific purpose. Joshua's specific role of bringing Israel into the land was completed at his death. More remained to be done but this was left to the people and to God. The second reason follows from this. The period of the judges was a time when leadership would be raised up where and when God willed it. It was not left to Joshua, nor the elders, nor even all of Israel, to make this decision. God would choose his future leadership according to his will.

For the Christian, as for Israel, this conclusion leaves an epitaph of faithful leadership and service. The bestowing of the epitaph *servant of the LORD* remains a challenge for all who would follow God. Thus Christians are confronted with the testimony of the apostle at the end of his life: 'I have fought the good fight, I have finished the race, I have kept the faith. Now there is in store for me the crown of righteousness, which the Lord, the righteous Judge, will award to me on that day – and not only to me, but also to all who have longed for his appearing' (2 Tim. 4:7–8).

---

[1] Boling and Wright, pp. 541–542.

[2] This was perceived in the LXX, where the book of Joshua closes with these additional words, which conclude with Jdg. 3:12, 14: 'On that day the Israelites took the ark of God and carried it by themselves. Phinehas held the priesthood in place of Eleazar his father until he died. He was then buried in his own tomb in Gabaath. The Israelites each returned to their own places and towns. There they worshipped Astarte and Astaroth and the gods of the surrounding nations. So the LORD gave them into the hand of Eglon, the Moabite king, who ruled them for eighteen years.'

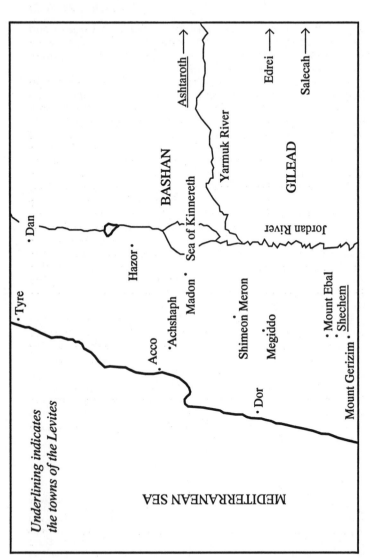

NORTHERN PLACES IN JOSHUA 1–12

Underlining indicates the towns of the Levites

MEDITERRANEAN SEA

Tyre

Acco

Achshaph

Madon

Hazor

Shimeon Meron

Megiddo

Dor

Mount Ebal
Shechem

Mount Gerizim

Dan

Sea of Kinnereth

BASHAN

Ashtaroth →

Yarmuk River

Jordan River

GILEAD

Edrei →

Salecah →

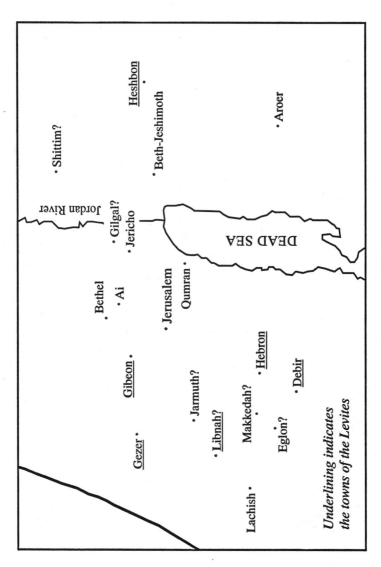

SOUTHERN PLACES IN JOSHUA 1–12

Underlining indicates the towns of the Levites

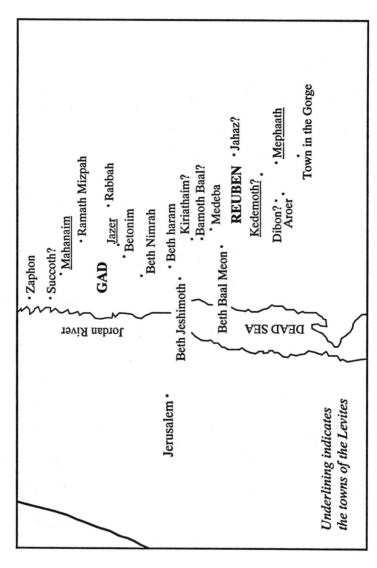

REUBEN AND GAD IN JOSHUA 13

Zaphon
Succoth?
Mahanaim
· Ramath Mizpah
Jazer · Rabbah
· Betonim

GAD

Beth Nimrah
· Beth haram
Kiriathaim?
Bamoth Baal?
· Medeba

REUBEN · Jahaz?

Kedemoth?
Dibon? · Mephaath
· Aroer
Town in the Gorge

Jordan River

Beth Jeshimoth ·

Beth Baal Meon ·

DEAD SEA

Jerusalem ·

Underlining indicates
the towns of the Levites

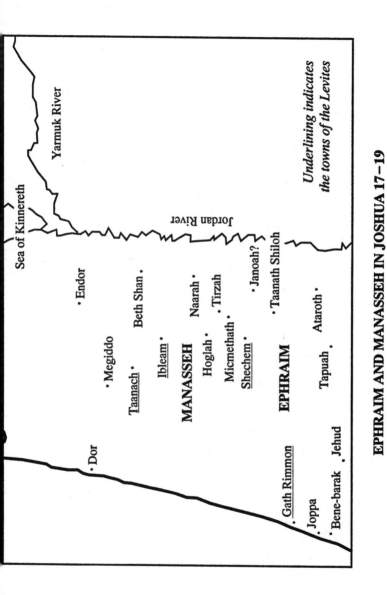

EPHRAIM AND MANASSEH IN JOSHUA 17–19

315

BENJAMIN AND DAN IN JOSHUA 17–19

Underlining indicates the towns of the Levites

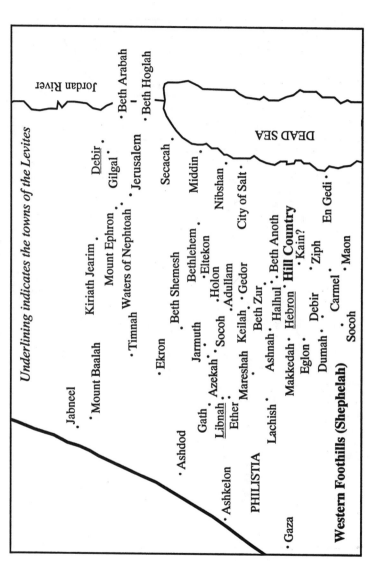

Underlining indicates the towns of the Levites

Jordan River

· Beth Arabah

· Beth Hoglah

DEAD SEA

· Debir

· Gilgal

· Jerusalem

· Secacah

· Middin

· Nibshan

· City of Salt

· En Gedi

· Kiriath Jearim

· Mount Ephron

· Waters of Nephtoah

· Timnah

· Beth Shemesh

· Bethlehem

· Eltekon

· Holon

· Adullam

· Gedor

· Beth Zur

· Halhul

· Beth Anoth

Hill Country

· Kain?

· Ziph

· Carmel

· Maon

· Mount Baalah

· Jabneel

· Ekron

· Jarmuth

· Socoh

· Keilah

· Ashnah

· Makkedah

· Eglon

· Debir

· Dumah

· Hebron

· Socoh

· Ashdod

· Gath

· Libnah

· Ether

· Mareshah

· Azekah

· Lachish

· Ashkelon

PHILISTIA

· Gaza

Western Foothills (Shephelah)

JUDAH IN JOSHUA 15

317

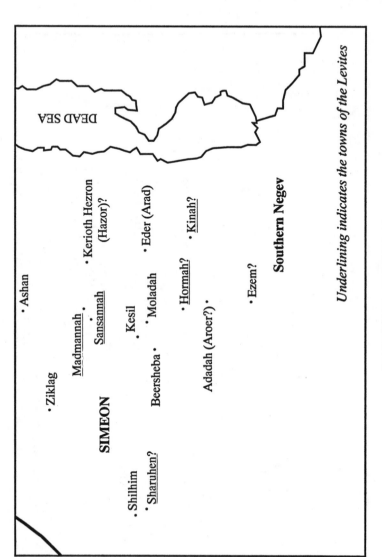

SIMEON IN JOSHUA 19

Underlining indicates the towns of the Levites

DEAD SEA

· Ashan

· Kerioth Hezron (Hazor)?

<u>Madmannah</u> ·

<u>Sansannah</u>

· Eder (Arad)

· Kesil

· <u>Kinah</u>?

· Ziklag

· Moladah

· <u>Hormah</u>?

SIMEON

Beersheba ·

Adadah (Aroer?) ·

· Ezem?

· Shilhim

· <u>Sharuhen</u>?

Southern Negev

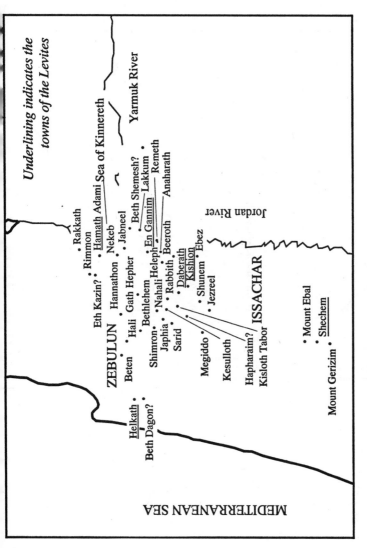

ZEBULUN AND ISSACHAR IN JOSHUA 19

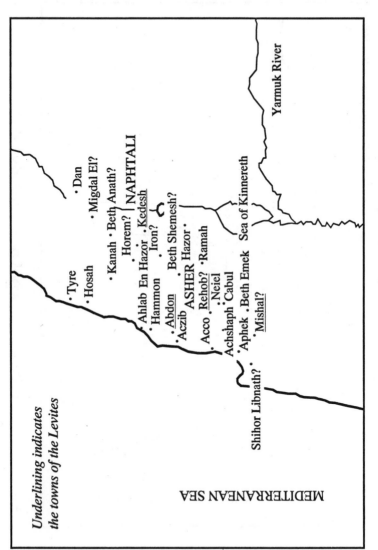

Underlining indicates
the towns of the Levites

· Tyre
· Hosah
· Dan
· Migdal El?

· Kanah · Beth Anath?
Horem? · Kedesh
· Ahlab En Hazor · Iron?
Hammon
· Abdon
· Aczib ASHER Hazor
Acco · Rehob? · Ramah
· Neiel
Achshaph Cabul
· Aphek · Beth Emek
· Mishal?

NAPHTALI

Beth Shemesh?

Sea of Kinnereth

Shihor Libnath?

Yarmuk River

MEDITERRANEAN SEA

ASHER AND NAPHTALI IN JOSHUA 19